College Essay ESSENTIALS

A Step-by-Step Guide to Writing a
Successful College Admissions Essay

Ethan Sawyer

College Essay Guy™

Published by Sourcebooks, Inc.
P.O. Box 4410, Naperville, Illinois 60567–4410
(630) 961-3900
Fax: (630) 961-2168
www.sourcebooks.com

Library of Congress Cataloging-in-Publication data is on file with the publisher.

Printed and bound in the United States of America.
VP 25 24 23 22 21

Testimonials

"Ethan Sawyer is an essay guru. His approach to essay work is insightful, inspirational, and fun. He helps students find their own unique voices and knows what colleges are looking for. Ethan is my number one choice for essay help."

—*Dr. Steven R. Antonoff, former dean of admission and financial aid, University of Denver, author of* College Match *and* College Finder

"Ethan teaches us the shape, the shift, the heft of the weapons, and the soft caresses that make words worth reading and remembering. His cinematic approach, his warm but literate and smart tone will help any student learn the beauty of shaping words into essays that work and play. This is one book applicants to college will want to read."

—*Parke Muth, consultant and former assistant dean of admission, University of Virginia*

"A must-have book for students and counselors! Sawyer's detailed steps make writing awesome college essays a breeze!"

—*Jennifer Kresock, independent counselor*

"Ethan's *College Essay Essentials* is the most concise and easy to follow 'how-to' guide out there... I cannot recommend Ethan and his approach more."

—*Rebekah Elmore, Peak College Consulting*

"With the gentle wisdom of a trusted shepherd, Ethan Sawyer brings the art of self-reflection and the craft of storytelling together brilliantly—and students respond with inspired, deep narratives worthy of respect by today's most discerning admissions officers. I can't imagine tackling an essay without it."

—*Jann Russell, College Fly*

"My advice to you if you are applying to college—get writing and get this book. Ethan will help guide them every step of the way until they have finished their college essays—ALL of them!"

—*Kelly Bates-Siegel, independent counselor*

"I've attended a lot of college essay classes, and read even more books on the subject, but nobody breaks it down quite so simply, yet elegantly, as Ethan. His essays and story examples are excellent and really highlight what college admissions departments are looking for. I highly recommend his new book!"

—*Gina Ney, college and career advisor*

"Yours was the best workshop I've attended in thirty years in the profession."

—*college counselor, on WACAC 2015 workshop session*

"If it weren't for your help and support, I don't think I would've gotten too 'personal' on my personal statement... Working with you was extremely helpful and rewarding... Thank you for loving what you do. Your love is now reflecting through us as we continue our journey."

—*Adriana S., student*

"By day two, [my daughter] was looking forward to going [to Ethan's class] and was so excited to see how her essay would develop by day's end. At the end of the three days, Dana's reaction was a sense of relief and excitement because she was completely done with her essay, she had crossed off a major task from her 'college to-do list,' and she was so very happy with how her essay turned out."

—*Erin C., parent*

Contents

WHY THIS BOOK   ix

Questions You Might Have and Where You Can Find the Answers   xi

WHY I'M THE PERFECT PERSON TO GUIDE YOU
THROUGH THE ESSAY-WRITING PROCESS   xii

HOW THIS BOOK WORKS   xvi

CHAPTER ONE   1

Brainstorming   1

→   Essence Objects Exercise   1

What's Your Story?   6

→   Core Values Exercise   8

How the Essence Objects and Core Values Exercises
Can Help You Write Your Essay (and Your Life)   10

CHAPTER TWO   13

Structure   13

Narrative vs. Montage Structure   13

Narrative vs. Montage Structure Takeaways   17

CHAPTER THREE 20

The Four Types of College Essays 20

Type A: "With Debate" 22

Type B: "Endodontics" 24

Type C: "Raising Anthony" 26

Type D: "Scrapbook" 28

What Makes These Essays Great: A Brief Structural Analysis 30

CHAPTER FOUR 39

**A Step-by-Step Guide to Writing Each of
the Four College Essay Types** 39

How to Write Essay Type A 40

How to Write Essay Type B 59

How to Write Essay Type C 71

How to Write Essay Type D 89

CHAPTER FIVE 102

How to Revise Your Essay in Five Steps 102

Revising the First Draft 102

Revising Drafts 2–50 106

CHAPTER SIX 107

How to Bring Your Essay to Life 107

How Do I Grab the Reader's Attention? 107

How Do I Show the Reader I'm Really Smart? 112

How Do I Brag without Seeming Like I'm Bragging? 119

How Do I Make My Essay, Like, Deep? 121

→ Feelings and Needs Exercise 127

How Do I End My Essay? 137

What Do I Do if I Feel Like I'm Falling Behind? 140

CHAPTER SEVEN 142

Advanced Techniques 142

Advanced Technique 1: Setup and Payoff 142

Advanced Technique 2: Verisimilitude 147

Advanced Technique 3: Turn Something Dark into Something Beautiful 149

Advanced Technique 4: Blow the Reader's Mind by Using *The Sixth Sense*
Ending (a.k.a. Create an Ending That's Surprising, but Inevitable) 150

Advanced Technique 5: Make It New 160

What Makes an Essay Amazing 172

CHAPTER EIGHT 183

How to Make Sure Your Essay Is Doing Its Job 183

→ The Great College Essay Test 186

How to Bring More Values, Vulnerability, and Insight into Your Essay 187

When to Scrap What You Have and Start Over 201

How to Write Your Essay in Just One Night 202

How and When to Ask for Feedback 204

CHAPTER NINE 207

A Few of My Favorite Essays 207

Analysis of a Few of My Favorite Essays 213

CHAPTER TEN 221

Finally 221

ADDITIONAL RESOURCES 222

1,000+ Ways to Get Inspired Right Now 222

How to Work with a Partner 223

Accountability Agreement 224

21 Details Exercise 225

Everything I Want Colleges to Know about Me List 226

Time Line of My Life Exercise 228

List of Real Student Essays Included in This Book 231

Acknowledgments 233

Index 234

About the Author 238

Why This Book

IMAGINE YOU'RE A SEVENTEEN-YEAR-OLD HIGH school senior given the task of writing a 650-word personal statement for your college application.

You're perplexed. Do you tell the story *of* your life or a story *from* your life? Do you choose a single moment? If so, which one? You feel your options are endless.

After an hour mulling over the possibilities, you're now more than perplexed—you're stressed. You start to wonder about what "they" (the admissions officers) want, even though you can neither predict nor have any control over their thoughts. So you start to panic. *What if they don't like what I write? What if I say the wrong thing? Is there a wrong thing?*

Then you remember you have just 650 words. That's one page of single-spaced Times New Roman to express the entire depth and complexity of who you are. You want to throw up.

Then you do.

★ ★ ★

This is the position many students find themselves in each year when it comes to writing the college application essay, an essay that—given the current landscape of college admissions—is arguably the most important 650 words a contemporary human will write.

But what if I told you, the seventeen-year-old high school senior, that your options aren't as endless as you might think? In fact, what if I told you that you only had *four* choices—just four potential paths you could take to write your essay?

And that, furthermore, you could choose a path by answering two simple questions.

Would that make things easier?

★ ★ ★

Tell me if this sounds like you:

a. You're worried about your essay because you don't know what you want to be when you grow up, or you don't have a sob story.
b. You do have a sob story, but you're worried it's too dramatic or that the reader will judge you for it.
c. You feel like you have too many options for stuff to write about, and you don't know how to pick.
d. You have a couple ideas, but you're not sure how to structure them.
e. You've written a draft, but you're not sure if it's any good.
f. You have some combination of all these, depending on the hour.

Here's the thing: no other college essay book out there helps you solve all these issues in an in-depth, step-by-step way.

But this book does.

QUESTIONS YOU MIGHT HAVE AND WHERE YOU CAN FIND THE ANSWERS

How do I figure out what to write about?	page 1
How do I structure my essay?	page 13
Is there a step-by-step process for writing the essay?	page 39
Are any topics off-limits?	page 75
How much sharing is too much?	page 77
How do I revise my essay?	page 102
How do I make my essay not boring?	page 107
What are some different ways I can start my essay?	page 107
How do I show the reader I'm really smart?	page 112
How do I brag in a way that doesn't sound like I'm bragging?	page 119
How do I make my essay, like, deep?	page 121
How do I end my essay?	page 137
How do I know whether my essay is good or not?	page 183
I'm in a jam: How do I write my essay in one night?	page 202
Should I share my essay? With how many people? When?	page 204

That's right. This book answers all these questions.

And you don't even have to read the whole book.

You can jump around.

In a few minutes, you'll already be writing your essay. But first, let me tell you why I'm the perfect person to guide you through this process.

Why I'm the Perfect Person to Guide You through the Essay-Writing Process

THIS MAY SOUND WEIRD, BUT being the College Essay Guy is my dream job. Why? Not because, as a kid, I thought to myself, "I really want to be the College Essay Guy when I grow up." In fact, I first studied to become a screenwriter (BS in speech, Northwestern), then an actor (MFA, UC–Irvine), and then a counselor (Interchange Counseling Institute). And when I considered all the things that I loved to do and that I'd trained for—writing, speaking, counseling—I realized that I'd uniquely equipped myself to become the College Essay Guy. So I created this really cool job for myself.

How? To paraphrase Joseph Campbell, I followed my bliss. I kept doing what I loved until I found myself in this place.

But things really clicked for me when I realized how being the College Essay Guy actually brought together some of my core values, and I think sharing those with you here might help you understand why I'm the only person who could have written this book.

Here are some of my core values:

Practicality. I can't stand general writing advice that suggests,

"Use your authentic voice!" or "Write what you know!" Why? Because I have no idea what these things mean, and because they do not tell me *how* to do these things. I prefer advice that actually gets me from point A to point B.

Efficiency. I love getting things done and I especially love finding ways to streamline my productivity. (It's something I'm actually kind of obsessed with, and my wife likes to joke that in one day I can get done what it usually takes three people combined to finish.) It's why the word "essentials" is in the title of this book.

Vulnerability. I grew up as a missionary kid, moving twenty times before I graduated high school. Even though I often found myself meeting new people, I began to dislike small talk (either because I knew I'd be leaving soon anyway or because, well, small talk sucks), which is why when you meet me, I'll probably ask you some deeply personal question within the first five minutes. I'm interested in your deepest story. And I believe vulnerability is a more efficient way of finding that story.

So here's something that feels vulnerable for me to admit: the number one thing I look for when I meet people is their ability to listen and be present. If I sense someone is unwilling to at least try to listen and be present, I tend to distance myself emotionally for fear of being hurt. This feels vulnerable to admit because I think it makes me sound super judgmental. But I'm about to ask you to get vulnerable, so I figured I'd go first.

Patterns and connections. I loved watching movies as a kid, and those stories helped me make sense of my world. When I started teaching story structure to my college essay students, I loved how it helped them make sense of their worlds.

But it wasn't until I was introduced to narrative therapy that I really began to understand how powerful personal statement writing could be. Through narrative therapy, I discovered how I could reframe events of my past and, in effect, rewrite my identity. It was like learning a super-power. And guess what? You have this superpower, too. It's one you'll be upgrading as you read this book.

Insight. In college, one of my theater professors wrote the word "Illuminate!" at the bottom of a performance analysis I'd turned in. He was challenging me to answer "So what?" in a compelling way. I took his note to heart, and it's become something I strive for both in my work and in my life. It's something I challenge you to do, too.

Inspiration. I thrive on helping others realize their own brilliance, and I have worked to weave inspiration into every chapter of this book. In fact, if I had to sum up the goal of this book into one phrase, it would be this: I WANT TO INSPIRE YOU. And that feels extra vulnerable to share with you.

Which brings me to...

You. I believe in the person you are and in the person you are becoming. And that's what I believe your personal statement is—a record of your becoming.

So here's what you'll find in these pages: an efficient, practical process that will help you access your deepest story, recognize new patterns and connections, and generate insights that express how brilliant you are. Because you are.

But there's one more thing I haven't told you yet.

This process could change your life.

That's right. The personal statement writing process can be empowering, therapeutic, and even life-altering. Why? To paraphrase Joseph Campbell:

[A] good life is one hero journey after another.
Over and over again, you are called to the realm of adventure, you are called to new horizons.

Each time, there is the same problem: do I dare?
And then if you do dare, the dangers are there, and the help also, and the fulfillment or the fiasco.

There's always the possibility of a fiasco.

But there's also the possibility of bliss.

Writing your personal statement is a hero's journey. There are dangers. And there is the possibility that you might fail. But there's also the possibility that, if you stick with it, something amazing might happen.

Do you dare?

If so, continue to the next page.

How This Book Works

FIRST, YOU'LL SPEND ABOUT TWENTY minutes brainstorming.

Next, you'll spend ten minutes learning story structure and ten more minutes reading some sample essays and analysis.

Then I'll ask you two questions that point to four essay paths and you'll get to decide if you'd like to:

a. choose a path and start writing your essay, or
b. read about all four paths before choosing.

Then you'll write a draft of your essay.

Once your draft is done, I'll show you how to revise your essay, bring it to life, make it "like, deep," and then I'll introduce a few advanced essay-writing techniques.

Then you'll write a second draft (or third, or ninth) and come back to take The Great College Essay Test.

After that, I'll give you a few more step-by-step exercises to help you make sure your essay is doing what you want it to be doing, and finally you'll be ready for feedback (but do read my feedback tips first).

Quick note:

Even if you've already written a draft, I recommend reading the first four chapters anyway. It won't take long—I've designed the first part of the book so you can read it and write a draft in a day.

Sound good?

Let's do this.

CHAPTER ONE

Brainstorming

BEFORE WE DISCUSS *HOW* TO write the essay (structure), we need to know *what* we're writing about (content). I've used many brainstorming exercises over the years, but the following two are my favorites. They generate lots of ideas, and they get my heart pounding while I write.

ESSENCE OBJECTS EXERCISE

For this, you'll need a quiet place (or headphones) and about fifteen minutes.

Ready? Here we go:

- I want you to imagine a box.
- In this box is a set of objects.
- Imagine that each one of these is an "essence object" for you.
- What do I mean?
- Each object represents one of your fundamental qualities.
- So each object is more than just an object.

Example 1: My green pen. Why a green pen? I always carry a green pen because, like my mentor Cliff Faulkner, I grade nearly all my students' essays in green. Why green? Because red carries so many negative connotations—bad, wrong, warning—and when a student gets an essay back and it's covered in red marks, it can tend to look bloody, like a battlefield. But if a student gets an essay back that's covered in green, it looks verdant. Also, red means "stop" (like a stoplight), but green says "keep going." And that's the essence I want to communicate to my students: keep going. So my green pen is more than just a green pen.

Example 2: A well-worn North Carolina Tar Heels basketball. Why? I came home from the hospital wearing Carolina Blue, so I've been a Carolina fan, literally, since birth. I've spent more time on a basketball court than almost anywhere else (which is why the ball is well worn), and basketball represents my connection with my dad: when I was a kid, we'd watch Carolina games and play basketball for hours. In fact, basketball was one important way my dad showed he loved me. So this basketball is more than just a basketball.

Example 3: The blue Bible my grandma gave me when I was seven. This represents my having been raised in the Presbyterian Church. It represents Wednesday night potluck dinners, summer camp adventures, and trips with my youth group. So this Bible is more than just a Bible.

You get the idea.

I want you to make a list of twenty essence objects. (Don't complain—you're infinitely complex and creative and could come up with a thousand—I'm asking for only twenty.)

Note: No need to write what the objects mean to you as I've just done if you don't want to. You can just do this:

- green Precise V5 extra-fine rolling-ball pen
- worn-down North Carolina basketball

- blue Bible with my name stitched on it in gold lettering
- BBQ sauce
- annotated copy of *The Brothers Karamazov*
- friendship bracelet
- black-and-white composition notebook
- *Amélie* DVD
- Evanston Hockey T-shirt

If it helps, put on some music. Let your mind wander.
Begin now.

MY ESSENCE OBJECTS

Use your imagination.

(If you get stuck, you'll find questions on the next page to inspire you.)

THE BIG LIST OF BRAINSTORMING QUESTIONS

- What's a food that reminds you of your grandmother?
- What's an object that reminds you of home?
- An object that represents your father?
- Or, if you don't have a relationship with your father, what object reminds you of that absence in your life?
- What about your mother?
- What's something that makes you feel safe?
- What's something you lost?
- Something you forgot?
- What—or who—makes you laugh?
- Best book ever?
- What would your desert island movie be—the one you'd watch again and again?
- What piece of art consistently blows your mind?
- What object represents something you regret— something you wish you'd done differently?
- What's a secret you have? (Don't worry, this stays here.)
- What's something about you that no one else knows?
- Something you stole?
- Something you found?
- Something that makes you feel safe?
- What do you wish you were better at being or doing?
- The worst thing that ever happened to you?
- The last time you cried so hard that your breath caught in that halting way that it does when little kids cry? What mattered to you so much that it brought forth your deepest sobs?
- What's a challenge you faced?
- When you think about that challenge, what brought you through—what resources did you develop to overcome that difficulty?
- What would the logo on your imaginary business card be?
- What image would you have carved into your tombstone?
- An object that represents: a smell you love, a smell you hate, a taste you love, a taste you hate, the sweetest sound in the world?

- ❏ What's the coolest thing about science?
- ❏ Something that reminds you of being a kid?
- ❏ Something that represents a dream you have?
- ❏ What object represents your best friend? Your grandmother?
- ❏ When did you know? (Yes, that's the whole question.)
- ❏ What object represents a quality you have that you love but that people don't often recognize?
- ❏ What object represents the best advice you ever received?
- ❏ What's the best money you ever spent?
- ❏ What's your favorite word?
- ❏ Something you'll never get rid of?
- ❏ A bad habit?
- ❏ A perfect moment?
- ❏ A time you laughed so hard you cried?
- ❏ A time you cried so hard you laughed?
- ❏ An image you'll never forget?
- ❏ What would they put in the museum of your life?
- ❏ The cover image on your first self-titled album?
- ❏ An object representing a near-death experience?
- ❏ When did you feel most alive?
- ❏ What does a perfect Saturday night look like to you?
- ❏ A perfect Sunday afternoon?
- ❏ Best game ever—real or made up?
- ❏ Your favorite metaphor for life?
- ❏ When were you so embarrassed you wanted to disappear?
- ❏ What's a recurring dream you have?
- ❏ Your worst (actual) nightmare?
- ❏ When were you most afraid?
- ❏ If you had a clone, what would you have the clone do?
- ❏ When's a time you were speechless?
- ❏ The moment you left childhood behind?
- ❏ A quotation you love?
- ❏ Your favorite photo?
- ❏ A word that you love from another language?
- ❏ The biggest decision you've ever made?

Now survey your list and ask: Which essences or qualities are missing? What else could I include?

Write down two to three more essence objects.

(Google "100 Brave and Interesting Questions" for more.)

WHAT'S YOUR STORY?

FINDING THE RIGHT CLAY

Think of essay writing as sculpting. You're working to sculpt an essay that reflects something true about who you are. The purpose of the Essence Objects Exercise is to help you find the right clay. How can you be absolutely sure you're sculpting with the right clay? You can't. Writing is an art, after all, not a science. But here's a tip:

Tell your deepest story.

I was part of a story circle once in which we were asked to tell our deepest story. How can you tell when you've found yours? You'll feel it in your gut. It'll feel vulnerable (more on this on page 189). If you read it aloud and the writing sounds superficial or like it could have been written by any number of people, it's probably not your deepest story. So:

What's your deepest story?

Before moving on, spend three minutes jotting down answers to these questions:

What's the toughest lesson you've ever had to learn?

What was the hardest thing you've ever had to overcome?

What's your actual superpower? When did you learn you had it? How'd you develop it?

I wouldn't be who I am today without _____ _____.

If you have a specific career/major in mind, answer: Why am I a [writer/doctor/teacher]?

Do any of these answers connect to any of your essence objects?

CORE VALUES EXERCISE

Here's my other favorite brainstorming exercise, and it'll help you figure out the second half of your essay in about five minutes. To begin, pick your Top Ten values from the following list.

What do I value?

- community
- inspiration
- serenity
- physical challenge
- responsibility
- competition
- career
- practicality
- working with others
- freedom
- security
- strength
- self-control
- hunger
- personal development
- respect
- mindfulness
- culture
- bravery
- communication
- change and variety
- compassion
- nature

- intuition
- trust
- social justice
- intellect
- self-reliance
- financial gain
- laughter
- faith
- involvement
- adventure
- vulnerability
- adaptability
- restraint
- healthy boundaries
- friendship
- excellence
- meaning
- power
- privacy
- self-expression
- stability
- diversity
- love
- control
- surprise

- nutrition
- competence
- risk
- balance
- self-discipline
- courage
- family
- empathy
- working alone
- fun
- humility
- efficiency
- intensity
- health and fitness
- meaningful work
- my country
- music
- truth
- resourcefulness
- awareness
- art
- autonomy
- wit
- patience
- listening
- commitment

- ☐ leadership
- ☐ helping others
- ☐ meditation
- ☐ practicality
- ☐ creativity
- ☐ excitement
- ☐ collaboration
- ☐ social change
- ☐ beauty
- ☐ passion
- ☐ integrity
- ☐ ecological awareness
- ☐ quality relationships
- ☐ travel
- ☐ logic
- ☐ curiosity
- ☐ spirituality
- ☐ directness
- ☐ honesty
- ☐ independence
- ☐ multiplicity
- ☐ supervising others
- ☐ cooperation
- ☐ affection
- ☐ wisdom
- ☐ knowledge
- ☐ growth
- ☐ mystery
- ☐ order
- ☐ innovation
- ☐ accountability
- ☐ democracy
- ☐ religion
- ☐ experience
- ☐ _____
- ☐ _____
- ☐ _____
- ☐ _____
- ☐ _____

Now pick your Top Five.

- ☐ _____
- ☐ _____
- ☐ _____
- ☐ _____
- ☐ _____

Once you have those, pick your Top Three.

- ☐ _____
- ☐ _____
- ☐ _____

And then, yes, pick your Number One value. Remember that you're not losing any of the others, you're just picking the most important value for you <u>today</u>.

- ☐ _____

Don't read ahead until you've done this.

Really.

Finally, if you know what career you'd like to pursue—engineering, for example—put the first letter of that career ("E") beside five values of a great engineer. Maybe you write an "E" next to collaboration, autonomy, innovation, and helping others, and for a fifth value, you write "working with my hands" in one of the blanks at the end of the list.

Once that's done, set these aside. I'll tell you what to do with them in a little bit.

HOW THE ESSENCE OBJECTS AND CORE VALUES EXERCISES CAN HELP YOU WRITE YOUR ESSAY (AND YOUR LIFE)

That's right. You're not just writing your essay. You're writing your life. I'll explain in a second. First, let's talk about:

How These Exercises Can Help You Write Your Essay

T. S. Eliot once wrote: "The only way of expressing emotion in the form of art is by finding an 'objective correlative.'"

What's an objective correlative? It's an object to which you correlate emotions, memories, and complex meanings. It's an object that's more than an object.

Every object in your essence object box is an objective correlative for some important, complex part of you.

Think of each one as a hyperlink to your soul. Click on any one of those essence objects and there's a story behind it. At this point we don't know how many will end up in your story—one, fifteen, or none—but the essences they represent most certainly will be the college essay you submit.

I love the Core Values Exercise for a few reasons:

1. If we sat down and I asked you why your top value is your top value, I'd probably learn something pretty great about you.
2. I believe your values can serve as a magic glue for your essay, helping to connect your past with your present and future (more on this in a bit).
3. It can also help generate material for my favorite prompt:

Describe the world you come from and tell us how your world has shaped your dreams and aspirations.

Why is this my favorite prompt? Because I believe that if a student answers this question—and answers it well—then this essay can work for most personal statement prompts and even some scholarship essays. Working on this particular question can also lead to a lot of personal growth. And how could you apply the material from the Essence Objects and Core Values exercises to this prompt?

Like this:

Your essence objects = your world
Your core values = your dreams and aspirations

I'll explain this in more detail in chapter four, but your essence objects will help you generate content for the first half of your essay (your past) and your core values will help you map out the second half (your present and your future).

How the Core Values Exercise Can Help You Write Your Life

Let me emphasize something: the process of writing your personal statement is more than just reporting on the facts of your life—you're actually assigning them meaning in the larger context of your life. As one of my students told me recently as she was finishing her essays, "I feel like this process has helped me realize the importance of everything I've experienced."

And check it out: this process can help you understand not only your past, but also your future. Here's how:

Some people think of their career as the end goal, their answer to the question, "What are your dreams and aspirations?" But I believe that thinking is flawed.

Why? I believe your career (doctor, lawyer, sports trainer, and so on) isn't actually your end goal. Instead, I think your career is the means by which you will experience and express your values. In other words:

Your values *are* your dreams and aspirations.

An example from my life: my goal in life is not to be the College Essay Guy, but to help people connect more deeply with themselves, realize that it's okay to be vulnerable, and tell the stories of their lives in ways that can be useful and empowering. The College Essay Guy just happens to be my current platform, the way I'm manifesting these values in the world right now.

That's why it's so important to begin identifying your core values. Understanding your core values can give you some criteria for judging what your priorities are and what it might take for you to find happiness—both in work and in life.

So if you skipped the Core Values Exercise on page 8, go back and do it!

The question to consider when writing your essay is: Should you focus on a single overarching value or a wide variety of your core values? Should you focus on a single essence object or several? That depends on which structure you choose.

CHAPTER TWO

Structure

NARRATIVE VS. MONTAGE STRUCTURE

A Quick Screenwriting Lesson

Ever seen a movie that didn't make sense at all? Probably not, as those films tend to not get made. But have you ever tried telling a friend about a movie you watched and wondered why it didn't sound right? Chances are it had something to do with the structure of your retelling.

What's structure? Simply put, it's how you organize and emphasize all the story moments or events (i.e., all the stuff you want to say) in your essay. And I believe there are just two ways.

Why just two? Because I believe you must choose whether you want to organize your story:

a. using cause and effect (where one moment leads to the next), in which case you'll use **narrative structure**, or
b. thematically (where all the moments relate under a common idea), in which case you'll use **montage structure**.

Are there other structures? Perhaps, but I believe every story that connects events must connect them in a way that is either causal or not causal, so any other structure would be a variation on either narrative or montage structure.

Can you combine narrative and montage structures? Yes, but now we're getting ahead of ourselves—let's first learn how each one works.

Narrative Structure

Let's unpack the structure that most American films use. Learning this may change the way you watch films (it did for me). It's a structure as old as time, one that storytellers have been using for centuries. Joseph Campbell, an American writer and mythologist, called it the monomyth, or Hero's Journey. I'll refer to it as narrative structure. Its basic elements are:

1. Status quo
2. Inciting incident/Status quo change
3. Raise the stakes
4. Turning point/Moment of truth
5. Denouement/The final act
6. Outcome/New status quo

STATUS QUO

The main character in the story (hint: in your essay, that's you) is living his or her normal life. Often, there is a Main Problem the Main Character Must Solve.

INCITING INCIDENT/STATUS QUO CHANGE

One day, something happens. A boy discovers he is a wizard (*Harry Potter*). A girl falls down a rabbit hole (*Alice in Wonderland*). A murder happens (almost every mystery ever). Or: The Worst Thing That Could Happen to the Main Character...happens. You get the idea. In short, the hero is called to adventure.

RAISE THE STAKES

Things get more dangerous and important.

- In small dramas, the events become more important inwardly—in our main characters' personal lives—and the events of the story gradually build until they threaten to change their lives forever.
- In action movies, events become more important outwardly, escalating until not only our main characters are threatened, but also the country, the world, or (in big budget films) civilization as we know it.
- In some films, the main characters' inward journey (what they must learn) and outward journey (what they must do) are intertwined. See: *Star Wars*, *Inside Out*, *Avatar*.

TURNING POINT/MOMENT OF TRUTH

Often this is the climax—the moment of highest tension. The character must make the Ultimate Choice or Fight the Ultimate Battle.

- Will Beauty kiss the Beast and save his life? (*Beauty and the Beast*)
- Will Neo realize—and accept—his role as The One before it's too late? (*The Matrix*)
- Will Frodo destroy the Ring and save Middle Earth? (*Lord of the Rings*)

Sometimes it's the character deciding, "I've got to do something about this" or, "I'm mad as heck and I'm not going to take it anymore."

DENOUEMENT/THE FINAL ACT

What does the hero or heroine (again, in your essay, that's you) do about it? Fight, run, apologize, start a movement, or something else?

OUTCOME/NEW STATUS QUO

The result. Note that this should be different from the original status quo.

Montage Structure

WHAT IS A MONTAGE?

Montage is a technique that involves creating a new whole from separate fragments (pictures, words, music). In filmmaking, a montage is used to condense space and time so that information can be delivered in a more efficient way.

Take the classic "falling in love" montage that's commonly used in romantic comedies. We don't see every single moment or interaction between the couple as their relationship grows; instead, we see: she surprises him at work with a card she made, they walk through the park, they dance in the rain, they move boxes into their new home. You get the idea—a few images tell the whole story. And you can use this technique for your essay.

But which moments from your life should you choose? That's something we won't decide right this second—it'll take some time—but it's what will ultimately provide the building blocks for your essay. And remember that there's no right answer to that question, since essay writing is an art, not a science.

FIND A FOCUSING LENS

Montage essays employ what I call a focusing lens. You can't discuss every single aspect of your life, but you can show us a few important elements through a single lens, or metaphor.

What type of focusing lens might you use to write your essay? A sport? A place? An art form? A hobby?

Tips for Finding a Good Focusing Lens

1. Make it visual. Storytelling is a visual medium. Use a lens that

will help conjure images in the reader's mind. And, by the way, I don't recommend writing "soundtrack" or "mixtape" essays in which your favorite songs provide the soundtrack for your life, as the reader can't hear the music (and often doesn't know or have the same emotional connection as you do to the songs referenced). Be a painter—conjure some images in our mind.

2. Consider using something you know a lot about. Know how to cook? Use food. Play chess? Use that! Use your essence objects list for ideas.

3. Find a focusing lens that allows you to "go wide." Use a metaphor that will allow you to discuss several different aspects of who you are.

For more narrative structure essay examples and analyses, see pages 22, 26, 54, 56, 85, 87, and 173.

For more montage structure essay examples and analyses, see pages 24, 28, 65, 96, 99, and 211.

NARRATIVE VS. MONTAGE STRUCTURE TAKEAWAYS

To make sure the difference between narrative and montage structures is really clear:

With Narrative Structure...

Think of the events being linked through cause and effect. For example:

I used to be really shy.

My shyness was really frustrating.

I knew I had to do something, so I tried a few different things. I failed at all of them.

Finally, I joined the debate club. At first it didn't go well.

But eventually I fell in love with it.

I started to come out of my shell and began improving in other areas of my life.

I'm no longer the shy kid—now I speak up and stand up for my beliefs.

This experience has led me to want to major in international relations and pursue a career in foreign diplomacy.

See how <u>one thing leads to another</u>, and how all the events are linked through cause and effect? That's what I'm calling narrative structure.

With Montage Structure...

Think of the events in a montage being linked <u>thematically</u>. For example:

My first lesson in behavioral economics came from my grandfather.

An experience with my dad taught me my second lesson in behavioral economics.

But it wasn't until I read *Freakonomics* that I began to actively examine the world through the lens of a behavioral economist.

Behavioral economics has provided me with an avenue to explore some of life's most complex questions.

Although there are no concrete answers to these questions, finding my passion for the social sciences has not only led me to a potential career path, but has also brought me closer to my family.

See how they're connected by a common theme? That <u>theme</u> is behavioral economics.

Remember that the key difference between narrative and montage structures is this:

- Narrative structure connects events <u>causally</u> (not "casually," but through cause and effect).
- Montage structure connects events <u>thematically</u>.

One final, important difference:

- With narrative structure, events are often chronological (they're mentioned in the order that they happened).
- With montage structure, there is more freedom to jump around in time.

Which structure should you choose?
That depends on the type of essay you're writing.
Unsure which type you want to write? Read on.

CHAPTER THREE

The Four Types of College Essays

I LOVE TO BEGIN MY private sessions and live workshops with these two questions:

1. Have you experienced challenges in your life?
2. Do you know what you want to be in the future?

So imagine I'm there right now, looking at you over a cup of tea, and I've just asked you these two questions.

Why these two questions? Because they point to four essay paths, and each path requires a different approach.

And before you choose a path, you must answer the questions.

No, really. This is an interactive book, so play along.

In fact, circle one:

1. Have you experienced significant challenges in your life?

        Yes   No

2. Do you know what you want to be in the future?

        Yes   No

Okay, the answers to these two questions break into four essay types:

A	B
Student **has** faced significant challenges and **does know** what he or she wants to study.	Student **has not** faced significant challenges and **does know** what he or she wants to study.
C	**D**
Student **has** faced significant challenges and **does not know** what he or she wants to study.	Student **has not** faced significant challenges and **does not know** what he or she wants to study.

Tip: Narrative structure tends to work well for essay types A and C, while montage structure tends to work well for types B and D. I'll say more in the upcoming step-by-step instructions, but I just wanted to plant this idea here.

Must you write about challenges in your essay if you have experienced them? No.

Must you write about your career if you know what it is? No.

You can write a great essay if you have or haven't experienced challenges and if you do or don't know what you want to study. Writing about challenges, however, can yield interesting material, and writing about a future career can help you shape your essay ending.

But you don't have to write about either. (I know I'm repeating myself, but I really want you to get that.)

In a moment I'll ask you to pick a type and dive in to the step-by-step guide for that type, but first let's look at an example of each one.

TYPE A: "WITH DEBATE"

Written by a student who did face significant challenges and did know what she wanted to study

The clock was remarkably slow as I sat, legs tightly crossed, squirming at my desk. "Just raise your hand," my mind pleaded, "ask." But despite my urgent need to visit the restroom, I remained seated, begging time to move faster. You see, I was that type of kid to eat French Fries dry because I couldn't confront the McDonalds cashier for some Heinz packets. I was also the type to sit crying in front of school instead of asking the office if it could check on my late ride. Essentially, I chose to struggle through a problem if the solution involved speaking out against it.

My diffidence was frustrating. My parents relied on me, the only one able to speak English, to guide them, and always anticipated the best from me. However, as calls for help grew, the more defunct I became. I felt that every move I made, it was a gamble between success and failure. For me, the fear of failure and disappointment far outweighed the possibility of triumph, so I took no action and chose to silently suffer under pressure.

Near meltdown, I knew something needed to be done. Mustering up the little courage I had, I sought ways to break out of my shell—without luck. Recreational art classes ended in three boring months. I gave up Self Defense after embarrassing myself in class. After-school band, library volunteering, and book clubs ended similarly. Continued effort yielded nothing.

Disillusioned and wrung dry of ideas, I followed my mom's advice and joined a debate club. As expected, the club only reaffirmed my self-doubt. Eye contact? Greater volume? No thanks.

But soon, the club moved on from "how to make a speech" lessons to the exploration of argumentation. We were taught to speak the language of Persuasion, and play the game of Debate. Eventually, I fell in love with it all.

By high school, I joined the school debate team, began socializing, and was even elected to head several clubs. I developed critical and analytical thinking skills, and learned how to think and speak spontaneously.

I became proud and confident. Moreover, I became eager to play my role in the family, and family relations strengthened. In fact, nowadays, my parents are interested in my school's newest gossip.

Four years with debate, and now I'm the kid up at the white board; the kid leading discussions; and the kid standing up for her beliefs.

More importantly, I now confront issues instead of avoiding them. It is exciting to discover solutions to problems that affect others, as I was able to do as part of the 1st Place team for the 2010 United Nations Global Debates Program on climate change and poverty. I take a natural interest in global issues, and plan to become a foreign affairs analyst or diplomat by studying international affairs with a focus on national identity.

In particular, I am interested in the North-South Korean tension. What irreconcilable differences have prompted a civilization to separate? Policy implications remain vague, and sovereignty theories have their limits—how do we determine what compromises are to be made? And on a personal level, why did my grandfather have to flee from his destroyed North Korean hometown—and why does it matter?

I see a reflection of myself in the divide at the 38th parallel because I see one part isolating itself in defense to outside threats, and another part coming out to face the world as one of the fastest-developing nations. Just as my shy persona before debate and extroverted character after debate are both part of who I am, the Korean civilization is also one. And just as my parents expect much from me, the first of my family to attend college, I have grand expectations for this field of study.

TYPE B: "ENDODONTICS"

Written by a student who did not *face significant challenges and* did know *what he wanted to study*

As a kid I was always curious. I was unafraid to ask questions and didn't worry how dumb they would make me sound. In second grade I enrolled in a summer science program and built a solar-powered oven that baked real cookies. I remember obsessing over the smallest details: Should I paint the oven black to absorb more heat? What about its shape? A spherical shape would allow for more volume, but would it trap heat as well as conventional rectangular ovens? Even then I was obsessed with the details of design.

And it didn't stop in second grade.

A few years later I designed my first pair of shoes, working for hours to perfect each detail, including whether the laces should be mineral white or diamond white. Even then I sensed that minor differences in tonality could make a huge impact and that different colors could evoke different responses.

In high school I moved on to more advanced projects, teaching myself how to take apart, repair, and customize cell phones. Whether I was adjusting the flex cords that connect the IPS LCD to the iPhone motherboard, or replacing the vibrator motor, I loved discovering the many engineering feats Apple overcame in its efforts to combine form with function.

And once I obtained my driver's license, I began working on cars. Many nights you'll find me in the garage replacing standard chrome trim with an elegant piano black finish or changing the threads on the stitching of the seats to add a personal touch, as I believe a few small changes can transform a generic product into a personalized work of art.

My love of details applies to my schoolwork too.

I'm the math geek who marvels at the fundamental theorems of Calculus, or who sees beauty in $A = (s(s-a)(s-b)(s-c))^{(1/2)}$. Again, it's in the details: one bracket off or one digit missing and the whole equation collapses. And details are more than details, they can mean the difference between negative and positive infinity, an impossible range of solutions.

I also love sharing this appreciation with others and have taken it upon myself to personally eradicate mathonumopho-biconfundosis, my Calculus teacher's term for "extreme fear of Math." A small group of other students and I have devoted our after-school time to tutoring our peers in everything from Pre-Algebra to AP Calculus B/C and I believe my fluency in Hebrew and Farsi has helped me connect with some of my school's Israeli and Iranian students. There's nothing better than seeing a student solve a difficult problem without me saying anything.

You probably think I want to be a designer. Or perhaps an engineer?

Wrong. Well, kind of.

Actually, I want to study Endodontics, which is (I'll save you the Wikipedia look-up) a branch of dentistry that deals with the tooth pulp and the tissues surrounding the root of a tooth. As an Endodontist, I'll be working to repair damaged teeth by performing precision root canals and implementing dental crowns. Sound exciting? It is to me.

The fact is, it's not unlike the work I've been doing repairing cellphone circuits and modifying cars, though there is one small difference. In the future I'll still be working to repair machines, but this machine is one of the most sophisticated machines ever created: the human body. Here, my obsession with details will be as crucial as ever. A one millimeter difference can mean the difference between a successful root canal and a lawsuit.

The question is: Will the toothbrushes I hand out be mineral white or diamond white?

TYPE C: "RAISING ANTHONY"

Written by a student who did *face significant challenges and* did not know *what she wanted to study*

At age three, I was separated from my mother. The court gave full custody of both my baby brother and me to my father. Of course, at my young age, I had no clue what was going on. However, it did not take me long to realize that life with my father would not be without its difficulties.

My brother, Anthony, was eleven months old when my father placed us in the hands of our first babysitter. I remember being confused at first, wondering where my father had gone and when he would be back, but after a while, I became accustomed to this routine of absence and the never ending babysitters that filled in for him. These strangers consisted of college students, chain-smokers, senile women, and foreigners—all were technically adults, but not one was a suitable substitute for a parent. When my father was home, he still seemed absent; he was distant both physically and emotionally. He was busy bouncing from one girlfriend to the next, sleeping in until 1:30 in the afternoon, and sitting on the couch watching television. He took us out to restaurants every night and wasted the money he earned on expensive dinners, his current girlfriend, and liquor. This continued for ten years.

Legally, we had all the necessities to survive, but in truth our home was devoid of structure. Schoolwork went unchecked. Bedtimes were unregulated. Dust accumulated in thick layers on the paperwork that overflowed on the dining table. Often times, Anthony and I would spend hours waiting at school for someone to pick us up, and most of our dinners were served well past eleven at night.

Consequentially, and quite unwittingly, I shed my childhood and assumed the role of "parent" for Anthony before my seventh birthday. I memorized the routes we took to school and led Anthony home myself. I watched professional chefs on PBS and learned how to cook basic meals for two. Unfortunately, as I progressively developed into the parent, Anthony took advantage of our lack of true authority and grew into the epitome of a problem child. He became unruly, and his behavior soon bled into his school life. His grades suffered and he seemed to act out more often. His rash temper continued to grow until one day the school called our home because he had tried to throw a chair at his teacher.

Anthony was the only kindergartner in our school's history to be suspended. The school counselor recommended that when my father was in town we attend therapy as a family. But that accomplished nothing—my father's initial attempts to implement authority devolved quickly into apathy, and then he was traveling again. I, on the other hand, would not give up so easily. I became the watchful eye and mentor that Anthony and I both needed. I soaked in the parenting videos that our family counselor had given my dad. I explained to Anthony why a structured lifestyle is important and why retribution is needed for one's misdeeds. To further instill self-discipline in him, I would have him formulate his own penalties. I also began to follow up on his schoolwork by contacting his teachers. On one particularly hopeful afternoon I even tried to introduce him to books that I had read— but I learned I can't win every battle. I wasn't satisfied with just giving a fish to my little brother; I wanted to teach him how to cast lines himself and learn the tools of self-reliance. Looking back at my hectic childhood, I am grateful for the insight it afforded me, and I am grateful for the effect my little brother had on me.

Inadvertently, by raising Anthony I ended up raising myself. Living with my unreliable father and reliant younger brother gave me the need and incentive to find myself and to mature quickly. At a very early age I became resourceful, independent, and responsible. It makes me proud to know that I single-handedly raised Anthony and myself. I now know that I can face any challenge with confidence. Even if I don't succeed, I know I will be stronger just for trying.

TYPE D: "SCRAPBOOK"

Written by a student who did not face significant challenges and did not know what she wanted to study

I look at the ticking, white clock: it's eleven at night, my prime-time. I clear the carpet of the Sony camera charger, the faded Levi's, and last week's Statistics homework. Having prepared my workspace, I pull out two 12 by 12 crème sheets and reproduce sketches of the layouts already imprinted in my head. Now I can really begin.

I leave a quarter inch border as I cut the first photograph, which I then adhere to a polka-dotted paper. For a sophisticated touch, I use needle and thread to sew the papers together. Loads of snipping and pasting later, the clock reads three in the morning. I glance down at the final product and feel an overwhelming sense of pride as I brush my fingers over the many layers and pages. For me, the act of taking pieces of my life and putting them together on a page is my way of organizing remnants of my past to make something whole and complete. This particular project is the most valuable one to date: the scrapbook of my life.

In the center of the first page are the words MY WORLD

in periwinkle letters. All four of my Korean grandparents sit in the top corner, looking over my first birthday—my ddol. Underneath them are my cousins trying not to let go of their overwhelming laughter while playing "red light, green light" at O'Melveney Park. Meanwhile, my Texas relatives watch Daniel, the youngest, throw autumn leaves into the air that someone had spent hours raking up. To the right, my friends miserably pose for our history teacher who documents our droopy faces the morning of our first AP exam. The largest photograph is that of my family huddled in front of the fireplace, drinking my brother's hot cocoa and listening to the pitter-patter of sporadic Los Angeles rain.

I move over to the right side of the page. At the top, I have delicately sewn on three items. The first is a page of a Bible that was given to the soldiers at a Cambodian base where I taught English. Beneath is the picture of my group of Guatemalan girls devouring *arroz con pollo*, red sauce slobbered all over our lips. I reread the third item, a short note that a student of mine from a rural Korean school had struggled to write in her broken English. Moving down the page, I see the shelf display of my vibrantly glazed ceramic projects. I have included a clipping of my page from the school newspaper, next to ticket stubs for Wicked from my date with Dad. I made sure to incorporate a snapshot of my first scrapbook page featuring a visit to Hearst Castle on my tenth birthday.

After proudly looking over each detail, I turn to the next page, which I've labeled: AND BEYOND. This page is not cluttered or crowded. There is my college diploma with International Relations listed and the school's name left blank. A map covers nearly half the paper with stickers pinpointing locations all over the world, but I cannot recognize the countries' names. The remainder of the page is a series of frames with captions underneath. Without the photographs, the descriptions are cryptic.

For now, that second page remains incomplete because I have no precise itinerary for my future. The red flags on the map represent the places I will travel to, possibly to teach English or to partner with a charity again. As for the empty frames, they will be filled with the people I will meet: a family of my own and the families I desire to help, through a career I have yet to adopt. Until these things unfold, all I can do is prepare. I'll continue to finalize the layout and gather materials so that I can start piecing together the next part, the next page of my life's scrapbook.

WHAT MAKES THESE ESSAYS GREAT: A BRIEF STRUCTURAL ANALYSIS

TYPE A: "WITH DEBATE"
Written by a student who did *face significant challenges and* did know *what she wanted to study*

Remember that narrative structure works well when relating challenges.

The clock was remarkably slow as I sat, legs tightly crossed, squirming at my desk. "Just raise your hand," my mind pleaded, "ask." But despite my urgent need to visit the restroom, I remained seated, begging time to move faster. You see, I was that type of kid to eat French Fries dry because I couldn't confront the McDonalds cashier for some Heinz packets. I was also the type to sit crying in front of school instead of asking the office if it could check on my late ride. Essentially, I chose to struggle through a problem if the solution involved speaking out against it.

Raise the stakes: it's important that she overcomes this problem not just for herself, but for her family.

Status quo (a.k.a. the main problem she must solve): she's really, really shy.

My diffidence was frustrating. My parents relied on me, the only one able to speak English, to guide them, and always anticipated the best from me. However, as calls for help grew, the more defunct I became.

I felt that every move I made, it was a gamble between success and failure. For me, the fear of failure and disappointment far outweighed the possibility of triumph, so I took no action and chose to silently suffer under pressure.

Near meltdown, I knew something needed to be done. Mustering up the little courage I had, I sought ways to break out of my shell—without luck. Recreational art classes ended in three boring months. I gave up Self Defense after embarrassing myself in class. After-school band, library volunteering, and book clubs ended similarly. Continued effort yielded nothing.

Raise the stakes even more: nothing is helping!

Disillusioned and wrung dry of ideas, I followed my mom's advice and joined a debate club. As expected, the club only reaffirmed my self-doubt. Eye contact? Greater volume? No thanks.

Inciting incident (a.k.a. the worst thing that could happen): Because what really shy kid would want to join the debate club?

But soon, the club moved on from "how to make a speech" lessons to the exploration of argumentation. We were taught to speak the language of Persuasion, and play the game of Debate. Eventually, I fell in love with it all.

By high school, I joined the school debate team, began socializing, and was even elected to head several clubs. I developed critical and analytical thinking skills, and learned how to think and speak spontaneously.

Side note: Look how many core values she gets into these thirty-four words. (I count at least five.)

I became proud and confident. Moreover, I became eager to play my role in the family, and family relations strengthened. In fact, nowadays, my parents are interested in my school's newest gossip.

Four years with debate, and now I'm the kid up at the white board; the kid leading discussions; and the kid standing up for her beliefs.

New status quo: though she was once too shy to ask for ketchup packets, look at her NOW.

More importantly, I now confront issues instead of avoiding them. It is exciting to discover solutions to problems that affect others, as I was able to do as part of the 1st Place team for the 2010 United Nations Global Debates Program on climate

Here she answers "so what" (see page 119 for how to brag in a subtle way).

change and poverty. I take a natural interest in global issues, and plan to become a foreign affairs analyst or diplomat by studying international affairs with a focus on national identity.

In particular, I am interested in the North-South Korean tension. What irreconcilable differences have prompted a civilization to separate? Policy implications remain vague, and sovereignty theories have their limits—how do we determine what compromises are to be made? And on a personal level, why did my grandfather have to flee from his destroyed North Korean hometown—and why does it matter?

I see a reflection of myself in the divide at the 38th parallel because I see one part isolating itself in defense to outside threats, and another part coming out to face the world as one of the fastest-developing nations. Just as my shy persona before debate and extroverted character after debate are both part of who I am, the Korean civilization is also one. And just as my parents expect much from me, the first of my family to attend college, I have grand expectations for this field of study.

Beautiful metaphor and wonderful insight to close.

Oh, and by the way.

TYPE B: "ENDODONTICS"
Written by a student who did not face significant challenges and did know what he wanted to study

Remember that montage structure works well for this type of essay.

As a kid I was always curious. I was unafraid to ask questions and didn't worry how dumb they would make me sound. In second grade I enrolled in a summer science program and built a solar-powered oven that baked real cookies. I remember obsessing over the smallest details: Should I paint the oven black to absorb more heat? What about its shape? A spherical shape would allow for more volume, but would it trap heat as well as conventional rectangular ovens? Even then I was obsessed with the details of design.

And it didn't stop in second grade.

In this montage essay, the author describes a variety of values, all of which connect under the lens of endodontics.

Core values: curiosity and meticulousness.

A few years later I designed my first pair of shoes, working for hours to perfect each detail, including whether the laces should be mineral white or diamond white. Even then I sensed that minor differences in tonality could make a huge impact and that different colors could evoke different responses.

Setup for final line of essay.

In high school I moved on to more advanced projects, teaching myself how to take apart, repair, and customize cell phones. Whether I was adjusting the flex cords that connect the IPS LCD to the iPhone motherboard, or replacing the vibrator motor, I loved discovering the many engineering feats Apple overcame in its efforts to combine form with function.

And once I obtained my driver's license, I began working on cars. Many nights you'll find me in the garage replacing standard chrome trim with an elegant piano black finish or changing the threads on the stitching of the seats to add a personal touch, as I believe a few small changes can transform a generic product into a personalized work of art.

Note this paragraph ends with a nice "so what" insight.

Again, core values—good with hands, attention to aesthetics—followed by a "so what" insight.

My love of details applies to my schoolwork too.

I'm the math geek who marvels at the fundamental theorems of Calculus, or who sees beauty in $A = (s(s - a)(s - b)(s - c))^{(1/2)}$. Again, it's in the details: one bracket off or one digit missing and the whole equation collapses. And details are more than details, they can mean the difference between negative and positive infinity, an impossible range of solutions.

I also love sharing this appreciation with others and have taken it upon myself to personally eradicate mathonumophobiconfundosis, my Calculus teacher's term for "extreme fear of Math." A small group of other students and I have devoted our after-school time to tutoring our peers in everything from Pre-Algebra to AP Calculus B/C and I believe my fluency in Hebrew and Farsi has helped me connect with some of my school's Israeli and Iranian students. There's nothing better than seeing a student solve a difficult problem without me saying anything.

Core value: helping others. And another subtle brag (see page 119).

You probably think I want to be a designer. Or perhaps an engineer?

Wrong. Well, kind of.

Actually, I want to study Endodontics, which is (I'll save you the Wikipedia look-up) a branch of dentistry that deals with the tooth pulp and the tissues surrounding the root of a tooth. As an Endodontist, I'll be working to repair damaged teeth by performing precision root canals and implementing dental crowns. Sound exciting? It is to me.

The fact is, it's not unlike the work I've been doing repairing cellphone circuits and modifying cars, though there is one small difference. In the future I'll still be working to repair machines, but this machine is one of the most sophisticated machines ever created: the human body. Here, my obsession with details will be as crucial as ever. A one millimeter difference can mean the difference between a successful root canal and a lawsuit.

The question is: Will the toothbrushes I hand out be mineral white or diamond white?

The ending is surprising, but inevitable. See page 150 for more.

This call-back to earlier in the essay helps us feel like we've come full circle.

TYPE C: "RAISING ANTHONY"

Written by a student who did face significant challenges, and did not know what she wanted to study

Again, narrative structure works well when relating challenges.

At age three, I was separated from my mother. The court gave full custody of both my baby brother and me to my father. Of course, at my young age, I had no clue what was going on. However, it did not take me long to realize that life with my father would not be without its difficulties.

My brother, Anthony, was eleven months old when my father placed us in the hands of our first babysitter. I remember being confused at first, wondering where my father had gone and when he would be back, but after a while, I became accustomed to this routine of absence and the never ending babysitters that

Inciting incident: we get why this might be the worst thing that could happen, so no need for status quo.

filled in for him. These strangers consisted of college students, chain-smokers, senile women, and foreigners—all were technically adults, but not one was a suitable substitute for a parent. When my father was home, he still seemed absent; he was distant both physically and emotionally. He was busy bouncing from one girlfriend to the next, sleeping in until 1:30 in the afternoon, and sitting on the couch watching television. He took us out to restaurants every night and wasted the money he earned on expensive dinners, his current girlfriend, and liquor. This continued for ten years.

Legally, we had all the necessities to survive, but in truth our home was devoid of structure. Schoolwork went unchecked. Bedtimes were unregulated. Dust accumulated in thick layers on the paperwork that overflowed on the dining table. Often times, Anthony and I would spend hours waiting at school for someone to pick us up, and most of our dinners were served well past eleven at night.

Consequentially, and quite unwittingly, I shed my childhood and assumed the role of "parent" for Anthony before my seventh birthday. I memorized the routes we took to school and led Anthony home myself. I watched professional chefs on PBS and learned how to cook basic meals for two. Unfortunately, as I progressively developed into the parent, Anthony took advantage of our lack of true authority and grew into the epitome of a problem child. He became unruly, and his behavior soon bled into his school life. His grades suffered and he seemed to act out more often. His rash temper continued to grow until one day the school called our home because he had tried to throw a chair at his teacher.

Anthony was the only kindergartner in our school's history to be suspended. The school counselor recommended that when my father was in town we attend therapy as a family. But that accomplished nothing—my father's initial attempts to

---

Margin notes (left):

Raise the stakes: not just bad babysitters, but absent father, too.

Raise the stakes even more: ten years is a long time.

What she did about it: Part 1.

This is the lowest point of the story, or what the late screenwriting guru Blake Snyder used to call "Dark Night of the Soul."

Margin notes (right):

Raise the stakes yet again: even more challenges.

implement authority devolved quickly into apathy, and then he
was traveling again. I, on the other hand, would not give up so
easily. I became the watchful eye and mentor that Anthony and
I both needed. I soaked in the parenting videos that our family
counselor had given my dad. I explained to Anthony why a
structured lifestyle is important and why retribution is needed
for one's misdeeds. To further instill self-discipline in him, I
would have him formulate his own penalties. I also began to
follow up on his schoolwork by contacting his teachers.

On one particularly hopeful afternoon I even tried to introduce him to books that I had read—but I learned I can't win
every battle. I wasn't satisfied with just giving a fish to my little
brother; I wanted to teach him how to cast lines himself and
learn the tools of self-reliance. Looking back at my hectic childhood, I am grateful for the insight it afforded me, and I am grateful for the effect my little brother had on me.

Inadvertently, by raising Anthony I ended up raising myself.
Living with my unreliable father and reliant younger brother
gave me the need and incentive to find myself and to mature
quickly. At a very early age I became resourceful, independent,
and responsible. It makes me proud to know that I single-
handedly raised Anthony and myself. I now know that I can
face any challenge with confidence. Even if I don't succeed, I
know I will be stronger just for trying.

What she did about it: Part 2.

Great verisimilitude: a detail that makes this feel like real life (see page 147 for more).

She clarifies her core values here, which she'll carry with her to college and beyond.

Remember that montage structure works well for this type of essay.

TYPE D: "SCRAPBOOK"
Written by a student who did not face significant challenges and did not know what she wanted to study

I look at the ticking, white clock: it's eleven at night, my prime-
time. I clear the carpet of the Sony camera charger, the faded
Levi's, and last week's Statistics homework. Having prepared
my workspace, I pull out two 12 by 12 crème sheets and

reproduce sketches of the layouts already imprinted in my head. Now I can really begin.

I leave a quarter inch border as I cut the first photograph, which I then adhere to a polka-dotted paper. For a sophisticated touch, I use needle and thread to sew the papers together. Loads of snipping and pasting later, the clock reads three in the morning. I glance down at the final product and feel an overwhelming sense of pride as I brush my fingers over the many layers and pages. For me, the act of taking pieces of my life and putting them together on a page is my way of organizing remnants of my past to make something whole and complete. This particular project is the most valuable one to date: the scrapbook of my life.

Focusing lens is made clear here, giving us context for the upcoming montage. It's also her thesis.

In the center of the first page are the words MY WORLD in periwinkle letters. All four of my Korean grandparents sit in the top corner, looking over my first birthday—my ddol. Underneath them are my cousins trying not to let go of their overwhelming laughter while playing "red light, green light" at O'Melveney Park. Meanwhile, my Texas relatives watch Daniel, the youngest, throw autumn leaves into the air that someone had spent hours raking up. To the right, my friends miserably pose for our history teacher who documents our droopy faces the morning of our first AP exam. The largest photograph is that of my family huddled in front of the fireplace, drinking my brother's hot cocoa and listening to the pitter-patter of sporadic Los Angles rain.

Core value: family.

Again, note how each object (or detail) reveals important values: diversity, culture, adventure, openness.

I move over to the right side of the page. At the top, I have delicately sewn on three items. The first is a page of a Bible that was given to the soldiers at a Cambodian base where I taught English. Beneath is the picture of my group of Guatemalan girls devouring *arroz con pollo*, red sauce slobbered all over our lips. I reread the third item, a short note that a student of mine from a rural Korean school had struggled to write in her broken

Note how these essence objects— fireplace, brother's hot cocoa, sound of rain—reveal her family values: warmth, connection, intimacy.

English. Moving down the page, I see the shelf display of my vibrantly glazed ceramic projects. I have included a clipping of my page from the school newspaper, next to ticket stubs for Wicked from my date with Dad. I made sure to incorporate a snapshot of my first scrapbook page featuring a visit to Hearst Castle on my tenth birthday.

After proudly looking over each detail, I turn to the next page, which I've labeled: AND BEYOND. This page is not cluttered or crowded. There is my college diploma with International Relations listed and the school's name left blank. A map covers nearly half the paper with stickers pinpointing locations all over the world, but I cannot recognize the countries' names. The remainder of the page is a series of frames with captions underneath. Without the photographs, the descriptions are cryptic.

For now, that second page remains incomplete because I have no precise itinerary for my future. The red flags on the map represent the places I will travel to, possibly to teach English or to partner with a charity again. As for the empty frames, they will be filled with the people I will meet: a family of my own and the families I desire to help, through a career I have yet to adopt. Until these things unfold, all I can do is prepare. I'll continue to finalize the layout and gather materials so that I can start piecing together the next part, the next page of my life's scrapbook.

She's setting up her conclusion, which answers "so what?"

Note the metaphors. She'll explain these in a second, but first she shows them.

Values that will be important to her no matter what career she chooses: travel, teaching, family, helping others.

She returns to the opening image, which, as in the "Endodontics" essay, lends a feeling of closure.

CHAPTER FOUR

A Step-by-Step Guide to Writing Each of the Four College Essay Types

OKAY, HERE'S THE PART WHERE you get to choose your own adventure.

Take a look at the diagram below and pick the path that sounds the most interesting and applicable. Keep in mind that these are not types of students, since you could use any of these paths. These are simply four different ways to tell your story.

A	B
Student **has** faced significant challenges and **does know** what he or she wants to study.	Student **has not** faced significant challenges and **does know** what he or she wants to study.
C	**D**
Student **has** faced significant challenges and **does not know** what he or she wants to study.	Student **has not** faced significant challenges and **does not know** what he or she wants to study.

For type A, turn to page 40.

For type B, turn to page 59.

For type C, turn to page 71.

For type D, turn to page 89.

If you're not sure yet, or want to see what each method has to offer, read through them all. One benefit of understanding all four methods is that you'll be able to combine elements of them to create your own.

All right, heeeeeeere we go.

HOW TO WRITE ESSAY TYPE A

For Students Who *Have* Faced Significant Challenges and *Do Know* What They Want to Study

You may be wondering: What counts as a "significant" challenge? Who decides? The answer is simple:

You decide what counts as a significant challenge.

But maybe you'd like some ideas. No problem.

A List of Challenges You Might Discuss in Your Essay

- single-parent household
- significant work hours while in high school, particularly if you contributed to the family income to help pay bills
- low-income family or large family with many dependents
- you're the first person in your family to attend college
- parents' disability or unemployment (specify what and how long)
- any physical or learning disabilities (diagnosed by a health professional; specify what and how long)
- language spoken at home other than English or any portion of your high school career that was taken outside of the United States

IMPORTANT NOTE: You don't *have* to write about these things in your main essay.

If you have faced significant challenges, this information could also be included in the additional information section or elsewhere in your application—and your challenge certainly doesn't have to dominate your essay. For example, if there are any potential red flags on your application (low grades, classes or activities dropped, important school changes), explanations for them can be mentioned in your additional information section or *very* briefly in your main essay, but your whole essay should not be solely about your grades or school change—you'll want to discuss those challenges in the context of a broader, more meaningful story.

ANOTHER IMPORTANT NOTE: If you don't believe you've experienced significant challenges, or if you believe you've been through "some stuff" but you're not sure that "stuff" would qualify as a "significant challenge," you can still use this type A step-by-step approach to write your essay—simply replace the word "challenge" or "challenges" in the following paragraphs with the word "experience" or "experiences."

Let's get to it.

THE SECRET TO WRITING ESSAY TYPE A

If you **have faced** significant challenges in your life and you **do know** what you want to study, the key question for your essay is this:

How do the challenges from my <u>past</u> connect to my <u>future</u> career?

And the secret is...

Through your values.

What do I mean? This:

1. You experienced **challenges**.
2. Those challenges had particular **effects** or repercussions, impacting you in a variety of ways.
3. To get through those challenges, **you took action**.
4. As a result, you developed certain resources, skills, or **values**.
5. And the resources, skills, and values you developed as a result of your challenges will serve you in [insert chosen **career** here].

Visually speaking, that looks something like this:

HOW TO CONNECT YOUR CHALLENGES TO YOUR INTENDED CAREER

Get out a blank sheet of paper, turn it sideways (horizontally), and write these words along the top:

1. Challenges	2. Effects	3. What I Did	4. Values	5. Amazing [insert chosen career here] (Doctor, Artist, and so on)

HERE'S WHAT TO WRITE IN EACH COLUMN:

Column 1: Challenges

What difficulties did you face or are you currently facing?

Feel free to list several. Perhaps not all of these challenges will end up in the essay, but we're just brainstorming right now, so at this point, list all that come to mind. Even write the one that feels edgy to talk about, that you think, "Nah, that's too personal." Write that one down, too, just for the sake of the exercise.

If you're wondering if any topics are off-limits or how much sharing is too much, see pages 75 and 76.

Examples of Challenges

❏ adapting to a new culture in a new country
❏ moving a lot and having no real place to call home

- ❐ divorce
- ❐ being afraid to come out as lesbian, gay, bisexual, transgender, queer
- ❐ having an extremely shy personality
- ❐ having to work to pay for groceries
- ❐ dealing with the death of a family member
- ❐ adjusting to a new school
- ❐ parents or siblings fighting a lot
- ❐ parents not being home a lot
- ❐ racism
- ❐ crime
- ❐ school or neighborhood violence
- ❐ failing to meet someone's expectations
- ❐ alcohol or drug abuse
- ❐ joblessness or unemployment
- ❐ illness (you or someone close to you)
- ❐ failure
- ❐ natural disaster (hurricane, earthquake)
- ❐ car crash
- ❐ war
- ❐ riots
- ❐ home invasion or break-in
- ❐ fire
- ❐ ignorance
- ❐ physical injury
- ❐ physical disability
- ❐ mental illness
- ❐ suicide
- ❐ sibling rivalry
- ❐ getting rejected
- ❐ a learning difference or disability
- ❐ sexism
- ❐ abuse

- ☐ controlling behavior from family or friends
- ☐ dealing with an excessively critical person
- ☐ aggression
- ☐ cruelty
- ☐ destructive behavior/bullying/cyberbullying
- ☐ peer pressure
- ☐ discrimination based on being a minority (race, sexual orientation, nationality, and so on)
- ☐ lack of access to educational resources
- ☐ parents not supportive of your dreams

Column 2: Effects

What negative effects did you experience as a result of your challenges? (Note that you probably experienced some positive effects, too, but save those for the fourth column.)

The purpose of this section is to differentiate *your* experiences from those of everyone else who went through (and is writing his or her college essay about) the challenges you faced.

For example, Student A and Student B might both write "my dad lost his job" as a challenge. However, for Student A, the effects might have been "domestic violence," "poverty," and "mom left us," whereas for Student B, the effects might have been "sleepless nights" and "we had to sell one of our cars."

Two important things to remember as you're brainstorming this section:

1. You don't need to match just one effect per challenge—one challenge can have several repercussions.
2. This part of the process can take some time, so be patient.

Column 3: What I Did

What actions did you take to change or improve your situation?

Examples: I started helping out more around the house; I got a part-time job; I quit Key Club, SADD, and French Club; or I secretly went into my brother's room and folded his unkempt pajamas.

In the third column, list all the positive actions you took.

Column 4: Values

What qualities/skills/values/resources did you develop during this time?

For ideas and examples, go back to the Core Values Exercise on page 8, but this time—rather than thinking of your core values—consider which values you developed as a result of the experiences you listed in the third column.

Make that list now.

Here's an example of how your brainstorm page may be shaping up. (Note that I list only one challenge, while you might list several.)

1. Challenges	2. Effects	3. What I Did	4. Values	5. Amazing [Doctor]
mom lost her job	no money	got a job	accountability	
			confidence	
			beauty	
	dad worked more	taught myself to cook	health	
			art	
	had to quit soccer	play w/ brothers	gratitude	
			listening	

IMPORTANT NOTE: See if you can include several *unexpected* connections or values. In the example, many of the connections between the "what I did" and the "values" are pretty obvious. But a few are not so obvious, such as the connections between how "[getting] a job" led to the value of "beauty" or how "[teaching] myself to cook" might lead to "art." It's these unusual values—or usual values developed in unusual ways—that can lead to unique insights and make your essay stand out.

And the point I just made is so important that I feel I must underscore it:

If you use only predictable values at the end of your essay and explain your values in usual ways, there is a good chance your essay will be boring.

- Examples of predictable values gained from working a job: discipline, commitment, hard work
- Examples of less predictable values gained from working a job: risk, social change, healthy boundaries

Which group of values makes for a more interesting essay? That's a rhetorical question, but just in case: the second group. Just to get your brain turning, here are a couple more examples:

- Predictable values gained from teaching yourself to cook: responsibility, health, helping others
- Less predictable values gained from teaching yourself to cook: art, privacy, practicality

IMPORTANT NOTE: Just because the values are predictable doesn't mean that they are wrong or boring or that you are wrong or boring. I've read great essays that have used predictable values, but here's the key: the more usual the values are, the more well-crafted (or unusual) the "so what" moments need to be. Look at the "With Debate" (page 22) or "Stomach Whisperer" (page 69) essays—in both of these, the authors developed confidence (which could be called a "predictable" value), but how the confidence was developed was told in an interesting and somewhat unusual way.

Also, just because you choose to write about unusual values doesn't mean you should necessarily use such words in a straightforward and direct way. In other words, I wouldn't recommend saying, "Teaching myself to cook taught me the values of art, privacy, and practicality." That can be really boring, too. Instead, show first how you developed the value, and then tell us anything else we might need to know or give us insight into why it was meaningful.

HOW CAN YOU BRAINSTORM LESS PREDICTABLE VALUES?

Try this: look at the Core Values Exercise on page 8 and see if you can choose a value you think will surprise me. (Yes, me, Ethan.) Imagine we're actually sitting across from each other and you've just told me about your challenge and what you did about it. Then pick a value on that list and imagine telling me what you gained from it. If you think I'll be able to guess the connection, chances are it'll be predictable for the reader. So pick something else. Keep going until you find something that you don't think I'd be able to guess right away.

Column 5: Amazing [Insert Chosen Career Here]

Ask yourself: What are the essential qualities of an amazing [whatever you want to be/study]? Don't worry about connecting these qualities to your values yet—we'll get there. Right now just list three to five essential qualities of someone who would be excellent in your potential future profession.

And, just as I've suggested earlier, make sure to not only include expected values, but also unusual values—values you wouldn't normally associate with that career. Consider that most essays on becoming a doctor, for example, will emphasize the value of "helping others." But what unusual values would you bring to the profession?

- Examples of predictable values in a doctor essay: responsibility, helping others, collaboration
- Examples of less predictable values in a doctor essay: laughter, restraint, balance

Will the reader be able to guess how those last values apply to being a doctor? Maybe, but at least you'd be making him or her do a little work. Think of the difference between a bad joke and a good one. If the punch line is predictable, the joke isn't funny. But if your brain has to do a little work, it's funnier. Usually.

Remember: The values *on their own* don't have to be strange or unusual; it can be the connection you make to the career that's unusual, as in the doctor examples. By this, I mean that "laughter" isn't on its own a weird value—it's just not likely to be the first value that comes to mind when you think of "doctor" and may be interesting to include in an essay that otherwise focuses solely on helping others.

If this is still unclear, the following essay is a quick example of a student who developed five values from playing a musical instrument. But, before you read it, try imagining what values most musical instrument essays focus on. In my experience, most of those essays focus on hard work, perseverance, excellence, and so on. But notice how this student doesn't focus on any of those.

"SANTUR"
150-word extracurricular statement

I've devoted thousands of hours to playing the santur, a classical Persian instrument that originated in the Middle East. Some think I'm strange: a Persian redheaded Jewish teenager obsessed with an ancient musical instrument. But many don't see what I see. My santur is King David's lyre: it can soothe, enrapture, mesmerize. It's also a tool for social change: many view Iran as a land of terrorists, but when I play, if just for a moment, the barrier is broken and the innocent of Iran, the educated, the artists, the innovators, come to life. The santur is also my way of connecting to my Persian grandfather, who was afflicted with Alzheimer's. In December I'll be releasing my first album and donating the proceeds to Alzheimer's research, doing my part to help eradicate the disease and preserve the voice of the santur so that it shall never be forgotten.

I count at least five values in 148 words. Pretty good.

So first ask yourself: What are the essential qualities of an amazing [insert chosen career here]? Write them down. Then ask: What will my secret sauce be? What, in other words, will make you (and your essay) different from all the other future doctors (and future doctor application essays)?

At this point, your brainstorm page might look something like this:

1. Challenges	2. Effects	3. What I Did	4. Values	5. Amazing [Doctor]
mom lost her job	no money	got a job	accountability	listening
			confidence	restraint
			beauty	improvisation
	dad worked more	taught myself to cook	health	efficiency
			art	accountability
	had to quit soccer	play w/ brothers	gratitude	fun
			listening	

Note that some of your values in the fourth column (Values) may overlap with the values in your fifth column (Amazing [Career]), and some may not. That's okay. You don't have to connect <u>all</u> the values right now, and you certainly don't have to use everything you've written down. At this point, we're still brainstorming.

What to do next:

START MAKING SOME CONNECTIONS

Here's the fun part. See if you notice any threads of connection between the challenges, effects, what you did, values you developed, and the qualities necessary to be a great [whatever you want to be].

You can even draw some arrows to help you see the connections. Note that if you spot a continuous thread of connection from the first column to the fifth column, that's great, as this could provide the connective thread for your entire story.

Example 1:
(Challenges, Effects, What I Did, Values, and Career are marked in bold.)

> I noticed that after **my father lost his job** that's when he started **drinking** and becoming **verbally abusive** and my **grades went down** and I started to become **angry**. Deep down all I really wanted was a mentor and someone I could talk to. It wasn't until 9th grade when I joined **wrestling** that I found a way to channel my frustrations and anger. That's when things shifted for me, **my grades went up**, and, though we were never able to fully connect, my **father quit drinking**. Wrestling really turned things around for me: it taught me to **channel my emotions** in more productive ways, **manage my time**, and even **inspired me** to work with other young men to help them learn the value of **healthy competition**, potentially as a **coach**. I hope to one day be there for other young men to listen to them and provide the positive role model I never had.

IMPORTANT NOTE: You don't have to connect ALL your challenges to the qualities of a great [whatever you want to be]. Try to find just two or three connective threads. Why? Because not <u>all</u> your great qualities were born from struggle—some were born out of curiosity or your innate awesomeness. So just try to make a few connections now. It's almost time to start writing.

WHAT NOW?

Here are a few options:

Option 1: Just write a draft.

That's right. You've got the content and you've identified a couple connective threads: jump in and start writing while you're inspired. (Tip: If you wait twenty-four hours, chances are you'll have forgotten some of the connections your brain just made—it starts to fade fast, like a dream—so capture the ideas now in a rough draft.)

Option 2: Read "How to Write Essay Type C" in this chapter for more tips on writing about challenges.

This section, which begins on page 71, is especially useful if you're interested in writing about challenges, but you're uncertain about your career path. It also answers "Are any topics off-limits?" and "How much sharing is too much?"

Option 3 (my favorite): Add emotional depth and layers by completing the Feelings and Needs Exercise.

For this, turn to the "How Do I Make My Essay, Like, Deep?" section on page 121.

Option 4: Create a simple three-part challenges essay outline using these elements:

1. Challenges and effects (≈ 1/3 of essay)
2. What I did (≈ 1/3 of essay)

3. What I learned that led me to discover my calling ($\approx 1/3$ of essay)

Note that sometimes it's difficult to get all the challenges into the first third. If so, make sure you at least get the challenges into the first half of your essay. But I'd recommend including a turning point (a.k.a. what you did about it) before the middle of the essay.

If it helps, give yourself a word budget. Say, for example, you're writing a 650-word essay. If so, that's:

1. Challenges and effects: 216.66 words
2. What I did: 216.66 words
3. What I learned that led me to discover my calling: 216.66 words

Must your essay follow this budget precisely? Of course not. That ".66 words" thing is a joke: How could you possibly write just part of a word? This is simply a rough guide for how much space you should spend on each part. But with this simple three-part structure, you should be able to start your essay.

Want a more in-depth outline?

Option 5: Use narrative structure to create your outline.

Note that this will work best after completing the Feelings and Needs Exercise mentioned in Option 3.

As a reminder, here are the six elements of narrative structure:

1. **Inciting Incident**: What moment or event launched your story? Often it's the worst thing that could have happened.
2. **Status Quo**: What do we need to know in order to understand why the inciting incident was the worst thing that could have happened to you? (Note that in the discussion of narrative structure on page 14, status quo is listed before inciting incident, but often it can be more exciting to switch the order. Remember: It's art, not science. If your inciting incident comes

first, your status quo provides the context for the opening
image or moment.)

3. **Raise the Stakes**: What happened to make things worse,
more important, serious, or dangerous? What else happened?

4. **Turning Point**: When did things shift? Often this involves a
choice that you made, perhaps a decision to take action.

5. **Denouement**: What did you do about it?

6. **New Status Quo**: How are things different now from the
original status quo?

Think of each of these parts as a paragraph. Then write your
essay draft.

Note: Once you've written a draft, turn to "How to Revise Your
Essay in Five Steps" on page 102.

**Want another example of narrative structure used to write
essay type A?**

Check out the "Porcelain God" essay that follows.

"PORCELAIN GOD"

*Written by a student who did face significant
challenges and did know what she wanted to study*

Bowing down to the porcelain god, I emptied the contents of
my stomach. Foaming at the mouth, I was ready to pass out.
My body couldn't stop shaking as I gasped for air, and the room
started spinning.

Ten minutes prior, I had been eating dinner with my family
at a Chinese restaurant, drinking chicken-feet soup. My mom
had specifically asked the waitress if there were peanuts in it,
because when I was two we found out that I am deathly allergic
to them. When the waitress replied no, I went for it. Suddenly I
started scratching my neck, feeling the hives that had started to

form. I rushed to the restroom to throw up because my throat was itchy and I felt a weight on my chest. I was experiencing anaphylactic shock, which prevented me from taking anything but shallow breaths. I was fighting the one thing that is meant to protect me and keep me alive—my own body.

At five years old, I couldn't comprehend what had happened. All I knew was that I felt sick, and I was waiting for my mom to give me something to make it better. I thought my parents were superheroes; surely they would be able to make me well again. But I became scared when I heard the fear in their voices as they rushed me to the ER.

After that incident, I began to fear. I became scared of death, eating, and even my own body. As I grew older, I became paranoid about checking food labels and I avoided eating if I didn't know what was in the food. I knew what could happen if I ate one wrong thing, and I wasn't willing to risk it for a snack. Ultimately, that fear turned into resentment; I resented my body for making me an outsider.

In the years that followed, this experience and my regular visits to my allergy specialist inspired me to become an allergy specialist. Even though I was probably only ten at the time, I wanted to find a way to help kids like me. I wanted to find a solution so that nobody would have to feel the way I did; nobody deserved to feel that pain, fear, and resentment. As I learned more about the medical world, I became more fascinated with the body's immune responses, specifically, how a body reacts to allergens. This past summer, I took a month-long course on human immunology at Stanford University. I learned about the different mechanisms and cells that our bodies use in order to fight off pathogens. My desire to major in biology in college has been stimulated by my fascination with the human body, its processes, and the desire to find a way to help people with allergies. I hope that one day I can find a way to stop allergic reactions or at least lessen the symptoms, so that children and adults don't have to feel the same fear and bitterness that I felt.

Note how the author's allergic reaction, brought on by anaphylactic shock (**Challenge**), led her to fear death, eating, and even her own body (**Effects**). This led her to a desire for knowledge about the body's immune responses and its reaction to allergens, which led her to take the course at Stanford (**What She Did**), and ultimately inspired her to become an allergy specialist (**Career**) so that children and adults don't have to feel the same fear and bitterness that she felt (**Values**). Note, too, that in her essay, she mentions her career before she mentions her values, which of course is fine. The brainstorming columns provided earlier aren't a mandate on how you must order everything in your essay. That goes for everything in this book, by the way: take these tools and make your essay your own.

> Fun fact: The admissions officers at Davidson College liked this essay so much that they asked the author if they could use it as a sample for how to write a great essay.

Here's one more type A essay example that illustrates narrative structure in a clear way:

"EASTER"

Written by a student who did *face significant challenges and* did know *what she wanted to study*

It was Easter and we should've been celebrating with our family, but my father had locked us in the house. If he wasn't going out, neither were my mother and I.

My mother came to the U.S. from Mexico to study English. She'd been an exceptional student and had a bright future ahead of her. But she fell in love and eloped with the man that eventually became my father. He loved her in an unhealthy way, and was both physically and verbally abusive. My mother lacked the courage to start over so she stayed with him and slowly let go of her dreams and aspirations. But she wouldn't allow for the same to happen to me.

In the summer before my junior year I was offered a scholarship to study abroad in Egypt. Not to my surprise, my father refused to let me go. But my mother wouldn't let him crush my dreams as well. I'd do this for myself and for my mother's unfulfilled aspirations. I accepted the scholarship.

I thought I'd finally have all the freedom I longed for in Egypt, but initially I didn't. On a weekly basis I heard insults and encountered harassment in the streets, yet I didn't yield to the societal expectations for women by staying indoors. I continued to roam throughout Egypt, exploring the Great Pyramids of Giza, cruising on the Nile, and traveling to Luxor and Aswan. And before I returned to the U.S. I received the unexpected opportunity to travel to London and Paris. It was surreal: a girl from the ghetto traveling alone around the world with a map in her hands and no man or cultural standards could dictate what I was to do. I rode the subway from Cambridge University to the British Museum. I took a train from London to Paris and in two days I visited the Eiffel Tower, the Louvre, Notre Dame Cathedral, and took a cruise on the Seine. Despite the language barrier I found I had the self-confidence to approach anyone for directions.

While I was in Europe enjoying my freedom, my mother moved out and rented her own place. It was as if we'd simultaneously gained our independence. We were proud of each other. And she vicariously lived through my experiences as I sent her pictures and told her about my adventures.

Finally, we were free.

I currently live in the U.S with my mother. My father has

gradually transformed from a frigid man to the loving father I had yearned for. Life isn't perfect, but for the moment I'm enjoying tranquility and stability with my family and are communicating much better than before.

I'm involved in my school's Leadership Council as leader of our events committee. We plan and execute school dances and create effective donation letters. I see this as a stepping-stone for my future, as I plan to double major in Women's Studies and International Relations with a focus on Middle Eastern studies. After the political turmoil of the Arab Spring many Middle Eastern countries refuse to grant women equal positions in society because that would contradict Islamic texts. By oppressing women they are silencing half of their population. I believe these Islamic texts have been misinterpreted throughout time, and my journey towards my own independence has inspired me to help other women find liberation as well.

My Easter will drastically differ from past years. Rather than being locked at home, my mother and I will celebrate outdoors our rebirth and renewal.

Note the narrative structure elements in this essay:

- **Inciting Incident**: Author and her mother are locked in the house by the author's father.
- **Status Quo** (which provides context): Father has been physically and verbally abusive for years, mother and daughter are trapped not only physically but psychologically. (Like the "Porcelain God" essay, the inciting incident comes first—that's the hook—then we get some background details.)
- **Raise the Stakes**: Author is offered a scholarship to study in Egypt and father initially won't let her go. We wonder: What will happen?

- **Turning Point 1**: Her mother gives her permission, and author accepts the scholarship.
- **Raise the Stakes Even More**: Rather than experiencing freedom in Egypt, author experiences sexism.
- **Turning Point 2**: Author describes the surreal experience of exploring Europe: "a girl from the ghetto traveling alone around the world with a map in her hands and no man or cultural standards could dictate what [she] was to do" (this line always makes me cry). She gains confidence and independence and learns that mom has moved out, in effect gaining her own independence.
- **New Status Quo**: "Finally, we were free." After being oppressed by men for years, the author decides to major in women's studies. The final sentence returns to the opening, but rather than being locked inside her house, in the future the author and her mother "will celebrate outdoors [their] rebirth and renewal." Boom.

HOW TO WRITE ESSAY TYPE B

For students who *have not* faced significant challenges and *do know* what they want to study

THE SECRET TO WRITING THIS TYPE OF ESSAY

Write your essay backward.

One of my favorite ways to outline a type B essay is to "write it backward," which essentially involves reverse engineering the essay using montage structure. Here's how it works:

Turn a piece of paper sideways (horizontally) and write these headings along the top:

How I've Developed These Values	Essential Values of a Great [insert chosen career here]	Insights

HERE'S WHAT TO WRITE IN EACH COLUMN:

Center Column: Essential Values of a Great [Insert Chosen Career Here]

1. Make a list of the qualities necessary to excel in whichever field you've chosen. If, for example, you want to study business, you might write "resourcefulness" or "autonomy" on your list.

> Tip: Brainstorm several unusual values. "Helping others" may be a common value for a doctor, for example, whereas "creativity" or "restraint" may be less common. Or "efficiency" might be common in an engineering essay, whereas "fun" or "beauty" may be less common.
>
> If you're having trouble coming up with a list, refer to the Core Values Exercise on page 8.

Another tip: You may want to do some research by asking a few people in your chosen field, "What's amazing about your job?" or "Why do you do what you do?" Note that phrasing your questions in this way might be more effective at eliciting values than asking a question like, "What are the necessary skills required of your career?" Why? You're not looking for what is most logical (head), but for purpose and meaning (heart). In other words: not *what*, but *why*. So phrase your question in a way that invites deeper reflection. Other possibilities are, "What would I find surprising about your work?" or "Why are you great at what you do?"

List at least five qualities in the center column. Challenge yourself to identify at least two unusual ones.

Left Column: How I've Developed These Values

1. For each quality in your center column, write a specific moment or example from your life that SHOWS that you've developed this quality. (For example, if you wrote "ability to work well with others" in your center column, write a specific instance that shows you work well with others—like the time you worked with a large group to organize the Dance Marathon at your school. Or if you wrote "good listener" in the center column, you might describe how, while volunteering at the hospital, you found that the patients often felt comfortable sharing their life stories with you.)

2. Keep going until the left column is filled with examples that demonstrate the qualities you've listed in the center column.

Here's an example of what your brainstorm might look like so far, based on the "Endodontics" essay on page 24:

How I've Developed These Values	Essential Values of a Great Endodontist	Insights
After-school math tutoring	Desire to help others	
Designing my own shoes	Detail-focused	
Taking apart machines	Interested in how human body works	
Always asked questions as a kid	Curiosity	

After you've finished the steps above, you'll have your basic outline. But there's one more part left to brainstorm, and it's key to making your essay stand out.

Right Column: Insights

An insight is something you know or see that another person may not. Why are moments of insight important in your essay? Because, if you describe the examples you've brainstormed in a simple and straightforward way, your essay might still sound a little flat or boring. You need insights, or what I call "so what" moments. So…

For each of your examples, write down a particular lesson or skill you learned that is beyond what the average person knows. How do you do this? Think about your example and simply ask yourself, "So what?" Then ask yourself, "So what?" again. Keep going to see where it leads.

Here are some examples from the "Endodontics" essay (and I've highlighted the insight/"so what" moments in bold):

> In high school I moved on to more advanced projects, teaching myself how to take apart, repair, and customize cell phones. Whether I was adjusting the flex cords that connect the IPS LCD

to the iPhone motherboard, or replacing the vibrator motor, **I loved discovering the many engineering feats Apple overcame in its efforts to combine form with function.**

And once I obtained my driver's license, I began working on cars. Many nights you'll find me in the garage replacing standard chrome trim with an elegant piano black finish or changing the threads on the stitching of the seats to add a personal touch, **as I believe a few small changes can transform a generic product into a personalized work of art.**

My love of details applies to my schoolwork too.

I'm the math geek who marvels at the fundamental theorems of Calculus, or who sees beauty in $A = (s(s - a)(s - b)(s - c))^{\wedge}(1 / 2)$. Again, **it's in the details: one bracket off or one digit missing and the whole equation collapses. And details are more than details, they can mean the difference between negative and positive infinity, an impossible range of solutions.**

Notice how each of these "so what" moments tells us something the reader probably wouldn't have been able to come up with on his or her own. These moments illuminate the author's unique perspective. For more on this, see "Analogy of the Painter, the Art Critic, and the Curator" on page 117.

ONE FINAL IMPORTANT NOTE: Be patient with this "insight" part. It's the toughest part of the essay, and you may not discover your "so what" moments until later in the writing process. You can either start writing before you have all the insights figured out, hoping to discover them along the way, or figure out the insights before you start a draft—either can work.

When you're ready to start writing, here are a few tips.

TIPS FOR WRITING A TYPE B ESSAY

1. Before you begin, decide on an order for your examples. One way might be chronologically—in other words, the order in which you developed the values.

2. Think of the first two-thirds or three-fourths of the essay as the "show," full of images, essence objects, and details that illustrate your values—but don't make the values too obvious or you might make the ending obvious. For example, suppose your essay opens with "I've always wanted to be a doctor." If your first paragraph is about how your father is a doctor (value: family), your second paragraph is about how your favorite class is anatomy (value: knowledge), and your third paragraph is about volunteering at your local hospital (value: helping others), then the ending better be about how you want to be a chef or sports agent (which all those values will work for, by the way). If your ending is "I want to be a doctor," then we're in trouble. And by "in trouble," I just mean bored. (For tips on avoiding being predictable, check out Advanced Technique 4 on how to blow the reader's mind by using *The Sixth Sense* ending on page 150.)

3. At some point—perhaps two-thirds or three-fourths of the way through the essay—you'll probably want to mention your potential career.

4. Think of the last one-third or one-fourth of the essay as the "tell," in which you help the reader make connections between the values you've shown and what you'd like to study.

5. Remember that montage structure works well for a type B essay. For a very clear example, check out the "Endodontics" essay on page 24. For another, check out the "Behavioral Economics" essay that follows.

WHAT NOW?

1. Brainstorm the qualities or values that will make you amazing at your career.
2. Come up with an example demonstrating how you've developed each quality or value.
3. Brainstorm insights you've developed based on each of the values (see examples of this in the "Endodontics" essay).
4. Focus on one major example/value/insight per paragraph (of course there can be multiple examples, values, or insights if they are short, but it's easiest to focus on one per paragraph).
5. Near the end of the essay, reveal what you want to study and perhaps say why.
6. Once you've written a draft, turn to page 102 to learn how to revise your essay in five steps.

"BEHAVIORAL ECONOMICS"
Written by a student who did not face significant challenges and did know what he wanted to study

Fact: my grandfather got Jack Ruby off of his death sentence. He also got murderer Nathan Leopold paroled.

When I learned this as a sixth grader, I couldn't comprehend why my benevolent Grandpa Elmer would fight so hard for the lives of two killers. My grandma Midge explained to me that my grandpa "would rather let a guilty man go free than have an innocent man wrongfully imprisoned," and by preventing people from being executed, he adhered to this philosophy.

That was my first lesson in behavioral economics: trade-offs are necessary for a just society.

An experience with my Dad taught me my second lesson.

As a young man, my Dad had trouble finding an activity

he liked, until he picked up the bass guitar. From that point on, he immersed himself in music, eventually earned a jazz scholarship, secured a PhD, and became a sociology professor. And to this day, my Dad insists that the work ethic and focus he developed through music helped him find the career he loves.

But, I'm different. I love football.

Unfortunately, my Dad always considered football a waste of time and, after my parents' divorce, he threatened to make me quit. But through football I'd met some of my best friends, developed confidence, and grown closer with my younger brothers.

So, to prove to him that football wasn't a waste of time, I worked extra hard in the classroom, and in the weight room, almost as if my football career depended on it—which it did. Eventually, my efforts led to me winning an all-Greater Spokane League first team academic award for having the highest GPA of any senior on my team.

When I got home from the awards banquet, a realization hit me: my Dad's initial disapproval had fueled me to work as hard as I had. So, ironically, winning that football award was an indirect result of my Dad's first moment with his guitar.

This was my second lesson in behavioral economics: dramatic events often have distant, even subtle causes.

But it wasn't until I read *Freakonomics* that I began to actively examine the world through the lens of a behavioral economist.

While mentoring Keaziah, an at-risk fourth grader at an elementary school in a rough part of town, I subconsciously used a lesson I learned from *Freakonomics* to mentor him more effectively. Keaziah would not respond to the structured activities instituted by the mentorship program: he was reticent to paint birdhouses, for example, or play board games with the others. Instead of insisting that he partake in the usual methodical activities, however, I had a different idea. I began to take him to the basketball court, or to the computer lab, where a lack of structure enabled him to open up to me more naturally.

I realized that conventional wisdom was not always correct because, as *Freakonomics* taught me, irrationality is paradoxically one of the main constants to be expected in human behavior, rather than easily predictable rationality.

Behavioral economics has provided me with an avenue to explore some of life's most complex questions: How does one judge if a trade-off ultimately benefits society as a whole? And how does one balance autonomy with the desires of an important family member?

Although there are no concrete answers to these questions, finding my passion for the social sciences has not only led me to a potential career path, but also has brought me closer to my family. I now have a better understanding of who my Grandpa Elmer was, while my dad and I have found something in common: appreciation for the social sciences.

Although my Dad and I never had the clichéd father-son bonding moment while tossing the football in the backyard, our dinner-time discussions about current socioeconomics and extensive talks about the difference between neoclassical and behavioral economics have created even more quintessential moments between a Dad and son.

Note the simple framing device the author uses: three lessons from behavioral economics that relate to his own life. As he lays out each lesson, he reveals several core values, saving the insight/"so what" moment for the end of each section, which gives a "surprising but inevitable" quality, something I discuss more on page 150. The ending also doesn't tie things up neatly, but instead acknowledges that, while his relationship with his father is complex, it has evolved from the old status quo (Dad and I are different) to the new status quo

(Dad and I now have something in common), which is an example of using a narrative structure element in an essay that largely employs montage structure.

HOW TO COMBINE NARRATIVE AND MONTAGE STRUCTURES

It's perfectly possible to use elements of both the structures we've discussed, as you'll see in the "Stomach Whisperer" essay that follows. As you read it, try to identify elements from each type of structure. As a quick reminder, they are:

Narrative Structure (generally recommended for type A and C essays):

♦ Inciting incident/Status quo change

♦ Status quo

♦ Raise the stakes

♦ Turning point/Moment of truth

♦ Denouement/The final act

♦ Outcome/New status quo

Montage Structure (generally recommended for type B and D essays): finding a focusing lens that organizes the elements of your essay (and by "elements" I mean all the stuff you want to say about yourself) under a common theme.

What qualities or values will serve this student in her future career, and how did she develop them? (Hint: I spot at least six.)

"STOMACH WHISPERER"

Written by a student who did not *face significant challenges and* did know *what she wanted to study*

I could taste tangy cinnamon, a dash of extra vanilla, the raw flavor of molasses, all overlaid with the smooth creamy base of buttermilk batter. I'd just eaten my first bite of my grandmother's spice cake. That night, I lay with my ear against her stomach, listening to her digestion as she told me a bedtime story. Drowsily, I wondered if the echoing gurgle I'd just heard was caused by the molasses or by the cinnamon.

In the ensuing years, I never thought too much about the days when I was the Stomach Whisperer. Cooking everything I could get a recipe for, and navigating by trial and error where no recipes were found, I took advantage of my ability to pick out ingredients in what I ate. Gradually, that early curiosity regarding the destiny of what we eat soon evolved into an intense love of science.

In high school, I fed my interest in science. Classes like Biology weren't simply lectures designed to drill knowledge into my head; they were an experience. What I learned in science became intermingled with how I saw my environment; I could clearly picture my surroundings as the sum of billions of cells working together, or grasp how nitrogen fixation fit into the biogeochemical cycle.

But regardless of my new curiosity about science, I tended to second guess myself, especially during labs. A snarky voice inside me whispered that I couldn't find success in science if I had no self-confidence, or if I kept questioning whether or not I was doing a lab right. Tentative goals were forming in my mind, visions of a white coat with my name embossed on it, but I told myself that becoming a doctor was a ridiculous aspiration for a cook.

Abruptly, during junior year, my beliefs about my scientific

capabilities underwent a metamorphosis. I was introduced to
a new type of lab: specimen dissections. Lab handouts were
scarce on instructions; once we delved into the anatomy of
the stomach, they became little more than pictorial references. When asked to obtain a sample of stomach epithe-
lium, I could make a lateral incision along the pylorus of the
stomach or choose to slice open the fundus along the greater
curvature. I was gleefully awed. Not only was I exploring the
organ that I found most interesting, but I was actually doing
a good job at it. No matter which way I chose to dissect, my
eyes were opened to the fact that I had the capacity to be an
independent thinker, someone who didn't necessarily need
the instructions.

Armed with a newfound degree of self-assurance, I applied
and was accepted to an internship at the Simi Dermatological
Group. My assumption had been that when doctors see a
patient, they deliberate briefly on treatment, and then prescribe
whatever care is necessary. But interning showed me how very
wrong I was. Patients came in daily with skin conditions that
the doctors couldn't diagnose immediately. I saw that before
they prescribed treatment, stellar doctors saw patients as a
mixture of physical and mental parts, not just equations to plug
various medicines into.

As a matter of fact, breaking a spice cake down to ingredients, I realized, isn't all that different from what a doctor does
when diagnosing a patient. And in the future, I'll be combining
cooking and science by becoming a gastroenterologist. With a
wide array of gastric disorders to treat, from gastritis to polyps,
I'll have to be self-assured, so my patients can get the best care
possible. Still, each patient won't have a recipe that I can follow
to cure them, so I'll draw on the thinking of the little girl in
the kitchen, using what I know to make my own recipes. And
simultaneously, I'll always be able to incorporate the mindset

of the girl wondering whether cinnamon or molasses was the cause of that gastric condition.

In terms of montage structure, here are the qualities/values that will one day serve the author as a gastroenterologist, in the approximate order that they appear in the essay: **listening, curiosity, desire for knowledge, experience, lack of squeamishness** (I'm calling this a value since it's important for her career), **confidence, ability to improvise, willingness to take risks**.

In terms of narrative structure, the elements are: **status quo** (becoming a doctor was a ridiculous aspiration for a cook), **inciting incident** (during a dissection in class, she realized she didn't always need the instructions), **turning point** (she witnessed doctors solving problems without the instructions), **new status quo** (she realized that she could actually draw on her cooking background in the future as a gastroenterologist). Note that the author breaks the usual form by bringing up her main challenge later than usual—almost four paragraphs into the essay!—and then resolving it two paragraphs later. It works well, though, as it gives us a sense that her journey hasn't been without challenges. (Technically, this could also be considered a type A essay, but honestly, the exact type matters little—what's important is that the essay works.)

HOW TO WRITE ESSAY TYPE C

For students who *have* faced significant challenges and *do not know* what they want to study

Note: If you've already read "How to Write Essay Type A," you'll notice some of the following brainstorm instructions are similar, so feel free to skip those parts. But there are some differences in terms of how to structure and conclude your essay, so don't skip this section altogether, especially if you're contemplating *not* mentioning your potential future career at the end of your essay.

You may be wondering: What counts as a "significant" challenge? Who decides? The answer is simple:

You decide what counts as a significant challenge.

But maybe you'd like some ideas. No problem.

A List of Challenges You Might Discuss in Your Essay

- single-parent household
- significant work hours while in high school, particularly if you contributed to the family income to help pay bills
- low-income family or large family with many dependents
- you're the first person in your family to attend college
- parents' disability or unemployment (specify what and how long)
- any physical or learning disabilities (diagnosed by a health professional; specify what and how long)
- language spoken at home other than English, or any portion of your high school career that was taken outside of the United States

IMPORTANT NOTE: You don't *have* to write about these things in your main essay.

If you have faced significant challenges, this information could also be included in the additional information section or elsewhere in your application—and no single bullet point listed above has to dominate your essay. For example, if there are any potential red flags on your application (low grades, classes or activities dropped, important school changes), these can be mentioned in your additional information section or *very* briefly in your main essay, but your whole essay should not be solely about your grades or school change—you'll want to discuss those challenges in the context of a broader, more meaningful story.

ANOTHER IMPORTANT NOTE: If you don't believe you've experienced significant challenges, or if you believe you've been through some "stuff" but you're not sure that "stuff" would qualify as a "significant challenge," you can still use this type C step-by-step approach to write your essay—simply replace the word "challenge" or "challenges" in the following paragraphs with the word "experience" or "experiences."

THE SECRET TO WRITING ESSAY TYPE C

Be a victor, not a victim.

How?

a. Describe your challenges at the start of your essay, but don't dwell there.
b. Emphasize how you metabolized your challenges—in other words, what you did about them and what you learned.

The key to doing this well is to spend some serious time processing the "what I did" and "what I learned" and then to create for yourself a word budget that forces you to communicate your challenges in a succinct way. How do you do that? Read on.

HOW TO CONNECT YOUR CHALLENGES TO YOUR VALUES

STEP 1: BRAINSTORM THE CONTENT.

This, too, will be somewhat familiar if you've already read "How to Write Essay Type A." However, since you're not sure what you want to study, your essay won't make connections to your future career at the end of your essay. (Note: If you are sure, or have an idea about what you might like to study, read "How to Write Essay Type A" first, then this section.)

Here's a quick play-by-play:

1. You experienced **challenges**.
2. Those challenges had particular **effects** or repercussions, impacting you in a variety of ways.
3. To get through those challenges, you took **action**.
4. As a result, you developed certain resources, skills, or **values** that will be with you no matter what you study.

So the four questions for your essay are:

1. What **challenges** did you experience?
2. What **effects** did you face as a result of those challenges?
3. What did you **do** about it?
4. What **values** did you develop while working to overcome those challenges?

Challenges   Effects   What You Did   Values

To Organize Your Brainstorm, Do This:

Get out a blank sheet of paper, turn it sideways (horizontally), divide it into four columns, and label the columns like this:

1. Challenges	2. Effects	3. What I Did	4. Values

HERE'S WHAT TO WRITE IN EACH COLUMN:

Column 1: Challenges

What difficulties did you face or are you currently facing? Not sure what I mean by "challenges"? For examples, go to page 43.

Feel free to list several. Perhaps not all of these challenges will end up in the essay, but we're just brainstorming right now, so at this point, list all that come to mind. Even write the one that feels edgy to talk about, that you think, "Nah, that's too personal." Write that one down, too, just for the sake of the exercise.

FAQ

1. Are any topics off-limits?

Broadly speaking, very few topics are off-limits; it all depends on how the story is told. I've had students write about domestic violence, mental illness, and even self-harm in ways that have demonstrated vulnerability, core values, and insight.

The key question I always ask is this: Do you have enough distance and perspective on your challenge that you can articulate what you learned from the experience, or are you still so immersed in it that it's hard to speak about it with objectivity? *In other words, are you still in it, or have you come through it?*

If you've (honestly) come through it, then it could be worth writing about. But if you're still in it, or your essay deadline is looming, I recommend finding something else to write about. I say this because I've seen situations where students were trying to write on a tight deadline while dealing with a lot of feelings, and it just made them more stressed. But I've also seen situations where, even though a student was "in it" when they began their essay, the process of working on the essay—and in some cases, seeing a therapist—allowed the student to work through the experience and write about a sensitive challenge in a powerful way. However, this takes time.

REMEMBER: What is most interesting to a college is not your challenge, but how you metabolized your challenge—in other words, what you did about it and what you learned. If you have already metabolized/worked through your challenge, or you have time to, go for it. But if you don't, or you're afraid you might not, look for another topic.

Every situation is different, and if you're uncertain, please ask your counselor or a trusted mentor. Do make sure the person you're asking has had some experience advising students on topics for college admissions essays. And here's a tip: chances are, the answer to, "Should I write about X?" will be, "It depends on how you write about it." And the rest of this section covers how to write about any challenge.

2. How much sharing is too much?

Generally speaking, we don't need to know all the details of the challenges you faced. In other words, we don't need, "My father punched me in the face, breaking my nose and sending blood spurting all over the kitchen floor. I watched the blood as it oozed between the cracks in the blue-and-white linoleum tiles..." We just need enough information to get a sense of what you experienced. So, in this case, it would be enough to say, "There were even times when my father was physically abusive."

As a general rule, you don't need to shock the reader to make your point.

Column 2: Effects

What negative effects did you experience as a result of the challenges you faced? (Note that you probably experienced some positive effects, too, but save those for the column 4, which is labeled "values.")

The purpose of this section is to differentiate <u>your</u> experiences from those of <u>everyone else</u> who went through (and is writing his or her college essay about) similar challenges.

For example, Student A and Student B may have both experienced the challenge of "bullying," but Student A might list "physical abuse," and "having to switch schools" in the "Effects" column, whereas Student B might list "ridicule" and "name-calling."

Or two students may have the same medical condition, but for one student that may have meant trips to the allergy specialist for several years (see the "Porcelain God" essay on page 54), while for another student that may have meant a week away from school (see the "Bowling" essay on page 85). And there's no better or worse here; the point is that by providing more information, you differentiate your experiences from those of others.

Two important things to remember as you're brainstorming this section:

1. You don't need precisely one effect per challenge—one challenge can have several repercussions.
2. This part can take some time, so be patient.

Column 3: What I Did

What actions did you take to improve your situation?

Examples: I started watching the parenting videos our family counselor had given my dad, I took a train from London to Paris, or I created two organizations to improve sustainability on campus.

Column 4: Values

What qualities/skills/values/resources did you develop during this time?

Here's an example based on the brainstorm for the "Bowling" essay on page 85:

1. Challenges	2. Effects	3. What I Did	4. Values
father's accident	Cup of Noodles soup	connected w/ mom more	family, sacrifice
baby sister car accident	I missed school to work	Leadership Council	confidence
mother's tumor	hurt myself (vein lea.k.a.ge)	GSA (anti-bullying)	self-love
		soccer (captain)	leadership
		job (bowling alley)	fun

IMPORTANT NOTE: See if you can include several *unexpected* connections or values. Let me explain. Some of the connections between the "what I did" and the "values" are pretty obvious. But a few of them are less obvious, such as the connections between "GSA (anti-bullying)" and "self-love" or between "connected with mom more" and "sacrifice." It's these unusual values—or usual values developed in unusual ways—that can lead to unique insights and make your essay stand out.

And the point I just made is so important that I feel I must underscore it:

If you use only predictable values at the end of your essay and explain your values in predictable ways, there is a good chance your essay will be boring.

- Examples of predictable values gained from being the captain of the soccer team: discipline, commitment, hard work
- Examples of unpredictable values gained from being the captain of the soccer team: emotional risk, autonomy, healthy boundaries

Which group of values might make for a more interesting essay? That's a rhetorical question, but just in case: the second group. Just to get your brain turning, here's one more set of examples:

- Predictable values gained from joining Model United Nations: responsibility, sacrifice, helping others
- Unpredictable values gained from joining Model United Nations: resourcefulness, art, privacy

IMPORTANT NOTE: Just because the values are predictable doesn't mean that they are wrong or boring or that you are wrong or boring. I've read great essays that have used predictable values, but here's the key: the more usual the values are, the more well-crafted (or unusual) the "so what" moments need to be. Notice, for example, that the "Bowling" essay on page 85 includes the theme of "hard work," which could be considered a predictable value—that's fine, and the essay still works. I'm simply suggesting you either include a couple unusual values or express your predictable values in an interesting (or at least succinct) way.

HOW CAN YOU BRAINSTORM LESS PREDICTABLE VALUES?

Try this: look at the Core Values Exercise on page 8 and see if you can choose a value you think will surprise me. (Yes, me, Ethan.) Imagine we're actually sitting across from each other and you've just told me about your challenge and what you did about it. Then pick a value on that list and imagine telling me what you gained from it. If you think I'll be able to guess the connection, chances are it'll be predictable for the reader. So pick something else. Keep going until you find something that you don't think I'd be able to guess right away.

STEP 2: DECIDE ON A STRUCTURE.

Here's a simple structure for organizing your essay:

1. What's the challenge I faced? ($\approx$ 1/3 of essay; it could be a bit more, but not more than 1/2! The essay should turn from negative "challenges" to positive "what I did" by the midway point.)
2. What did I do about it? ($\approx$ 1/3 of essay)
3. How did this make me a better person? ($\approx$ 1/3 of essay)

So, if you're writing a 650-word essay, the math works out like this:

1. Challenge(s): $\approx$ 150–250 words
2. What I did: $\approx$ 150–250 words
3. What I learned: $\approx$ 150–250 words

This is just a guide. It's totally possible to break from this form and still write a great essay, but this is a good starting point to keep you on track.

Two Common Pitfalls When Discussing Challenges in an Essay (and How to Avoid Them)

1. Avoid articulating the "challenge" and the "what I did" in the same sentence, like this:

   My mother injured her back, so I had to take on more responsibility around the house by cleaning the house and cooking meals for my brothers.

This ruins the ending of the story. Why? I'll explain in a second.

2. Avoid jumping back and forth between the "challenge" and "what I did" several times in the same paragraph, like this:

   My mother hurt her back, so I started helping more around the house, I started falling behind in school, so I taught myself to manage my time better, and responsibilities as soccer captain increased, so I learned to delegate responsibilities better.

This creates two problems:

1. It can ruin the ending (thanks, that's the whole essay, goodbye!).
2. It can lead to an essay that feels disorganized.

How do you solve this?

Group all the challenges into one paragraph and don't solve the problems until later in the essay, in a separate paragraph.

Why should you do this?

1. Grouping all the challenges into an early paragraph allows time for the reader to wonder, "Are things going to work out? If so, how?" It builds tension.

2. It organizes the information in a way that allows you to have a narrative arc that looks something like this:

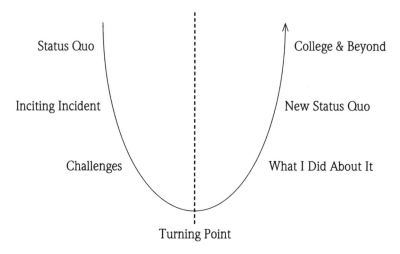

You'll notice this follows the narrative structure. That's the idea. To review:

- **Status Quo**: how things were at one point
- **Inciting Incident**: the moment the changes began
- **Raise the Stakes**: the tough stuff
- **Turning Point/Moment of Truth**: the moment you decided to do something about it
- **Denouement/What I Did**: describe in detail the specific actions you took
- **New Status Quo**: what changed, or how things are now

Interesting note: The "Raising Anthony" essay on page 26 does not follow this structure. In fact, its arc looks more like this:

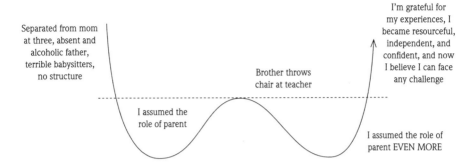

Why this structure? Because otherwise it's too easy to spend most of the essay describing the "challenges" and not enough time describing "what I did" or "what I learned"—which is what admissions officers are most interested in knowing.

Want an even more specific outline? I'll give you one in just a second, and I'll even include some paragraph starters to give you a sense of how the essay might flow. But remember this: don't use this sample outline if it feels too confining. Use it only if you're feeling lost or if you really need a more specific structure. With those qualifiers, here is:

A PAINT-BY-NUMBER OUTLINE FOR A TYPE C ESSAY

1. THE CHALLENGES (OR) THE EFFECTS: ≈ 1/3 OF ESSAY (AND NO MORE THAN 1/2!)

- ❏ **Paragraph 1**: My life was forever changed when…
- ❏ **Paragraph 2**: To make matters worse…
  - ❏ Transition sentences (the lowest point of the story):
    - ❏ Sentence 1 (the breaking point): The toughest part came when…
    - ❏ Sentence 2 (the turning point): I realized I had to do something.

2. WHAT I DID (OR) THE WORK I PUT IN: ≈ 1/3 OF ESSAY

☐ **Paragraph 3**: So I started… (Describe the specific things you did to make things better.)

☐ **Paragraph 4**: I also… (What else did you do? Describe the specifics here.)

> Tip for increasing the drama: In these two paragraphs, build the details from smallest to largest.
>
> Example: "I started helping my brother with his homework" should come before "I founded an environmental science club at my school and began holding weekly meetings," since presumably the homework help required less work than founding a club and holding weekly meetings.

> Tip for the transition between paragraphs 4 and 5: In order to clearly demonstrate that things have improved, create a "stand up and cheer" moment at the end of paragraph 4 that involves one specific detail or image that shows you at your best.
>
> Example: "And to top it all off, I got straight As for the first time ever" or "Then I did something with my brother that I hadn't done in six years: I ate dinner with him." This moment represents an opportunity to show how far you've come. (See the "Bowling" or "I Shot My Brother" essay for an example.)

3. WHAT I LEARNED (OR) THE RESULT: ≈ 1/3 OF ESSAY

☐ **Paragraph 5**: Turn your difficulties into strengths.

Example 1: Having to balance schoolwork, plus chores, plus a job, taught me the value of time management.

Example 2: Overcommitting myself with four AP classes, six clubs, and two jobs taught me how important it is to prioritize and how to say "no."

WHAT NOW?

Time to outline and write a draft using the instructions in this section. You can use any of the following:

- The simple three-part outline (Challenges, What I did, What I learned) described on page 80
- The narrative structure described on page 82
- The paint-by-number outline for a type C essay on page 83
- The Feelings and Needs Exercise on page 127 (if you really want to take your essay to the next level)

Once you've written a draft, turn to "How to Revise Your Essay in Five Steps" on page 102.

Want two more examples of type C essays?

Here you go:

"BOWLING"

Written by a student who did *face significant challenges and* did not know *what she wanted to study*

Every weekend, my family and I go to the bowling alley. We either go to Lucky Strike in Orange County, to 300 in Pasadena or the AMF Bowladrome in Torrance. It's been a tradition for us ever since I turned 11. But here's a secret:

I've never bowled a game in my life.

I began going when I was 11 because that's when I was old enough to adroitly wipe down a table and spray Windex on a window without making a mess. Every Saturday night from 10pm to 4am, after entering the bowling alley through a back door, my parents dispatch my older sister Marlene and me to the lanes armed with broomsticks.

"Try to clean around the bowlers," she always says.

We always do.

In 2003 my family's stability was put to the test when my father suffered an accident: he was bitten by a horse and unable to work for three years. Some months later my year-old baby sister was hit by a car. My mother was our only financial support, so we often ate Cup of Noodles for breakfast, lunch and dinner. I prayed every night that things got [sic] better but first they got worse.

In the eleventh grade my father suffered a muscle failure and my mother was diagnosed with a tumor. Due to my parents' health problems I took on more responsibilities, sometimes missing school to care for my younger sisters and helping my father and mother at their work. Unfortunately, I pushed myself so hard that I ended up hurting myself, suffering a vain [sic] lea.k.a.ge in my brain. I was the fighter, the protector, and now I found myself needing someone to protect me. I was glad to have my mother by my side because she gave the strength I needed.

After some rest, I returned to school more focused than ever on preparing for my future. I got involved in Leadership Council where I'm now part of the civics committee, planning events such as Day at the Park and school dances. I've also become a big supporter of the Gay Straight Alliance that deals with anti-bullying, and through this club I've given presentations that address unfairness and promote equity. But perhaps my biggest support system has come through the four years on my high school soccer team, where my commitment and love for soccer won me the captain position for the past two years.

I know I'm not like many students my age, but I'm happy with who I am. I am the student who works on the weekends scrubbing restrooms, carrying trash bags and mopping kitchen floors. I am the student who won't give a second thought to missing a party to help my parents babysit my sisters or accompany them to a new job. I know that one day I will not take my family to a bowling alley to clean it but to enjoy it.

And who knows, maybe one day I will learn to bowl.

Note that this essay follows the recommended structure, but with a slight variation: rather than describing the "challenge," "what [she] did," and "what [she] learned" in one-third chunks, the author instead dedicates the first one-fourth of the essay to setting up a hook, then devotes one-fourth to each of the other parts. This is fine and good. Again, the suggested structure is just a guide to get you to communicate the challenges succinctly so you can focus on other elements in the essay.

"WHAT I FOUND ON THE FARM"
Written by a student who did *face significant challenges* *and* did not know *what he wanted to study*

"In the first six years of my life, my family moved exactly thirteen times. By the fifth move, the security of 'home' was gone. By the ninth, my eyes had adjusted to the aggressive two-dimensionality of the Affordable Housing Authority's drab brick walls. This was my life: only drifting, transience. No roots, no permanence."

My voice trembled beneath the dim dining hall lights as I sat before sixty students and two dozen faculty members. I shared my world as a first-generation Asian-American, how my mother's first job in America had been a seamstress in an overstuffed Chinese garment factory, and how my grandmother, in her seventies, spent her last years in the Land of Opportunity scavenging cans on city streets.

Here I was, three hundred miles from home in the Colorado backcountry, opening my heart to strangers. Why?

For the past few years, I'd found myself the bearer of rather peculiar labels from my peers, creative terms like "banana" and "golden Oreo." Perhaps it was because my Chinese language ability (or lack thereof) was my family's shame, or because I absolutely could not use chopsticks for the life of me. Maybe it was because even though I tried and tried, I could not play Pachelbel's Canon in D. Whatever it was, I was accused of letting my "Chinese-ness" slip. I was stuck in limbo, truly belonging to neither the Chinese nor the American community. I felt closed-off and lost.

I yearned for a place to belong. But where? In my junior year, I found it—in Colorado, of all places.

At the Colorado Ranch School, a summer program on a farm in rural Colorado, I bucked my home culture of over-scheduling and over-stimulation. Living together with my teachers and their children, witnessing one too many animal slaughters with my classmates, and harvesting all 2,000 pounds of sweet potatoes until our nails caked with dried dirt, I felt comfortable enough, for the very first time, to share my deepest stories.

I also discovered a refreshing approach to activism, one that valued student voices, respected individualism, and championed student-led change—values not as esteemed at my home school. When the issue of racial microaggressions emerged, for example, I created an affinity group to increase awareness about diversity issues, holding conversations that unified students and staff to effect change in our school.

But most importantly, I found a place where I belonged, and with it, a sense of community and acceptance.

In the spring, I returned to high school refreshed and empowered. I created two organizations to improve sustainability on campus, fundraising thousands to install water stations to reduce plastic bottle consumption. Realizing the value of fighting for change, I protested outside the White House at the Keystone XL Dissent rally and marched alongside a legion of 400,000 at the People's Climate March, demanding action to save our planet.

Before the Colorado Ranch School, I let others define me, based on the titles they chose to bestow upon me: "banana," "golden Oreo," even tree-hugger. But in Colorado, despite the rootlessness and transience of my upbringing, I was able to solidify a strengthened sense of self: environmentalist, activist, Asian-American. By showing my authentic self to a group of compassionate individuals, I realized that I'm so much more than those confining titles: I'm the son of hardworking immigrant parents, the lover of anything by Junot Diaz, the one for whom mixing cereal and milk is a personal sin.

Chopsticks still fluster me, and I can't magically play Pachelbel, but so be it. My identity is just that: mine to own, and mine to shape. In time, I've learned that while my identity already has, and will continue to change, I can embrace it for what it is: a medley of unorthodox traits, passions, and dreams, blending into a singular vibrant whole.

Note that this essay basically uses the one–third, one–third, one–third structure suggested earlier, as the "challenge," "what I did," and "what I learned" sections are all about the same length. Also note that the author begins the essay not with his inciting incident, but with the turning point—in other words, he starts with the moment that he was able to find what he was looking for—a community where he could feel safe enough to be vulnerable. This works great.

HOW TO WRITE ESSAY TYPE D

For Students Who *Have Not* Faced Significant Challenges and *Do Not Know* What They Want to Study

If you haven't experienced significant challenges and aren't sure what you'd like to study, you may be wondering what to write about. Don't worry. You'll be generating ideas in a few minutes.

Consider that in broad terms you're looking for:

1. **Content**: some stuff (values or qualities) that you want to discuss
2. **Structure**: a way to frame all the stuff—an angle, a focusing lens

How do you find a great focusing lens? We'll get to that in a second. But first, I want to emphasize something.

The Importance of Being Patient

Type D essays are the most open-ended of the four types. Think for a second about why that may be.

Type A and C essays dedicate a lot of their word count to describing the author's challenges and efforts to overcome them, while type B essays are dedicated to describing values that will serve the author in a particular career.

But for type D essays, nothing is set. It's wide open. What does this mean for you?

You'll need to be patient.

It's very possible to write an interesting essay that has no major conflict and mentions no definitive career choice in its conclusion. (You'll find examples on pages 28, 96, 99, 152, and 207.) Because your options are wide open, it just might take you a little longer. How much longer? As a reference point, the type D essays mentioned above took at least eight to ten drafts to complete.

THE SECRET TO WRITING THIS TYPE OF ESSAY

Find a focusing lens that allows you to discuss a wide range of values or qualities.

The type D essays in this book (see list on page 231) all utilize a framing device that allowed their authors to demonstrate a variety of values. In the "Scrapbook" essay on page 28, for example, the author was able to bring to life the values of travel, teaching, family, and helping others through the "scrapbook of [her] life." In the "Five Families" essay on page 152, the author describes how living in five different homes helped him learn the importance of humility, intimacy, openness, discipline, diversity, and adaptability.

How did these authors do this? First, they generated some stuff to write about, and then they figured out a way to organize all their stuff. Did they have to start over several times? Yes. Did they get frustrated along the way? Definitely. But both authors worked hard, they didn't give up, and ultimately they wrote great essays.

It's your turn. First, you need your content, so here are:

SIX WAYS TO GENERATE YOUR CONTENT (A.K.A. SOME STUFF YOU WANT THE READER TO KNOW ABOUT YOU)

Complete the following exercises:

1. Essence Objects Exercise (page 1)
2. Core Values Exercise (page 8)
3. 21 Details Exercise (page 225)
4. Everything I Want Colleges to Know about Me List (page 226)

5. Time Line of My Life Exercise (page 228), either alone or with someone else

6. Complete a personality assessment online (many are available and some are free).

Once you've finished these exercises, most of which should take between five and twenty minutes, you should have several (or many) gems—qualities or values that you definitely want to communicate in your essay. If not, keep going—you may have rushed through the process.

Once you've completed the exercises, look for a way to organize your content—in other words, a structure. Here are:

SIX WAYS TO IDENTIFY A FRAMING DEVICE FOR YOUR ESSAY

Remember: A great framing device (i.e., focusing lens) is one that allows you to discuss a wide variety of values. Here are some ideas.

Option 1: Use a placeholder career and discuss values essential to that career (i.e., write a type B essay).
That's right—before we even get into the type D tips—ask yourself if you could actually write a type B essay using a placeholder.

What's a placeholder career? It means picking something you're interested in and mentioning it as a potential future career at the end of your essay. Say, for example, you love math, you're interested in studying business, and you love helping others—you might say at the end of your essay that you're interested in being a "socially conscious entrepreneur."

Fun Fact: Some of the essays in this book actually have career placeholders. But I'm not going to tell you which ones, and *you'll never be able to guess them.*

And, by the way, isn't *every* career a placeholder in the long run?

Here are two benefits to this method:

1. **A placeholder can actually help you find your calling**. It's true. I once worked with a student who wasn't sure what she wanted to study, but she knew she was interested in travel, working with people, and global issues. So she chose a travel-related major (international relations) as a placeholder and was able to write an essay describing how her interests and family background led her to become interested in this field. And guess what? By researching international relations, she actually ended up becoming more interested in it, and it went from being a placeholder to a college major that she was excited about. Will choosing a placeholder always lead you to find your calling? Not always. But it might.

2. **Focusing on how you developed a core set of values might also save you time**. I recently worked with a student who thought he wanted to major in computer science, so we started brainstorming an essay by naming some of the values that had led him to that field: autonomy, creativity, and helping others. A few weeks before his essay was due, however, he decided he was interested in studying psychology and potentially becoming a counselor. Fortunately, he didn't have to start his essay over from scratch. Why? We'd been focusing on core values that connected to many majors, so he was able to salvage a good portion of his essay. How? Because while computer scientists value autonomy, creativity, and helping others, so do counselors. So he was able to keep most of his essay, which detailed how he'd developed these values. He simply rewrote the ending, explaining what these values all added up to. Just to clarify: this will work as long as the values you've been focusing on in your essay will connect to your new career path—and, by the way, most values will connect to most careers.

My main point here is this: Because I believe that, ultimately, every career is a placeholder, what's most important is not where we end up, but how we get there. Put another way, admissions officers are less interested in what you want to be (career) and more interested in how you arrived there (values). In short, prioritize process over product, journey over destination.

What's the best way to discover a potential major or career? I use the book *Do What You Are*, by Paul D. Tieger, Barbara Barron, and Kelly Tieger, which provides profiles for different careers based on a student's personality.

If you would rather not write about a potential career or major, here are some other ways to find a focusing lens.

Option 2: Search for common themes among your brainstorm exercises.

Ask yourself: Do any themes repeat in my brainstorming material?

Example: *I'm noticing the theme of "home" coming up a lot. What does "home" really mean to me? Could I write an essay exploring my relationship to home, and how the meaning of "home" has shifted for me throughout my life?*

Another example: *I'm noticing the theme of "being a man" has come up a few times. What does it mean to me to "be a man" and how has my thinking on that evolved over the years?*

Option 3: Look for interesting contradictions.

Ask yourself: Do I spot any interesting opposites, contradictions, or paradoxes in my brainstorming material?

Example from a past student: *Some of my essence objects demonstrate my passion for collaboration, while a few of my 21 details mention how much I love working by myself. What does this say about me? Could I write an essay exploring these two parts of myself—my desire for both autonomy and connectedness?*

Another example from a past student: *Some of my essence objects represent my connection to Korean culture, while other details represent my connection to American culture. How do I feel about this? Am I torn between the two, connected to them equally, or both?* (Apologies to you, dear reader, that I can't include all these essays—this book would be crazy long. But many are available on the College Essay Guy website: www.collegeessayguy.com.)

Option 4: Look for a potential negative and turn it into a positive.

Ask yourself: Is there a potential red flag on my application? Anything the reader might question? How could I reframe this so that it might actually be seen as a strength?

Example from a past student: *I feel like I'm all over the place with my extracurricular activities. What positive quality could all this jumping around represent? Ooh! How about an ability to adapt to all sorts of scenarios—like a chameleon?* (Careful here: make sure your essay doesn't sound like an elaborate excuse. How will you do this? Over the course of several drafts, my friend.)

Option 5: List your top three (or five) life lessons.

Ask yourself: What three to five moments, events, or lessons really shaped who I am?

Example from an essay in this book: *Some people see me as "the debate guy" or "the writer" or even the guy who got a great SAT score. But that's not really me—I'm more of a punk rock philosopher. Could I write about how I became that?* (Yes. See the "Punk Rock Philosopher" essay that on page 96.)

Option 6: Choose something that you love and write about it unabashedly.

Is there anything in your life that you love to do that could serve as a focusing lens?

Example from a past student: *I love beekeeping. Seriously, it's like my favorite thing. It's helped me connect with my dad, it's taught me about nature, and even about business, since I've started selling the honey that our bees have produced. Could I write an essay on The Top Five Lessons I've Learned from Beekeeping?* (Um, yes. Absolutely.)

Another example: *I love reading. Could my essay be all about how books have shaped me?* Yes—see the "If Ink Were Ants" essay on page 99.

Ready for some examples of essays built from these options? You'll find two here and others by searching the index at the back of the book.

"PUNK ROCK PHILOSOPHER"
Written by a student who did not *face significant challenges and* did not know *what he wanted to study*

I am on Oxford Academy's Speech and Debate Team, in both the Parliamentary Debate division and the Lincoln-Douglass debate division. I write screenplays, short stories, and opinionated blogs and am a regular contributor to my school literary magazine, *The Gluestick.* I have accumulated over 300 community service hours that includes work at homeless shelters, libraries, and special education youth camps. I have been evaluated by the College Board and have placed within the top percentile.

But I am not any of these things. I am not a test score, nor a debater, nor a writer. I am an anti-nihilist punk rock philosopher. And I became so when I realized three things:

1) That the world is ruled by underwear. There is a variety of underwear for a variety of people. You have your ironed briefs for your businessmen, your soft cottons for the average, and hemp-based underwear for your environmental romantics. But underwear do [sic] not only tell us about who we are, they [sic] also influence our daily interactions in ways most of us don't even understand. For example, I have a specific pair of underwear that is holey, worn out but surprisingly comfortable. And despite how trivial underwear might be, when I am wearing my

favorite pair, I feel as if I am on top of the world. In any case, these articles of clothing affect our being and are the unsung heroes of comfort.

2) When I realized I cannot understand the world. I recently debated at the Orange County Speech League Tournament, within the Parliamentary Division. This specific branch of debate is an hour long, and consists of two parties debating either side of a current political issue. In one particular debate, I was assigned the topic: "Should Nation States eliminate nuclear arms?" It so happened that I was on the negative side and it was my job to convince the judges that countries should continue manufacturing nuclear weapons. During the debate, something strange happened: I realized that we are a special breed of species, that so much effort and resources are invested to ensure mutual destruction. And I felt that this debate in a small college classroom had elucidated something much more profound about the scale of human existence. In any case, I won 1st place at the tournament, but as the crowd cheered when my name was called to stand before an audience of hundreds of other debaters, and I flashed a victorious smile at the cameras, I couldn't help but imagine that somewhere at that moment a nuclear bomb was being manufactured, adding to an ever-growing stockpile of doom. And that's when I realized that the world was something I will never understand.

3) When I realized I was a punk rocker philosopher. One summer night, my friend took me to an underground hardcore punk rock show. It was inside a small abandoned church. After the show, I met and became a part of this small community. Many were lost and on a constant soul-search, and to my surprise, many, like myself, did not have a blue Mohawk or a nose piercing. Many were just ordinary people discussing Nietzsche, string theory, and governmental ideologies. Many were also artists creating promotional posters and inventive

slogans for stickers. They were all people my age who could not afford to be part of a record label and did something extraordinary by playing in these abandoned churches, making their own CDs and making thousands of promotional buttons by hand. I realized then that punk rock is not about music nor is it a guy with a blue Mohawk screaming protests. Punk rock is an attitude, a mindset, and very much a culture. It is an antagonist to the conventional. It means making the best with what you have to contribute to a community. This was when I realized that I was a punk rock philosopher.

The world I come from consists of underwear, nuclear bombs, and punk rockers. And I love this world. My world is inherently complex, mysterious, and anti-nihilist. I am Daniel Bak, somebody who spends his weekends debating in a three-piece suit, other days immersed within the punk rock culture, and some days writing opinionated blogs about underwear.

But why college? I want a higher education. I want more than just the textbook fed classrooms in high school. A community which prizes revolutionary ideals, a sharing of multi-dynamical perspectives, an environment that ultimately acts as a medium for movement, similar to the punk rock community. I do not see college as a mere stepping stone for a stable career or a prosperous life, but as a supplement for knowledge and self-empowerment; it is a social engine that will jettison us to our next paradigm shift.

Note the simple framing device. The author names all his achievements and then undercuts them by writing, "But I am not any of these things. I am not a test score, nor a debater, nor a writer. I am an anti–nihilist punk rock philosopher. And I became so when I realized three things…" and just like that, I'm hooked. I totally want to know what those three things are. He does so by raising a question that's interesting enough to keep our attention for the length of the essay (something that's discussed more on page 112). In this case, the question is simple: What were the three lessons the author learned that led him to become an anti–nihilist punk rock philosopher?

"IF INK WERE ANTS"

Written by a student who did not *face significant challenges and* did not know *what she wanted to study*

"If the ink of my writing morphed into ants, would they march along with my thoughts?" ~ Jarod Kintz

Wooden bookshelves protrude regally from my wall. The wall's deep purple stucco contrasts starkly with the boards' glossy white granules. Atop the shelves, several volumes rise in lofty columns. The columns tremble. A strange commotion ripples through their pages.

Sprawled upon one such page, I feel the parchment beneath me shuddering like the earth beneath a wild stampede. Before my incredulous eyes, the typed letters before me quiver, totter… morph into ants! The ants march to and fro across the page, ravenously following thoughts of quarks, hidden dimensions, and string theory. I am in Brian Greene's scientific novel, *The Elegant Universe*. I want to join the ants and delve into the author's thoughts. Instead, I reflect on my memories:

Awe overwhelmed my middle-school mind. My hand, a bottle cap, everything, was composed of not only atoms, but of smaller quarks, which were not static points, but oscillating strings. Everything in my life might be controlled by infinitesimal, interconnected loops… the universe, a mind-bogglingly large space, might be only one of an infinite number of universes. After studying cosmology at an extra-curricular astro-camp, I was certain: I wanted to be a theoretical physicist.

I haul myself out of Greene's novel and observe a stream of ants spilling from *Pride and Prejudice, Gone with the Wind,* and *Crime and Punishment.* I join their ranks, revisiting scenes of ballrooms, Civil War battles, 19th century St. Petersburg. Again, my thoughts wander:

As a sophomore, I loved venturing into the worlds of historic characters. AP European History quickly became my favorite class. I obsessed with particulars: Queen Elizabeth I and her rumored romantic interest in Sir Walter Raleigh, the infamous schemes and bizarre execution of the Russian monk, Rasputin. Studying history was like reading a novel, and I was determined to uncover the plots. I aspired to become an historian.

As we vacate *Crime and Punishment,* the ant before me halts jarringly. I pitch forward precariously. My arms whirl in a windmill-like motion. I plunge over the ant's back into another novel.

An ant nudges me from the left. Another from the right. All around me, the ants career spasmodically—here, there, everywhere! As I listen to the thoughts swirling about I deduce the cause of the chaos: the little creatures cannot decipher my Latin copy of *Carmina.*

I remembered translating Catullus' poetry, analyzing his dysfunctional relationship with Lesbia. Wishing to grasp Catullus' motivations and thought processes, I realized that it would be fascinating to study psychology.

I squeeze beneath *Carmina*'s cover and spot my ceramic teddy-bear bookend looming above me. Struck by a sudden impulse, I scale its towering form and settle comfortably between the figurine's ears, my legs dangling over its eyes, and survey my bedroom. Around me, my books pitch and heave mightily as ants swell from their covers. A black sea of scuttling limbs, the ants pour out of *Atlas Shrugged, A Long Way Gone, Star Trek, Harry Potter,* and Dickens novels, and dozens more. They surge toward the center of my room, billow beneath my bed, and... disappear. The boisterous, animate rabble of thoughts vanishes, leaving behind the whisper of empty pages rustling blankly.

I withdraw from my daydream and scrutinize my college application. The old, but now more pressing, question batters my brain: "What do you want to be when you grow up?" I contemplate my bookshelves and the stories that have shaped my identity and aspirations and am struck by the power of ink on paper to persuade, inform, and inspire. I select the English option from the application menu. My future might be undecided but surely pursuing my passionate interest in litera-ture is the best way to fill its pages. I eye my copy of *One L.*

Perhaps an English degree will lead to a J.D. in law...

Again, note the simple framing device. The author seems to say, *Here are a few ways that books have shaped my interests.* Straightforward enough. But the way the author tells of their influence is unusual, unexpected, and beautifully crafted. In fact, note that the insights and craft in both this essay and the "Punk Rock Philosopher" essay are on another level. I believe that for an essay that does not address a particular challenge to really stand out, careful attention must be paid to the insights (or "so what" moments) and the craft (*how* the story is told). To be sure, these elements are always important, but I think they are especially important when writing the type D essay. As I've mentioned, it can sometimes take longer to find an unusual framing device and to craft the insights, but it is possible with some hard work and patience. As a point of reference, the author of the "If Ink Were Ants" essay and I had a conversation about an entirely different essay, which she ultimately decided to scrap after our conversation. Several weeks later, after not hearing from her, she wrote me an email that read, "I finally finished the new draft of my essay (after 10 revisions!)" and she attached the essay you just read. Because, sometimes, that's what it takes.

CHAPTER FIVE

How to Revise Your Essay in Five Steps

REVISING THE FIRST DRAFT

Some of the essays you've read so far have a structure that is rock solid. Not only is it rock solid, it's one we can learn from.

Take a look at the first sentence of each paragraph from type A essay "With Debate" (page 22) and type B essay "Endodontics" (page 24).

Notice something?

If you read just those sentences, each essay still makes sense. They're like mini-essays. Take a look:

Here's the first line of each paragraph of the "With Debate" essay:

> The clock was remarkably slow as I sat, legs tightly crossed, squirming at my desk.

> My diffidence was frustrating.

> Near meltdown, I knew something needed to be done.

> Disillusioned and wrung dry of ideas, I followed my mom's advice and joined a debate club.

But soon, the club moved on from "how to make a speech" lessons to the exploration of argumentation.

By high school, I joined the school debate team, began socializing, and was even elected to head several clubs.

I became proud and confident.

Four years with debate, and now I'm the kid up at the white board; the kid leading discussions; and the kid standing up for her beliefs.

More importantly, I now confront issues instead of avoiding them.

In particular, I am interested in the North-South Korean tension.

I see a reflection of myself in the divide at the 38th parallel because I see one part isolating itself in defense to outside threats, and another part coming out to face the world as one of the fastest-developing nations.

And here's the first line of each paragraph of the "Endodontics" essay:

As a kid I was always curious.

And it didn't stop in second grade.

A few years later I designed my first pair of shoes, working for hours to perfect each detail, including whether the laces should be mineral white or diamond white.

In high school I moved on to more advanced projects, teaching myself how to take apart, repair, and customize cell phones.

And once I obtained my driver's license, I began working on cars.

My love of details applies to my schoolwork too.

I'm the math geek who marvels at the fundamental theorems of Calculus, or who sees beauty in $A = (s(s - a)(s - b)(s - c))^{(1/2)}$.

I also love sharing this appreciation with others and have taken it upon myself to personally eradicate mathonumopho-biconfundosis, my Calculus teacher's term for "extreme fear of Math."

You probably think I want to be a designer. Or perhaps an engineer?

Wrong. Well, kind of.

Actually, I want to study Endodontics, which is (I'll save you the Wikipedia look-up) a branch of dentistry that deals with the tooth pulp and the tissues surrounding the root of a tooth.

The fact is, it's not unlike the work I've been doing repairing cellphone circuits and modifying cars, though there is one small difference.

The question is: Will the toothbrushes I hand out be mineral white or diamond white?

Kind of awesome. Almost as if the whole essay could be boiled down to those first sentences.

How can this help you revise your essay? Like this:

1. Go through your essay and highlight the first sentence of each

paragraph in bold. Then read the bolded lines aloud. (Side note: I once heard that Anton Chekhov would read all his work aloud to his wife to check for sense and errors—it's a great practice. Even if you have no wife.)

As you read, you'll probably notice that some parts make sense and some parts don't.

So:

2. Write a new outline in which all of the first sentences flow together like a mini-version of your essay.
3. Once you've written this new outline, paste the bolded lines onto a brand new blank document.

Then:

4. Rewrite your paragraphs so that each paragraph fleshes out the topic sentence.

This may not sound like a very romantic or creative way of writing an essay, but it works. It'll also help you clarify what you're trying to say. "Foggy writing is foggy thinking," my favorite English teacher, Mrs. Clark, used to say.

Why do I suggest you paste the new outline onto a new document and start over? Because, in short, it'll take longer if you don't. Chances are you'll have fallen in love with your first way of phrasing something. Once you've written the new outline, though, that old phrasing dies. And if you're trying to create a new and living thing out of old, dead parts, you're no better than Dr. Frankenstein. And we all know what happened to him.

5. Step away from the essay for at least thirty minutes. Go for a walk, get something to eat, do something else to clear your mind.

Then come back to the essay and read it aloud. When you do:

- Highlight the first sentence of each paragraph in bold.
- Read the bolded sentences aloud in order to see if they now tell a short version of your essay. (If not, rewrite them.) If they do...
- Read the whole essay aloud, checking to see if what's in each paragraph supports the sentences in bold.

If they do, you should have a very solid revision, maybe even one that's ready for feedback.

REVISING DRAFTS 2–50

What if you've just done the first sentence revision exercise and your essay still doesn't flow? Make sure you've tried it a couple times or even had someone else guide you through it—sometimes an outside eye can help. Also make sure this person has read the description of this exercise, so he or she understands what you're trying to do here.

Still isn't working? It may be that your problem isn't the "flow" of your ideas at all. It may actually be that your essay doesn't reveal much about you or that it's not that deep.

If you suspect that one of these things is the case, turn to page 186 and read "The Great College Essay Test" or to page 121 to learn how to make your essay, like, deep.

CHAPTER SIX

How to Bring Your Essay to Life

(or) How to Make It Not Boring

HERE ARE SOME QUESTIONS I get a lot:

- How do I grab the reader's attention?
- How do I show the reader that I'm really smart?
- How do I brag in a way that doesn't sound like I'm bragging?
- How do I make my essay, like, deep?
- How do I end my essay?

And here are my thoughts on these matters.

HOW DO I GRAB THE READER'S ATTENTION?

Your English teacher has probably told you, "Your essay needs a hook!" or "You've gotta draw 'em in!"

Thanks. The question is: How?

Here's my favorite way:

Begin with a Problem That Must Be Solved

Examples:

"Porcelain God" (page 54)

> Bowing down to the porcelain god, I emptied the contents of
> my stomach. Foaming at the mouth, I was ready to pass out.
> My body couldn't stop shaking as I gasped for air, and the room
> started spinning.

Problem: What happened? Why is she throwing up? Will she be
okay? Will she die?

"I Shot My Brother" (page 173)

> From page 54 of the maroon notebook sitting on my mahogany
> desk:
> *Then Cain said to the Lord, "My punishment is greater*
> *than I can bear. I shall be a fugitive and a wanderer on the*
> *earth and whoever finds me will kill me."—Genesis 4:13*
> Here is a secret that no one in my family knows: I shot my
> brother when I was six. Luckily, it was a BB gun. But to this
> day, my older brother Jonathan does not know who shot him.
> And I have finally promised myself to confess this eleven year
> old secret to him after I write this essay.

Problem: Why did he shoot his brother? How? Will he actually get
up the nerve to confess? How will his brother react?

"Rock, Paper, Scissors" (page 169)

> **Prompt:**
> Dear Christian, The admissions staff at the University of

Chicago would like to inform you that your application has been "put on the line." We have one spot left and can't decide if we should admit you or another equally qualified applicant. To resolve the matter, please choose one of the following:

Rock, paper, or scissors.

You will be notified of our decision shortly.

Response:

Rock beats scissors, scissors beats paper, and paper beats rock. Wait… paper beats rock? Since when has a sheet of loose leaf paper ever defeated a solid block of granite? Do we assume that the paper wraps around the rock, smothering the rock into submission? When exposed to paper, is rock somehow immobilized, unable to fulfill its primary function of smashing scissors? What constitutes defeat between two inanimate objects?

Problem: Which will he choose? How will he decide? What if he makes the wrong choice?

IMPORTANT NOTE: Don't solve the problem until the end of the essay. OR: If you choose to solve the problem or answer the question partway through the essay, make sure you create a new problem or ask a new question that won't be answered until the end. In the "I Shot My Brother" essay, for example, the author answers the question of *how* he shot him (with a BB gun) in the first paragraph. But he doesn't answer *why* he shot him until later in the essay, and (advanced technique) he never tells us in the essay how his brother reacted to finding out who shot him, something that gives the essay an elliptical ending. (See "Four Qualities of an Amazing Essay" on page 178 for more on this.)

Variation: Start with an Image That Doesn't Make Any Sense

It can also be effective to begin with something that makes the reader wonder, "How in the world is this relevant for a college admissions essay?"

Examples:

"Dying Bird" (page 176)

> Smeared blood, shredded feathers. Clearly, the bird was dead. But wait, the slight fluctuation of its chest, the slow blinking of its shiny black eyes. No, it was alive.

"Knife" (page 144)

> I can do this by myself.
>
> I held the blade, watched it slide across my flesh. The knife was just like Richard Selzer described: cold, gleaming, silent. Red drops of blood trailed the slightly serrated edge. I let out a long sigh.

Two Keys to Making This Kind of Opening Work

1. Make sure you give us context very soon after establishing the unusual image—maybe in the second paragraph. In a movie, if the viewers don't know what's happening, you'll lose them in about seven minutes—but college essay readers have a much shorter attention span, and if you keep yours in the dark for more than a paragraph or two, you're likely to lose them.

2. Don't use an image *solely* for its shock value. It can have shock value, but the image must be tied in some important way to one of the major themes or lessons of the story. In the "Dying Bird" essay, for example, the opening image functions in

several ways by (1) setting up the author's Want (to save the dying bird), which is the larger arc of the story, and (2) setting up the author's Need (to let the bird—and, by extension, her friend who died—go). For more on creating a Want vs. Need dynamic, see page 131.

IMPORTANT NOTE: Although both these openings begin with an unusual or striking image, they ALSO begin with a problem that must be solved.

Variation: Just Start Your Darn Essay

It's easy to obsess over finding the *perfect* essay opening and delay (read: stall, procrastinate) writing your essay until you've found that perfect beginning. Here's a secret: often, that opening is going to get rewritten because, once you write the middle of the essay, you discover the topic needs to change. Or you realize you need to start your essay at a later point in the story—right at the crucial moment of decision, for example.

So here's some advice for those looking for that perfect opening: just write your essay. Get started. You'll find an opening later.

Another secret: some of the best essays I've read didn't have mind-blowing openings. Some of the best essays start quietly. Examples:

"Grandma's Kimchi" (page 209)

Every Saturday morning, I'd awaken to the smell of crushed garlic and piquant pepper. I would stumble into the kitchen to find my grandma squatting over a large silver bowl, mixing fat lips of fresh cabbages with garlic, salt, and red pepper. That was how the delectable Korean dish, kimchi, was born every weekend at my home.

"Breaking Up with Mom" (page 192)

I stare into my cappuccino to try to avoid looking at my teary eyed mom, who had just found a hole in her favorite bright pink floral print scarf.

"Barbie vs. Terrorism and the Patriarchy" (page 207)

Much of my early knowledge of how the world works was formed through countless hours spent playing with Barbie dolls.

HOW DO I SHOW THE READER I'M REALLY SMART?

IMPORTANT NOTE: The primary aim of your essay shouldn't be to prove your intelligence—it should be to demonstrate core values that are central to who you are. Also, if you're a smart person, trust that your intelligence will come through in your selection of topic, your articulation of your values, and your insights.

Having said this, here are some techniques that I've seen students use that really helped me see their intelligence. Just so I'm clear, though, this should not be where you primarily focus your attention. Don't just put lipstick on a pig. First, make sure you've got a really fine pig. Then consider the techniques presented here to be some different shades of lipstick to make that pig look fabulous.

Also, do not assume that just because you litter your paper with big words that you will sound really smart (see the "Use Big Words Selectively" section on page 199).

Method 1: Ask Great Questions

My favorite way that I've seen students demonstrate their intelligence in an essay isn't through smart statements—it's through smart questions. Take a look at these examples:

"Rock, Paper, Scissors" (page 169)

> Rock beats scissors, scissors beats paper, and paper beats rock. Wait... paper beats rock? Since when has a sheet of loose leaf paper ever defeated a solid block of granite? Do we assume that the paper wraps around the rock, smothering the rock into submission? When exposed to paper, is rock somehow immobilized, unable to fulfill its primary function of smashing scissors? What constitutes defeat between two inanimate objects?

Such great questions. Two possible benefits of smart questions:

1. You can help the reader see something ordinary in a new and unusual way.
2. Your questions might inspire the reader's imagination, making him or her wonder how you'll answer those questions.

But there's another value to asking questions:

"Endodontics" (page 24)

> As a kid I was always curious. I was unafraid to ask questions and didn't worry how dumb they would make me sound. In second grade I enrolled in a summer science program and built a solar-powered oven that baked real cookies. I remember obsessing over the smallest details: Should I paint the oven black to absorb more heat? What about its shape? A spherical shape would allow for more volume, but would it trap heat as well as conventional rectangular ovens? Even then I was obsessed with the details of design.

Notice how these questions demonstrate the core value of this paragraph: curiosity. And while these may not be mind-blowing questions, they sure are smart—especially for a second grader.

And here's one more great thing about questions—you don't have to actually answer them in your essay. Here's what I mean...

"With Debate" (page 22)

> In particular, I am interested in the North-South Korean tension. What irreconcilable differences have prompted a civilization to separate? Policy implications remain vague, and sovereignty theories have their limits—how do we determine what compromises are to be made? And on a personal level, why did my grandfather have to flee from his destroyed North Korean hometown—and why does it matter?

See? These questions don't get answered here. Why? They'd be impossible to answer in a thorough way in such a short personal statement—and that's totally fine. Just ask the questions and make sure, as this writer has done, that your questions are complex enough that they might engage your interest through college and beyond.

Fun fact: This writer didn't have these questions in her head when she started writing this essay. She had to do some research.

Tip: Research your topic to discover what other smart questions people in your intended field of study are asking or have already asked. Then use those questions to inspire your own.

Method 2: Use Geeky Language

If you know a subject really well, and can speak about it in ways that are shining, shimmering, and splendid, then go for it.

Just Enough Geeky Language

> Through switch-side policy debate I not only discuss a multitude
> of competing ideas, but also argue from both sides of widely
> disputed issues. By equipping me with Protagoras' antilogic and
> Dissoi Logoi, switch-side policy debate has provided me with
> a forum to cultivate a diversity of intellectual perspectives that
> has informed my own intellectual growth.

Notice how the writer uses a bit of jargon to demonstrate that he
knows some stuff about some stuff.

But don't use so much jargon that you alienate the reader. Here's
what I mean:

Too Much Geeky Language

> The first project that I was involved with investigated the
> extraintestinal manifestations of IBD. Patients who suffer from
> IBD often have diseases called extraintestinal manifestations
> that also affect multiple other organ systems and can be just as,
> if not more debilitating than the intestinal inflammation itself.
> My contribution involved examining data in Dr. Shih's clinical
> database, which led me to discover that the skin is one of the
> most commonly affected organ systems in patients who suffer
> from IBD. I contributed to Dr. Shih's review article to give an
> overview of the types of skin diseases typically seen with IBD
> and their respective pathogenesis, proposed mechanisms, and
> treatments, and my contributions were significant enough to
> earn recognition as a second author.

Using too much jargon can leave the reader wondering: *Who cares?
What's the takeaway?*

> Tip: To avoid going overboard with jargon, insert a phrase after your geeky language that helps contextualize things for the reader.

"Endodontics" (Geeky Language + "So What")

I'm the math geek who marvels at the fundamental theorems of Calculus, or who sees beauty in A = $(s(s-a)(s-b)(s-c))^{\wedge}(1/2)$. Again, it's in the details: one bracket off or one digit missing and the whole equation collapses. **And details are more than details, they can mean the difference between negative and positive infinity, an impossible range of solutions.**

This is great because we get the geeky language, but we also get some insight into why this is a big deal for the writer—so we learn something more about the writer than just that he or she is smart.

Method 3: Show First, Then Tell

"Show, don't tell" is another phrase you've probably heard from your English teacher. It's an invitation to use images (i.e., create a pretty picture) to illustrate ideas, which is a good starting point. But I think a college admissions officer is interested in not only the pretty picture you paint, but also your reflections and insights on what the pretty picture means to you, the writer. Let me show you what I mean.

Here's an example of a nice "show," again from the "Endodontics" essay:

Many nights you'll find me in the garage replacing standard chrome trim with an elegant piano black finish or changing the threads on the stitching of the seats to add a personal touch...

Great start. But if the writer stops there, we're not sure what his perspective on these details is. That's why I advocate for a little "tell" after the "show."

Example of "show" followed by "tell":

> Many nights you'll find me in the garage replacing standard chrome trim with an elegant piano black finish or changing the threads on the stitching of the seats to add a personal touch, **as I believe a few small changes can transform a generic product into a personalized work of art.**

The "show" demonstrates you're a talented writer.

The "tell" demonstrates you're a critical thinker.

Be both.

Analogy of the Painter, the Art Critic, and the Curator

Consider that, in a college essay:

- the painter is in charge of creating the beautiful images
- the art critic is in charge of saying smart stuff about the images

So, when dreaming up beautiful images and examples for your essay, think of yourself as a painter.

But here's the thing: your responsibility is to also be the art critic, in charge of saying something smart about the images. Your goal is to illuminate something about the work that we might otherwise miss.

And what if you don't have anything smart to say about the image?

That's the best part:

You are also the curator, in charge of deciding whether the image/example stays or goes. And you can elect to change out the painting at any time…preferably for an image/example about which you do have something smart/interesting/illuminating to say.

TIP: Put the "show" <u>before</u> the "tell," as opposed to the other way around.

Version A (Show before Tell)

Many nights you'll find me in the garage replacing standard chrome trim with an elegant piano black finish or changing the threads on the stitching of the seats to add a personal touch, **as I believe a few small changes can transform a generic product into a personalized work of art.**

Version B (Tell before Show)

I believe a few small changes can transform a generic product into a personalized work of art, which is why many nights you'll find me in the garage replacing standard chrome trim with an elegant piano black finish or changing the threads on the stitching of the seats to add a personal touch.

See how Version A is a little better?

Putting the images (show) before your interpretation of them (tell) accomplishes two things:

1. It creates an interesting puzzle in the reader's mind: What do these images mean? What will they add up to? This engages the reader's imagination.
2. Once you deliver your interpretation, the specificity of your articulation will be more surprising because it will be something the reader won't have thought of (and by the way, make sure it's something the reader won't have thought of).

And the way you can ensure this is by choosing images and examples that you can provide insight about—that's your job as curator. And what is insight? It's something you see that the reader doesn't.

> Tip: Include "insight" moments three to five times in your essay. (Look at the "Endodontics" essay on page 24 and see if you can spot how many times he offers insights. Hint: Look at the ends of his paragraphs.)

HOW DO I BRAG WITHOUT SEEMING LIKE I'M BRAGGING?

Let's be honest. If there were ever a time to talk about how awesome you are, it's in your college application. But how do you do it in a way that doesn't sound like that's all you're doing? Here's my advice:

Connect your achievement or skill to an important value.

What do I mean? Weave your brag into a paragraph that is really (or primarily) about something else.

Examples:

"With Debate" (page 22)

> More importantly, I now confront issues instead of avoiding them. It is exciting to discover solutions to problems that affect others, as I was able to do as part of the 1st Place team for the 2010 United Nations Global Debates Program on climate change and poverty. I take a natural interest in global issues,

and plan to become a foreign affairs analyst or diplomat by studying international affairs with a focus on national identity.

Note that this paragraph is primarily about how the author has developed courage and is discovering solutions to problems that affect others, so her fancy UN Global Debates award isn't (only) a brag, it's evidence that she has developed, or is in the process of developing, this value.

"Endodontics" (page 24)

I also love sharing this appreciation with others and have taken it upon myself to personally eradicate mathonumophobiconfundosis, my Calculus teacher's term for "extreme fear of Math." A small group of other students and I have devoted our after-school time to tutoring our peers in everything from Pre-Algebra to AP Calculus B/C and I believe my fluency in Hebrew and Farsi has helped me connect with some of my school's Israeli and Iranian students. There's nothing better than seeing a student solve a difficult problem without me saying anything.

Same technique: this paragraph is primarily about helping others. But the author works in a brag (his ability to speak Hebrew and Farsi) by connecting it to this value—in other words, his fluency in multiple languages has helped him pursue this deeper (and altruistic) value.

Note on technique: See how in both these examples the important value is established in the first sentence of the paragraph? That's good. You don't have to do this, of course, but it can really help make the value clear, especially if you're about to slide in an "Oh, by the way, I'm a rock star" detail.

HOW DO I MAKE MY ESSAY, LIKE, DEEP?

Here are two ways to add depth and complexity to your essay:

Method 1: Feelings and Needs Exercise

This first exercise is adapted from an exercise inspired by Nonviolent Communication (NVC), which is a communication process that supposes that we all have the same needs, and when we can identify those needs and the feelings surrounding those needs, we become better equipped to communicate about our experiences. In NVC, this can lead to a higher likelihood of our getting our needs met. In college essay writing, it can lead to a higher likelihood of writing an awesome essay.

The purpose of this exercise is to take you deeper into your experiences and help you metabolize them by thinking about how your experiences led to feelings and needs that you worked to meet in creative ways. Sound abstract? Don't worry, we're about to get really specific. And I'll explain the steps of the exercise first, then offer a worksheet that you can fill out, if you like.

As before, if you don't feel you've experienced difficulties in life, simply replace "challenge" or "challenges" with the word "experience" or "experiences."

Take a blank sheet of paper, turn it sideways (horizontally), and write these words along the top:

1. Challenges	2. Effects	3. Feelings	4. Needs	5. What I Did	6. Other Values I Gained

If you've done an outline for "How to Write Essay Type A" on page 40, this may look similar, but this version is more comprehensive and it's the key to making your essay, like, deep.

HERE'S WHAT TO WRITE IN EACH COLUMN:

Column 1: Challenges

Write a challenge or a few challenges you've faced in your life, and then…

Column 2: Effects

Write the things that happened to you as a result of your challenge(s). In other words, the repercussions.

If you're unsure what I mean by "Challenges" and "Effects," and you skipped the "How to Write Essay Type A" section, go to page 40 for an explanation.

Note that most students list more than just two challenges, and I invite you to do the same. Take some time with this; it's really worth spending five to ten minutes per column.

Okay, here's where I invite you to be a little vulnerable.

Column 3: Feelings

Make a list of emotions that you felt as a result of the effects you've listed in column 2.

If it would help to see a list emotions—and it always helps me, since they're weirdly difficult to think of on the spot—take a look at the Feelings and Needs Exercise worksheet on page 127. And I'm so grateful that NVC expert LaShelle Lowe-Chardé (http://www .wiseheartpdx.org/) has allowed me to adapt her exercise for our purposes in this chapter.

> Tip: Don't move on until you've completed column 3.

In fact, here's a little white space to remind you to actually do this step and not read ahead.

Have you created your list of feelings?

Do you promise?

Okay, so far your brainstorm might look something like this:

1. Challenges	2. Effects	3. Feelings
Moved around a lot	No security or "home"	Anxious, lonely, stressed
Stuck in between cultures	Family shame, ridicule	Isolated, disconnected

Next step:

Column 4: Needs

Broadly speaking, Nonviolent Communication posits that when we feel negative emotions, it's due to an unmet need. So for each feeling you've listed, ask yourself, *What need wasn't being met?*

Examples

Let's say you moved around a lot (**Challenge**), which resulted in having no security or "home" (**Effect**), which led to your feeling anxious, lonely, and stressed (**Feelings**). Maybe what you lacked was consistency and stability (**Needs**), so you'd write those in column 4.

Or let's say that, growing up, you felt stuck between cultures (**Challenge**), which led to shame and ridicule (**Feelings**), causing you to feel isolated and disconnected (**Feelings**). It could be that your unmet needs were community and support.

So, right now, take a few minutes to brainstorm the unmet needs that may have been motivating each of the emotions listed in column 3.

To help you brainstorm, complete the Feelings and Needs Exercise on page 121.

Did you do it? Promise?

Okay, before moving on, let's go one level deeper.

Did you identify any emotions or needs that *surprised* you? Here's what I mean: sometimes we think we understand our past, but it's not until someone questions us that we realize that *there are multiple ways of making sense of our past*—some of which are unexpected.

Here's an example from my own life: if you'd asked me ten years ago what I thought of my parents' divorce, I'd have probably said, "Whatever, I didn't really feel any particular way about it."

But when I did this exercise I realized something...

When I, Ethan, experienced...my parents' divorce

I felt...disconnected and detached

Because I needed...intimacy, community, and connection.

And, I kid you not, I had this realization *while I was leading this exercise in front of a class*. I was like, "Whoa, didn't think about it that way." But it helped me better understand myself.

So here's my challenge: spend one more minute with this and ask yourself, "Are there any emotions or needs that might actually surprise me?" Maybe you skipped over something the first time, but once you went back and thought about it a little more you realized, "Oh wait... Yeah, I kinda *did* feel that" or "Maybe I *did* need that."

My challenge to you is this: **take a moment here**. Maybe close your eyes, take a deep breath, and feel into this. (I know, that's counseling talk, but go with me here.)

Take a few moments to meditate on this until you make a realization. It could be the key to your whole essay.

More white space because I really want you to do this.

Okay, next:

Column 5: What I Did

What did you do to meet your unmet need(s)? In my case, in order to meet my need for connection, community, and intimacy, I got involved in theater. As my parents were divorcing, I became much more involved with my theater friends—both in and out of school—and essentially formed a new family. I found my community. I didn't know at the time that this was connected to my parents' divorce, but when I look back, it makes a lot of sense.

And you may be thinking, *Well, I didn't actually do anything to try to meet that need; I just lived my life.* But think about things in a broader sense. For example, I initially thought I got more involved in theater just because I liked acting in and writing plays, but when I thought about theater for a bit (seriously, while doing this exercise), I realized that theater really did help me meet my unmet needs.

So here you can either (a) list some things you know you did to meet your needs, or (b) list some of your favorite activities and ask, "Could it be that [this activity] was helping me meet my deeper needs? If so, which one(s)?" Spend a few minutes with this.

Column 6: Other Values I Gained

In my case, by joining theater I not only met my need for intimacy/community, I also found new ways to express my creativity (performing, writing), I gained the confidence to apply to one of the top universities for theater in the country, and I even got to travel to New York City and perform on a Broadway stage. So, in a weird, roundabout way, my parents' divorce helped me cultivate my passion for theater and the arts. Thanks, Mom and Dad!

So make a list of skills/qualities/values you developed in column 6.

If you need ideas, take a look once more at the "What Did I Learn" part of the Feelings and Needs Exercise that follows.

FEELINGS AND NEEDS EXERCISE

When I experienced_____,
I felt_____,
because I needed_____.

FEELINGS

Delighted	Healthy	Peaceful	Hurt	Shocked
Joyful	Empowered	Tranquil	Pain	Disturbed
Happy	Alive	Serene	Agony	Stunned
Amused	Robust	Calm	Anguish	Alarmed
Adventurous			Heartbroken	Appalled
Blissful	**Relaxed**	**Confident**	Lonely	Concerned
Elated	Relieved	Secure		Horrified
	Rested	Safe	**Depressed**	
Thankful	Mellow	Hopeful	Disconnected	**Sad**
Appreciative	At ease		Detached	Grief
Moved	Light		Despondent	Despair
Touched		**Scared**	Dejected	Gloomy
Tender	**Content**	Apprehensive	Bored	Sullen
Expansive	Cheerful	Dread		Downhearted
Grateful	Glad	Worried	**Tired**	Hopeless
	Comfortable	Panicky	Burned out	
Excited	Pleased	Frightened	Exhausted	**Torn**
Enthusiastic		Vulnerable	Lethargic	Ambivalent
Overjoyed	**Friendly**			Confused
Fervent	Affectionate	**Nervous**	**Angry**	Puzzled
Giddy	Loving	Jittery	Furious	
Eager	Passionate	Anxious	Rage	**Jealous**
Ecstatic		Restless	Irate	Envious
Thrilled	**Energetic**	Vulnerable	Resentful	Bitter
	Exhilarated		Irritated	
Satisfied	Exuberant	**Tense**		**Embarrassed**
Fulfilled	Vigorous	Cranky	**Frustrated**	Ashamed
Gratified		Stiff	Disappointed	Contrite
	Alert	Stressed	Discouraged	Guilty
Interested	Focused	Overwhelmed	Disheartened	
Curious	Awake	Agitated	Impatient	
Absorbed	Clearheaded			

NEEDS

Intimacy
Empathy
Connection
Affection
Warmth
Love
Understanding
Acceptance
Caring
Bonding
Compassion
Communion
Divine union
Sexuality

Autonomy
Choice
Freedom
Spontaneity
Independence
Respect
Honor

Security
Predictability
Consistency
Stability
Trust
Reassurance

Partnership
Mutuality
Friendship
Companionship
Support
Collaboration
Belonging
Community
Consideration
Seen/Heard
Appreciation

Purpose
Competence
Contribution
Efficiency
Growth
Learning
Challenge
Discovery

Order
Structure
Clarity
Focus
Information

Celebration
Aliveness
Humor
Beauty
Play
Creativity
Joy
Mourning

Honesty
Integrity
Authenticity
Wholeness
Fairness

Peace
Groundedness
Hope
Healing
Harmony

Nurturing
Food/Water
Rest/Sleep
Safety
Shelter

WHAT DID I DO ABOUT IT?

To meet the need(s) just mentioned, I _____.

(What did you do? Example: I learned time management.)

If you're still in process (i.e., haven't done anything yet), what could you do to meet those needs?

As a result, I developed _____.

(What values did you develop? Choose a few from the list that follows.)

Again, if you haven't done anything yet, what values do you anticipate developing?

WHAT DID I LEARN?

Community

Inspiration

Serenity

Physical challenge

Responsibility

Competition

Career

Practicality

Working with others

Freedom

Security

Strength

Self-control

Hunger

Personal development

Respect

Mindfulness

Culture

Bravery

Communication

Change and variety

Compassion

Nature

Intuition

Trust

Social justice

Intellect

Self-reliance

Financial gain

Laughter

Faith

Involvement

Adventure

Vulnerability

Adaptability

Restraint

Healthy boundaries

Friendship

Excellence

Meaning

Power

Privacy

Self-expression

Stability

Diversity

Love

Control

Surprise

Nutrition

Competence

Risk

Balance

Self-discipline

Courage

Family

Empathy

Working alone

Fun

Humility

Efficiency

Intensity

Health and fitness

Meaningful work

My country

Music

Truth

Resourcefulness

Awareness

Art

Autonomy

Wit

Patience

Listening

Commitment

Leadership

Helping others

Meditation

Practicality

Creativity

Excitement

Collaboration

Social change

Beauty

Passion

Integrity

Ecological awareness

Quality relationships

Travel

Logic

Curiosity

Spirituality

Directness

Honesty

Independence

Multiplicity

Supervising others

Cooperation

Affection

Wisdom

Knowledge

Growth

Mystery

Order

Innovation

Accountability

Democracy

Religion

Experience

_____

_____

_____

_____

_____

_____

What to Do Next: Start Making Some Connections

Once you've filled in all the columns, see if you can formulate a sentence or two that connects all the columns:

1. Challenges 2. Effects 3. Feelings 4. Needs 5. What I Did 6. Other Values I Gained

Example from my own life (key points in bold): After my **parents' divorce**, we spent less time together as a family, which led to me feeling somewhat **detached** and **disconnected**. I think deep down I needed **intimacy**, **connection**, and **belonging**. During this time, I got more involved with the **theater** program at my school, and not only found the **community** that I wanted, but also became more **independent** and **creative**. I even got the chance to **travel** to New York City.

If You Know Your Future Career...

Feel free to connect the "Other Values I Gained" to your career at the end of your essay—you might even create one more column right now, if you like, to brainstorm some connections. For more ideas on how to do this, see "How to Write Essay Type A" on page 40.

Once you've done this, chances are you should have a thread or two that will connect your story elements. As with the type A and type C approaches, I'd recommend using narrative structure to outline your essay.

If you'd like to see example essays that are "deep"—and by "deep," I mean essays in which the author discusses a deeper need—check out the "Porcelain God," "Easter," "What I Found on the Farm," "Knife," and "Breaking Up with Mom" essays. There are other essays in the book that do this, but I think these are the clearest examples.

The "Burying Grandma" essay discussed in the next section addresses a deeper need, but the author takes a slightly different approach to structuring the essay.

Method 2: Setting Up a Want vs. Need Dynamic

Here's a screenwriting secret: in most popular films you've seen, there are two stories unfolding.

1. The Outside Story: These are the external circumstances of the story, typically the main plot.
2. The Inside Story: The main character's inner journey, typically some sort of emotional shift marked by a realization that the way he or she has been doing things has been wrong (or at least not ideal).

Examples:

Star Wars

- Outside Story: Luke wants to keep the universe from being taken over by the Dark Side.
- Inside Story: Luke needs to learn to believe in himself in order to use The Force.

Finding Nemo

- Outside Story: Nemo's dad, Marlin, wants to find Nemo.
- Inside Story: Marlin needs to overcome his overprotective nature and ultimately let Nemo go.

Toy Story

- Outside Story: Woody wants to get rid of Buzz Lightyear so that Woody can go back to being Andy's favorite toy.
- Inside Story: Instead of getting Buzz out, Woody needs to get over his jealousy and, essentially, let Buzz in.

Notice the way I've phrased those:

- Outside Story = main character's **want**
- Inside Story = main character's **need**

Here's another way of thinking about this:

- What the movie is about on the surface = **Outside Story/want**
- What the film is *really* about = **Inside Story/need**

And that's what gives these films depth, *particularly if the want and need are, at some point in the story, in direct opposition.* Look at *Toy Story* and *Finding Nemo*, for example. In both cases, the main character spends the first part of the movie pursuing the thing he thinks is going to make him happy (getting rid of Buzz Lightyear, finding Nemo). But we, the wise audience members, know that there's a deeper lesson the character needs to learn (to accept Buzz Lightyear, to let Nemo go).

What does this have to do with your essay?

Ask yourself this question: Was there ever a time in your life when you were pursuing one thing (a want), but once you thought about it, you realized there was something deeper that you were really searching for (a need)?

It's kind of a huge question. In fact, you probably didn't just read that and think, "Oh yeah, totally." It takes some thought, and sometimes even a little creative reframing. But if you can do this, it can add real dimension to your essay.

Several of the sample essays in this book employ this want/need dynamic, and I don't think all the authors knew they were doing it. Take a look:

"With Debate" (Type A)

> **Want**: to get over her shyness, which she does by joining debate and coming out of her shell

> **Need**: to accept her shyness—rather than try to get over it—and ultimately accept that she isn't two separate parts, but one whole being...just as "the Korean civilization is also one," as she says in the last paragraph

"I Shot My Brother" (Type C)

> **Want**: to get rid of his brother (on a subconscious level, it could be argued, he wants to "kill" him)

> **Need**: to get over his jealousy and reconcile with his brother

"Dying Bird" (Type C)

> **External Want**: to save the bird

> **External Need**: to let the bird go

But the "Dying Bird" essay is particularly satisfying because it actually has a...

> **Deeper Want**: to save her friend

> **Deeper Need**: to let her friend go

That's next level stuff.

"Why Did the Chicken Cross the Road?"

Even this essay on page 162 has a version of the want/need dynamic at work.

Chicken's **want**: to get to the other side of the road

Chicken's **need**: to get back *from* the other side of the road

That's what makes that story so satisfying—it provides an ending that's surprising, but inevitable (see page 150 for more on this).

So How Do You Do This in Your Essay?

Notice that in each of the essays I just mentioned, there's a moment when the author shifts from pursuing his or her want to pursuing his or her need. Ask yourself: Could I work such a moment into my story?

The essay below provides a clear example. Try to identify the want, the need, and the moment when the shift happens.

"BURYING GRANDMA"

They covered the precious mahogany coffin with a brown amalgam of rocks, decomposed organisms, and weeds. It was my turn to take the shovel, but I felt too ashamed to dutifully send her off when I had not properly said goodbye. I refused to throw dirt on her. I refused to let go of my grandmother, to accept a death I had not seen coming, to believe that an illness could not only interrupt, but steal a beloved life.

When my parents finally revealed to me that my grandmother had been battling liver cancer, I was twelve and I was angry—mostly with myself. They had wanted to protect me—only six years old at the time—from the complex and morose concept of death. However, when the end inevitably arrived, I wasn't trying to comprehend what dying was; I was trying to understand how

I had been able to abandon my sick grandmother in favor of playing with friends and watching TV. Hurt that my parents had deceived me and resentful of my own oblivion, I committed myself to preventing such blindness from resurfacing.

I became desperately devoted to my education because I saw knowledge as the key to freeing myself from the chains of ignorance. While learning about cancer in school I promised myself that I would memorize every fact and absorb every detail in textbooks and online medical journals. And as I began to consider my future, I realized that what I learned in school would allow me to silence that which had silenced my grandmother. However, I was focused not with learning itself, but with good grades and high test scores. I started to believe that academic perfection would be the only way to redeem myself in her eyes—to make up for what I had not done as a granddaughter.

However, a simple walk on a hiking trail behind my house made me open my own eyes to the truth. Over the years, everything—even honoring my grandmother—had become second to school and grades. As my shoes humbly tapped against the Earth, the towering trees blackened by the forest fire a few years ago, the faintly colorful pebbles embedded in the sidewalk, and the wispy white clouds hanging in the sky reminded me of my small though nonetheless significant part in a larger whole that is humankind and this Earth. Before I could resolve my guilt, I had to broaden my perspective of the world as well as my responsibilities to my fellow humans.

Volunteering at a cancer treatment center has helped me discover my path. When I see patients trapped in not only the hospital but also a moment in time by their diseases, I talk to them. For six hours a day, three times a week, Ivana is surrounded by IV stands, empty walls, and busy nurses that quietly yet constantly remind her of her breast cancer. Her face is pale and tired, yet kind—not unlike my grandmother's. I need only to smile and say hello to see her brighten up as life returns to her face. Upon our first meeting, she opened up about her two sons, her hometown, and her knitting group—no mention of her disease. Without even standing up, the three of us—Ivana, me, and my grandmother—had taken a walk together.

Cancer, as powerful and invincible as it may seem, is a mere fraction of a person's life. It's easy to forget when one's mind and body are so weak and vulnerable. I want to be there as an oncologist to remind them to take a walk once in awhile, to remember that there's so much more to life than a disease. While I physically treat their cancer, I want to lend patients emotional support and mental strength to escape the interruption and continue living. Through my work, I can accept the shovel without burying my grandmother's memory.

So what was the author's want? What about her need?

There's no perfect answer here, but here's my version: the author's **want** was to deal with her guilt around her grandma's death by burying herself in her studies. Her **need** was to heal from her grandma's death by broadening "[her] perspective of the world," as she puts it, "as well as [her] responsibilities to [her] fellow humans," something she ends up doing through her volunteer work at the hospital.

Here are two tips for applying this technique:

1. Once you've shifted from the want to the need, demonstrate what you did about it. Think, for example, how that essay would be different if she'd ended it with this sentence: "Before I could resolve my guilt, I had to broaden my perspective of the world as well as my responsibilities to my fellow humans." We wouldn't get a chance to see that she actually externalized the lesson—that she actually did something about it.

2. For the first part of the essay, try solving your problem in a "bad" way (by pursuing the want), then include a turning

point/realization and begin to work on your problem in a "good" way (pursuing the need).

Finally, if you're writing a type B or D essay, you may be wondering if these two methods for adding depth apply mostly to type A and C (challenges) essays. Yes, they do, since both exercises rely on challenges. If you'd like to add depth and complexity to a type B essay, either turn to page 196 to learn how to make sure your insights are actually insightful, or turn to page 68 to learn how to combine narrative and montage structures by including a challenge in a montage essay.

HOW DO I END MY ESSAY?

The best endings have two things in common. And I won't make you guess what they are; I'll just tell you.

The best endings are surprising, but inevitable.

Take a look at two examples from essays in this book.

At the end of the "Endodontics" essay, the author reveals that he wants to study dentistry (specifically, endodontics). This is somewhat surprising, as we might have pegged him for an engineering guy. But when we look back at his essay, we see that the values he has been describing in the essay will actually make him a great dentist. So even though "endodontist" initially catches us off-guard, once we think about it (and once he makes that "machines" connection near the end), the ending feels, well, kind of inevitable.

The "Easter" essay begins with the author trapped (physically and psychologically) at home with her mother. At the end of the essay, the author notes that she will celebrate Easter again, but next time will be different—rather than being trapped indoors, she and her mother will celebrate outdoors their rebirth and renewal. In this case, what's surprising is that she brought up Easter again in the essay. But of course she did, since it's the perfect metaphor for the rebirth that she and her mother have experienced in the story. So, in a way, the ending feels inevitable.

Think about your favorite movie or play: you probably knew how it was going to end, but something about it still surprised you. Or, alternately, perhaps you had no idea how it was going to end. But once it was over, you thought, "Yeah, that makes sense."

Examples:

- You know by the end of every romantic comedy that the two main characters will end up together (it's inevitable); you're just waiting to find out *how* (and that's the surprising part).
- In every epic action film, you know that OF COURSE they'll save the planet before it's destroyed (that's inevitable), but you're still watching the film because you want to see *how* (that's the surprise).

Here's something to keep in mind: if your ending is too "inevitable," it means that we saw it coming a mile away, and it will feel boring, like the punch line to a bad joke. But, on the other hand, if the ending is too "surprising," then it probably means we didn't see it coming at all, and it might feel random. The key is the sweet spot in the middle:

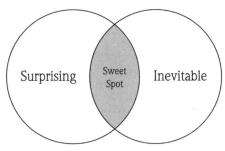

Are all great endings both surprising and inevitable?

No. The ending of the "Porcelain God" essay, for example, feels, at least to me, more inevitable than surprising. (I mean, come on, "my regular visits to my allergy specialist inspired me to become an allergy specialist." *Super* inevitable.) Also, as you read the "With Debate" essay, some part of you knew the author would inevitably overcome her shyness. But in both cases, there were elements at the end that were surprising. The "Porcelain God" author, for example, attended the program at Stanford (that's somewhat unexpected), while the "With Debate" author lays out a beautiful metaphor describing how the North-South Korean dividing line actually represents the introverted and extroverted parts of herself. So, while part of their stories may have been inevitable, what they say at the end answers "so what?" in a surprising way.

Keep that in mind, by the way: if this "surprising, but inevitable" technique seems too complex, just answer "so what" at the end of your essay, ideally in an unexpected way.

HOW TO WRITE A GREAT LAST LINE FOR YOUR ESSAY

Look at the final lines of some of the essays mentioned earlier. What do they all have in common?

→ "Endodontics" essay: *The question is: Will the toothbrushes I hand out be mineral white or diamond white?*

→ "Bowling" essay: *I know that one day I will not take my family to a bowling alley to clean it but to enjoy it. And who knows, maybe one day I will learn to bowl.*

→ "Easter" essay: *My Easter will drastically differ from past years. Rather than being locked at home, my mother and I will celebrate outdoors our rebirth and renewal.*

Cudgel thy brains no more about it, I'll tell you:

All these endings return to some earlier moment in the essay, but from a different perspective.

> T. S. Eliot put it best in the *Four Quartets:* "In my beginning is my end"
> and "In my end is my beginning."
>
> That's the goal.

You may still be wondering: How do I implement the "surprising, but inevitable" technique? Can I see an example in a full essay?

Yes, indeed. In fact, I'll give you three example essays that use this technique: "I Shot My Brother," "Dying Bird," and "Five Families." I analyze the first two in the "Four Qualities of an Amazing Essay" section that begins on page 178, and I analyze the third in the "Advanced Technique 4" section that begins on page 150.

But in order to understand the "surprising, but inevitable" concept fully, I recommend learning more about setup and payoff, which is the foundation of this approach and something I explain in the next chapter, "Advanced Techniques." Just one quick note before we get there on what to do if you're feeling like you're behind in the process.

WHAT DO I DO IF I FEEL LIKE I'M FALLING BEHIND?

You might be whizzing right along at this point and you're hard at work on your third or eighth draft. Good for you. But maybe you're not quite there yet—maybe you're still struggling to nail down your structure or even decide on your topic.

Listen, it's totally fine. You aren't falling behind. Writing is a strange and unpredictable process. The best thing you can do is to keep at it—keep reading, keep writing, and, above all, keep trying new things. What sorts of new things?

Here are a few ideas:

If you're still struggling to find your topic…

What's wrong with you? I'm kidding. Some options:

1. Try writing Morning Pages, as Julia Cameron suggests in *The Artist's Way,* which are three pages of longhand, stream-of-consciousness writing done first thing in the morning..
2. Have you tried brainstorming with a partner yet? If not, try it. Maybe you tried brainstorming with someone and it didn't work? Try someone else!
3. Just pick something and start writing. That simple? Yep. It's better than doing nothing.

You've Got Your Topic, but Aren't Sure That the Structure Is Right or That the Essay Flows

- First, go back to page 102 and review "How to Revise Your Essay in Five Steps."
- Repeat those steps until, when you read your essay aloud, you can hear the ideas flow together in a clear way.
- Get feedback from someone else. Does that person agree? Super. You're on your way.
- Maybe you asked someone else but didn't get useful feedback? Try another person. Keep going until you get the help you need.

Just Need Some Inspiration?

I have a whole website dedicated to college essay inspiration that I update weekly: http://collegeessayguy.tumblr.com/.

CHAPTER SEVEN

Advanced Techniques

MANY OF THE TOOLS DISCUSSED in this chapter come from screenwriting. Why? Because I have spent a whole lot of time studying screenwriting structure and have learned that screenwriting structure works *beautifully* for college essay structure. Oh, and because you've probably watched movies, and because the visual images you'll use in your essay will mean your essay is basically a short film.

Here are five techniques I call "advanced," not because they are necessarily difficult to understand, but because they can be a bit more difficult to do well. But if you can pull these off, the payoff can be big. Speaking of payoff...

ADVANCED TECHNIQUE 1: SETUP AND PAYOFF

Degree of difficulty: 5.2

Setup and payoff is a narrative technique that involves "setting up" a detail or a statement that initially seems irrelevant, and then later making the relevance very clear—in other words, "paying it off."

As Chekhov said:

If you say in the first chapter that there is a rifle hanging on the wall, in the second or third chapter it absolutely must go off.

It can also be useful to cut extraneous setups that promise or imply certain payoffs that never arrive. Here's the rest of that Chekhov quotation:

If [the gun is] not going to be fired, it shouldn't be hanging there.

Three Simple "Setup" Examples from Film

1. At the beginning of *The Wizard of Oz*, Dorothy sings "Somewhere Over the Rainbow." Guess where she goes?
2. At the opening of *Citizen Kane*, a dying man's last word is "Rosebud." Guess what "Rosebud" is? (Actually, I won't ruin it for you.)
3. A troll in *Frozen* explains that only an "act of true love" will prevent Anna's heart from freezing forever. And, well, you get it…

Who This Technique Is For

This technique is for:

a. students who have been through a particularly big change in their lives and are having difficulty finding a larger structure, or
b. any student looking to make his or her essay more interesting.

In short, this technique can be used to structure an entire essay (as the "Knife" essay that follows does) or small moments throughout the essay (as the "Knife" essay also does).

And here's an important qualifier: what the sample essay "Knife" attempts is extremely difficult, given the sensitivity of the topic, and I did not, for the record, advise the student to write about this. She wrote about it without consulting me, sent it to me, and when I read it, I thought, *This is incredibly risky, but the story is told so well that I feel she has truly moved through this and learned from it.* How risky was it? A colleague of mine and former admissions officer at Mills College noted that, after reading this essay, she would have had to flag it for the college's psychological services office, and there's no telling how many hands this essay would have had to pass through at Stanford, where the student was ultimately accepted.

Having said all this, her technique here is wonderful, and we can learn a lot from it. Read the essay first without my notes.

"KNIFE"

I can do this by myself.

I held the blade, watched it slide across my flesh. The knife was just like Richard Selzer described: cold, gleaming, silent. Red drops of blood trailed the slightly serrated edge. I let out a long sigh.

I was at my most desperate. My friend had died in September of my junior year. Five AP classes, weekly volunteering, and a tutoring job had provided added stress. I needed reprieve. And I found it in the knife.

Two months later, my French teacher, Madame Deleuze, discovered my secret. That day in AP French while everyone else drilled vocabulary, she called me out to have a talk.

Bubbly and smiling, I chatted about the test we were about to take.

"I know what you're doing, Sara. I know you cut yourself."

My breath caught in my throat. My hands grew cold. My pulse sped up. I looked down at my shoes, then at the green planter next to me. This can't be happening. I dug my nails into my hands to stop them from shaking. I began to cry.

Shame. I had wanted to be the perfect student, an effort-less model of fortitude. School, volunteering, work. I can do it. I will do it. Bring it on. I had wanted to be that girl, the teacher's pet, the lone wolf, the ambitious go-getter with big dreams and even bigger expectations. What I had not wanted to be was a victim.

But as Madame Deleuze held me, her voice cracking, she spoke words of compassion.

"You're beautiful. You're valuable. You're amazing and so, so precious. Don't ever let yourself think otherwise."

Enclosed in her arms, I realized that I had been a victim—a victim of my own relentless standards.

Since that day, my every flaw, my every hurt has been laid bare. My mother cried for hours when she first found out. My father said nothing. In fact, he remained silent for a week. My brother and my teachers were shocked. I seemed a stranger to them.

Yet in their despair, they chose to love me.

My mother drove me to therapy every week with tears staining her makeup. My father, though quiet, left me breakfast every morning when I woke up. My brother, a freshman at CalArts, sent me text messages and braved LA traffic every weekend to see me. Mrs. Risher gave me tight hugs. Mrs. Natanzi, my counselor, sat me down, concern marking her face.

Their compassion allowed me to replace ambition for passion. I quit Key Club, SADD, French Club. Passion grew for the written word, journalism, speech and debate. It led me away from the pharmacy to forensics, pathology, pediatrics.

Failure seemed less a tragedy, more an opportunity. To ask for help was not weakness. To endure alone was not strength.

I can't do this by myself. I don't need to.

Analysis of "Knife"

I can do this by myself.

Setup 1: This sets up the final line of the essay.

I held the blade, watched it slide across my flesh. The knife was just like Richard Selzer described: cold, gleaming, silent. Red drops of blood trailed the slightly serrated edge. I let out a long sigh.

Setup 2: This builds suspense, raises the stakes, and launches the question of the essay: How will she overcome this?

I was at my most desperate. My friend had died in September of my junior year. Five AP classes, weekly volunteering, and a tutoring job had provided added stress. I needed reprieve. And I found it in the knife.

Setup 3: *Uh-oh*, we think. *What's going to happen outside the room?* (Mini setup, which helps build suspense.)

Setup 4: Establish that the narrator doesn't see this coming. (Dramatic irony.)

Two months later, my French teacher, Madame Deleuze, discovered my secret. That day in AP French while everyone else drilled vocabulary, she called me out to have a talk. Bubbly and smiling, I chatted about the test we were about to take.

"I know what you're doing, Sara. I know you cut yourself."

Great verisimilitude (see page 147).

My breath caught in my throat. My hands grew cold. My pulse sped up. I looked down at my shoes, then at the green planter next to me. This can't be happening. I dug my nails into my hands to stop them from shaking. I began to cry.

Payoff for setups 3 and 4.

(Unexpected) payoff for setups 3 and 4: We didn't expect the teacher to say this.

Shame. I had wanted to be the perfect student, an effortless model of fortitude. School, volunteering, work. I can do it. I will do it. Bring it on. I had wanted to be that girl, the teacher's pet, the lone wolf, the ambitious go-getter with big dreams and even bigger expectations. What I had not wanted to be was a victim.

Setup 5: This echoes and amplifies setup 1. She goes from "can" to "will" and then "Bring it on."

But as Madame Deleuze held me, her voice cracking, she spoke words of compassion.

"You're beautiful. You're valuable. You're amazing and so, so precious. Don't ever let yourself think otherwise."

Enclosed in her arms, I realized that I had been a victim—a victim of my own relentless standards.

First payoff for setup 1.

Since that day, my every flaw, my every hurt has been laid

bare. My mother cried for hours when she first found out. My father said nothing. In fact, he remained silent for a week. My brother and my teachers were shocked. I seemed a stranger to them.

This pays off setup 2 in that it shows the consequences of her actions. It's also setup 6.

Yet in their despair, they chose to love me.

Major turning point in the essay.

My mother drove me to therapy every week with tears staining her makeup. My father, though quiet, left me breakfast every morning when I woke up. My brother, a freshman at CalArts, sent me text messages and braved LA traffic every weekend to see me. Mrs. Risher gave me tight hugs. Mrs. Natanzi, my counselor, sat me down, concern marking her face.

Pays off setup 6.

Their compassion allowed me to replace ambition for passion. I quit Key Club, SADD, French Club. Passion grew for the written word, journalism, speech and debate. It led me away from the pharmacy to forensics, pathology, pediatrics.

Pays off setup 5.

Failure seemed less a tragedy, more an opportunity. To ask for help was not weakness. To endure alone was not strength.

I can't do this by myself. I don't need to.

Final and most satisfying payoff, as it pays off setup 1 (at the start) and its echo in setup 5 (in the middle), giving the essay a feeling of roundedness and a through line.

ADVANCED TECHNIQUE 2: VERISIMILITUDE

Degree of difficulty: 4.4

The word "verisimilitude" comes from Latin: *veri similis* means "like the truth." This technique involves the use of specific details to give the story the ring of truth. In the previous essay, a detail such as "slightly serrated edge [of the knife]" gives the sense that this was an actual knife and, by extension, that this story really happened. Verisimilitude can help bring a story to life in a way that makes us believe, and often feel, the story more.

Here's another example from the "Raising Anthony" essay on page 26:

> On one particularly hopeful afternoon I even tried to introduce him
> to books that I had read—but I learned I can't win every battle.

Why this moment feels so true to life: at this point in the story, everything is working well—the author is soaking in parenting videos, having her little brother formulate his own penalties, and following up on his homework—but this moment brings us back to earth. It's useful because it saves the essay from having an ending that sounds like a Hallmark card, in which everything works out perfectly.

And here's one more example, from the "Knife" essay you just read:

> My breath caught in my throat. My hands grew cold. My pulse
> sped up. I looked down at my shoes, then at the green planter
> next to me.

Why did the author choose a "green" planter—why not blue or red? Does green symbolize something—nature, perhaps, or safety, or even envy? No! She notes that it was a green planter because that was *the actual color of the actual planter.*

Here's one of my favorite quotations from Gustave Flaubert:

> If I say the stones are blue it is because blue is the precise word,
> believe me.

Read that again. It's a good one.

There are other wonderful moments of verisimilitude in the essays in this book, particularly in the "Grandma's Kimchi" (page 209) and "Breaking Up with Mom" (page 192) essays.

ADVANCED TECHNIQUE 3: TURN SOMETHING DARK INTO SOMETHING BEAUTIFUL

Degree of difficulty: 9.1

One more strategy the author of the "Knife" essay uses to address the difficult, not-often-talked-about topic of cutting is giving us insight into why she did it. How does she do so? Look again at the second paragraph. She makes it sound almost…well, beautiful. And, if you possess all parts of humanity inside you—if, in other words, there is a part of you deep down that has ever seen something that other people might think was "gross" and you've found yourself thinking "that's actually kind of interesting"—*you kind of get it.* I'm not suggesting that you would cut yourself, but you see her perspective. So that's one possibility:

Turn something dark into something beautiful.

But there's a larger lesson here. For students who are struggling to find a way to talk about a challenge that either they are ashamed of or that is stigmatized in our culture, here is my invitation:

Get creative.

You don't have to give a straightforward account of your challenges, and you certainly don't have to describe every gory detail. Choose your details. Find what's interesting or compelling, and select the pieces that connect to the values we can all relate to. In the "Knife" essay, for example, I believe the story isn't primarily about cutting; I believe it's about someone who pushed herself too hard (I've done that), who got some support, and who is beginning to learn to accept help from others, which is something I (and perhaps you) can really relate to. In short:

Find what's universal about your experience.

That's something this author does very well in her essay, and it's a big part of why I think the essay works.

Although this student did end up at Stanford, I caution anyone against drawing too direct a conclusion from this, such as, "If I write about something really deep and dark, then I'll get into Stanford" or "This essay is why she got into Stanford." Why? Because her 2320 SAT score and near-perfect grades had a lot to do with her acceptance. But I offer this tidbit to note that it is possible to write about a topic like this and still be accepted to a great school. But, as I noted, the degree of difficulty is much higher.

ADVANCED TECHNIQUE 4: BLOW THE READER'S MIND BY USING *THE SIXTH SENSE* ENDING (A.K.A. CREATE AN ENDING THAT'S SURPRISING, BUT INEVITABLE)

Degree of difficulty: 7.5

Okay, we're about to take this setup and payoff thing to the next level.

Have you seen *The Sixth Sense*? Because I'm about to ruin it for you.

Haley Joel Osment's character sees dead people.

I'm kidding. Well, I'm not kidding, but you knew that. Actually, I'm about to give a plot summary, so if you haven't seen the film, consider watching it. But if you won't watch it, or don't care if I spoil the ending, read on.

Short Plot Summary of *The Sixth Sense*

The life of psychologist Dr. Crowe, played by Bruce Willis, changes forever when a disgruntled former patient walks into his house one night and puts a bullet in his gut (**Inciting Incident**). Soon after recovery, Crowe begins seeing a new patient named Cole, played by Haley Joel Osment, who swears he sees dead people (**Raise the Stakes**). Dr. Crowe, who seems to have trouble opening his basement office (**Setup**), tries to diagnose Cole, only to realize that he is telling the truth—he does actually see dead people (**Raise the Stakes Even More**). Dr. Crowe agrees to help Cole resolve these ghosts' problems so they can finally be at peace (**Turning Point**).

At the end of the film, Dr. Crowe goes home to his wife, whom he had estranged by working too hard. She drifts off to sleep while watching their wedding video. Then his wedding ring slips out of her fingers. Dr. Crowe, not remembering ever taking it off, realizes that he has actually been dead the whole time (**Payoff and another Turning Point**) and TA DA! Multiple story elements suddenly make more sense given this bit of information—even moments that you didn't even think about before. (So *that's* why Dr. Crowe talks to Cole only when they're alone! *That's* why he couldn't open the basement office door!)

What Can We Learn from This Technique?

The key moment—the final reveal at the end—works like any great "Whodunit" mystery in that it "pays off" all these little clues that have been buried or hidden along the way. In a well-made film, we don't make sense of these hints until the final reveal, which, as screenwriting teacher Robert McKee points out, is like a giant explosion that detonates all these little explosions in our minds and sends us mentally hurtling back through the film to connect all the hints that we were only partially aware of along the way.

And, if done really well:

It's *surprising* as in, "I totally didn't see that coming."

But it's *inevitable*, as in, "Now that I think about it, of *course* that's how it had to end."

> Fun fact: Almost every single example essay in this book has a conclusion that is somehow both surprising and inevitable.

If you can achieve both, you've got a winner. How can you do this? Two tips:

1. Set up your hints so that they're clear enough to be remembered at the payoff moment, but also buried enough so that we don't expect the payoff.

How do you "bury" them? Here's an idea:

2. Give us something else to focus on, or something that's interesting enough to capture our attention so we're not aware that you're burying a hint. It's kind of like a magic trick; it's a misdirect.

Want a clear example with some analysis?

I'll give you a whole essay. Read the "Five Families" essay that follows and see if you can spot the buried hints along the way. There's something toward the end that connects all the separate parts of the story.

I'll let you read it first without analysis so you can just enjoy it. Then we'll dissect it together.

"FIVE FAMILIES"

When I was 16, I lived with the Watkins family in Wichita, Kansas. Mrs. Watkins was the coordinator of the foreign exchange student program I was enrolled in. She had a nine year old son named Cody. I would babysit Cody every day after school for at least two to three hours. We would play Scrabble or he would read to me from *Charlotte's Web* or *The Ugly Duckling*. He would talk a lot about his friends and school life, and I would listen to him and ask him the meanings of certain words. He was my first friend in the New World.

My second family was the Martinez family, who were friends of the Watkins's. The host dad Michael was a high school English teacher and the host mom Jennifer (who had me call her "Jen") taught elementary school. She had recently delivered a baby, so she was still in the hospital when I moved into their house. The Martinez family did almost everything together. We made pizza together, watched *Shrek* on their cozy couch together, and went fishing on Sunday together. On rainy days, Michael, Jen and I would sit on the porch and listen to the rain, talking about our dreams and thoughts. Within two months I was calling them mom and dad.

After I finished the exchange student program, I had the option of returning to Korea but I decided to stay in America. I wanted to see new places and meet different people. Since I wasn't an exchange student anymore, I had the freedom—and burden—of finding a new school and host family on my own. After a few days of thorough investigation, I found the Struiksma family in California. They were a unique group.

The host mom Shellie was a single mom who had two of her own sons and two Russian daughters that she had adopted. The kids always had something warm to eat, and were always on their best behavior at home and in school. It would be fair to say that this was all due to Shellie's upbringing. My room was on the first floor, right in front of Shellie's hair salon, a small business that she ran out of her home. In the living room were six or seven huge amplifiers and a gigantic chandelier hung from the high ceiling. The kitchen had a bar. At first, the non-stop visits from strangers made me nervous, but soon I got used to them. I remember one night, a couple barged into my room while I was sleeping. It was awkward.

After a few months I realized we weren't the best fit. In the nicest way possible, I told them I had to leave. They understood.

The Ortiz family was my fourth family. Kimberly, the host mom, treated me the same way she treated her own son. She made me do chores: I fixed dinner, fed their two dogs Sassy and Lady, and once a week I cleaned the bathroom. I also had to follow some rules: No food in my room, no using the family computer, no lights on after midnight, and no ride unless it was an emergency. The first couple of months were really hard to get used to, but eventually I adjusted.

I lived with the Ortiz family for seven months like a monk in the deep forest. However, the host dad Greg's asthma got worse after winter, so he wanted to move to the countryside. It was unexpected and I only had a week to find a new host family. I asked my friend Danielle if I could live with her until I found a new home. That's how I met the Dirksen family, my fifth family.

The Dirksen family had three kids. They were all different. Danielle liked bitter black coffee, Christian liked energy drinks, and Becca liked sweet lemon tea. Dawn, the host mom didn't like winter, and Mark, the host dad, didn't like summer. After dinner, we would all play Wii Sports together. I was the king of bowling, and Dawn was the queen of tennis. I don't remember a single time that they argued about the games. Afterward, we would gather in the living room and Danielle would play the piano while the rest of us sang hymns.

Of course, those 28 months were too short to fully understand all five families, but I learned from and was shaped by each of them. By teaching me English, nine year-old Cody taught me the importance of being able to learn from anyone;

the Martinez family showed me the value of spending time together as a family; the Struiksma family taught me to reserve judgment about divorced women and adopted children; Mrs. Ortiz taught me the value of discipline and the Dirksen family taught me the importance of appreciating one another's different qualities.

Getting along with other people is necessary for anyone and living with five families has made me more sensitive to others' needs: I have learned how to recognize when someone needs to talk, when I should give advice and when to simply listen, and when someone needs to be left alone; in the process, I have become much more adaptable. I'm ready to change, learn, and be shaped by my future families.

Analysis of "Five Families"

When I was 16, I lived with the Watkins family in Wichita, Kansas. Mrs. Watkins was the coordinator of the foreign exchange student program I was enrolled in. She had a nine year old son named Cody. I would babysit Cody every day after school for at least two to three hours. We would play Scrabble or he would read to me from *Charlotte's Web* or *The Ugly Duckling.* He would talk a lot about his friends and school life, and I would listen to him and ask him the meanings of certain words. He was my first friend in the New World.

Is this just a sweet image? Or Top Secret Buried Hint 1? Both.

My second family was the Martinez family, who were friends of the Watkins's. The host dad Michael was a high school English teacher and the host mom Jennifer (who had me call her "Jen") taught elementary school. She had recently delivered a baby, so she was still in the hospital when I moved into their house. The Martinez family did almost everything together. We made pizza together, watched *Shrek* on their cozy

Hint 2.

couch together, and went fishing on Sunday together. On rainy days, Michael, Jen and I would sit on the porch and listen to the rain, talking about our dreams and thoughts. Within two months I was calling them mom and dad.

After I finished the exchange student program, I had the option of returning to Korea but I decided to stay in America. I wanted to see new places and meet different people. Since I wasn't an exchange student anymore, I had the freedom—and burden—of finding a new school and host family on my own. After a few days of thorough investigation, I found the Struiksma family in California. They were a unique group.

The host mom Shellie was a single mom who had two of her own sons and two Russian daughters that she had adopted. The kids always had something warm to eat, and were always on their best behavior at home and in school. It would be fair to say that this was all due to Shellie's upbringing. My room was on the first floor, right in front of Shellie's hair salon, a small business that she ran out of her home. In the living room were six or seven huge amplifiers and a gigantic chandelier hung from the high ceiling. The kitchen had a bar. At first, the non-stop visits from strangers made me nervous, but soon I got used to them. I remember one night, a couple barged into my room while I was sleeping. It was awkward.

After a few months I realized we weren't the best fit. In the nicest way possible, I told them I had to leave. They understood.

The Ortiz family was my fourth family. Kimberly, the host mom, treated me the same way she treated her own son. She made me do chores: I fixed dinner, fed their two dogs Sassy and Lady, and once a week I cleaned the bathroom. I also had to follow some rules: No food in my room, no using the family computer, no lights on after midnight, and no ride unless it was an emergency. The first couple of months were really hard to get used to, but eventually I adjusted.

Hint 3.

Hint 4.

I lived with the Ortiz family for seven months like a monk in the deep forest. However, the host dad Greg's asthma got worse after winter, so he wanted to move to the countryside. It was unexpected and I only had a week to find a new host family. I asked my friend Danielle if I could live with her until I found a new home. That's how I met the Dirksen family, my fifth family.

The Dirksen family had three kids. They were all different. Danielle liked bitter black coffee, Christian liked energy drinks, and Becca liked sweet lemon tea. Dawn, the host mom didn't like winter, and Mark, the host dad, didn't like summer. After dinner, we would all play Wii Sports together. I was the king of bowling, and Dawn was the queen of tennis. I don't remember a single time that they argued about the games. Afterward, we would gather in the living room and Danielle would play the piano while the rest of us sang hymns.

Of course, those 28 months were too short to fully understand all five families, but I learned from and was shaped by each of them. By teaching me English, nine year-old Cody taught me the importance of being able to learn from anyone; the Martinez family showed me the value of spending time together as a family; the Struiksma family taught me to reserve judgment about divorced women and adopted children; Mrs. Ortiz taught me the value of discipline and the Dirksen family taught me the importance of appreciating one another's different qualities.

Getting along with other people is necessary for anyone and living with five families has made me more sensitive to others' needs: I have learned how to recognize when someone needs to talk, when I should give advice and when to simply listen, and when someone needs to be left alone; in the process, I have become much more adaptable. I'm ready to change, learn, and be shaped by my future families.

It's this final value, being "adaptable," that connects ALL his experiences with the five families, and it's a value he'll carry on to his future families—in college and beyond. Final boom.

Margin notes (left):
All along he was weaving in these little tiny lessons that he learned. It's satisfying to reveal the connection here at the end. But wait, he's not finished.

Boom: Payoff/ Lesson 2.
Boom: Payoff/ Lesson 4.

Such a beautiful last line. Don't you just wanna hug him?

Margin notes (right):
Hint 5.

So what has all this been leading up to?

Let the series of explosions in your mind begin...Boom: Payoff/Lesson 1.

Boom: Payoff/ Lesson 3.

Boom: Payoff/ Lesson 5.

How can you use this technique for your essay?

You can't.

I'm kidding again. You actually can. The key is this... Wait, before I tell you, here's a word of warning:

Don't try to preplan this too much.

The author of the "Five Families" essay was able to discover this approach only *after* he'd written some really detailed paragraphs about the experience of living with these families. By trying to find an interesting way to connect the five families, he discovered there were lessons buried in a couple of the family descriptions, and he thought he might be able to set up some lessons in the other family paragraphs and then reveal all the lessons at the end. Again, it was important that his "hints" (the lessons) were clear enough for us to remember, but not so obvious that it'd be predictable where he was headed with the essay while we were reading it. How did he do this? On a basic level, he chose to "show" (set up) his lessons in the first few paragraphs, and then chose to "tell" all the lessons at the end. And I just want to reiterate that this was *discovered* and not preplanned.

Wait, so how did the author do this?

Here's a breakdown:

LEVEL 1.0

First, he found some interesting things to talk about. Essentially, he found a variety of interesting experiences to describe. So he had an initial framing device: *I'm going to give a variety of details about my experiences with these five families.* But then...

LEVEL 2.0

He found *a deeper way that they were all connected.* How? He realized that he "learned from and was shaped by each of [these families]" (see next to last paragraph). Nice! This connected them all. But he didn't stop there.

LEVEL 3.0

He found yet *another* way they were all connected. How? All of them taught him the value of…adaptability (see last paragraph). Great. So it's like Level 2.0 drew out something the families had in common (he learned a lesson from each), and Level 3.0 identified a value he gained from living with all of them (adaptability).

Together, these threads give the essay a feeling of inevitability, as though the author knew where he was taking us the whole time (even though, at first, he didn't). And it's surprising because we didn't necessarily think that all the families were going to connect in any particular way—we certainly didn't see there was a lesson buried in each paragraph as we were reading—and we didn't know they would all be tied together with a common value.

That's what makes it surprising *and* inevitable—we had some sense that the paragraphs probably *would* connect, but as we read through the essay, we didn't really know *how*.

Final Words on This Technique

Again, don't try to preplan too much. Why?

1. Preplanning can get really frustrating if you're trying to make this structure work, but you find the events of your life simply don't work with this structure. It can feel forced. So don't force it. Preplanning can actually prevent or postpone you from finding a structure and a flow that will work for *your* life story.
2. It can end up sounding pretty mechanical and obvious if you're too aware of your ending when you begin your story. In other words, sometimes if you're trying to Set Up Something, the "surprise" ending won't be very surprising because the Buried Hints won't be sufficiently buried. They may all be kind of

obvious and on-the-surface, and there won't be enough interesting stuff around the hints to distract us from what you're doing. (Remember, this is like a magic trick, and we need a misdirect—something shiny or pretty to focus on while the magic is happening behind the scenes.)

Instead, write interesting paragraphs with interesting details that correspond to the *original* focusing lens. Let me clarify what I mean by that. In the "Five Families" essay, the author began by writing some nice details about each family. So the reader is able to get pulled into *that* and perhaps be lulled into thinking that maybe this is as deep as it goes.

Then: BAM—an aha moment for the reader. And you want to know how to get the most aha into your aha moment? If you discover it yourself along the way. It takes patience and a trust of the process (or openness to the possibility that you may not actually discover a deeper connection), but chances are the thing you discover as you write will be much more interesting than the thing you preplan. Let me say that again, and make it look like an epic quote, so you remember it:

> "The connections that you discover along the way will be much more interesting than those you try to plan."
>
> —ME

ADVANCED TECHNIQUE 5: MAKE IT NEW

Degree of difficulty: 8.0–10.0★ (depends on what you're making new)

> "Make it new."
>
> —EZRA POUND

I know it seems redundant to put a quote with the exact same words as the technique, but doing so gives this final point *legitimacy*. Because Ezra Pound said this, too. And Ezra Pound is *legit*.

What does it mean to "make it new"?

For years, filmmakers have been taking familiar stories and recontextualizing them.

Some examples include:

- *Apocalypse Now*: Joseph Conrad's *Heart of Darkness* set during the Vietnam War
- *O Brother, Where Art Thou?*: Homer's *Odyssey* adapted to the 1930s American South
- The updated *Annie* musical, produced by Jay Z and Will Smith and starring Quvenzhané Wallis, which is set in modern-day New York City and is a remake of the original *Annie* musical that was based on the *Little Orphan Annie* comic strip.

You can do this with your essay, too.

Which essay prompts will this technique work best with?

I think it works best for creative, open-ended supplemental essay prompts such as:

- the University of Chicago "Create your own prompt" essay, or
- any school that asks, "What else would you like us to know about you?" (Note that some schools, in particular a few Ivies, ask this at the very end of the application. This is your opportunity to show one more side of yourself. Don't pass up this chance!)

This can also definitely work for your main essay, but it's just a bit more difficult to pull off—thus the "advanced technique" label.

What "it" should you be making new?

That's up to you. Want some options? Take a look at Greek, Roman, Jewish, Christian, or Islamic stories and myths. Or consider remaking a fairy tale (What's the *real* Cinderella story?), a holiday origin story (How did Christmas *really* begin?), or even doing an alternate take on an old joke (Why do firemen actually wear red suspenders?).

This last option—a new take on an old joke—is exactly what this next student does. And note that everything under the title is her writing.

"WHY DID THE CHICKEN CROSS THE ROAD?"

Note to reader: I plan to double major in biochemistry and English and my main essay explains my passion for the former; here is a writing sample that illustrates my enthusiasm for the latter.

In my AP Literature class, my teacher posed a question to which students had to write a creative response. My response is framed around the ideas of Plato's "Allegory of the Cave."

Q: Why did the chicken cross the road?

A: A manicured green field of grass blades cut to perfectly matched lengths; a blue expanse ornamented with puffy cotton clouds; an immaculately painted red barn centered exactly at the top of a hill—the chicken gazes contentedly at his picturesque world. Within an area surrounded by a shiny silver fence, he looks around at his friends: roosters pecking at a feast of grains and hens lounging on luxurious cushions of hay. As the nice man in a plaid shirt and blue jeans collects the hens' eggs, the chicken feels an overwhelming sense of indebtedness to him for providing this idyllic lifestyle.

On a day as pristine as all the others, the chicken is happily eating his lunchtime meal as the nice man carefully gathers the smooth white eggs when it notices that the man has left one behind. Strangely located at the empty end of the metal enclosure, highlighted by the bright yellow sun, the white egg appears to the chicken different from the rest. The chicken moves towards the light to tacitly inform the man of his mistake. But then the chicken notices a jagged gray line on the otherwise flawless egg. Hypnotized and appalled, the chicken watches as the line turns into a crack and a small beak attached to a fuzzy yellow head pokes out. Suddenly a shadow descends over the chicken and the nice man snatches the egg—the baby chick— and stomps off.

The chicken—confused, betrayed, disturbed—slowly lifts its eyes from the now empty ground. For the first time, it looks past the silver fence of the cage and notices an unkempt sweep of colossal brown and green grasses opposite its impeccably crafted surroundings. Cautiously, it inches closer to the barrier, farther from the unbelievable perfection of the farm, and discovers a wide sea of black gravel. Stained with gray stones and marked with yellow lines, it separates the chicken from the opposite field.

The curious chicken quickly shuffles to Mother Hen, who has just settled on to her throne of hay and is closing her eyes. He is sure that the always composed and compassionate chicken will help him make sense of what he's just seen.

"Mother Hen, Mother Hen! I-I just saw one of those eggs, cracking, and there was a small yellow bird inside. It was a baby. Are those eggs that the nice man takes away babies? And that black ground! What is it?" the chicken blurts out.

Her eyes flick open. "BOK BOK! Don't you ever dare speak of what you have seen again," Mother Hen snaps in a low and violent whisper, "or all of this will be taken away." Closing her eyes again, she dismisses the chicken.

Frozen in disbelief, the chicken tries to make sense of her

harsh words. It replays the incident in its head. "All the food, the nice soft hay, the flawless red barn—maybe all of this isn't worth giving up. Maybe Mother Hen is right. She just wants to protect me from losing it all." The chicken replays the incident again. "But it was a baby. What if it was hers? She still wouldn't care. She's being selfish; all she cares about is this perfect life." A final replay, and the chicken realizes and accepts that Mother Hen knows, has known, that the man is doing something wrong; yet she has yielded to the cruelty for her own comfort. A fissure in the chicken's unawareness, a plan begins to hatch. The chicken knows it must escape; it has to get to the other side.

"That man in the plaid shirt is stealing the eggs from their mothers again," the chicken thinks the next day as he unlocks the cage. Then the man reaches into the wooden coop, his back to the entrance. "Now!" At its own cue, the chicken scurries towards the opening and exits unseen. With a backwards glance at his friends, the chicken feels a profound sadness and pity for their ignorance. It wants to urge them to open their eyes, to see what they are sacrificing for materialistic pleasures, but he knows they will not surrender the false reality. Alone, the chicken dashes away.

The chicken stands at the line between green grass and black gravel. As it prepares to take its first step into the unknown, a monstrous vehicle with 18 wheels made of metal whizzes by, leaving behind a trail of gray exhaust. Once it regains its breath, it moves a few inches onto the asphalt. Three more speeding trucks stop its chicken heart.

"I can't do this," it says to itself. "These monsters are a sign. They're telling me to go back. Besides, a few lost chicks aren't so bad. The man's not that evil. He gives us food, and a home." But the chicken dismisses the cowardly voice in its head, reminding itself of the injustice back in the deceptively charming prison. Over the next several hours, it learns to strategically position itself so that it is in line with the empty space between the tires of passing trucks. It reaches the yellow dashes. A black blanket gradually pushes away the glowing sun and replaces it with diamond stars and a glowing crescent. It reaches the untouched field.

With a deep breath, the chicken steps into the swathe, a world of tall beige grass made brown by the darkness. Unsure of what it may discover, it determines to simply walk straight through the brush, out on to the other side. For what seems like forever, it continues forward, as the black sky turns to purple, then blue, then pink. Just as the chicken begins to regret its journey, the grass gives way to a vast landscape of trees, bushes, flowers—heterogeneous and variable, but nonetheless perfect. In a nearby tree, the chicken spots two adult birds tending to a nest of babies—a natural dynamic of individuals unaltered by corrupt influence.

And then it dawns on him. It has escaped from a contrived and perverted domain as well as its own unawareness; it has arrived in a place where the pure order of the world reigns.

"I know the truth now," it thinks to himself as the sun rises. "But here, in Nature, it is of no use. Back home, I need to try to foster awareness among my friends, share this understanding with them. Otherwise, I am as cruel as the man in the plaid shirt, taking away the opportunity to overcome ignorance.

I must return now, thought the chicken. *I have to get to the other side.*

Analysis of "Why Did the Chicken Cross the Road?"

Note to reader: I plan to double major in biochemistry and English and my main essay explains my passion for the

former; here is a writing sample that illustrates my enthusi-
asm for the latter.

In my AP Literature class, my teacher posed a question to which students had to write a creative response. My response is framed around the ideas of Plato's "Allegory of the Cave."

Q: Why did the chicken cross the road?

A: A manicured green field of grass blades cut to perfectly matched lengths; a blue expanse ornamented with puffy cotton clouds; an immaculately painted red barn centered exactly at the top of a hill—the chicken gazes contentedly at his picturesque world. Within an area surrounded by a shiny silver fence, he looks around at his friends: roosters pecking at a feast of grains and hens lounging on luxurious cushions of hay. As the nice man in a plaid shirt and blue jeans collects the hens' eggs, the chicken feels an overwhelming sense of indebtedness to him for providing this idyllic lifestyle.

On a day as pristine as all the others, the chicken is happily eating his lunchtime meal as the nice man carefully gathers the smooth white eggs when it notices that the man has left one behind. Strangely located at the empty end of the metal enclosure, highlighted by the bright yellow sun, the white egg appears to the chicken different from the rest. The chicken moves towards the light to tacitly inform the man of his mistake. But then the chicken notices a jagged gray line on the otherwise flawless egg. Hypnotized and appalled, the chicken watches as the line turns into a crack and a small beak attached to a fuzzy yellow head pokes out. Suddenly a shadow descends over the chicken and the nice man snatches the egg—the baby chick—and stomps off.

The chicken—confused, betrayed, disturbed—slowly lifts its eyes from the now empty ground. For the first time, it looks past the silver fence of the cage and notices an unkempt sweep of colossal brown and green grasses opposite its impeccably

---

Marginal notes:

Love the context. Otherwise we might wonder, "What the heck is she talking about?"

She debated for a week on whether or not to include this note, and ultimately she wanted to make sure the reader really got it. I think she made the right choice.

Status quo: Note the great details.

Setup for raising of the stakes.

Inciting incident.

crafted surroundings. Cautiously, it inches closer to the barrier, farther from the unbelievable perfection of the farm, and discovers a wide sea of black gravel. Stained with gray stones and marked with yellow lines, it separates the chicken from the opposite field.

The curious chicken quickly shuffles to Mother Hen, who has just settled on to her throne of hay and is closing her eyes. He is sure that the always composed and compassionate chicken will help him make sense of what he's just seen.

"Mother Hen, Mother Hen! I-I just saw one of those eggs, cracking, and there was a small yellow bird inside. It was a baby. Are those eggs that the nice man takes away babies? And that black ground! What is it?" the chicken blurts out.

Her eyes flick open. "BOK BOK! Don't you ever dare speak of what you have seen again," Mother Hen snaps in a low and violent whisper, "or all of this will be taken away." Closing her eyes again, she dismisses the chicken.

Frozen in disbelief, the chicken tries to make sense of her harsh words. It replays the incident in its head. "All the food, the nice soft hay, the flawless red barn—maybe all of this isn't worth giving up. Maybe Mother Hen is right. She just wants to protect me from losing it all." The chicken replays the incident again. "But it was a baby. What if it was hers? She still wouldn't care. She's being selfish; all she cares about is this perfect life." A final replay, and the chicken realizes and accepts that Mother Hen knows, has known, that the man is doing something wrong; yet she has yielded to the cruelty for her own comfort. A fissure in the chicken's unawareness, a plan begins to hatch. The chicken knows it must escape; it has to get to the other side.

"That man in the plaid shirt is stealing the eggs from their mothers again," the chicken thinks the next day as he unlocks the cage. Then the man reaches into the wooden coop, his back

I love that the chicken can talk.

Raise the stakes.

Reiterating the raising of the stakes (just to make sure we get it).

The question of the essay—Why did the chicken cross the road?—is answered here. End of essay? No way. Why? Because now we're waiting to find out *how*.

to the entrance. "Now!" At its own cue, the chicken scurries towards the opening and exits unseen. With a backwards glance at his friends, the chicken feels a profound sadness and pity for their ignorance. It wants to urge them to open their eyes, to see what they are sacrificing for materialistic pleasures, but he knows they will not surrender the false reality. Alone, the chicken dashes away.

Raise the stakes; also a setup for the ending.

The chicken stands at the line between green grass and black gravel. As it prepares to take its first step into the unknown, a monstrous vehicle with 18 wheels made of metal whizzes by, leaving behind a trail of gray exhaust. Once it regains its breath, it moves a few inches onto the asphalt. Three more speeding trucks stop its chicken heart.

Raise the stakes.

Funny. Intelligent humor = great.

"I can't do this," it says to itself. "These monsters are a sign. They're telling me to go back. Besides, a few lost chicks aren't so bad. The man's not that evil. He gives us food, and a home."

Raise the stakes: The chicken is going to give up!

But the chicken dismisses the cowardly voice in its head, reminding itself of the injustice back in the deceptively charming prison. Over the next several hours, it learns to strategically position itself so that it is in line with the empty space between the tires of passing trucks. It reaches the yellow dashes. A black blanket gradually pushes away the glowing sun and replaces it with diamond stars and a glowing crescent. It reaches the untouched field.

In film terms, this is the end of the climax. Chicken has arrived! We sigh. Next is the denouement.

With a deep breath, the chicken steps into the swathe, a world of tall beige grass made brown by the darkness. Unsure of what it may discover, it determines to simply walk straight through the brush, out on to the other side. For what seems like forever, it continues forward, as the black sky turns to purple, then blue, then pink. Just as the chicken begins to regret its journey, the grass gives way to a vast landscape of trees, bushes, flowers—heterogeneous and variable, but nonetheless perfect. In a nearby tree, the chicken spots two adult birds tending to

New status quo.

a nest of babies—a natural dynamic of individuals unaltered by corrupt influence.

And then it dawns on him. It has escaped from a contrived and perverted domain as well as its own unawareness; it has arrived in a place where the pure order of the world reigns.

"I know the truth now," it thinks to himself as the sun rises. "But here, in Nature, it is of no use. Back home, I need to try to foster awareness among my friends, share this understanding with them. Otherwise, I am as cruel as the man in the plaid shirt, taking away the opportunity to overcome ignorance.

I must return now, thought the chicken. *I have to get to the other side.*

Amazing final line. It's inevitable (because it references the familiar joke), but it's surprising because you probably thought the "Why did the chicken cross the road" was referring to the first time the chicken crosses the road in the essay, BUT IT'S ACTUALLY ABOUT CROSSING BACK. And that wasn't easy to predict. It also gives the essay a kind of circularity (it's a payoff!), plus it sets up beautifully for her sequel.

Here's one more "make it new" example:

"ROCK, PAPER, SCISSORS"
Written for the University of Chicago prompt, which asked applicants to create their own prompt

Prompt:

Dear Christian,

The admissions staff at the University of Chicago would like to inform you that your application has been "put on the line." We have one spot left and can't decide if we should admit you or another equally qualified applicant. To resolve the matter, please choose one of the following:

Rock, paper, or scissors.

You will be notified of our decision shortly.

Response:

Rock beats scissors, scissors beats paper, and paper beats rock. Wait… paper beats rock? Since when has a sheet of loose leaf paper ever defeated a solid block of granite? Do we assume that the paper wraps around the rock, smothering the rock into submission? When exposed to paper, is rock somehow immobilized, unable to fulfill its primary function of smashing scissors? What constitutes defeat between two inanimate objects?

Maybe it's all a metaphor for larger ideals. Perhaps paper is rooted in the symbolism of diplomacy while rock suggests coercion. But does compromise necessarily trump brute force? And where do scissors lie in this chain of symbolism?

I guess the reasoning behind this game has a lot to do with context. If we are to rationalize the logic behind this game, we have to assume some kind of narrative, an instance in which paper might beat rock. Unfortunately, I can't argue for a convincing one.

As with rock-paper-scissors, we often cut our narratives short to make the games we play easier, ignoring the intricate assumptions that keep the game running smoothly. Like rock-paper-scissors, we tend to accept something not because it's true, but because it's the convenient route to getting things accomplished. We accept incomplete narratives when they serve us well, overlooking their logical gaps. Other times, we exaggerate even the smallest defects and uncertainties in narratives we don't want to deal with. In a world where we know very little about the nature of "Truth," it's very easy—and tempting—to construct stories around truth claims that unfairly legitimize or delegitimize the games we play.

Or maybe I'm just making a big deal out of nothing…

Fine. I'll stop with the semantics and play your game.

But who actually wants to play a game of rock-paper-scissors? After all, isn't it just a game of random luck, requiring zero skill and talent? That's no way to admit someone!

Wrong.

Studies have shown that there are winning strategies to rock-paper-scissors by making critical assumptions about those we play against before the round has even started. Douglas Walker, host of the Rock-Paper-Scissors World Championships (didn't know that existed either), conducted research indicating that males will use rock as their opening move 50% of the time, a gesture Walker believes is due to rock's symbolic association with strength and force. In this sense, the seemingly innocuous game of rock-paper-scissors has revealed something quite discomforting about gender-related dispositions in our society. Why did so many males think that brute strength was the best option? If social standards have subliminally influenced the way males and females play rock-paper-scissors, than [sic] what is to prevent such biases from skewing more important decisions? Should your decision to go to war or to feed the hungry depend on your gender, race, creed, etc?

Perhaps the narratives I spoke of earlier, the stories I mistakenly labeled as "semantics," carry real weight in our everyday decisions. In the case of Walker's study, men unconsciously created an irrational narrative around an abstract rock. We all tell slightly different narratives when we independently consider notions ranging from rocks to war to existence. It is ultimately the unconscious gaps in these narratives that are responsible for many of the man-made problems this world faces. In order for the "life of the mind" to be a worthwhile endeavor, we must challenge the unconscious narratives we attach to the larger games we play—the truths we tell (or don't tell), the lessons we learn (or haven't really learned), the people we meet (or haven't truly met).

> But even after all of this, we still don't completely under-
> stand the narrative behind rock-paper-scissors.
>
> I guess it all comes down to who actually made this silly
> game in the first place… I'd like to think it was some snotty 3rd
> grader, but then again, that's just another incomplete narrative.

Just to reiterate: the topic of this essay (and the "Why Did the Chicken Cross the Road?" essay) may not be ideal topics for a main personal statement. Why? I'm not sure I learn a ton about the student's world or dreams and aspirations from these—or, to put it another way, I prefer personal statements that are a little more, well, personal. How do you get personal? I think vulnerability is the key (something I discuss in more depth on page 183 in "How to Make Sure Your Essay Is Doing Its Job"), and I like to be able to name a greater number and variety of a student's values by the end of the essay than I can name with these. But both of these make great supplemental essays (and along with the "Santur" essay, they are the only supplemental essays in this book) because they demonstrate intelligence, writing ability, and tons of intellectual curiosity, all of which colleges appreciate. Personally, I love this essay, not just because it's so darn fun to read, but also because (get this) it was a first draft. I know this because I was present for the moment when, days before the deadline, the author landed on the idea. I received an email less than twenty–four hours later with this essay. I read it on my phone and wrote back the words "Nice job."

WHAT MAKES AN ESSAY AMAZING

Following are two essays that I find to be, well, amazing. Read them first, without analysis, and then we'll look at four elements that make them amazing.

This first essay was originally written for a "topic of your choice" prompt, but it could work for any number of prompts. It's more than 1,000 words, but I'm including it as is, since this was how the author submitted it.

"I SHOT MY BROTHER"

From page 54 of the maroon notebook sitting on my mahogany desk:

Then Cain said to the Lord, "My punishment is greater than I can bear. I shall be a fugitive and a wanderer on the earth and whoever finds me will kill me."—Genesis 4:13

Here is a secret that no one in my family knows: I shot my brother when I was six. Luckily, it was [with] a BB gun. But to this day, my older brother Jonathan does not know who shot him. And I have finally promised myself to confess this eleven year old secret to him after I write this essay.

The truth is, I was always jealous of my brother. Our grandparents, with whom we lived as children in Daegu, a rural city in South Korea, showered my brother with endless accolades: he was bright, athletic, and charismatic.

"Why can't you be more like Jon?" my grandmother used to nag, pointing at me with a carrot stick. To me, Jon was just cocky. He would scoff at me when he would beat me in basketball, and when he brought home his painting of Bambi with the teacher's sticker "Awesome!" on top, he would make several copies of it and showcase them on the refrigerator door. But I retreated to my desk where a pile of "Please draw this again and bring it to me tomorrow" papers lay, desperate for immediate treatment. Later, I even refused to attend the same elementary school and wouldn't even eat meals with him.

Deep down I knew I had to get the chip off my shoulder. But I didn't know how.

That is, until March 11th, 2001.

That day around six o'clock, juvenile combatants appeared in Kyung Mountain for their weekly battle, with cheeks smeared in mud and empty BB guns in their hands. The Korean War game was simple: to kill your opponent you had to shout "pow!" before he did. Once we situated ourselves, our captain blew the pinkie whistle and the war began. My friend Min-young and I hid behind a willow tree, eagerly awaiting our orders.

Beside us, our comrades were dying, each falling to the ground crying in "agony," their hands clasping their "wounds." Suddenly a wish for heroism surged within me: I grabbed Min-young's arms and rushed towards the enemies' headquarters, disobeying our orders to remain sentry duty. To tip the tide of the war, I had to kill their captain. We infiltrated the enemy lines, narrowly dodging each attack. We then cleared the pillars of asparagus ferns until the Captain's lair came into view. I quickly pulled my clueless friend back into the bush.

Hearing us, the alarmed captain turned around: It was my brother.

He saw Min-young's right arm sticking out from the bush and hurled a "grenade," (a rock), bruising his arm.

"That's not fair!" I roared in the loudest and most unrecognizable voice I could manage.

Startled, the Captain and his generals abandoned their post. Vengeance replaced my wish for heroism and I took off after the fleeing perpetrator. Streams of sweat ran down my face and I pursued him for several minutes until suddenly I was arrested by a small, yellow sign that read in Korean: DO NOT TRESPASS: Boar Traps Ahead. (Two summers ago, my five year old cousin, who insisted on joining the ranks, had wandered off-course during the battle; we found him at the bottom of a 20 ft deep pit with a deep gash in his forehead and shirt soaked in blood.) "Hey, stop!" I shouted, heart pounding. "STOP!"

My mind froze. My eyes just gazed at the fleeing object; what should I do?

I looked on as my shivering hand reached for the canister of BBs. The next second, I heard two shots followed by a cry. I opened my eyes just enough to see two village men carrying my brother away from the warning sign. I turned around, hurled my BB gun into the nearby Kyung Creek and ran home as fast as I could.

***

Days passed. My brother and I did not talk about the incident.

'Maybe he knew it was me,' I thought in fear as I tried to eavesdrop on his conversation with grandpa one day. When the door suddenly opened, I blurted, "Is anything wrong?"

"Nothing," he said pushing past me, "Just a rough sleep."

But in the next few weeks, something was happening inside me.

All the jealousy and anger I'd once felt had been replaced by a new feeling: guilt.

That night when my brother was gone I went to a local store and bought a piece of chocolate taffy, his favorite. I returned home and placed it on my brother's bed with a note attached: "Love, Grandma."

Several days later, I secretly went into his room and folded his unkempt pajamas.

Then, other things began to change. We began sharing clothes (something we had never done), started watching Pokémon episodes together, and then, on his ninth birthday, I did something with Jon that I hadn't done in six years: I ate dinner with him. I even ate fishcakes, which he loved but I hated. And I didn't complain.

Today, my brother is one of my closest friends. Every week I accompany him to Carlson Hospital where he receives treatment for his obsessive compulsive disorder and schizophrenia.

While in the waiting room, we play a noisy game of Zenga, comment on the Lakers' performance or listen to the radio on the registrar's desk.

Then, the door to the doctor's office opens.

"Jonathan Lee, please come in."

I tap his shoulder and whisper, "Rock it, bro."

After he leaves, I take out my notebook and begin writing where I left off.

Beside me, the receptionist's fingers hover over the radio in search of a new station, eventually settling on one. I hear LeAnn Rimes singing "Amazing Grace." Her voice slowly rises over the noise of the bustling room.

"'Twas Grace that taught my heart to fear. And Grace, my fears relieved..."

Smiling, I open Jon's Jansport backpack and neatly place this essay inside and a chocolate taffy with a note attached.

Twenty minutes have passed when the door abruptly opens.

"Guess what the doctor just said?" my brother cries, unable to hide his exhilaration.

I look up and I smile too.

This next essay was originally written for a prompt that read, "Evaluate a significant experience, risk, achievement, or ethical dilemma you have faced and its impact on you."

"DYING BIRD"

Smeared blood, shredded feathers. Clearly, the bird was dead. But wait, the slight fluctuation of its chest, the slow blinking of its shiny black eyes. No, it was alive.

I had been typing an English essay when I heard my cat's loud meows and the flutter of wings. I had turned slightly at the noise and had found the barely breathing bird in front of me.

The shock came first. Mind racing, heart beating faster, blood draining from my face. I instinctively reached out my hand to hold it, like a long-lost keepsake from my youth. But then I remembered that birds had life, flesh, blood.

Death. Dare I say it out loud? Here, in my own home?

Within seconds, my reflexes kicked in. Get over the shock. Gloves, napkins, towels. Band-aid? How does one heal a bird? I rummaged through the house, keeping a wary eye on my cat. Donning yellow rubber gloves, I tentatively picked up the bird. Never mind the cat's hissing and protesting scratches, you need to save the bird. You need to ease its pain.

But my mind was blank. I stroked the bird with a paper towel to clear away the blood, see the wound. The wings were crumpled, the feet mangled. A large gash extended close to its jugular rendering its breathing shallow, unsteady. The rising and falling of its small breast slowed. Was the bird dying? No, please, not yet.

Why was this feeling so familiar, so tangible?

Oh. Yes. The long drive, the green hills, the white church, the funeral. The Chinese mass, the resounding amens, the flower arrangements. Me, crying silently, huddled in the corner. The Hsieh family huddled around the casket. Apologies. So many apologies. Finally, the body lowered to rest. The body. Kari Hsieh. Still familiar, still tangible.

Hugging Mrs. Hsieh, I was a ghost, a statue. My brain and my body competed. Emotion wrestled with fact. Kari Hsieh, aged 17, my friend of four years, had died in the Chatsworth Metrolink Crash on Sep. 12, 2008. Kari was dead, I thought. Dead.

But I could still save the bird.

My frantic actions heightened my senses, mobilized my spirit. Cupping the bird, I ran outside, hoping the cool air outdoors would suture every wound, cause the bird to miraculously fly away. Yet there lay the bird in my hands, still gasping, still dying. Bird, human, human, bird. What was the difference? Both were the same. Mortal.

But couldn't I do something? Hold the bird longer, de-claw the cat? I wanted to go to my bedroom, confine myself to tears, replay my memories, never come out.

The bird's warmth faded away. Its heartbeat slowed along with its breath. For a long time, I stared thoughtlessly at it, so still in my hands.

Slowly, I dug a small hole in the black earth. As it disappeared under handfuls of dirt, my own heart grew stronger, my own breath more steady.

The wind, the sky, the dampness of the soil on my hands whispered to me, "The bird is dead. Kari has passed. But you are alive." My breath, my heartbeat, my sweat sighed back, "I am alive. I am alive. I am alive."

Four Qualities of an Amazing Essay

Before I discuss the four qualities, here's an important qualifier:

When I share the two essays you just read in my workshops, readers tend to fall into two camps. Some say:

1. "Great story! But NOT a great college essay."

While others say:

2. "Great story AND a great college essay!"

Those in the first camp argue that the authors do not sufficiently demonstrate the qualities, skills, and values that they would bring to a college campus—in short, readers feel they don't really get a sense of who the student is.

Those in the second camp note that the authors' writing ability, attention to detail, and emotional intelligence are enough to let them know they'd contribute a lot to a college.

There is, of course, no right answer.

I see both sides. To be honest, I worked with these students several years ago. If I were to work with them today, I think I'd actually advise different topics, or different treatments of the topics, simply because I've become more conservative in how I advise students and, frankly, I think these essays are risky. (And by "conservative," I mean that I tend to advise students according to the criteria outlined in "How to Make Sure Your Essay Is Doing Its Job" on page 183, which these essays may or may not pass.)

With that said, my goal here is not to tell you what you must do, but instead to offer you creative options and let you make up your own mind. Whether or not the two essays would make great essays, I believe they are great pieces of writing and have a lot to teach us. So let's get to it!

A great story has two parts: a narrative that engages, often through a series of images, and an insight that illuminates something about the images and essentially answers "so what?" Although I've read a lot of essays, the two you've just read have two of the most interesting narrative and "so what" combinations I've ever seen. As I looked at them side-by-side, I realized they had a few things in common, traits that I now refer to as my "Four Qualities of an Amazing Essay."

Here are four qualities that these essays share:

1. The story is unusual in either content, structure, or both.
2. The story has at least one "wow" moment.
3. The ending is both surprising and inevitable.
4. The ending makes the reader do a little bit of work.

Note that these are not the *only* qualities of an amazing essay, but they are qualities that these amazing essays share.

Analysis of "I Shot My Brother"

1. Unusual elements

a. Unusual content (the "what"): How many people shoot their brother? Beyond that, how many shoot their brother *in order to save his life?* Not many.

b. Unusual structure (the "how"): Nonchronological order of events (essay begins with the ending). Includes cinematic time jumps.

c. Unusual style (the "how"): Great dialogue. Realistic characters. Memorable visual details. One of the best essay openings I have ever read.

2. The "wow" moment

a. The moment he has to shoot his brother in order to save his life.

b. Double wow: He's also been looking to get back at his brother, so shooting him is both an "I love you" and "I hate you" moment.

c. Triple wow: The moment of violence ends up being the catalyst for ultimately bringing them together.

3. The ending is both surprising and inevitable

a. Surprising: No way will these two reconcile.

b. Inevitable: Of course they'll reconcile.

c. Also surprising: Even if we suspected they would reconcile, we didn't expect it would happen in this way.

4. The ending makes the reader do a little bit of work

Look at that ending again—what does it mean?

> Smiling, I open Jon's Jansport backpack and neatly place this essay inside and a chocolate taffy with a note attached.

Twenty minutes have passed when the door abruptly opens.

"Guess what the doctor just said?" my brother cries, unable to hide his exhilaration.

I look up and I smile too.

I won't spell it out. Just think about where his relationship with his brother was at the start of the story (status quo) and think about where it is now (new status quo).

Analysis of "Dying Bird"

1. Unusual elements

    a. Unusual content (the "what"): Who gets the chance to save a dying bird? Who makes a connection to a friend while the bird is dying? Not many people.

    b. Unusual structure (the "how"): The nonchronological opening—she starts with an arresting image, then does a flashback to fill us in on the context.

    c. Unusual style (the "how"): The clipped style of the writing. Like a series of snapshots or a film with very quick takes.

2. The "wow" moment

    a. The moment when she realizes that her struggle to let the bird go parallels her struggle to let her friend go. It's not explicit, so you have to look for it. But it's there.

3. The ending is both surprising and inevitable

    a. Why surprising? We didn't expect her to make peace with the bird's death or her friend's.

    b. Why inevitable? Once we think about it, of course she'd have to accept the bird's death and her friend's.

4. The ending makes the reader do a little bit of work

Look at that ending again—what does it mean?

> The wind, the sky, the dampness of the soil on my hands whispered to me, "The bird is dead. Kari has passed. But you are alive." My breath, my heartbeat, my sweat sighed back, "I am alive. I am alive. I am alive."

It's subtle, what I would call a poetic ending, and I'll define "poetic" in this way—it leaves something unaccounted for. To get the meaning, you have to think about it a little, and different readers may have different interpretations. Note that it's easy to do this poorly and hard to do this well. In terms of what the ending to this essay means, I won't ruin it by trying to explain it. I'll let you decide for yourself.

Also, both of these essays end with some kind of redemption. I'm not saying that's required for an amazing essay, but I think it's part of what makes my heart swell each time I read them.

Again, these are not the *only* qualities of an amazing essay, nor are they required to make your essay amazing. These are simply qualities that I have observed in two essays that I find amazing. Incorporating these concepts can help you create a piece of writing that will amaze the reader and may even be considered by some to be a work of art.

But many students haven't experienced crazy, unusual circumstances, and some students aren't necessarily looking to create a piece of art.

Is it still possible to write an excellent college essay despite the fact that you didn't shoot your brother when you were six or see a bird die and recognize it as a metaphor for your friend's death?

Of course it is. The next chapter explains how.

CHAPTER EIGHT

How to Make Sure Your Essay Is Doing Its Job

IT'S STILL POSSIBLE TO WRITE a great college essay even if you haven't undergone crazy, unusual circumstances. In fact, maybe you just want to make sure your essay is doing its job. And what is its job? Well, think about it a second. The colleges you apply to will have a record of your grades, test scores, and extracurricular activities. So clearly your essay should show something that hasn't already been made evident. But that's kind of an obvious answer. Your essay might also contextualize or explain any red flags on your application (like bad grades) so that you're not judged too harshly. But that shouldn't be the main point of your essay. I believe the main point of your essay—actually, hang on, let me say this in bold and italics:

The aim of your college essay is to illustrate that you will make valuable contributions in college and beyond.

Why? Because college admissions offices are putting together a team...no, wait, they're hosting a dinner party and there's just one seat left...no, actually they're inviting you into their family—okay, enough analogies, you get the point. In short, colleges want to know how you'd contribute to life on campus. And they want to imagine you'll do amazing things once you graduate.

How do you illustrate that you will make valuable contributions in college and beyond? I believe it's by demonstrating these qualities:

1. Core values (a.k.a. *information*)
2. Vulnerability
3. "So what" moments (a.k.a. *important and interesting connections*)

If you work to incorporate all these things into your essay over a series of drafts, and you work to tell a story that is both compelling and succinct, you will end up with something called:

4. Craft

Here's why I believe each of these qualities is important:

1. **Core values (a.k.a. information)**: The best essays provide valuable information about the author. And I'm not talking about trivial facts—your favorite basketball team, for example, or whether you prefer brown or green M&M's—I'm talking about four to five values that are essential to who you are.
2. **Vulnerability**: The best essays offer more than superficial information; they hit you in the gut and make you feel things—the ups and downs, the passions and frustrations of the author.
3. **"So what" moments (a.k.a. important and interesting connections)**: "The best way for me to tell if a student is college-ready," says Kati Sweaney of Reed College, "is if the student can answer 'So what?' in the essay." I agree.

And I believe it's important to do so several times through-out the essay.

4. **Craft**: The best essays demonstrate a series of carefully consid-ered choices. And in the best essays, every word counts.

How can you tell if your essay is great?

Turn the page and take The Great College Essay Test.

THE GREAT COLLEGE ESSAY TEST

Is your essay great? The criteria below will help you decide. And, as in the "Four Qualities of an Amazing Essay" section, these are not the *only* qualities of a great essay—these are just a few qualities that I have observed in essays that I find to be great.

How might you use these criteria? Read your essay aloud, or have someone else read it aloud. Then ask these questions:

1. Core values (a.k.a. information)
   → Can you name at least four to five of the author's core values?
   → Do you detect a variety of values, or do the values repeat?
     Examples of NOT varied values: hard work, determination, perseverance
     Examples of more varied values: autonomy, resourcefulness, healthy boundaries, diversity

2. Vulnerability
   → Does the essay sound like it's mostly analytical or like it's coming from a deeper, more vulnerable place? (Another way of asking this: Does it sound like the author wrote it using mostly his or her head [intellect] or his or her heart and gut?)
   → After reading the essay, do you know more about the author AND feel closer to him or her?

3. "So what" moments (a.k.a. important and interesting connections)
   → Can you identify at least three to five "so what" moments of insight in the essay?
   → Are these moments predictable, or are they truly illuminating?

4. Craft
   → Do the ideas in the essay connect in a way that is logical, but not too obvious (boring)?

→ Can you tell that the essay represents a series of carefully considered choices and that the author spent a lot of time revising the essay over the course of several drafts?

→ Is it interesting and succinct throughout? If not, where do you lose interest? Where could words be cut or which part isn't revealing as much as it could be?

If you're feeling bold...

Give your essay to someone else and ask him or her to evaluate it based on these elements. But before you do, read "How and When to Ask for Feedback" on page 204.

Want to read some example essays that incorporate all these elements?

Guess what: I've already given you a bunch of examples, since most of the essays in this book illustrate these qualities.

To clarify these qualities, you'll find four of my favorite essays in chapter nine, and in the analysis that follows each one, I've highlighted the qualities discussed in The Great College Essay Test (see page 186).

If you don't want to read examples right now, though, and you just want to know how to improve your own essay based on these criteria, keep reading.

HOW TO BRING MORE VALUES, VULNERABILITY, AND INSIGHT INTO YOUR ESSAY (OR HOW TO IMPROVE YOUR ESSAY IF YOU FEEL IT'S "JUST OKAY")

In this section I address:

1. How to Bring More Values (and Information!) into Your Essay
2. How to Be Vulnerable in Your Essay
3. How to Make Sure Your Insights Are Actually Insightful

If you've skipped to this section and you're not yet sure if your essay is great or just okay, flip back to page 186 and give your essay The Great College Essay Test.

1. How to Bring More Values (and Information!) into Your Essay

Just a reminder that when I say it's important to include "information" in your essay, I don't mean trivial facts; I mean core values (see the Core Values Exercise on page 8 for examples).

I believe it's important to clearly express four to five of your core values in the essay. Here's how:

Make sure you've done the Core Values Exercise on page 8. And, if you know what career you're aiming for, make sure you've identified the values necessary for that career (see page 59 in the "How to Write Essay Type B" section for more on how to do this).

Then ask yourself these three questions:

1. Which values are clearly coming through in the essay? Highlight the lines that clearly demonstrate those values.
2. Which values are kind of coming through but could be expressed more clearly?
3. Which values aren't there yet, but could be?

> Tip: Delete any repetitive values. Examples: "determination" and "perseverance" are basically the same thing, as are "collaboration" and "working with others." But if you feel they are definitely different, just make sure to articulate why they're different.

In short, make sure you're exhibiting a variety of values. Then:

CUT sections where no values are clearly being communicated, REWRITE sections where the values aren't super clear, and ADD sections that will clearly communicate values that aren't there yet, but that you'd like to include.

2. How to Be Vulnerable in Your Essay

I'm sometimes asked: Must you be vulnerable to write a great essay? The answer is no. I've read some great essays that are not, in some way, vulnerable. (Pause.) Okay, actually, I just went through this book looking for examples of great essays that aren't in some way vulnerable, and I couldn't find one. So the answer might be yes.

Why? Because there are so many ways to be vulnerable in your essay. Here are a few of those ways:

Reveal Something That You Worry People Might Judge You For

This is a common way to define vulnerability: we fear revealing something that might lead us to feel isolated, ashamed, or unloved. But I find that vulnerability can, in fact, have the opposite effect. By discussing our deepest fears, we can actually draw people closer to us, since deep down we often share those same fears.

Here are some essays by students who were worried that they might be judged for their essay content: "Raising Anthony," "Easter," "Bowling," "What I Found on the Farm," "I Shot My Brother," "Breaking Up with Mom," and especially "Knife."

I want to emphasize that, by the end of each of the essays listed, I don't feel repelled by the authors—quite the opposite, actually. I want to know them better because the choice to be vulnerable is a brave and risky choice, and I like brave people who take risks.

The other benefit is a little more mysterious—the vulnerable place is, I believe, where the magic happens. Venture down the path of vulnerability and who knows where it might lead, but chances are it will be somewhere interesting.

Discuss a Challenge or Contradiction That Is Unresolved or Unresolvable

One thing I don't find very interesting in a personal statement is a student presenting his or her résumé or activities list. Here's why: Admissions officers are less interested in who you have been, and they're more interested in who you are becoming. I sometimes describe this difference as writing to report vs. writing to discover. Writing to report says, "I'm finished and here is what I'm presenting," whereas writing to discover says, "I'm very much in process and this is what I've figured out so far, but here are one or two things I haven't figured out yet." In essence, while answers are okay, good questions are more interesting.

So where can you search for your own unresolved challenges or contradictions? Often these are the result of a conflict between important values. What do I mean?

Here are some personal examples of my own unresolved challenges and the values that I believe are in conflict:

- I want to eat foods that are good for me (value: health), but this is at odds with my desire to eat every different kind of pizza on the planet (values: freedom, curiosity, variety, authenticity).
- I want to be present with my daughter (values: family, connection), but I also really love traveling to deliver workshops for students, parents, and counselors (values: meaningful work, variety, connection).

See what I mean? And note that this concept of conflicting values is actually the essence of drama. Think about that: drama doesn't exist if you hate X but love Y. Drama exists when you love two things that are in opposition. (There's no drama if I love eating healthy foods and hate eating pizza, since the choice is simple: don't eat pizza. Drama exists when I crave eating a whole pizza, but I also want to lead a healthy, balanced lifestyle.)

In terms of your essay, these types of conflict can create what I call a productive tension, one that may be worth exploring in an essay.

How can you discover these for yourself?

Review your top values from the Core Values Exercise on page 8 and ask: Which of my other top values tends to conflict with this one? (Here's an example, with values marked in bold: my desire for **consistency** sometimes conflicts with my desire to **travel**, or my desire to **express myself** often conflicts with my desire to **listen**.) And here's the key: try to find something that you haven't figured out yet (in other words, an unresolved conflict), and then go write about it. See what happens. Or if you've written a draft already that you feel isn't all that deep, use the Feelings and Needs Exercise on page 127 and see if you can determine which needs are in conflict. Note that sometimes we encounter conflicts that aren't just unresolved, but are actually unresolvable. And that can be even more interesting.

For example, sometimes I will listen to meditation CDs while I'm driving in order to be productive and efficient. But think about that. This represents two directly opposed values—my desire to do more (multitask) and my desire to just be (meditate). What does this say about me? It's a complex question. When should I do, and when should I just be? It's the dance of life, and I don't know that I can actually resolve it. But that's okay. I believe facing down our unresolved or unresolvable conflicts and contradictions reveals us as vulnerable, as human.

For an example of an essay that addresses an unresolvable contradiction or paradox, check out the "Barbie vs. Terrorism and the Patriarchy" essay on page 207.

Describe Your Passion and Do Not Apologize for It

How does this show vulnerability? Because it takes guts to stand up and say what you love, or what you stand for, especially if your passion is something other people might consider nerdy, like reading or, God forbid, endodontics. (I say this with love: I am a nerd too—for college essays, board games, and puns.) But it's possible to scream to the heavens "I LOVE MATH" unapologetically, and people will love you for it.

But here's the key: you can't just say, "I love math so, so, so much." You still need to make sure that your essay reveals core values, includes "so what" moments of insight, and is well-crafted.

Three essays that I find to be unapologetically passionate are the "Endodontics," "If Ink Were Ants," and "Mazes" essays.

But want to get next-level vulnerable?

Discuss a Challenge and Don't Actually Resolve It at the End

Like this student did:

"BREAKING UP WITH MOM"

I stare into my cappuccino to try to avoid looking at my teary eyed mom, who had just found a hole in her favorite bright pink floral print scarf.

"I'm your mother, Katyush," she says in her heavy Russian accent.

A tiny bird of a woman with clipped wings.

I remember white walls, bottles upon bottles of acrylic paint, and a mortgage on a two-bedroom apartment in Lomita, California: my mother's dream. Together, we unpacked the painting box and started a mural on my new bedroom wall. "Let it Be", my new wall read, with an array of squares and swirls in every shade of blue imaginable. We proudly took a step back, then unpacked the Jasmine Fancy tea leaves and floral teapot.

Her trembling hands reach for her coffee.

"You're supposed to take care of me. That's what family does. I don't have anyone else."

Her mom in Moscow, her ex-husband remarried, and her oldest son avoiding her at all costs. Unemployed and unwilling.

"I'll get my pills eventually, but family has responsibilities."

Her depression plummeting, her sanity dwindling, her only lifeline dying for freedom from her confines.

I flash back to the terror in her eyes as she noticed a chip on the teapot's spout—a spark of fear that transformed into a thunderstorm. How she crumpled in the old kitchen chair across from me. From that moment on, life became a broken record. I walked her to bed, kissed her goodnight, reminded her that I had school the next day. Asleep by 3 am. Late to class. Come home stressed. Start homework. Take care of mom. Finish homework. 3 am.

My mother was in a state of stagnation, and she had a hold on me like quicksand.

Though living with my dad and stepmom was its own ticking timebomb, for the most part I was left alone long enough to do schoolwork and get to class on time—but every moment away from my mom felt like I was tying a noose around her neck. Nothing I did could bring her the peace she wanted from me.

When I was fifteen years old I broke up with my mother. We could still be friends, I told her, but I needed my space, and she couldn't give me that.

For the first time in my life, I had taken action. I was never again going to passively let life happen to me.

During four long months of separation, I filled the space that my mom previously dominated with learning: everything and anything. I began teaching myself rudimentary French through an online program, learned basic HTML coding and website design, and began editing my drawings on Photoshop so that I could sell them online. When my dad lost his job, I learned to sew my own clothing, and applied my new knowledge to costume design within the Drama department.

On stage, I learned to stand up and say things that mattered. Backstage, I worked with teams of dedicated students who wanted each other to succeed. In our improv group, I gained the confidence to act on my instincts. In the classroom, my Drama teacher emulated the person I wanted to be. She gave me hugs on days that wouldn't end, insisted that taking care of myself was not the same thing as being selfish, and most importantly, taught me how to ask for help.

A year later, it all culminated in One Bad Apple—a full length musical that I produced with my best friend. Managing the budget, scheduling rehearsals, and working with a cast and crew of students was easily the most difficult thing I have ever done—but it was my choice. The challenge, and the reward, belonged to me.

On my sixteenth birthday, I picked up the phone and dialed my mom. I waited through three agonizingly long pauses between rings.

"Katyush?"

"Hi mom, it's me."

I absolutely love this essay. Why? Because the author doesn't follow the standard "...but I learned from and was shaped by this experience," a common trope for failure essays. *Yet I still learn a lot about this student's core values, plus it's loaded with "so what" moments.* And in terms of craft, this is next-level stuff; it's clear that the words were carefully chosen and that the author revised over several drafts.

What can we learn from this?

1. You don't need to tie things up at the end with a nice little bow. Your essay can finish in an open-ended way.

2. If you decide not to tie things up at the end, the rest of the essay had better be amazing. And how do you know if your essay is amazing? Write ten drafts until you find it to be amazing, then give it to five people and ask them if they agree.

3. There are many ways to be vulnerable, and this essay employs all the methods I've described so far. The author:

a. reveals something people might judge her for (her tumultuous relationship with her family, in particular her mom),

b. addresses an unresolved challenge (inner conflict between her desire to help her mom, which has led her to frustration, and her desire to be free and focus on her own needs—put simply, the conflicting values might be "helping others" vs. "helping herself"), and

c. names a passion for which she does not apologize (it could be argued that this is theater—and if you met this student you'd know this is her passion—but I think there's a deeper passion unfolding here, since by the end of the essay she is learning to fall in love with herself).

> Tip: One variation on the method just described is to discuss a failure you experienced and to not (as most students do) actually resolve everything at the end. One student I worked with, for example, discussed how a student he was tutoring in an after-school program ended up quitting the program. Rather than making things nice in the conclusion of his essay, though, he reflected on how he felt he had failed that student and in the end is left with the burden of that failure. It was powerful.

So ask yourself: What would the Hollywood ending to my essay be? Then reject that Hollywood ending and ask yourself: What really happened? And what's the deeper lesson I can learn based on that?

How to Practice Being Vulnerable: Complete the Feelings and Needs Exercise on Page 127 with Someone You Know

Here's an idea: complete the Feelings and Needs Exercise on page 127 by picking something that really bothers you about someone you know (maybe you feel that a friend doesn't really listen to you, for example, or that your coach doesn't treat you as being equal to the others on your team). Then tell the person how you feel about that and what your deeper needs are. This may or may not give you

content for your essay, but it should give you a pretty good reference point for what vulnerability feels like! Also, imagining that
conversation may have made your stomach drop just now. If so,
that may be an indication you're on the right path to vulnerability.

3. How to Make Sure Your Insights Are Actually Insightful

Consider that providing insight is like telling a joke, and that joke
telling is basic setup and payoff. A funny joke positions the setup and
payoff just the right mental distance apart. If the setup and payoff are
too close to each other, the joke isn't that funny:

Q: Why did the chicken cross the road?
A: To get to the other side.

But if the setup and payoff are too far apart, the joke isn't funny either:

Q: What's the difference between a watermelon and a sweet pea?
A: About ten minutes.

(This is an old family joke that relies on telling the joke aloud.
Good luck. It took me years to get it.)

For an insight to be satisfying, your setup has to be just the right
mental distance from your payoff. Here's what I mean by "mental
distance" and how to do this:

Separate several of your "show" moments from your "tell" moments.

To clarify, a "show" moment is an interesting image, detail, example,
or story that illustrates a core value or an important point, and a "tell"
moment offers some comment on or interpretation of that "show."

Example "show" moment:

> Many nights you'll find me in the garage replacing standard chrome trim with an elegant piano black finish or changing the threads on the stitching of the seats to add a personal touch...

Example "tell" moment:

> ...as I believe a few small changes can transform a generic product into a personalized work of art.

Note: I think these are the right "mental distance" from each other because I wouldn't be likely to guess the "tell" simply by reading the "show."

Okay, once you've separated your "show" and "tell" moments:

a. Read your "show" moments aloud to someone else and see if he or she can predict what your insight will be.
b. If that person can predict your insight, chances are your current insight isn't surprising or unusual. So rewrite the insight. And if you can't come up with something insightful, consider cutting the image/detail/example/story altogether.

What about Craft?

You'll notice that I included four qualities in The Great College Essay Test, but I only discuss how to do the first three here. Why? Because, in some sense, this whole book is about craft—and to try to say in a few paragraphs, "Here's how to craft your essay" would be just plain silly. So if you're looking for my answer to how to write a well-crafted college essay, my answer is this book. All of it.

But there is a little something called "style" that I'd love to offer a few tips on, and it's not unrelated to craft. So here are:

A Few Ways to Score Style Points (Once Your Essay Is Mostly Written)

1. Express complex thoughts in succinct ways

This simply means taking something elaborate and saying it in fewer words.

Examples:

In the "Breaking Up with Mom" essay (page 192), the author details a complicated relationship with her mother. But rather than going into all the details of how complicated her mother is, she evokes it in these two lines:

> "I'm your mother, Katyush," she says in her heavy Russian accent.
> A tiny bird of a woman with clipped wings.

And just like that we learn a whole lot. Does she spell it out? No. But we do learn something valuable about the way the author sees her mother.

Here's another example, from the "Grandma's Kimchi" essay (page 209):

> A piece of writing is more than just a piece of writing. It evokes. It inspires. It captures what time takes away.
>
> My grandma used to say: "Tigers leave furs when they die, humans leave their names." Her legacy was the smell of garlic that lingered around my house. Mine will be these words.

Again, the author communicates so much in just a few words. And in this essay, those last five words deliver that satisfying "surprising, but inevitable" conclusion that I'm such a fan of (see page 150 for more).

How to express a complex thought in a succinct way:

First, you'll need a complex thought. To get one, you'll need to think deeply about your world, and you'll need to question your own assumptions.

Can't think of a complex thought? You're in trouble. Give up writing an essay altogether.

I'm kidding.

Instead, try looking through your essay and, for each major point you make, ask yourself these four questions:

1. What are the positive/negative consequences of this belief?
2. What's a potential counterargument for this belief that I can debunk?
3. What's a call to action? (What must I do as a result?)
4. What's an unexpected value? (Is there something else that I or we will gain if we learn from or put this belief into action?)

In essence, you're answering "So what?" These four questions are designed to help you do that. Your goal is to come up with a fresh idea.

Next, you'll need to find a succinct way to explain your fresh idea. How? By revising, revising, and revising some more. If you've written something, revised it, and it's still unclear, chances are it's because your thoughts aren't clear—yet. Keep going. Keep whittling away the unnecessary. You'll get there.

2. Use big words selectively

First, some examples:

From the "With Debate" essay (page 22): "My diffidence was frustrating" and "as calls for help grew, the more defunct I became." Note the simple but effective use of the words "diffidence" and "defunct." Their use isn't showy, the words are used correctly, and there are only two big words—not six.

From the "Knife" essay (page 144): "I was at my most desperate. My friend had died in September of my junior year. Five AP classes, weekly volunteering, and a tutoring job had provided added stress. I needed reprieve. And I found it in the knife." Note the use of the word "reprieve." Again, simple.

From the "Mazes" essay (page 211): "...I created several computer games, incorporating such unordinary aspects of gameplay as the avoidance of time-travel paradoxes, and the control of 'jounce,' the fourth derivative of position with respect to time." Okay, so this example is a little less selective in terms of its usage of big words, and you'll need to decide for yourself how far you want to go with this, but I wanted to show you an example that was a little more showy. But I wouldn't go too much further than this example with your jargon/geeky language (see page 114 for more on using geeky language).

What not to do:

Don't add needless complexity. "Obscurantism is obscurantism," as my English teacher Mrs. Clark used to say.

What do I mean? Don't do this:

> I have experienced the unbridgeable paradigm between a dissipated way of life and a miring in depression and lack of motivation. The moment I apprehended the myriad of consistencies between the diversified fields of religion, philosophy, and existence, I eliminated the sufferings caused by my inextricable subjectivity, and eventually surrendered to the conclusion—after analyzing the mechanism of the universe and the history of evolution—that everything is without clear meaning.

In short, when it comes to big words, be like my man Prufrock: politic, cautious, and meticulous.

3. Make the reader cry

This one's kind of a joke because I mean, really, how do you *make* the reader cry?

Well, I'll tell you.

1. Tap into something so deep and important to you that just thinking about it makes you cry. Then:

2. Write about it in a way that never, ever, makes the reader feel like you're trying to make him or her cry.

3. Finally, make sure to leave something unaccounted for. (The best essays don't explain everything.)

Examples of essays that have made me cry: the "Bowling," "Dying Bird," "I Shot My Brother," "Grandma's Kimchi," and "Breaking Up with Mom" essays.

How do you test this? Keep revising it until your essay makes five different people cry.

But remember: Do it without trying to do it.

WHEN TO SCRAP WHAT YOU HAVE AND START OVER

When is it time to start over? Simple:

Any time you want.

As long as it's before the deadline, you have time.

Really?

In the words of Shrek, "Really, really." As writers, we can some-times grow pretty attached to what we've written. We think, "But I've spent so much time on it!" or "I'm invested!" or my favorite, "If I start over now, I'll *lose* everything I've written!"

But it's not true. You won't *lose* anything. Just because you choose new examples, a new structure, or even a new topic doesn't mean you lose everything from before. The work you've done clears the way for the work you've yet to do.

"Sacrifice the essay of yesterday to the essay of tomorrow."

—ME (I THINK)

If you're feeling kind of "meh" about your essay, or like you haven't found your deepest story yet, just remember:

There's an extraordinary story inside you waiting to be told.

"Ditch your crappy story so your extraordinary story can come forth."

—ALBERT EINSTEIN (I'M KIDDING. THAT'S ME, TOO.)

HOW TO WRITE YOUR ESSAY IN JUST ONE NIGHT (BREAK ONLY IN CASE OF EMERGENCY)

Please. Try *everything* else before you try this. Why? Because writing a great personal statement takes time. How much time? In my experience, a great essay takes several weeks to write, and most of the essays in this book represent the fifth, sixth, or fifteenth draft.

But what if you don't have the luxury of time? Say you're in a jam and, for whatever reason, your essay is due in a few days (or hours). That's what this section is for.

Here's what to do:

Create an outline based on qualities or values you'd like to show, but instead of ending the essay with your future career, end with values that will be important to you no matter what career you choose.

Here's how to do it:

1. Complete the first five items on the "Six Ways to Generate Your Content" list on page 91.
2. Get a blank sheet of paper, draw a vertical line down the middle, write the words "My values" at the top of the right column, and list your four to five most important values with space in between. (Example: "knowledge"—skip an inch—"nature"—skip an inch—"music.") That's right, you're doing a modified type B essay.
3. In the left column, beside each value, describe an image that shows how you developed that value. (Examples: Beside the value of "knowledge" you write, "I sometimes stay up until 3 a.m. surfing obscure Wikipedia articles," or beside the value of "nature" you write, "Going camping alone with just a tent, my journal, and 5 lbs. of trail mix.") You get the idea. Everything in the left column should be visual, like a snapshot or a scene from a movie.
4. Put your little movies in order—chronological often works—and describe each image or movie in a brief paragraph. (Important: Don't mention your values yet.)
5. Write transitions between the ideas so there is some sense of flow. This part will take the longest. (Hint: If you write them chronologically, you can use basic transitions such as "A few years later..." or "When I entered high school..." as place-holders and tweak later.)
6. At the end, describe some of the values that you'll carry with you into college and beyond.

This will at least yield an essay that demonstrates a few of your core values. With any extra time you have, try including a "so what" moment after each value. For more on this, turn to page 62.

For examples of what this might look like, check out the "Scrapbook" (page 28) and "Punk Rock Philosopher" (page 96) essays, both of which use a simple framing device to lay out some important details and then end with some core values. I'm not saying, by the way, that these essays were written in one night, but they were written more quickly than some of the other essays in this book.

HOW AND WHEN TO ASK FOR FEEDBACK

Getting opinions from others is a great idea—when it's done the right way. Here are some common mistakes to avoid and some tips for what to do instead.

1. Don't ask for feedback too early.

When an idea is newly hatched, it's very fragile. A harsh word can stop it dead.

> Tip: Wait 'til you're really, really ready.

2. Don't ask for feedback from too many people.

"Too many cooks spoil the broth," goes the old saying. It's so true.

> Tip: During the writing process, I recommend working with one person at a time. Once you're clear on what every single paragraph is doing and why every single sentence and word is there, then it's safe to ask a few more people. But wait until you feel really solid about what you've produced.

3. Don't be vague (or lie to yourself) about what kind of feedback you want.

> Tip: If you know or sense that you're looking for something specific, do your reader (and yourself) a favor and ask for that specific thing. (Example

> email: "Hi, Mrs. Clark! I've written a draft of my college essay and I'm wondering if you would mind proofreading it. I'm happy with the topic and the structure, so I don't need feedback on that; I just want to make sure I don't have any glaring grammatical errors. Thanks!") It's such a big help to your teachers/counselors/friends/family-members-turned-editors.

Sometimes you honestly just want to hear, "Great essay! Submit it!" Or say it's twenty-four hours from a submission deadline. Who wants to be told, "I think you should write about your involvement with wrestling instead." Yikes. Nobody. The more specific you are with your feedback request, the more likely you are to get what you want from the exchange.

Something to keep in mind: consider that essays work in three parts—content (what the essay is about), structure (how the ideas connect to one another), and details—and it's sometimes hard to give notes on one without giving notes on the other. If you ask for someone to give notes on the "structure" or "flow" of the essay, that can be difficult because sometimes an essay isn't working because of the topic, not because of the structure. So don't be afraid to ask your reader for feedback on the topic and structure—just be ready to hear that person say, "I'm not sure this is the best topic for you," since that may mean that the reader is suggesting you start over. Must you start over? No (see next point). But you might want to consider it (see earlier section "When to Scrap What You Have and Start Over" on page 201).

4. Don't allow one person's opinion to be more important than your own.

Who knows, objectively, what every single college admissions reader will think? No one. And anyone who claims to know "what colleges want" is often really saying, "Here is what I've seen work for some other students."

Tip: If you hear someone giving general writing advice, request specificity. (Example: If your counselor, or even a college admissions person, says
something like, "The essay should be in your authentic voice," feel free to
ask, "What does 'authentic voice' mean to you?" or "How do I do that?".)
If you agree with what the person says and it's useful, great! If it's vague
or doesn't resonate with you, then see my note below.

A Quick Final Note on How to Receive Feedback

Remember: Anyone's input is just that—input. It doesn't mean you
have to follow it. If you're given advice on how to write your essay
that you don't agree with—either from your parents, your friend,
your counselor, or even from me—don't be afraid to ask, "Why?"
And if the answer doesn't make sense, or you don't think it will
help, just nod graciously and thank the person for the input. Deep
down, that person likely has your best interests at heart and is just
trying to help.

But it's your essay. It's your story. You get final say.

CHAPTER NINE

A Few of My Favorite Essays

I LOVE ALL THE ESSAYS in this book, but coming up are a few that I believe pass The Great College Essay Test, as they exhibit core values, vulnerability, "so what" moments, and craft. Read them first here, without comment, then read my analysis afterward.

"BARBIE VS. TERRORISM AND THE PATRIARCHY"

Much of my early knowledge of how the world works was formed through countless hours spent playing with Barbie dolls. My sister, Taylor, and I had a plethora of toys, filling our basement's cabinets and often littering our brightly checkered IKEA rug, but Barbie was our favorite. We gave her choppy, unfortunate haircuts, houses constructed out of large wooden dominoes, and a variety of cars—a neon orange truck, a convertible with a bubblegum-pink steering wheel, and a Volkswagen Beetle with a missing back tire.

Above the basement, the kitchen radio spewed out information—the news of the 9/11 attacks on our friends' parents at the Pentagon, the War in Afghanistan, and the D.C. area snipers' attacks on our entire community—but Taylor and I had trouble understanding what the information meant.

As my mom drove me to a doctor's appointment, our local station announced that the snipers had shot someone just miles away. After I "raced" her inside into the waiting room, I soaked in the murmur about guns, a white van, and two very bad men. In the car ride home, I asked her a myriad of questions about terrorism including, "Do bullets go through glass?" Her responses left me still craving answers, so I took matters into my own hands. At five years old, I decided to enlist Barbie in the army.

While I fought against my penetrating fear of the world outside our haven of toys, Barbie herself fought against the very terrorism I was afraid of. In what we called our "Barbie Afghanistan," Taylor and I worked through our confusion by making Barbie fight the battles, still wearing her high heels and ball gowns.

I no longer play with Barbie, but she has fought another war in my adolescence. I'm a passionate feminist, and my opinions about Barbie have caused an internal tug-of-war on my beliefs. As I sit in my basement now, surrounded by books and my laptop, I have just as many questions as I did at five years old.

I've desperately attempted to consolidate my opposing opinions of Barbie into a single belief, but I've accepted that they're separate. In one, she has perpetuated physical ideals unrepresentative of how real female bodies are built. Striving to look like Barbie is not only striving for the impossible—the effort is detrimental to women's psychological and physical health, including my own. In the other, Barbie has inspired me in her breaking of the plastic ceiling. She has dabbled in close to 150 careers, including some I'd love to have: a UNICEF Ambassador, teacher, and business executive. And although it's not officially listed on her résumé, Barbie served honorably in the War in Afghanistan.

Barbie has proven to be an 11.5-inch-tall embodiment of both what frustrates and excites me. From terrorism to feminism and beyond, I am vexed by the complexities of the world but eager to piece things together. Although I'm frustrated by what I can't understand, I've realized that confusion is okay.

With Barbie as my weapon, I've continued to fight in the many "wars" in my life. I've found great value in the questions I ask and in my attempts to reconcile our world's inevitable contradictions. Things can be innocent yet mature, they can be detrimental yet empowering, and they can even wear high heels and a ball gown while fighting in a war.

"GRANDMA'S KIMCHI"

Every Saturday morning, I'd awaken to the smell of crushed garlic and piquant pepper. I would stumble into the kitchen to find my grandma squatting over a large silver bowl, mixing fat lips of fresh cabbages with garlic, salt, and red pepper. That was how the delectable Korean dish, kimchi, was born every weekend at my home.

My grandma's specialty always dominated the dinner table as kimchi filled every plate. And like my grandma who had always been living with us, it seemed as though the luscious smell of garlic would never leave our home. But even the prided recipe was defenseless against the ravages of Alzheimer's that inflicted my grandma's mind.

Dementia slowly fed on her memories until she became as blank as a brand-new notebook. The ritualistic rigor of Saturday mornings came to a pause, and during dinner, the artificial taste of vacuum-packaged factory kimchi only emphasized the absence of the family tradition. I would look at her and ask,

"Grandma, what's my name?" But she would stare back at me with a clueless expression. Within a year of diagnosis, she lived with us like a total stranger.

One day, my mom brought home fresh cabbages and red pepper sauce. She brought out the old silver bowl and poured out the cabbages, smothering them with garlic and salt and pepper. The familiar tangy smell tingled my nose. Gingerly, my grandma stood up from the couch in the living room, and as if lured by the smell, sat by the silver bowl and dug her hands into the spiced cabbages. As her bony hands shredded the green lips, a look of determination grew on her face. Though her withered hands no longer displayed the swiftness and precision they once did, her face showed the aged rigor of a professional. For the first time in years, the smell of garlic filled the air and the rattling of the silver bowl resonated throughout the house.

That night, we ate kimchi. It wasn't perfect; the cabbages were clumsily cut and the garlic was a little too strong. But kimchi had never tasted better. I still remember my grandma putting a piece in my mouth and saying, "Here, Dong Jin. Try it, my boy."

Seeing grandma again this summer, that moment of clarity seemed ephemeral. Her disheveled hair and expressionless face told of the aggressive development of her illness.

But holding her hands, looking into her eyes, I could still smell that garlic. The moments of Saturday mornings remain ingrained in my mind. Grandma was an artist who painted the cabbages with strokes of red pepper. Like the sweet taste of kimchi, I hope to capture those memories in my keystrokes as I type away these words.

A piece of writing is more than just a piece of writing. It evokes. It inspires. It captures what time takes away.

My grandma used to say: "Tigers leave furs when they die, humans leave their names." Her legacy was the smell of garlic that lingered around my house. Mine will be these words.

"MAZES"

My story begins at about the age of two, when I first learned what a maze was. For most people, solving mazes is a childish phase, but I enjoyed artistically designing them. Eventually my creations jumped from their two dimensional confinement, requiring the solver to dive through holes to the other side, or fold part of the paper over, then right back again. At around the age of eight, I invented a way for mazes to carry binary-encoded messages, with left turns and right turns representing 0s and 1s. This evolved into a base-3 maze on the surface of a tetrahedron, with crossing an edge representing a 2. For me, a blank piece of paper represented the freedom to explore new dimensions, pushing the boundaries of traditional maze making.

I found a similar freedom in mathematics. Here's what I wrote when I was 9:

$N + B = Z$

$M^2 = P$

$E - (L + B) = G$

$C / Y = Z - Q$

$B + B = Y$

$(D - V)^9 - (P*L) = J$

$W = (I - V)^2$

$Y + B + C = R$

$O^2 + (Y*O) = T$

$F^3 - (T + W) = F^2$

$V - R = H - U$

$A^3 - C = N$

$Y^2 + B = L$

$J^2 - J = J + (P + I)$

$Y^3 = X$

$X - R = M - O$

$D*A - B - (V + Y) = E$

$$U - X - O = W$$
$$P / P = B$$
$$S - A = U$$
$$(Z + B)*C = P$$
$$C(+ / -)B = A$$
$$U + C = H$$
$$R - L = S - T$$

The object of puzzles like these was to solve for every letter, assuming they each represented a unique positive integer, and that both sides of each equation are positive. These are not typical assumptions for practical mathematics, and I didn't even need 26 equations. Upon formally learning algebra, I was dismayed that "proper math" operated under a different set of assumptions, that two variables can be equal, or be non-integers, and that you always need as many equations as variables. Yet looking back, I now see that mathematics was so inspirational because there really is no "proper" way, no convention to hold me from discovering a completely original method of thought. Math was, and still is, yet another way for me to freely express my creativity and different way of thinking without constraint.

It's all about freedom. The thoughts are there, they just need a way to escape. The greatest single advancement that delivered even more freedom was my first computer, and on it, one of the first computer games I ever played: "Maze Madness." It was a silly and simple game, but I remember being awed that I could create my own levels. Through the years, I've made thousands (not exaggerating) of levels in a variety of different computer games. I get most excited when I discover a bug that I can incorporate to add a new twist to the traditional gameplay.

A few years ago I grew tired of working within the constraints of most internet games and I wanted to program my own, so I decided to learn the language of Scratch. With it, I created several computer games, incorporating such unordinary aspects of gameplay as the avoidance of time-travel paradoxes, and the control of "jounce," the fourth derivative of position with respect to time. Eventually, I came to realize that Scratch was too limited to implement some of my ideas, so I learned C#, and my potential expanded exponentially. I continue to study programming knowing that the more I learn, the more tools I have to express my creativity.

I plan to design computer systems that are as outside of the box as my thoughts. And who knows where it will lead? My way of thinking in different dimensions could be the very thing separating computers from humans, and it could motivate the creation of true artificial intelligence. To me, studying computer science is the next step of an evolution of boundary breaking that has been underway since my first maze.

ANALYSIS OF A FEW OF MY FAVORITE ESSAYS

As I've already analyzed a few essays based on narrative structure or montage structure (page 30) and the "Four Qualities of an Amazing Essay" (page 178), I'll analyze the following essays in terms of the qualities of The Great College Essay Test, which are:

1. Core values (information)
2. Vulnerability
3. "So what" moments (insights or important and interesting connections)
4. Craft

"BARBIE VS. TERRORISM AND THE PATRIARCHY"

Much of my early knowledge of how the world works was formed through countless hours spent playing with Barbie dolls. My sister, Taylor, and I had a plethora of toys, filling our basement's cabinets and often littering our brightly checkered IKEA rug, but Barbie was our favorite. We gave her choppy, unfortunate haircuts, houses constructed out of large wooden dominoes, and a variety of cars—a neon orange truck, a convertible with a bubblegum-pink steering wheel, and a Volkswagen Beetle with a missing back tire.

Craft. Love the details/ verisimilitude here. And not too much, just enough.

Above the basement, the kitchen radio spewed out information—the news of the 9/11 attacks on our friends' parents at the Pentagon, the War in Afghanistan, and the D.C. area snipers' attacks on our entire community—but Taylor and I had trouble understanding what the information meant.

As my mom drove me to a doctor's appointment, our local station announced that the snipers had shot someone just miles away. After I "raced" her inside into the waiting room, I soaked in the murmur about guns, a white van, and two very bad men. In the car ride home, I asked her a myriad of questions about terrorism including, "Do bullets go through glass?" Her responses left me still craving answers, so I took matters into my own hands. At five years old, I decided to enlist Barbie in the army.

Information. Core value: curiosity.

While I fought against my penetrating fear of the world outside our haven of toys, Barbie herself fought against the very terrorism I was afraid of. In what we called our "Barbie Afghanistan," Taylor and I worked through our confusion by making Barbie fight the battles, still wearing her high heels and ball gowns.

Information. Core values: creativity and social consciousness (even at a young age).

I no longer play with Barbie, but she has fought another war in my adolescence. I'm a passionate feminist, and my opinions about Barbie have caused an internal tug-of-war on my beliefs. As I sit in my basement now, surrounded by books and my laptop, I have just as many questions as I did at five years old.

I've desperately attempted to consolidate my opposing opinions of Barbie into a single belief, but I've accepted that they're separate. In one, she has perpetuated physical ideals unrepresentative of how real female bodies are built. Striving to look like Barbie is not only striving for the impossible—the effort is detrimental to women's psychological and physical health, including my own. In the other, Barbie has inspired me in her breaking of the plastic ceiling. She has dabbled in close to 150 careers, including some I'd love to have: a UNICEF Ambassador, teacher, and business executive. And although it's not officially listed on her résumé, Barbie served honorably in the War in Afghanistan.

Barbie has proven to be an 11.5-inch-tall embodiment of both what frustrates and excites me. From terrorism to feminism and beyond, I am vexed by the complexities of the world but eager to piece things together. Although I'm frustrated by what I can't understand, I've realized that confusion is okay.

With Barbie as my weapon, I've continued to fight in the many "wars" in my life. I've found great value in the questions I ask and in my attempts to reconcile our world's inevitable contradictions. Things can be innocent yet mature, they can be detrimental yet empowering, and they can even wear high heels and a ball gown while fighting in a war.

Margin notes (left): Important and interesting connection (a.k.a. "so what" moment). In a society that sometimes insists students have their lives mapped out, this can be a scary thing to admit. Important and interesting connections. GREAT "so what." Vulnerability!

Margin notes (right): Information, important and interesting connections, craft, vulnerability (and humor). Amazing paragraph—this one hits all the marks. Great "so what," and the turn of phrase she uses at the end is beautifully crafted.

I learn so much about this student and her values. I learn that she is curious, funny, intelligent, socially aware, mature, and willing to be vulnerable. Plus, she's able to include some memorable turns of phrase and express complex thoughts in succinct ways. All without having to shoot her brother or watch a bird die.

"GRANDMA'S KIMCHI"

Note how this essay does NOT begin with a hook in the traditional sense of "grabbing the reader's attention." Instead, it begins quietly, with a dash of verisimilitude.

Information and craft. Values of family, ritual, tradition, and community are established here in just a few words.

Craft. Note the subtle double meaning of "fed."

More craft. This is even more subtle, but it's foreshadowing the ending.

Every Saturday morning, I'd awaken to the smell of crushed garlic and piquant pepper. I would stumble into the kitchen to find my grandma squatting over a large silver bowl, mixing fat lips of fresh cabbages with garlic, salt, and red pepper. That was how the delectable Korean dish, kimchi, was born every weekend at my home.

My grandma's specialty always dominated the dinner table as kimchi filled every plate. And like my grandma who had always been living with us, it seemed as though the luscious smell of garlic would never leave our home. But even the prided recipe was defenseless against the ravages of Alzheimer's that inflicted my grandma's mind.

Dementia slowly fed on her memories until she became as blank as a brand-new notebook. The ritualistic rigor of Saturday mornings came to a pause, and during dinner, the artificial taste of vacuum-packaged factory kimchi only emphasized the absence of the family tradition. I would look at her and ask, "Grandma, what's my name?" But she would stare back at me with a clueless expression. Within a year of diagnosis, she lived with us like a total stranger.

One day, my mom brought home fresh cabbages and red pepper sauce. She brought out the old silver bowl and poured out the cabbages, smothering them with garlic and salt and pepper. The familiar tangy smell tingled my nose. Gingerly, my grandma stood up from the couch in the living room, and as if lured by the smell, sat by the silver bowl and dug her hands into the spiced cabbages. As her bony hands shredded the green lips, a look of determination grew on her face. Though her withered hands no longer displayed the swiftness and precision they once did, her face showed the aged rigor of a professional. For the first time in years, the smell of garlic filled the air and the rattling of the silver bowl resonated throughout the house.

That night, we ate kimchi. It wasn't perfect; the cabbages were clumsily cut and the garlic was a little too strong. But kimchi had never tasted better. I still remember my grandma putting a piece in my mouth and saying, "Here, Dong Jin. Try it, my boy."

Holy craft, Batman. (I don't know about you, but I'm in tears.)

Seeing grandma again this summer, that moment of clarity seemed ephemeral. Her disheveled hair and expressionless face told of the aggressive development of her illness.

More craft. This is a student with some writing experience.

But holding her hands, looking into her eyes, I could still smell that garlic. The moments of Saturday mornings remain ingrained in my mind. Grandma was an artist who painted the cabbages with strokes of red pepper. Like the sweet taste of kimchi, I hope to capture those memories in my keystrokes as I type away these words.

BOOM. Super "so what" moment. And it's hugely vulnerable, too.

A piece of writing is more than just a piece of writing. It evokes. It inspires. It captures what time takes away.

My grandma used to say: "Tigers leave furs when they die, humans leave their names." Her legacy was the smell of garlic that lingered around my house. Mine will be these words.

I've been tempted to frame this and put it above my writing table. And I don't even need to say it, but CRAFT.

This is one of the very few effective uses of a quotation that I've ever seen. And it makes this ending so succinct, so memorable, and so...wow. Amazing use of craft, great "so what" moment, plus this clarifies some important values.

Again, I learn so much about this student through this essay. I learn that he values family, tradition, relationships, legacy, and the written word. This is one of the most well-crafted college essays I've read, and it makes me cry almost every time I read it.

"MAZES"

Information.
Core values:
creativity,
knowledge.

My story begins at about the age of two, when I first learned what a maze was. For most people, solving mazes is a childish phase, but I enjoyed artistically designing them. Eventually my creations jumped from their two dimensional confinement, requiring the solver to dive through holes to the other side, or fold part of the paper over, then right back again. At around the age of eight, I invented a way for mazes to carry binary-encoded messages, with left turns and right turns representing 0s and 1s. This evolved into a base-3 maze on the surface of a tetrahedron, with crossing an edge representing a 2.

For me, a blank piece of paper represented the freedom to explore new dimensions, pushing the boundaries of traditional maze making.

"So what" moment/insight.

I found a similar freedom in mathematics. Here's what I wrote when I was 9:

$$N + B = Z$$
$$M\hat{\ }2 = P$$
$$E - (L + B) = G$$
$$C / Y = Z - Q$$
$$B + B = Y$$
$$(D - V)\hat{\ }9 - (P*L) = J$$
$$W = (I - V)\hat{\ }2$$
$$Y + B + C = R$$
$$O\hat{\ }2 + (Y*O) = T$$
$$F\hat{\ }3 - (T + W) = F\hat{\ }2$$
$$V - R = H - U$$
$$A\hat{\ }3 - C = N$$
$$Y\hat{\ }2 + B = L$$
$$J\hat{\ }2 - J = J + (P + I)$$
$$Y\hat{\ }3 = X$$
$$X - R = M - O$$

$$D*A - B - (V + Y) = E$$
$$U - X - O = W$$
$$P / P = B$$
$$S - A = U$$
$$(Z + B)*C = P$$
$$C(+/-)B = A$$
$$U + C = H$$
$$R - L = S - T$$

Values: creativity and risk. (How many students would have the guts to do this in an essay?)

The object of puzzles like these was to solve for every letter, assuming they each represented a unique positive integer, and that both sides of each equation are positive. These are not typical assumptions for practical mathematics, and I didn't even need 26 equations. Upon formally learning algebra, I was dismayed that "proper math" operated under a different set of assumptions, that two variables can be equal, or be non-integers, and that you always need as many equations as variables. Yet looking back, I now see that mathematics was so inspirational because there really is no "proper" way, no convention to hold me from discovering a completely original method of thought. Math was, and still is, yet another way for me to freely express my creativity and different way of thinking without constraint.

"So what" moment.

Craft. While he's expressing an important value (breaking convention), the content matches the form, since his equations break the convention of the standard college essay.

"So what" moment.

Value: freedom. In this case, he uses the value as a transition between his paragraphs.

It's all about freedom. The thoughts are there, they just need a way to escape. The greatest single advancement that delivered even more freedom was my first computer, and on it, one of the first computer games I ever played: "Maze Madness." It was a silly and simple game, but I remember being awed that I could create my own levels. Through the years, I've made thousands (not exaggerating) of levels in a variety of different computer games. I get most excited when I discover a bug that I can incorporate to add a new twist to the traditional gameplay.

Values: personal development, challenge, self-expression.

A few years ago I grew tired of working within the constraints of most internet games and I wanted to program my own, so I decided to learn the language of Scratch. With it, I

Values: personal development, challenge, self-expression.

created several computer games, incorporating such unordinary aspects of gameplay as the avoidance of time-travel paradoxes, and the control of "jounce," the fourth derivative of position with respect to time. Eventually, I came to realize that Scratch was too limited to implement some of my ideas, so I learned C#, and my potential expanded exponentially. I continue to study programming knowing that the more I learn, the more tools I have to express my creativity.

"So what" moment.

    I plan to design computer systems that are as outside of the box as my thoughts. And who knows where it will lead? My way of thinking in different dimensions could be the very thing separating computers from humans, and it could motivate the creation of true artificial intelligence. To me, studying computer science is the next step of an evolution of boundary breaking that has been underway since my first maze.

Vulnerability. I believe he shows this through his passion. Why? It takes guts to say "I love math" in such a—and I say this with love—geeky way. He does it beautifully.

I love how this student's brain works. I love how much more he knows about math than I do, and I love how he makes math fun, creative, and inspiring—just like he is! I can feel his passion through his words, and this essay makes me curious to know more about him and the other amazing things he will create.

CHAPTER TEN

Finally

I'VE BEEN WORKING ON THIS book for a while. But my ideas keep evolving, and I feel I still haven't gotten it quite right. Here I sit, going over the manuscript five days before it's due to my editor, and I've got this T. S. Eliot line in my head: "That is not what I meant at all. That is not it, at all."

I stare at the blinking cursor, and I'm tempted to hit "delete" even on the end of the previous sentence, and to try saying it again, to say it better. Beckett is in my head now: "Try again. Fail again. Fail better."

But at some point, I know I've got to abandon the thing and send it out into the world.

Actually, I think that's the last thing I want to say to you.

I had a much longer speech prepared. But that thing that I just wrote is more important than what I had prepared.

Sometimes, writing is like this.

You work really hard to say a thing in just the right way, and then, after a little while, it's time to abandon it and send it out into the world.

So work really, really hard, my friend,

then let go.

Additional Resources

1,000+ WAYS TO GET INSPIRED RIGHT NOW

1. collegeessayguy.tumblr.com

   My Tumblr site is specifically dedicated to inspiring you as you work through the college essay process. It's updated almost daily, so you'll get up-to-date content that's specific to the time of year (i.e., essay tips in the fall, interview and financial aid tips in the winter, and so on).

2. collegeessayguy.com

   Here you'll find my most up-to-date resources for other parts of the application process, including:
   - How to Create a Great College List
   - How to Write a "Why Us" Essay
   - Five FAFSA Myths—Busted
   - College Interviews: How Much Do They Really Matter?
   - Five Common Myths about College Majors
   - Five Ways to Make Your Activities List Awesome
   - How to Decide Which Extracurricular Activity to Write About
   - How Much Do SAT Scores Matter? (A Paradox)

- How to Create the Simplest, Best To-Do List Ever
- 5 Resources That Will Save You $3,480
3. Google "100 Brave and Interesting Questions"
   This list is guaranteed to get your brain (and heart) going.

HOW TO WORK WITH A PARTNER

Why work with a partner?

1. He or she can hold you accountable.
2. He or she can serve as a mirror, reflecting things about yourself that you may not notice.
3. It's more fun.
4. Chances are you'll grow closer through the process and learn a lot about yourselves and each other.

Who might make a good partner?

A smart friend, a teacher, a mentor, an older sibling—basically anyone whose opinion you trust and whom you believe will hold you accountable.

Can I be a writing partner for someone who is my writing partner?

Of course! Supporting each other in this way is great.

How do I make sure that person holds me accountable?

Copy and paste the agreement on the next page into an email, or write your own version.

ACCOUNTABILITY AGREEMENT

Dear [enter name here]:

I'm going through a personal statement writing process, and I'm writing to ask if you'd be my accountability partner.

Why am I choosing you?

- Because you are awesome.
- Because I need someone to provide an outside perspective on my writing, and I think you would be a good person to help me.
- Because [enter other reason] _____.

What does it mean to be accountability partners? It means that I am committing to the following:

- Completing each of the goals listed below on each of the days listed.
- Letting you know by email (or text) if for some reason I am going to miss a deadline.
- Working hard on my assignments and doing my very best.

It means that you are committing to the following:

- Meeting with me to complete each of the goals listed below on each of the days listed.
- Letting me know by email (or text) if for some reason you have to reschedule with me.
- Being kind with criticisms and offering useful notes for improvement.

Goals and potential meeting dates:

1. Select a topic for main personal statement. [Enter potential date here.]

2. Create an outline. [Enter potential date here.]
3. Write a first draft. [Enter potential date here.]
4. Write a second draft. [Enter potential date here.]
5. Write a third draft. [Enter potential date here.]

Are you willing to agree? If so, type your name in the blank below and email it back to me:

I, _____[your name here]_____,
do hereby agree to serve as accountability partner for _____
_____[my name here]_____ according
to the terms listed above. I recognize that this is not a legally binding agreement, but that if I fail to fulfill my duties, I will be leaving my partner (that's me) hanging.

Signed, _____.

21 DETAILS EXERCISE

Make a list of twenty-one details from your life—interesting facts that describe some small, random part of who you are.

Here are eleven of my twenty-one details:

1. We moved twenty times while I was growing up, and I attended thirteen schools.
2. My biggest pet peeve is when the waiter takes my food before I've finished.
3. I eat salad with my hands. And never with dressing.
4. The worst feeling in the world is the dentist's air suction tube sucking air over my teeth.
5. I love popping bubble wrap.
6. When I was young, I used to use my finger to wipe off the top layer of toothpaste that I shared with my sister so I wouldn't get her germs.

7. I've never, ever seriously contemplated suicide.

8. I find most people fascinating and can talk to just about anyone.

9. I've won several awards in my life, but I'm most proud of these two: finishing second in the elementary school spelling bee when I was nine and being named MVP of the middle school floor hockey all-star game when I was eleven.

10. The most painful thing I ever experienced was breaking my kneecap in the tenth grade during a basketball game. The physical pain wasn't the worst part, though: it was losing the rest of the season and watching my team go 0–18.

11. My three younger brothers and I have never, as far as I can remember, ever had a fight.

See how each is a little tiny glimpse into my world? It's impossible to capture all of who you are in twenty-five or even 650 words, but with a few carefully chosen details, a portrait begins to emerge. Think of these twenty-one details as a collage.

Once you've written your twenty-one details, look for themes. Is there anything that comes up again and again? That may be a good theme for an essay, and this list can be especially useful for a supplemental essay that asks you to write a letter to your future roommate.

EVERYTHING I WANT COLLEGES TO KNOW ABOUT ME LIST

This exercise is simple, but extremely useful, especially in the middle or near the end of the process.

STEP 1: MAKE A LIST OF ALL THE THINGS YOU WANT COLLEGES TO KNOW ABOUT YOU.

How? Either:

- In a bullet-point format (organized, easy to read)

- On a blank sheet of paper (with drawings; get creative)
- On a time line (map out the major events in your life)

Note: I don't recommend a stream-of-consciousness free-write because those tend to get a little messy. By "messy," I mean they tend to bring forth a lot of words, but not a lot of specific, bullet point-able qualities that will help you get into college.

And that's the point of this list—to provide your counselor (or yourself) with a solid list of qualities, values, and cool stuff that might be interesting to a college admissions officer.

The main reason that this list is a good idea: it generates a list of details and possible topics for your personal statement, supplements, activities list, and additional information section.

Tips for creating a great list:

- **Have fun**. This doesn't have to be a chore. You're basically making a list of everything that's awesome about who you are and what you've done, which can be pretty darn affirming.
- **Create the list with a parent or friend**. Say to him or her: "Hey, I'm trying to make a list of all the reasons why a college should love me as much as you do—can you help me?"
- **Back up general stuff with specific examples**. For instance, suppose you think, "I can motivate people!" or "I stick with things I'm passionate about!" Provide a specific example to support your claim—or, better yet, one example that supports both claims! (Like the fact that you helped raise debate membership from nineteen to ninety-six at your school over four years.)

STEP 2 (OPTIONAL): ASK SOMEONE FOR HELP.

Once you've created your list, it can be great to get an outside perspective, so consider sharing it with whoever is helping you with your applications (friend/parent/counselor) and ask that person, "Can you help me make sure that all this stuff makes it into my application?"

Could you do this once your application is almost finished?

Absolutely. In fact, this will provide a checklist for making sure all the important parts of you are represented somewhere in your application.

STEP 3: DECIDE WHERE THE INFORMATION SHOULD GO IN YOUR APPLICATION.

Some options include:

1. Main statement
2. Activities list
3. Additional information section
4. Extracurricular essay (required only for some schools)
5. Another supplemental essay (required only for some schools)

TIME LINE OF MY LIFE EXERCISE

Here's one more exercise I love. This can be especially useful for students who have faced challenges, but it can also be useful for any student seeking perspective on the events of his or her life.

Step 1: Take out a blank sheet of paper and draw a line down the middle.

Step 2: Chart the major events of your life on the time line: any moves from one location to another, any births and deaths in the family, and anything else that you feel has shaped or changed you.

> Tip: Make room on your time line for "Before I was born" (Example: my parents came to the United States) and also for "After college" (Example: I will invent a cure for cancer).

Step 3: Once you've created your life time line, tell your life story to someone while that person just listens.

Step 4: Ask that person to help you identify the different "phases" of your life.

- Example 1: Life in Texas, Life in California (private school), Life in California (public school).
- Example 2: Pre-Divorce, The Divorce, Post-Divorce.
- Or, if you've experienced challenges, it might be: Challenges, What I Did, and What I Learned. (Turn to page 80 for more on this.)

CREATE A TIME LINE (VARIATION)

Step 1: Draw a line down the middle of a blank sheet of paper and hand it to a partner or mentor.

Step 2: Rather than creating your own time line, speak your life story aloud to a partner or mentor and have that person chart your life events on the time line for you. This frees you up as you talk.

Step 3: Once you've finished, have your partner tell you your life story back to you while you listen.

I actually prefer this variation because it allows the rare opportunity to hear someone else tell you your life story. The retelling can be done in pairs or before a larger group.

Once you've created the time line, work with your partner to identify the beginning, middle, and end of your essay. If possible, you can use narrative structure by identifying:

Type A

- Status quo: How did things used to be?
- Inciting incident: The event that started it all. The moment things began to change.
- Raise the stakes: What happened to build suspense for you—and others?
- Moment of truth/Turning point: Was there a moment when you had to make a big choice? Or when things were in danger of going down a dark path, but then turned around?
- New status quo: How are things now? (and perhaps) How have these experiences shaped you for [insert chosen career here]?

Or simply:

Type C

- Challenges
- What I did
- What I learned

Turn to page 74 for more on this.

List of Real Student Essays Included in This Book*

Title*	Essay Type	Page Number
With Debate by Anna Kang	A	22
Endodontics by Parham Natanzi	B	24
Raising Anthony by Crystal Cunanan	C	26
Scrapbook by Veronica Lee	D	28
**Santur by Parham Natanzi	D	49
Porcelain God by Kailynn Best	A	54
Easter by Citlalli Velasquez	A	56
Behavioral Economics by Devon Killian	B	65
Stomach Whisperer by Amanat Bal	B	69
Bowling by Zuleyma Guillermo	C	85
What I Found on the Farm by Joseph Lin	C	87
Punk Rock Philosopher by Daniel Bak	D	96
If Ink Were Ants by Ivana Valdez	D	99
Burying Grandma by Jacqueline Kwon	A	134

Knife by Hye Jeong Yoon	C	144
Five Families by Jesper Kim	D	152
**Why Did the Chicken Cross the Road? by Jacqueline Kwon	D	162
**Rock, Paper, Scissors by Christian Lau	D	169
I Shot My Brother by Alex Park	C	173
Dying Bird by Hye Jeong Yoon	C	176
Breaking Up with Mom by Katya Forsyth	C	192
Barbie vs. Terrorism and the Patriarchy by Tess Joseph	D	207
Grandma's Kimchi by Dong Jin Oh	A	209
Mazes by Jamie Tucker-Foltz	B	211

*Almost none of these students titled their essays (the exception is "Barbie vs. Terrorism and the Patriarchy"); I gave them titles to make referring to them easier.

**These are supplemental essays, submitted in addition to the main personal statement, while the rest of the essays in the book are main personal statements.

Acknowledgments

I STARTED MAKING A LIST of all those who have contributed to this book, then felt like I was planning a wedding and started to get nervous about the people I'd forget to mention. So I stopped and wrote this instead.

Thank you to all the amazing friends, mentors, and colleagues who've contributed so much, both directly and indirectly, to this book. You know who you are.

And thank you, in particular, to the students who so generously allowed me to use their essays for this book; to my best friend, Ryan Maldonado, who has taught me so much about writing; and to my wife, Veronica, and my daughter, Zola, who are my favorites.

Index

A

Amazing essays, qualities of, 172–182

B

"Barbie vs. Terrorism and the Patriarchy," 112, 207–209, 214–215

"Behavioral Economics," 65–68

"Bowling," 76, 78, 85–87

Bragging, 119–120

Brainstorming content, 1–12, 140–141, 225–230

"Breaking Up with Mom," 112, 192–195, 198

"Burying Grandma," 134–137

C

Career, future, 10, 12, 21, 114. See also specific essay type

Career placeholders, 92–94

Challenges. See also specific essay type; technique

connecting to career, 41–59

connecting to values, 74–84

examples, 40, 43–45, 72

unresolved conflicts, 190–191, 192–195

writing tips, 40–41, 72–73, 75–77, 81–83

Conclusions. See Endings

Conflicts. See Challenges

Core values, xii–xiv, 119–120, 126, 128–129, 184, 186. See also specific essay type

Core Values Exercise, 8–12

essay analyses, 30–38, 49–50, 213–220

examples, 8–9

of intended career, 60–62

predictable vs. unexpected, 46–51, 78–80

tips for improving your essay, 188–189, 190–191

Craft, 101, 185, 186–187, 197, 213–220

D

Depth and complexity, adding, 121–137, 198–201

"Dying Bird," 110–111, 133, 176–178, 181–182

E

"Easter," 56–59, 137–138

Emotion. See Depth and complexity, adding

Endings

elliptical, 109, 179–182

surprising, but inevitable, 137–140, 150–160, 179–182

unresolved challenges, 192–195

"Endodontics," 24–26, 32–34, 61–63, 103–104, 116–117, 120, 137

Essays, four types of, 20–21

Essays, goal of, 183–185

Essays for students who did not face significant challenges and do know future career

examples and analyses, 24–26, 32–34, 65–68, 69–71

writing guide for, 59–71

Essays for students who did not face significant challenges and do not know future career

examples and analyses, 28–30, 36–38, 96–101, 152–155, 207–209

writing guide for, 89–101

Essays for students who faced significant challenges and do know future career

examples and analyses, 22–24, 30–32, 54–59

writing guide for, 40–59

Essays for students who faced significant challenges and do not know future career

examples and analyses, 26–28, 34–36, 85–89

writing guide for, 71–89

Essence Objects Exercise, 1–7, 10–11

Everything I Want Colleges to Know about Me List, 226–228

F

Failures, writing about, 195

Feedback, 204–206

Feelings and Needs Exercise, 121–130

"Five Families," 91, 152–160

Flow, essay, 102–106, 141, 203

Focusing lens (framing device), 16–17, 37, 91, 92–101

G

Geeky language, 114–116

"Grandma's Kimchi," 111, 198, 209–210, 216–217

Great College Essay Test, The, 186–187, 213–220

I

"If Ink Were Ants," 99–101

Images, use of, 16–17, 110–111, 116–119

Insights ("so what" moments), 47–48, 79, 139, 186

essay examples and analyses, 213–220

importance, 62–63, 101, 184

show first, then tell, 64, 116–119, 196–197

Intelligence, demonstrating, 112–119, 199–200

"I Shot My Brother," 108, 109, 133, 173–176, 180–181

K

"Knife," 110, 143–147, 148, 149–150, 199

M

"Make it new" technique, 160–172

"Mazes," 199–200, 211–213, 218–220

Metaphors, 32, 38, 138, 139

Montage structure, 13, 21. *See also* Focusing lens

basic elements, 16–19

combining with narrative structure, 68–71

essay examples and analyses, 24–26, 28–30, 32–34, 36–38, 65–71, 96–101, 211–213

N

Narrative arc, 82–83

Narrative structure, 13, 21, 53–54

basic elements, 14–16

combining with montage structure, 68–71

essay examples and analyses, 22–24, 26–28, 30–32, 34–36, 54–59, 71, 85–89, 173–176

vs. montage structure, 17–19

Need vs. Want Dynamic, 131–137

O

Objective correlative, 10–11

Off-limit topics, 75–76

Opening sentences, 107–112

Outlines, 52–54, 80–84

P

Painter/art critic/curator analogy, 117–119

Partner, working with, 223–225

Passion, writing about, 95–96, 191–192, 195

"Porcelain God," 54–56, 108, 139

Predictable vs. unexpected values, 46–51, 78–80

"Punk Rock Philosopher," 96–99

Q

Questions, asking, 112–114

R

"Raising Anthony," 26–28, 34–36, 82–83, 148

Revising and improving your essay, 102–106, 141, 187–202

"Rock, Paper, Scissors," 108–109, 169–172

S

"Santur," 49–50

"Scrapbook," 28–30, 36–38, 91

Setup and payoff technique, 142–147, 150–160, 196

Sharing too much, 77

Show first, then tell, 64, 116–119, 196–197

Sixth Sense, The ending technique, 150–160

"So what" moments. See Insights

Starting over, 201–202

"Stomach Whisperer," 47–48, 69–71

Structure, 102–106, 141. See also Montage structure; Narrative structure; Outlines

Style tips, 198–201

Succinct language, 198–199

Supplemental essays, 49–50, 160–172

T

Time Line of My Life Exercise, 228–230

Topic selection. See Brainstorming content

"Turning dark into beautiful" technique, 149–150

21 Details Exercise, 225–226

V

Values. See Core values

Verisimilitude, 147–148, 214

Vulnerability, 172, 184, 186, 189–196, 213–220

W

Want vs. Need Dynamic, 131–137

"What I Found on the Farm," 87–89

"Why Did the Chicken Cross the Road," 134, 162–169

"With Debate," 22–24, 30–32, 47–48, 102–103, 114, 119–120, 133, 139, 199

Word choice, 114–116, 198–200

Writing, struggling with, 140–141

Writing your essay in one night, 202–204

About the Author

ETHAN SAWYER IS A NATIONALLY recognized college essay expert and a sought-after speaker. Each year he helps thousands of students and counselors through his webinars, workshops, articles, products, and books, and works privately with a small number of students.

Raised in Spain, Ecuador, and Colombia, Ethan has studied at seventeen different schools and has worked as a teacher, curriculum writer, voice actor, motivational speaker, community organizer, and truck driver. He is a certified Myers-Briggs™ specialist, and his type (ENFJ) will tell you that he will show up on time, that he'll be excited to meet you, and that, more than anything, he is committed to—and an expert in—helping you realize your potential.

A graduate of Northwestern University, Ethan holds an MFA from UC–Irvine and two counseling certificates. He lives in Los Angeles with his beautiful wife, Veronica, and their amazing daughter, Zola.

To arrange for Ethan to speak at your school, conference, or event, go to www.collegeessayguy.com.

Testimonials

"A comprehensive guide to navigating college admission with an emphasis on values that are important *to you*."

Edward Fiske, author of the Fiske Guide to Colleges

"Ethan has a natural ability to draw readers in with his poignant writing and thought-provoking insight. This book touches on some of the fundamental questions families have and will serve as an important and enjoyable resource in their college admission experience."

Rick Clark, Director of Undergraduate Admission at Georgia Tech University, coauthor of The Truth about College Admission: A Family Guide to Getting In and Staying Together

"Ethan is my go-to resource for college essay advice. I'll be giving this book to all my friends with children in high school."

Mignon Fogarty, author of the New York Times *bestseller* Grammar Girl's Quick and Dirty Tips for Better Writing

"Anyone with ties to the world of admission and writing essays will tell you they are a fan of Ethan. In this book, he clearly, concisely, and professionally gives parents, students, and schools a way to think about the whole college process in ways that will help. By help, I mean not just help students to 'get in,' but help lower the stress for all. A must read."

Parke Muth, consultant and former assistant dean of admission at University of Virginia

"Ethan has established himself as a credible and knowledgeable resource for students seeking useful and practical tips for their college essays. I'm excited to see that he is expanding his scope by providing this guide to the overall college application process. His ability to help students discover their voice is valuable as they figure out which schools they should apply to and how to best present themselves in their applications."

Falone Serna, Vice President of Enrollment Management at Whittier College

COLLEGE ADMISSION ESSENTIALS

A Step-by-Step Guide to Showing Colleges Who You Are and What Matters to You

Ethan Sawyer
↪ *The College Essay Guy*™

sourcebooks

Published by Sourcebooks
P.O. Box 4410, Naperville, Illinois 60567-4410
(630) 961-3900
sourcebooks.com

Library of Congress Cataloging-in-Publication Data

Names: Sawyer, Ethan (College essay expert), author.
Title: College admission essentials : a step-by-step guide to showing
   colleges who you are and what matters to you / Ethan Sawyer, college
   essay guy.
Description: Naperville, IL : Sourcebooks, [2020] | Includes
   bibliographical references and index.
Identifiers: LCCN 2019053665 | (trade paperback)
Subjects: LCSH: Universities and colleges--Admissions. | College
   applications.
Classification: LCC LB2351 .S29 2020 | DDC 378.1/61--dc23

LC record available at https://lccn.loc.gov/2019053665

Printed and bound in the United States of America.
DR 10 9 8

Contents

Introduction   ix

The Inciting Incident   ix

Why This Book and Who I Am   xi

The Treasure Trove   xiii

Housekeeping   xiv

Gratitude   xiv

Part I: What Admission Officers Want to Know   xvii

CHAPTER 1: How to Discover and Connect with What You Care about in Twenty Minutes   1

Part II: Ninth Grade to Eleventh Grade Essentials   9

CHAPTER 2: High School Essentials   11

CHAPTER 3: ACT and SAT Essentials   22

Part III: Essentials before You Apply   39

CHAPTER 4: How to Create a Balanced College List   41

CHAPTER 5: Early Decision and Early Action   67

CHAPTER 6: Demonstrated Interest   73

Part IV: The College Application   81

CHAPTER 7: Adrian's Brainstorming Exercises   83

CHAPTER 8: Essential Application Prework   91

CHAPTER 9: How to Up-Level Your Activities List in Thirty Minutes (and Why You Should)   107

CHAPTER 10: How to Write the Additional Information Section   126

Part V: The Personal Statement   141

CHAPTER 11: How to Write a Personal Statement That Matters   143

Part VI: The Supplemental Essays   181

CHAPTER 12: Creating Your Supplemental Essay Tracker   183

CHAPTER 13: The Super Essay (Combining Essay Prompts to Write Better Essays in Less Time)   186

CHAPTER 14: How to Write the "Why Us?" Essay   196

CHAPTER 15: How to Write the Extracurricular Activity Essay   222

CHAPTER 16: How to Write the "Why Major?" Essay   241

CHAPTER 17: The Dos and Don'ts of the Short Answers   249

Part VII: The Other Parts of the Application Process   255

CHAPTER 18: How to Get Great Letters of Recommendation   257

CHAPTER 19: How to Do the College Interview   267

Part VIII: How to Make Sure Your Application Is Doing Its Job   275

CHAPTER 20: The Values Scan   277

Part IX: More Resources for More Students   291

CHAPTER 21: Artists   293

CHAPTER 22: Athletes   302

CHAPTER 23: International Students   306

CHAPTER 24: Homeschoolers   309

CHAPTER 25: Students Interested in Historically Black Colleges and
Universities (HBCUs) and Tribal Colleges and Universities (TCUs)   315

CHAPTER 26: First-Generation and Low-Income Students   322

CHAPTER 27: Undocumented Students   331

CHAPTER 28: Students with Learning Differences   334

CHAPTER 29: LGBTQ+ Students   339

CHAPTER 30: Self-Directed Students   343

CHAPTER 31: Transfer Students   353

CHAPTER 32: Veterans   357

CHAPTER 33: Students Interested in Women's Colleges   361

Part X: After You Apply   365

CHAPTER 34: How to Write a Great Letter of Continued Interest   367

CHAPTER 35: How Senioritis Can Earn You a "Fear of God" Letter   371

Part XI: After You're Accepted   375

CHAPTER 36: Financial Aid Awards, and How to Write a Financial
Aid Award Appeal Letter   377

CHAPTER 37: How to Decide Where to Attend   390

CHAPTER 38: What to Do If You're Not Accepted Anywhere   393

A Final Request   395

Appendix and Additional Resources   397

   College Planning Timeline (a.k.a. What Should I Be
Doing Right Now?)   399

   Additional Resources for Students, Counselors, and Teachers   409

About the Author   411

Introduction

The Inciting Incident

Ten years ago I did an exercise that changed my life.

I'd just finished grad school and was working at Cornerstone Theater Company. One afternoon during a professional development workshop, the artistic director, Michael John Garcés, handed each of the staff members a list of personal values. "Pick your top ten," he told us.

I read through the list.

Huh, I thought. *How do I pick? Do I choose "creativity" or "collaboration"? "Family" or "community"? This feels impossible.*

But it wasn't. In the next few minutes I gave it some thought, made some tough choices, and ended up with ten values. "Okay," said Michael, "Now pick five…" A minute passed. "Now three…" Another minute. "Now pick your top value." Each time was harder, but eventually I ended up with one.*

Next, he asked us to turn to a partner and share our top value and why we picked it. I did and I learned something about my partner that I didn't know. Then I shared something with them that I'd never shared.

I looked at my list. *Wow*, I thought. *That was deep. And it only took a few minutes.* I put the list in my backpack and didn't think about it for a while.

---

*   That day, I believe I ended up with "variety." Although I'll admit, it's tempting to choose another value so I can set it up as a thematic thread for this book.

One night, a week later, I was working my second job helping students with their college essays. I found myself in a jam. I was trying to help a student figure out why he cared about basketball, and he was having trouble explaining.

"I don't know," he said, "I guess I just like it."

I remembered the exercise I'd done the previous week. "Here," I said, retrieving the exercise from my backpack. "Which of these values could you connect to basketball?"

He looked at the list for a minute.

"A few," he said.

"Which ones?"

"Family…discipline…variety…" he paused. "Beauty, I guess."

"Ooh," I said. "Tell me about beauty…" And we were off.

Little did I know how much that exercise would come to shape my approach to counseling. Over the next few weeks, I edited the list and began carrying a stack of copies in my backpack. At first, I'd use it only when my students got stuck. Eventually, I made it a required prework assignment. It ended up as one of the first exercises I shared when, a few months later, I launched the College Essay Guy blog.

Through that blog and my social media I now reach more than one million students, parents, and counselors each year, and the Values Exercise has become one of the cornerstones of my approach.

In the years since, here's what I've learned:

Values can work like a compass.

This is especially true when it comes to decision-making. I realized that my values pointed me toward what I cared about. Did I want to spend a Thursday evening playing board games with my friends, for example (values: connection, fun, laughter), or finish sending that student notes on their essay (values: contribution, creativity, meaningful work)? Even if I couldn't choose right away, my values helped me get a deeper understanding of what I was *actually* choosing. When faced with a tough choice, I began asking myself: "What value am I choosing right now?"

And I get it—the word "values" may sound kinda boring. Like one of those things old people ask about when they're trying to "get to know you better." But working with my students helped me discover something else about values…

You can actually *do* stuff with them.

In fact, when it comes to the college application process, values can help you:

- Figure out which classes to take
- Know what to look for in a college
- Up-level the activities list
- Brainstorm and revise the personal statement and supplemental essays
- Prepare for the interview
- Understand if your college application is doing its job
- Deal with disappointment
- And so much more

Values are more than a compass pointing the way…

In some cases, your values *are* the way.

I'll show you what I mean in a few minutes. But first, a few details on who I am and why I wrote this book.

Why This Book and Who I Am

Note: This is formatted like an additional information section on a college application. Why? (1) It communicates the information without the fluff, (2) I thought it'd be fun, and (3) You're probably skimming this anyway. So I'm limited to 650 words. Starting…now.

Why This Book

- While other books about the college application process exist, most focus either on the informational (*what*) or philosophical (*why*). This book focuses on the practical (*how*).

This Book's Core Values (and Mine)

- Bias toward action: I learn by doing. Through this book, you will too.

- Personal growth: I see the college application process as a modern rite of passage.
- Fun: Wait 'til you hear my demonstrated interest jokes.
- Community: This book is the result of dozens of podcast interviews and input from more than one hundred counselors and admission officers. I didn't write this book—*we* did.

What Makes This Book Different

- A values-based approach
- Real student examples, which are beautiful
- Fun footnotes*
- The Treasure Trove: a website I've created to accompany this book that has So. Many. Resources.
- The level of depth in a variety of areas. In fact…

This Book Will Teach You How to:

- Discover and connect with what you care about (in twenty minutes) (page 1).
- Create a college list with schools you're excited about *and* can get into (page 41).
- Figure out which schools will likely make themselves affordable to you (page 51).
- Decide whether to apply early or not (page 67).
- Make your activities list clear and attention grabbing (page 107).
- Make the most of your additional information section (page 126).
- Brainstorm and structure your personal statement (page 143).
- Save hours of time on your supplemental essays (page 186).
- Write a "Why Us?" essay that shows why you're a great fit for a school (page 196).
- Get a great letter of recommendation from people who know and like you (page 257).
- Develop a "message box" for your interview (page 267).
- Make sure your application is doing its job (page 277).
- Analyze your financial aid award and write an appeal (page 377).

---

* See how fun?

- Plus, tips and resources for students who identify as Artists, Athletes, First-Gen, Undocumented, LGBTQ+, Self-Directed, and much more (pages 293–361).

Who I Am

- Ethan Sawyer, a.k.a. College Essay Guy
- My mission: To bring more ease, joy, and purpose to the college application process
- Graduate of Northwestern University (BS) and UC-Irvine (MFA)
- Author of the Amazon #1 bestseller *College Essay Essentials*
- Since 2003 I've been working with students on their college essays and applications.
- Each year I reach over one million students, teachers, counselors, and parents through my website and blog (collegeessayguy.com), podcast, email newsletter, social media, online courses, workshops, and one-on-one work.
- Personal paradox: I love to go fast (values: productivity, efficiency, breadth) and slow (values: meditation, reflection, depth).
- Favorite way to say goodbye: "Stay curious."
- Favorite line from *Hamilton*: "How lucky we are to be alive right now."

In short...

- I want to make this process easier, more fun, and more meaningful for you.
- I want to help you discover who you are.
- This book is an extension and expression of my core values.

I'm excited to be on this journey with you.

The Treasure Trove

In an effort to focus this book on the "essentials," I've created a companion site that has TONS of resources. Like, hundreds. I call it the Treasure Trove. I'll reference it throughout the book. And while I'll update the book every few years, the Treasure Trove can and will be updated much more frequently.

That's in part why I created it. You can find the Treasure Trove by going to collegeessayguy.com/treasuretrove.

Housekeeping

WHAT I MEAN WHEN I SAY "COLLEGES" OR "SCHOOLS"

I've limited the scope of this book to colleges and universities in the United States, so when I say "colleges," I mean those in the United States. Sometimes I use the word "schools" to mean "colleges." But if I mean high school, I'll say "high school."

A WORD ON PRONOUNS

I also use the grammatically acceptable singular "they" throughout this book. (I already have!) Some folks don't identify as "he" or "she," and I want this book to be for everyone.

STYLE AND VOICE

You'll notice I sometimes end sentences with prepositions and use sentence fragments. Like this. Why? I'm writing the way I talk. The goal here is not to offend your grammar sensibilities (although that might happen), but to invite you into my world. I want you to feel like I'm sitting right next to you telling you this stuff. Because I literally am.[*]

Gratitude (a.k.a. Acknowledgments and Shout-outs)

This book represents a huge team effort. You know those action movies where the protagonist brings in the ballistics specialist, the expert driver, and the martial artist to pull off *one last job*? Yeah, this was kind of like that.

---

[*]   Kidding. I mean figuratively.

Except my experts just happened to specialize in things like college list development and standardized testing. And I didn't do it in three days. I spent three years.

Some folks contributed substantially to a chapter (or wrote it) and are named at the start of their chapter, while others provided invaluable input or feedback and are named below. In short, this book wouldn't be this book without…

Aarushi Machavarapu
Adam Ingersoll
Adrian Castaneda-Juarez
Adrienne Amador Oddi
Ah Young Chi
Aimee Kahn-Foss
Alex Bryson
Alexis Allison
Dr. Aliza Gilbert
Alyssa Muramatsu
Amanda Miller
Amanda Schwartz
Andrew Moe
Angel Perez
Ann Rossbach
Anne Wager
Anthony Russomanno
Anushka Subrahmanian
April Crabtree
Audrey Slaughter
Aviva Legatt
Blake Boles
Bob Dannenhold
Bob Schaeffer

Bonnie Swift
Brooke Cutler
Bruce Reed
Casey Rowley
Cathy McMeekan
Charles
Charlotte West
Chris Andersson
Chris Francis
Chris Reeves
Christine Butler
Clara Lieu
Dale Tritschler
Danny Dolan
David Hawkins
David Stoeckel
Deborah Wong
Devon Sawyer
Dewey Wilmot
Dong Jin "DJ" Oh
Dori Middlebrook
Ed Devine
Erica Flener
Erika Coplon
Erin Kim
Evan Antich
Foster Cournoyer Hogan

Frank Anderson
Hanah Moon
Harlan Cohen
Heath Einstein
Imy Wax
Ish Sethi
Jade Jewell
Jamiere Abney
Jamon Pulliam
Javaria Khan
Jeanette Spires
Jed Applerouth
Jeff Levy
Jennie Kent
Jennifer Blask
Jennifer Pollard
Joan Jacobs
Joan Liu
Joanne LaSpina
Jodi Okun
Joe Tavares
John Sy
Jorge Delgado
Juan Cai
Kati Sweaney
Katie Andersen
Kelly Goyette
Kelly Wescott
Kiersten Murphy

Kristen Adaway
Lars Peterson
Laura Kazan
Laura Young
Lauren Calahan
Lauren Schandevel
Lee Ann Backlund
Leslie Cohen
Lily Ge
Lindsay Reid
Lisa Carlton
Lisa Davis
Lisa
   Rubin-Johnson
Luci Jones
Maha Almatari
Mandy Herrera
Margaret Cortes
Margot Hutchison
Maria Furtado
Marie Bigham
Martin Walsh
Mary
   Kolbenschlag
Marybeth Kravets
Matt Rubinoff
Meredith
   Lombardi

Michael John
   Garcés
Michelle G.
Michelle
   McAnaney
Michelle Myers
Michelle Rasich
Michelle
   Silbernagel
Monica James
Narisa Svetvilas
Natasha de
   Sherbinin
Nikki Pitre
Noah Hechtman
Parke Muth
Patricia M. Soares
Patricia Peek
Paul Sweet
Peggy Jenkins
Rachel Tiersky
Rachel West
Rebecca Blackelari
Rebecca Orlowski
Reon Sines-Sheaff
Rick Diaz
Sabrina Moss
Sandra Furth

Sandy Clingman
Sandy Longworth
Sara Ness
Sara Urquidez
Sarah VonBargen
Shane Windmeyer
Shannon Harrison
Sonja Iribarren
Sophia Corwin
Stacy Hernandez
Steven Antonoff
Steven Smith
Sunday Salter
Susan Dabbar
Susan Tree
Swastid Badve
Tara Dowling
Ted Fiske
Trevor Rusert
Dr. Wendy Bigler
Wes Waggoner
Whitney
   Enwemeka
Whitney Soule
Veronica Sawyer
Zola Sawyer

Part 1

What Admission Officers Want to Know

How to Discover and Connect with What You Care about in Twenty Minutes

"I'm looking for a student to focus more on a genuine self-presentation than trying to communicate what they think we want to hear."

FALONE SERNA, VICE PRESIDENT FOR ENROLLMENT MANAGEMENT AT WHITTIER UNIVERSITY

In short, admission officers want to know *what matters to you* (a.k.a., "what are your values?") and how these things *manifest in your life*. Put a slightly different way, the goal of your application is to illuminate the skills, qualities, interests, and values you'll bring with you to college. The question is: How do you show these things?

First, it's a good idea to get a sense of what you care about. So, as I've done with many students before you, I'll ask you to begin with a few simple but (ahem) essential exercises.

In this chapter, we'll cover the:

- Essence Objects Exercise
- Values Exercise
- Core Memories Exercise

These will lay the groundwork for the entire journey of applying to college (and, hopefully, beyond). And, because I'll repeatedly refer to these exercises, don't skip 'em.

First, let's figure out what you care about.

ESSENCE OBJECTS EXERCISE

Time: 10–15 minutes

Instructions:

Imagine a box. In this box is a set of what we'll call "essence objects." What are these, you ask? Specific things that remind you of important moments, relationships, or values in your life. For example, some of my essence objects are:

> **A blue, red, and purple friendship bracelet.** My wife makes a friendship bracelet for me each year for my birthday. It takes about a year for the bracelet to wear off. As she ties the new bracelet onto my wrist, I can't help but feel like I'm marrying her again—remaking my connection with my best friend.
>
> **Pork xiao long bao dumplings from Din Tai Fung.** My daughter's favorite food. Besides representing pure deliciousness, they remind me of laughter, our dad-daughter dates, and our friends the Rizzos.
>
> **My Google doc spreadsheet.** Since 2017, I've kept a spreadsheet with my friend Sara where we track different habits we'd like to learn and the goals we want to accomplish. On my current spreadsheet, I'm tracking a variety of things including my caffeine intake, whether I meditated or not, and my main work objective for each day. This spreadsheet represents my commitment to self-improvement, as well as a list of completed action items to remind me each day that I've done enough (which is something I need).
>
> **A Neumann TLM 103 microphone.** I use this to record voiceovers, which represent my connection to my creativity, my love of storytelling, and a way I support my family.
>
> *The Brothers Karamazov.* This book changed my life. I read it in a college course with some of my friends during a time when we were learning and growing so fast. Also, the last play I performed in was an adaptation of the book; I played Alyosha.

As you create your list, I'd recommend briefly describing each essence object's meaning, as I'm doing. Get the idea?

Over the next ten to fifteen minutes, make a list of at least twenty of your essence objects.

Prefer the audio version of this exercise? Check out the Essence Objects Exercise in the Treasure Trove* or simply google "College Essay Guy Essence Objects Exercise."

Here are some questions to generate some ideas:

1. What's an object that reminds you of home?
2. What object makes you feel safe?
3. What's something that inspires you?
4. What's a food that reminds you of your family?
5. What's a book that changed your life?
6. What object represents a challenge you've faced?
7. What's a dream or goal you have for the future?
8. What's something about you that sometimes surprises people?
9. Who are you with and what are you doing when you feel most like yourself?
10. What makes your heart skip a beat?
11. What brings you joy?
12. What's hanging on your bedroom walls?
13. What are you proud of?
14. What's the last spontaneous thing you did?
15. What's your earliest memory?
16. What's an object that reminds you of something that still feels unresolved in your life?
17. What's an object that represents something you know now that you didn't know five years ago?
18. What action or gesture represents love to you?
19. What do you like to do that does not involve technology?
20. What will you save for your child someday?
21. What's the most memorable meal you've ever eaten or made?
22. Is there a book that you are always lending to people?

---

*   In case you missed it, the Treasure Trove is a web page full of companion resources for this book at www.collegeessayguy.com/treasuretrove.

23. What's in your bag right now? Anything that's always there?
24. What do you like to collect?
25. What have you kept from a trip?
26. What reminds you of summer?
27. What's something that people associate with you?
28. What's your favorite smell? Your favorite thing to look at? Your favorite thing to touch? Your favorite ambient noise?

The next questions may be a bit more difficult to connect to an object, but try! If you can't, don't worry. Just write down what comes to mind...

29. What's your actual superpower?
30. What's your favorite story to tell?
31. What traditions have been passed down in your family?
32. What's perfect about your life?
33. What do you want to be able to say about your life when you're 90?
34. When is a time you forgave someone or were forgiven for something?
35. What's a class you'd love to take, even if no such class exists?
36. What's a moment you'd like to go back and redo?
37. What's your theme song?
38. Is there a dream you've had that you've never forgotten? Or one that you recurrently have that feels important to you?
39. How do you make people laugh?
40. When in life have you felt most alone?
41. What's your biggest secret?
42. What would you tell your younger self?
43. If the zombie apocalypse came tomorrow, what particular skill would you use to survive?
44. What does your inner voice tell you?
45. What's missing from your life?
46. What thing could you never give up?
47. What's one thing you wake up to in the middle of the night worrying about?
48. What are you hiding?
49. Who or what makes you laugh?
50. What are you ready to let go of?

For more, check out the "100 Brave and Interesting Questions" in the Treasure Trove.

Once you've finished creating your Essence Objects List...

Spend a minute looking over your list, then ask yourself: *Which parts of my life aren't yet represented here?* Any significant memories or relationships? If someone were to really understand who you are, what would that person need to know? Then write down three more objects.

Now go right into the next exercise.

VALUES EXERCISE

Time: 5 minutes

Instructions:

First, select your top ten values from the following list. Spend maybe two to three minutes.

❑ personal development	❑ second chances	❑ knowledge
❑ recognition	❑ listening	❑ inclusion
❑ accountability	❑ family	❑ curiosity
❑ inspiration	❑ excitement	❑ gratitude
❑ music	❑ travel	❑ faith
❑ helping others	❑ adventure	❑ communication
❑ peace	❑ laughter	❑ interdependence
❑ diversity	❑ entrepreneurship	❑ efficiency
❑ expertise	❑ wonder	❑ stability
❑ vulnerability	❑ health and fitness	❑ humor
❑ global awareness	❑ love	❑ truth
❑ hunger	❑ close relationships	❑ order
❑ my country	❑ humility	❑ excellence
❑ sleep	❑ art	❑ religion
❑ productivity	❑ responsibility	❑ beauty
❑ intuition	❑ safety	❑ meaningful work
❑ culture	❑ wealth	❑ trust
❑ healthy boundaries	❑ creativity	❑ self-expression
		❑ fun
		❑ rationality

- ☐ democracy
- ☐ self-control
- ☐ balance
- ☐ adaptability
- ☐ success
- ☐ independence
- ☐ variety
- ☐ community
- ☐ patience
- ☐ challenges
- ☐ autonomy
- ☐ loyalty
- ☐ courage
- ☐ self-love
- ☐ ritual

- ☐ purpose
- ☐ privacy
- ☐ freedom
- ☐ quiet
- ☐ compassion
- ☐ cooperation
- ☐ growth
- ☐ authenticity
- ☐ practicality
- ☐ nature
- ☐ objectivity
- ☐ leadership
- ☐ wisdom
- ☐ respect
- ☐ strength

- ☐ flexibility
- ☐ financial stability
- ☐ empathy
- ☐ belonging
- ☐ equity
- ☐ resourcefulness
- ☐ decisiveness
- ☐ competence
- ☐ collaboration
- ☐ spirituality
- ☐ social change
- ☐ honesty
- ☐ mindfulness
- ☐ grace

Once you've picked your top ten, choose your top five...then your top three...then choose your number one value for today.

Then choose five of the essence objects from the previous exercise that mean the most to you. Next to each one, list a few values you connect with each of those five objects. Like this:

A blue, red, and purple friendship bracelet: love, ritual, friendship, family, connection

Pork xiao long bao dumplings from Din Tai Fung: laughter, love, tradition, family

My Google doc spreadsheet: accountability, health, stability, growth

A Neumann TLM 103 microphone: creativity, play, security, adventure, listening

The Brothers Karamazov: inspiration, friendship, connection, personal development

Listing values next to each object helps you begin to understand why each object is meaningful. It also helps you recognize values more easily, a skill that will come in handy later in this process.

Write down the values beside the essence objects now.

Together, these essence objects and values create a collage of details that point to some of the things you care about.

Let's add just a few more...

CORE MEMORIES EXERCISE

Remember *Inside Out*, that Pixar film that depicts emotions running around inside the brain of a young girl named Riley? It's one of my favorite movies and just so happens to offer a great metaphor for personal statements. (And don't worry, you don't have to have seen the film to get the value of this exercise.)

Here's the gist: Early in the film, the narrator, Joy, describes something called "core memories." Each core memory comes from an important time in Riley's life and powers a different aspect of her personality, creating what Joy calls Riley's "islands of personality." Riley's islands are Friendship, Honesty, Family, Goofball, and Hockey.

According to Joy, these islands are "what make Riley...Riley."

What does this have to do with your college application? Each of these islands—Friendship, Family, Honesty, Goofball (i.e., fun or humor), Hockey (i.e., teamwork or competition)—are also values.

Now that you've identified your top five values, I want you to imagine that these are the islands of your personality. What core memory would you associate with each one? What image? What essence object?

Time: 5–10 minutes

Instructions:

For each of your top five values, write down either a core memory, an image, or an essence object you associate with each value.

Before you begin, here are some examples:

Community (memory): Our volleyball team crying together in the locker room after we lost States—and the saddest/best team meal at In-N-Out afterward.

Social change (image): Standing on 47th Street surrounded by thousands of pink pussy hats and handmade signs.

Hard work (essence object): battered ballet slippers

If you like, imagine a series of images—almost like a mini-movie—that represents that value, like these:

Family: I've worked several different construction jobs over the past few years—tearing up carpets, breaking down walls and driveways, installing cabinets and flooring—and most of the money has gone to help my mom pay for rent and groceries.*

Home: Last summer I loved working under the fume hood with platinum nanoparticles, manipulating raw integration data, or spraying a thin platinum film over pieces of copper in Lab 304 in Hudson Hall.†

Okay, your turn. For each of your top five values, write down a core memory, image, or essence object.

Do this now. Spend five to ten minutes before moving on.

═══════

These exercises are just the start of our values work. They'll give us the foundation for our journey ahead.

---

*   See page 288 for this essay.
†   See page 171 for this essay.

Part II

Ninth Grade to Eleventh Grade Essentials

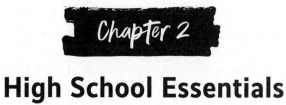

High School Essentials

Written with college counselors Erika Coplon and Sandy Longworth,
with special thanks to Stacy Hernandez and Devon Sawyer

Now that you've done the Essence Objects, Values, and Core Memories Exercises, let's talk about what those mean for you and your high school experience (if you currently have one).

Parts of this chapter are designed for students who are earlier in their high school career—first-years and sophomores. But there's still lots of useful insight for those of you who are juniors and seniors, so read this chapter if you have time. If you don't, feel free to skip ahead to the next chapter, "ACT and SAT Essentials," on page 22.

In this chapter, we'll cover:

- What your values have to do with school
- What colleges value
- How you can learn more about yourself
- How extracurricular activities fit into your journey
- How you can plan a fulfilling and productive summer

What do my values have to do with school?

The answer is…a lot.

There are many decisions you have to make while in high school, including which classes you take and what activities you do. If you're interested in attending college, the decisions you make should be partially guided by your values and partially guided by the values that colleges have.

Wait, colleges have values? Yup! Just like people, different colleges have different values. By the time you're ready to leave high school, you want to be confident that you and your future college are a great match.

But you might be wondering whether your values will change between now and when you actually go to college. The answer is yes, they probably will. Don't worry, that's normal. You're still (and always will be) figuring out what's important to you, and those developing ideas may lead to shifting values.

In fact, at the start of each school year, you can try revisiting the values exercises you just completed as a back-to-school ritual. You may be surprised by what you discover about yourself.

How do I find out what colleges value?

Some values are shared by all colleges. But each college has a unique culture that differentiates it from others. We'll talk more about how to discover those college-specific values when we get to developing your college list, but first let's talk about the values all colleges share.

As institutions of higher learning, colleges obviously value **education**. That's an easy one. They also value **challenge** and **self-knowledge**.

COLLEGES VALUE EDUCATION

Kind of a no-brainer. It's a school, so of course they're going to value education, but it's worth digging into what that means.

To evaluate your education, colleges will ask for an official copy of your transcript. High school transcripts are documents your high school creates for you that list every class you've taken, how many credits you received for each class, and the grades you earned. Your school assigns a point value for each grade, then averages those points to calculate a grade point average (GPA). It's easy to guess that they're interested in how good your grades are, but colleges also want to know what classes you've taken.

What are the right classes?

To get a broad educational base that will prepare you for any career, high schools require students to take classes in the core academic subjects: English, math, science, and social studies. And some states also require students to take foreign language, arts, and physical education classes.

Completing your high school's graduation requirements will make you eligible for acceptance at some colleges. But other colleges will suggest or even require that you take many more. The most selective colleges look for four years of classes in each of the core academic subjects, including two or more years of a foreign language.

A simple rule for class selection:
Take **four years** of each of the **four core academic subjects**: math, science, English, social sciences. And take two or more years of a world language.

After accounting for the core academic subjects, you may have time to take elective classes. This is your chance to explore possible interests. Think you may want to open a business someday? Take a business class. Love baking in your spare time? Take a culinary arts class.

Angel Perez, Vice President for Enrollment and Student Success at Trinity College, says, "High school is where students should start feeding their curiosities. Students should take courses because they find them interesting, or because they feed a passion. These will help them become better students and citizens, and in the end, that's what colleges are looking for."

If you're considering a specific major or program, elective courses become even more important, since colleges sometimes look for specific classes in student transcripts when they're interested in a career path.

For example, if you plan to go into a STEM field like engineering, it's strongly recommended you take math and science classes all four years. For competitive programs, colleges like to see calculus, biology, chemistry, and physics on your high school transcripts.

But don't think that we're going to leave you without a resource for this. For a list of high school courses that colleges like to see for particular pre-professional paths such as engineering and business, check out the chart on page 406. Keep in mind this isn't a "must-have" list; it's more of a "would be nice to have" list.

Words of Wisdom from an Admission Officer

Brooke Cutler, Director of the Office of International Student Services at Pepperdine

Oftentimes students' education systems compel them to prematurely decide which track or "what they want to do" before they've truly been exposed, when an inter-disciplinary foundation would serve them best. We know that innovations and challenges our communities face will inevitably change by the time they graduate, as will the corresponding careers. Therefore, students need to be diligent to select classes that ensure they are educated broadly enough to discover fields they didn't know would exist and be nimble critical thinkers that can solve the problems of tomorrow.

COLLEGES VALUE CHALLENGES

Beyond looking at the subjects you're taking, colleges will look at the rigor of your classes to tell whether you have the will and ability to take on increasingly difficult challenges.

One way to show clearly that you also value challenge is to take harder classes. Most high schools offer a wide range of classes in the core academic subjects that will do just that. Honors, Advanced Placement (AP), International Baccalaureate (IB), dual enrollment, or accelerated classes let you choose the challenge that's right for you. Are you acing standard-level classes when your school offers honors level? Maybe see this as an opportunity to challenge yourself with some more advanced classes.

If your school doesn't offer enough challenging classes, consider taking AP classes online. You can also enroll in college-level classes online or at your local community college.

April Crabtree, Assistant Vice Provost at the University of San Francisco, notes that "class selection should be about pushing for growth as an emerging scholar with time to reflect on what those experiences have taught you."

But be careful to not overdo it. Knowing how much you should challenge yourself is one of the trickiest things you'll do in life, but checking in with your values can help you make those decisions. Remember, *balance* is also a value, as is *happiness*. Take classes that challenge you but still allow you to maintain good grades, stay sane, and have a life.

COLLEGES VALUE SELF-KNOWLEDGE

Education and challenge form the core of what higher education is about, but colleges also deeply value students who are mature and self-reflective. Knowing yourself means knowing your ambitions, drives, and limits, and also knowing what makes you and your perspective unique. All these are things that enrich a college's student body.

But how can you know yourself, especially when you're always evolving? And what do I mean by self-knowledge? An answer to the question of who you really are can be tough to pin down. Some angles that might help you develop a response are:

- Your personality: Personality is the mix of behavior, emotion, motivation, and thought patterns that makes each person unique. So how are you uniquely you?
- Your interests: What do you wish you had more time to do? What really makes you geek out?
- Your aptitudes: What are you innately good at? How is your brain wired? Which subjects or activities come easy for you?
- Your core values: What's important to you?

Learning More about Yourself

Personality assessments:

- ***Do What You Are.*** This book is based on Carl Jung and the Myers-Briggs Personality Type, which looks at four personality dimensions: extraversion-introversion, sensing-intuition, thinking-feeling, and judging-perceiving. Through self-report, it helps you understand how you relate to the world and suggests potential career paths based on your personality type.* ($10–$15)

---

*   You'll find a link to an online version in the Treasure Trove.

- **The Big Five personality inventory.** Also known as the five-factor model, the Big Five assessment allows you to self-rate on the following five personality traits: openness to experience, neuroticism, extraversion, agreeableness, and conscientiousness. (Free)
- **The Enneagram.** A typology of nine interrelated personality types that can help students develop self-awareness, self-understanding, and self-development. (Free)

Interest and aptitudes assessments:

- **YouScience.** This assessment combines personality, interest, and aptitude testing to generate a comprehensive report that includes a career-matching feature. ($29)
- **Strong Interest Inventory.** This is the first test to look at likes and dislikes to determine what type of careers would be suitable. (Free)
- **Naviance Career Interest Profiler and Career Cluster Finder.** Naviance offers career-interest exploration through two separate assessments. (It's only available to schools that use Naviance, but many school districts pay for student access.)
- **StrengthsFinder**. This is one of the most popular self-assessments. You can discover your top five strengths, understand how to develop them, and use this information to live your best life. It's available in both book and online format. ($20)

Values assessments:

- Already done! Check out the exercises you did in chapter 1.

Self-assessments can be enlightening, but the best way to really learn about yourself is to go out into the world and try stuff. Speaking of which…

How Extracurricular Activities Fit into All This

Just like the classes you choose, what you do outside of school says a lot about you, your priorities, and (yup) your values. One question students often ask is, "What activities *should* I be doing?"

Some students think certain activities "look better" to colleges than others. But that's not necessarily the case. Admission officers are trying to learn who you are. They learn that by looking at your activities in school and beyond. Specifically, they're looking at where you're **engaged**, **taking initiative**, and **demonstrating leadership**.

So spend your time doing the things you love most. Remember your Values Exercise? Take another look and ask yourself how you can connect with these values outside of school. Let's say your top values are *community*, *helping others*, and *challenges*. You could challenge yourself by starting a community organization that helps others.

WHAT COUNTS AS AN EXTRACURRICULAR ACTIVITY?

Lots of things you do outside of classes count. Does playing video games count? Not quite. But if you teach coding to younger kids, that counts. Same with volunteer work. Taking care of a sick family member counts. So does your job.

Depending on where you go to school, you may or may not have tons of clubs and teams to choose from. If you don't, don't be discouraged. Plenty of things exist for you to do outside of school.

Many high schools require community service. Rather than just checking that box, find a way to incorporate your interests into your volunteer time. Do you love sports and teamwork? Then how about leading an after-school basketball program for kids at a local community center? Are you a voracious reader? Libraries and after-school tutoring programs offer great service opportunities. And you don't have to jet halfway around the world to log volunteer time. While international programs can be fun and rewarding, you can discover plenty of opportunities right in your own backyard.

Do you have an idea of your own and value independence and risk? Consider starting your own neighborhood organization or school initiative. You could launch a documentary film club or a dog-walking business. For more ideas and tips on how to start your own initiative, check out "Self-Directed Students" (chapter 30).

Or, if you're having a hard time thinking about what you've done, here's a list of...

Extracurricular activities that you may not have considered, but that count!

Job shadowing
Building your own projects
Being a go-to tech person
Running a small business
Photography
Writing
Ventriloquism
Self-taught language courses
Taking massive open online
      courses
Composing EDM
Selling stuff on eBay
Arts and crafts
Fashion blogging
Beekeeping
Glassblowing
Scuba diving certification
EMT certification

Part-time jobs
Summer academic program
Online class certifications
Maintenance for high school
      sporting events
Juggling
Unicycling
Yoga
Mountain biking
Bird watching
Sport refereeing
Book club (outside of school)
Cosplay + designing costumes
Fantasy football statistician,
      manager, recruiter
Creating a curated list of books
      you've read

If I stop doing an activity, does that show I'm not committed?

Nope. It shows you're a normal human being with evolving interests. Just as your values may shift over time, your interests will naturally change too. If you're feeling uninspired or unmotivated, it might be a sign that your priorities have shifted. If so, take the time to reflect, take an Interest or Values Assessment, and find some activities that *do* light you up.

But where will I find the time to do this stuff?

I get it. The school year is packed with homework, testing, sports, and more. But how about the summer? Those three months are a great time to have fun and explore opportunities that you don't have time for during the week. Plus, taking time off provides great perspective. Want some ideas? Here are…

Five Great Ways to Spend Your Summer

1. **Read.** Curious what first-year college students are reading? Google "college summer reading lists" and you'll find a range of fiction and nonfiction reads that colleges across the country are assigning to their incoming freshman class.
2. **Binge-watch some TED talks.** Get your mind blown every eighteen minutes. Too lazy to search the website? In the Treasure Trove, you'll find a Google spreadsheet with every single TED Talk. That should keep you busy for a year or so.
3. **Take an online course in something that fascinates you.** Google "free and low-cost online courses from top universities" to find every topic from How to Draw Good and Evil Comic Book Characters to How to Market and Monetize on YouTube.
4. **Do one good deed a day for thirty days, then blog about it.** Look to similar projects for inspiration, but be creative and focus on doing what will help your family, friends, and community in particular.
5. **Pretend you're a tourist in your own town.** Take some time to explore, learn, and experience your home.

But what if you want to explore careers during the summer? You can do that too. In fact, here are some...

Ways You Can Explore Your Career Interests over the Summer

1. **Shadow relatives or family friends at work.** Even if you just go out for coffee with someone you admire. Many successful people are happy to "send the elevator back down" by passing along their experiences and wisdom. It can be intimidating to reach out, but don't be afraid. You may even find a mentor.
2. **Spend a full day researching potential majors and careers.** After taking one of the interest and aptitude assessments, check out one of these websites:

   a. bigfuture.collegeboard.or g/majors-careers
   b. collegemajors101.com
   c. www.mymajors.com
   d. O*NET OnLine—www.one tonline.org

3. **Get a formal internship.** Browse www.internships.com for positions in your area.

4. **Hack your own internship.** Don't feel limited if a company doesn't have a formal internship available. Ask yourself, "Can I create my own?" Generate a list of a few small- to medium-size companies near you. Find a contact there, either through their website, a referral, or LinkedIn. Outline your background, why you're interested in working with that company, and how you can see yourself contributing to their organization in a cover letter. Email it to your new contact along with a great résumé.

5. **Do research with a local professor.** Find two to three professors at a local college who are teaching or doing research in an area you're excited about. Attach a résumé to a brief email that highlights a bit about yourself and why you're interested in their area of expertise. Ask how you can help them. It might take emailing twenty different professors, but don't get discouraged. (Fun fact: one student I worked with emailed seventy-four professors before getting a response. But that response led to two internships.)

6. **Start a podcast.** Are you an expert on a niche topic? Or is there something you're really curious about? Host a weekly or monthly podcast series. Reach out to interesting people for interviews. Pitch the head of your school's newspaper about starting the paper's official podcast. Engage your school community by interviewing students and faculty about stories and issues in your school, community, or the world.

What if none of these appeal to me?

In the Treasure Trove, you'll find a link to a two-minute exercise that will help you make your summer more fun and productive, and on the College Essay Guy podcast you can catch my interview with Jill Tipograph, in which we discuss whether expensive summer programs are likely to help your admission chances or not. Regardless of your career interests, remember that high school is a time to explore who you're becoming and what your evolving interests are.

In the Treasure Trove, you'll find:

→ A list of specific high school courses that colleges like to see for students preparing for particular career paths

→ Do What You Are and YouScience: personality assessment and career exploration tools

→ Twenty-one books that showed up on college reading lists across the United States

→ Every TED Talk ever on one Google spreadsheet

→ A database with tons of volunteer opportunities in your area

→ A two-minute guided meditation to make your summer more fun and productive

→ A podcast with Jill Tipograph: "How to Plan a Fulfilling and Productive Summer"

→ The Peace Corps' list of top volunteer-producing schools

→ A list of schools that send on the most students to earn doctorate degrees

→ A ranking of schools based on the number of graduates who go on to earn venture capital funding

ACT and SAT Essentials

Written by Bruce Reed and Adam Ingersoll (Compass Education Group)

The best advice we have about college admission testing is this:

Give it the time it deserves
and not a second more.

And that's coming from a couple of test prep guys.

We (the test prep guys) think testing can be managed in ways that are both effective *and* efficient. This chapter will explain how to do just that.

In this chapter, we'll cover:

- Whether you need to take standardized tests
- What counts as a "good" score
- How much time you should spend preparing for standardized tests
- When you should start testing, and when you should stop
- How to choose between the ACT and SAT
- Where to find practice tests
- Whether to do the optional essay section
- How retesting works

- Whether you need to take SAT Subject Tests
- A simple three-step testing plan and free resources

Testing, Testing. Do You Even Need to Do This?

Hmm, well, *maybe* not. While many colleges continue to require ACT or SAT scores, a growing number (more than one thousand and counting) no longer do! Fairtest.org maintains a complete list of U.S. colleges that have gone "test optional" or "test flexible."* The rationales for these policies are commonly that the school has found test scores just don't add much that isn't already provided by your high school transcript, and that not requiring tests encourages more applications from underrepresented and under-resourced students (and from otherwise strong students who don't test well).

As this movement gains steam, this path represents an increasingly viable alternative for many students. In fact, if you are a ninth or tenth grader today, you can bet there will be even more test-optional colleges when you are a twelfth grader than there are now.

What's more, a fast-growing subset of test-optional schools are moderately to highly selective, admitting fewer than half of their applicants. Half of the so-called "top 100" liberal arts colleges (LACs) are now test-optional.[†] And a few national universities (NUs) are too, like the University of Chicago, Bowdoin, and Wake Forest.

This is what Whitney Soule, Dean of Admissions and Financial Aid at Bowdoin, has to say about it:

> We have had many years to create and refine an academic review process for applicants that does not require test scores. If we have the test results, we use them as part of the review. If testing is absent, our review process, which is built on the required materials in the application, is a reliable predictor for how well a student will adapt to the academic work in the first year at Bowdoin. In other words, we don't

---

[*]   In the Treasure Trove, you'll find links to the full database of test-optional schools.

[†]   "Half of 'Top 100' National Liberal Arts Colleges Do Not Require ACT/SAT," Fair Test. fairtest.org/half-top-100-national-liberal-arts-colleges-do-not.

hit a speed bump when reading an application and realize there are no scores—we are comfortable with completing an academic assessment without scores—we have designed our process to work that way!

But deciding where you want to apply will typically happen after you've started the testing process. So ultimately, the answer is that **you probably should go ahead and test**. Your SAT, ACT, and Subject Test scores may or may not put you in a favorable light, but you won't know that until after you have completed your testing. And despite the significant number of colleges that have gone test optional, you probably shouldn't limit your choices before the application process begins.

When to Start Testing and When to Stop

We preach a two-part theme when we work with students on testing timelines: Be Patient, Be Sensible. The right balance involves resisting the urge to get testing out of the way too early and recognizing when enough is enough.

Good test taking starts with good planning. No matter how far into high school you are now, a good testing plan can take shape by working backward from the fall of senior year. Frame your testing window and then pencil in what you already have on your plate in that time span, whether that's a stretch of weeks, months, or years. From there you can map out test dates thoughtfully based on realistic timelines that work for you.

A common game plan looks like this:

- Take the PSAT (if offered at school) in tenth grade as a no-stakes introduction to testing.
- Take the PreACT (if offered at school) in tenth grade for comparison purposes.
- Retake the PSAT in October of eleventh grade, especially if you plan to take the SAT. (This is also the National Merit qualifying test for juniors.)
- Choose the ACT or SAT and select a date for your first official sitting (most students start official testing in the spring of eleventh grade).
- Consider taking Subject Tests at the end of eleventh grade.
- Retake the ACT or SAT at least once to improve in one or more sections (over the summer or early in the fall of twelfth grade).

We generally discourage taking an official college admission test during (or before) the first semester of junior year unless you are clearly ready to go. If you're tempted to test that early, it's better to do so off the record with practice tests.

At the start of summer before your senior year, you'll have time to reflect on your cumulative GPA, your first set of official test scores, and your preliminary list of potential colleges. It'll be time to reconcile these factors and decide what you need to align your scores and goals. You may determine that you are done with testing. Or you may opt to gear up for one final sitting.

For the SAT, that could be in August or October. For the ACT, it could be in July,[*] September, or October. Note that while some Early Decision/Early Action deadlines still accommodate the October ACT and SAT dates, unexpected scoring delays can create headaches. It is therefore safest to reserve November and December dates for regular decision applications only.

Your odds of having a successful and low-stress testing experience increase by anticipating and sticking to the best possible timeline for you. What works for your friends doesn't matter. Think it through carefully and you can avoid the common mistakes of starting too soon (or too late) and doing too much (or too little). *Stay patient, stay sensible.*

WHERE TO FIND PRACTICE TESTS

Full-length practice ACTs and SATs are free to download from the respective websites of the two testing agencies (www.act.org and www.collegeboard.org). Stick with those practice tests if you can. ACT and College Board offer additional real practice tests for a fee through their online stores. Taking practice tests in a simulated, proctored environment would be ideal, but you can also self-proctor a test at home. Just find a quiet space and a block of time to complete a full test in one sitting.

Third-party mock tests can be used for additional practice, but they don't necessarily predict scores accurately. Be particularly wary of any mock test that claims to "hybridize" parts of both tests. That's more of a test prep marketing tool than a worthwhile resource for you.

We like practice tests because they are actionable. Unlike officially administered tests, practice tests are truly helpful in that you receive scores with little delay, and you can review the items you missed. The PSAT is also a good tool

---

[*]   Not currently in California or New York.

for reviewing questions, but the two-month lag in receiving scores can be a costly period of time for juniors targeting the March SAT.

The ACT vs. the SAT

First, let's compare and contrast the tests side-by-side in broad terms:

Reading

- The ACT Reading section is shorter (35 minutes versus 65 minutes for the SAT).
- The ACT requires you to read and respond at a faster pace (more questions per minute).
- The ACT will focus more directly on what the passage contains.
- The SAT will focus more on the author (tone, inference, words in context).

English (Grammar)

- The two tests use similar formats (passage-based proofreading tasks).
- They both test common grammar rules and punctuation.
- They both assess your grasp of effective writing (organization, conciseness).

MATH

Math differs significantly between the ACT and SAT in form, content, and pace. Students preparing for each test should employ different strategies and review different math topics.

	SAT Math		ACT Math
Section placement	3rd	4th	2nd
Calculator	No calculator	Calculator	Calculator
Time allotted	25 minutes	55 minutes	60 minutes
Number of questions	20	38	60
Question types	Multiple choice and grid-in		Multiple choice
Topics tested	Emphasis on algebra I and II topics and data analysis		Broad but shallow approach to math topics ranging from pre-algebra to trigonometry

While both tests are built on a broad survey of high school "math class" math, they favor different topics. You'll see more Algebra I and II on the SAT; more Geometry/Trig on the ACT.

SCIENCE

Unlike the SAT, the ACT has a discrete Science section, which measures interpretation, analysis, evaluation, reasoning, and problem-solving skills. Although it uses scientific language, very little prior science knowledge is needed to do well. When the ACT does call for prior knowledge, it's typically something basic (e.g., that H_2O is water). It's more about interpreting information you're given and understanding the nature of scientific experiments. The questions may have very little to do with what you've actually learned in your science classes.

What the ACT Science does require is an ability to navigate a multilevel maze of information. Nowhere else on the ACT do they give you so much data to parse through. Clues are often deeply embedded within complicated diagrams, tables, and research summaries. Long lab write-ups or large data sets may be helpful for only a single question.

The triple whammy is that there is lots of dense information and it's a fast-paced section (forty questions in just thirty-five minutes) *and* it's at the end of the test when you may be running low on energy. The upside is that ACT Science rewards preparation. Success on ACT Science is not about learning science as much as it is about combining reading and data analysis skills, and learning to do that rapidly. Here's the content and structure:

Passage Type	Passages per ACT	Number of Questions per Passage	Characteristics
Data Representation	2–3	5–6	Scientific information is presented in charts, graphs, tables, and diagrams. Questions require interpretation and analysis of the information.
Research Summaries	2–3	6–8	One or more related experiments are described with the results of the experiment(s) typically summarized in graphs and/or tables. Questions cover the design, execution, and results.
Conflicting Viewpoints	1	6–8	Two or more incompatible theories, hypotheses, or viewpoints on a specific observable phenomenon are offered. Questions will evaluate your ability to analyze and compare the different viewpoints.

For its part, the SAT mixes in a number of science-themed questions throughout the exam, enough to form the backbone of the "Analysis in Science" cross-test score that you'll see in your score report's fine print.

The Test That's Best for You

Every U.S. college that requires a standardized test as part of the application for admission now accepts the ACT and SAT interchangeably, and they can do that because the two exams are pretty darn similar.

Even so, we highly recommend that you focus your preparation primarily on one test, not both. Doing both tests will not doubly impress anyone, we promise. Use practice tests (or the PSAT and/or PreACT) to generate baseline scores you can use to gauge your relative performance on each one. Here's a simple chart that will help you figure which test came out on top for you:

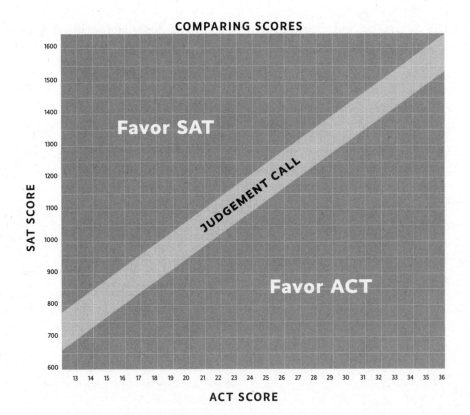

Sources: 2018 SAT/ACT Concordance; Compass analysis

Simply find where your scores intersect to see if there's a clear winner. If practice test scores suggest you should favor one test over the other, great! Move forward with that test and let the other one go. However, a majority of students land somewhere in the "judgment call" zone. If you find yourself in this crowded space, there are more factors to consider in picking a test.

THE SUBJECT TESTS

Though only a few colleges still require SAT Subject Tests in addition to the ACT or SAT, dozens more recommend or consider them. Some accept the ACT in lieu of the SAT/Subject Test combination, and some others will even accept Subject Tests in lieu of the ACT or SAT.

Confused? Yeah, it's confusing, but you'll find an updated resource that tracks all Subject Test requirements and recommendations, by school, in the Treasure Trove.

If Subject Test colleges are in play for you, you should set aside a spring test date to do those. May or June is a sensible option because year-long coursework will be nearly completed, and preparation for AP or final exams will have begun. Subject Tests are offered only on dates that conflict with the SAT, so calendaring is an important exercise to begin early.

A word of caution: Subject Tests should be used to demonstrate mastery of a subject. So if you haven't (yet) mastered a subject, don't demonstrate that. Subject Test scores are only helpful if they enhance your testing portfolio.

In other words, we don't recommend Subject Tests unless you are highly confident that your scores will exceed your SAT score (or ACT equivalent).

When evaluating your Subject Test scores, focus on the scaled score from 200–800. Percentile scores for Subject Tests are misleading because they reflect a smaller and more accomplished testing population.

For example, only about 27,000 students take the physics Subject Test each year, and we can assume that most are quite good at physics. And how can a perfect 800 on the Math Level 2 put you at only the 75th percentile? Well, because about one out of four test takers also got a perfect score. Yep, it's a tough crowd.

When to Take the Subject Tests

We recommend waiting until March or April of eleventh grade before taking a practice test to see where you stand. That's late enough in the course to get a basic sense of your readiness while leaving enough time to brush up a little more before May or June on gaps identified by the practice test. It's also a good idea to talk to your teacher about how well the class has prepared students for the corresponding Subject Test in the past.

Each Subject Test is an hour long, so you can take up to three in one official sitting. But there is no reason to go overboard, especially if you don't feel you have mastered more than two subjects. Very few students have, which is why very few students take Subject Tests in the first place.

When colleges receive Subject Test scores, they generally expect to get two scores from you, and they typically consider your two best scores anyway. A competitive STEM program, however, will understandably look for mastery in math/science, but undeclared majors can submit scores from any subjects—as long as they're good scores!

You can retake a Subject Test, but first ask yourself why. Your score is unlikely to improve much unless a significant change in your level of mastery occurs.

HOW RETESTING WORKS

Taking the ACT or SAT twice is almost a given for many students. We even recommend penciling an "emergency" third sitting into your testing timeline in case you need it. (Of course, one-and-done is even better, and you'll know if that's you when you see your scores.) After three tries, though, it starts to get excessive. Retesting (within reason) is absolutely an option, but it's not an obligation.

This is a good time to remind you of our advice at the beginning of this chapter: *give testing the time it deserves and not a second more.*

Retesting once (or maybe twice) should be done with a specific purpose and reasonable goal in mind. Don't keep testing just because. Read our "What counts as a good score?" discussion in the FAQs at the end of this chapter and ask, "Have my test scores done their job?" If you're unsure about retesting, ask your college counselor or another admission expert.

Three Steps for Standardized Testing

With an understanding of testing basics, you can begin to tailor a testing plan that suits you. Let's get you started down that path.

STEP 1: MAP YOUR FULL TESTING PLAN

Grab your calendar and make note of the upcoming slate of official test dates, which are published on the respective websites of the two testing agencies. Both offer testing several times a year.

Count the number of weeks (and conflicts) you have leading up to different test dates. Test date selection should be based on academic readiness, test preference, desired preparation timelines, date conflicts, and application deadlines. There's no such thing as predictably "easier" or "harder" test dates, and whoever else is testing on a given day has no bearing on your score.

Once again, it's smart to complete at least one ACT or SAT before the end of junior year and to remain open to retesting in the summer or early fall of senior year. Juniors should consider Subject Tests while the material is freshest. If you're taking an AP, Honors, or advanced course in a given subject, you are an especially good candidate for a corresponding Subject Test.

STEP 2: CREATE TESTING ACCOUNTS

After plotting a comprehensive testing plan, don't neglect the critical mechanics. If you take the PSAT, you'll set up a College Board account, which you'll use to register for the SAT and Subject Tests, access those results, and eventually submit those scores to colleges. A separate ACT account is required to manage your ACT testing.

Most colleges want official score reports sent via the testing agencies. However, some colleges now allow applicants to initially self-report scores and then provide official reports only after being admitted and prior to enrollment.*

Registering early increases your chance of securing a seat at your first-choice venue. Tests are not offered at every high school, so you may need to travel to another school in your region.

---

*   For an updated list of colleges that allow self-reporting of SAT and ACT scores, check out the Treasure Trove.

Opt in for (or opt out of) the essay during registration and take note of what's required (and forbidden) on test day. Certain test dates offer you the option of purchasing an expanded score report, which gives you a chance to review any questions you missed. Decide if this is something you'll use, especially if you think you'll retest.

Finally, if you need special testing accommodations due to a diagnosed learning, physical, or medical disability, be sure to have those approvals in place in advance. The testing organizations have crucial differences in their accommodation policies. Get help from your high school if you are unsure how to seek those accommodations.[*]

STEP 3: MAKE A TEST PREP AND PRACTICE PLAN

We recommend spending three to four months preparing for the ACT or SAT. This gives you enough room to work test prep into an active teenage life without sacrificing other interests. And with enough time, good test preparation will clean up content gaps identified by practice tests, and it will give insight into subtle but predictable patterns in the test as well as any negative testing habits you may not realize you have.

What is good test prep? At its heart it involves a commitment to evaluated practice over a reasonable amount of time, exposure to authentic study material, and some dry runs on full-length exams. Both ACT and College Board offer free or low-cost access to practice material, and there's an established commercial test prep industry that delivers resources and instruction.[†]

Self-starters can pull off a good three to four months of preparation by committing to the persistent use of tools found online and in bookstores, while other students will benefit from the structure and discipline of a regularly scheduled group class.

Test Prep Services

Other students will feel that the individualized approach of one-on-one tutoring works best for them and their busy schedules. This is a totally viable

---

[*] You'll find a library of resources on testing accommodations in the Treasure Trove.

[†] You'll find links to great free and low-cost test prep options in the Treasure Trove.

option, but it's good to be armed with questions to ask of a prospective test prep provider to help you determine the best fit when checking out commercial options.

- Do they specialize in test prep, or is test prep on a long list of their college-related offerings?
- Is testing their true area of expertise? Do they publish ongoing research and resources demonstrating their expertise?
- Are they equipped to handle all of your test prep needs (SAT, ACT, Subject Tests) with subject-matter experts? Do they have strong curricula and sufficient study materials?
- What is their history with college admission testing and preparation? Who provides leadership?
- Is their test prep recommendation placed within the context of your needs and goals? Did they take the time to ask thoughtful questions and listen to you?
- Who are the instructors? How are the instructors hired, trained, supervised, supported, evaluated, and professionally developed?
- How does the student-instructor match process work to ensure a good fit?
- Who is accountable for a satisfying experience and outcome? Who is in charge of resolving issues along the way?
- What exactly will test preparation involve on a daily, weekly, and monthly basis?
- How are goals determined, pursued, and measured? What happens if goals are not reached?
- What are the contractual terms of the program? Are the terms client friendly? Are they student centric? Are they easy to understand?
- What are the firm's expectations for the student? For the parents?

Standardized Testing FAQs

WHAT COUNTS AS A GOOD SCORE?

Ah, a trick question, but we'll take this one anyway. A "good" test score of course depends on the college, but in all cases, a "good" score is one that did its job for you. That's right, it served your needs!

Colleges use test scores as a way of gauging a student's relative standing in a larger pool. Your test score represents your "place in line" to an extent, and colleges have a good handle on where that score stands. We often tell students: "If your score isn't good enough to stand out, you at least want it to blend in."

Application readers are short on time, and a test score is like a headline—its job is to pull the reader into the full story, and a good one does just that. A score that blends into the range of scores submitted by most of a college's admitted pool (colleges usually publish the middle 50 percent of test scores submitted by a competitive mix of admitted students) will have done its job, but being a little higher than average is even better. It'll prompt the reader to delve into the more interesting aspects of your application that factor into final decisions. That's where you want them spending their time on you.

At the more selective colleges in particular, a good score is necessary but not sufficient. In those rare cases, a perfect test score won't guarantee admission by itself, but a below-average one may make a decision to reject a lot easier, unfortunately.

Know that when you're looking at score ranges of colleges, you're seeing a class year's final product. In most cases, those scores happened in the latter part of eleventh grade or later, and roughly two-thirds of college applicants take their final admission test in the fall of senior year. You'll get there too.

DO SCHOOLS GET TO SEE ALL OF MY SCORES?

College Board and ACT have "Score Choice" policies that give you some control over how scores are reported, but each college has the final word on what should be submitted and how those submitted scores get sent and used.

It would be great to know the score-reporting policy of every college you're considering, but you might not know where you're applying yet. The most prudent approach is to pretend you'll send all scores to all schools; that will make you more carefully consider the timing, frequency, and level of readiness for your official sittings.

Some admission offices, for example, will create "superscores" by combining your highest section scores from multiple sittings. They don't want you to inadvertently exclude a high section score. Colleges that don't superscore will typically consider only your highest total score, regardless of when it happened, so don't worry if a retake results in a lower score.

To find all the score choice and superscore policies by college, check out the Treasure Trove.

CAN I OPT OUT OF THE OPTIONAL ESSAY?

We'll answer that question with a question: might you apply to any of the University of California campuses (the UCs)? If so, you'll definitely need to do the essay. If not, you probably won't need to, but you should. Beyond the UCs, a handful of other schools ask for the essay too, and while not required, it's sort of expected. We maintain a current list of essay policies by college at www.compassprep.com/act-writing-and-sat-essay-requirements.

The safest approach is to just include the essay when you're testing in case you end up needing it. It will have no impact at colleges that don't consider it, but failing to complete the essay may disqualify the entire test sitting at colleges that do require it.

If you do register for the essay, here's what you need to know:

- The SAT has you first read a short passage. You'll then be instructed to leave your personal opinions out of your essay and instead provide a critique of the author.
- The ACT makes room for you to include your opinions on a stated topic while you analyze three provided perspectives and discuss how these positions relate to one another.
- Both tests assign multiple scores based on particular areas, or "domains," of the writing process. SAT keeps these scores separate while ACT averages them into a single writing test score.

Reducing Test Anxiety

Testing for college admissions is a huge source of stress for students applying to college. Hopefully the info in this chapter has helped you feel like you can handle it confidently, but there's always going to be some nerves as you go into the process. To give you some tools to manage those feelings of anxiety, Dr. Jed Applerouth, founder of Applerouth Tutoring Services and a nationally certified counselor with a doctoral degree in educational psychology (also an expert on standardized testing), shared some of his tips on how to keep the stress from becoming too much. Check out the Treasure Trove for even more techniques.

- **Normalize test anxiety.** Knowing that test anxiety is remarkably common can help reduce stress levels. Most everyone experiences anxiety in some area of life, and knowing that one in four high school students regularly experience test anxiety can take away that feeling of being alone in dealing with this. "This is not my thing, this is just a human thing. My peers can manage this, and I can too."
- **Identify the source of the anxiety.** In many cases students internalize anxiety from an outside source and make it their own. Sometimes parental anxiety can manifest as student anxiety. Check out if any outside sources of pressure may be affecting your own level of anxiety. You might need to create some space and distance from the emotions of others to reduce this external pressure and decrease your own level of anxiety.
- **Learn a little about your biology and neurochemistry.** Students who understand how anxiety functions in the brain and in the body will have an edge on self-regulation. Students should understand the primary function of the amygdala, a region of the brain in the temporal lobe, responsible for identifying threats and activating stress hormones to rally the body's defenses. If you come to understand how stress hormones affect the body and mind, you will be able to quickly identify the earliest signs of anxiety and begin to use interventions to regain your center.
- **Draw from other domains of competence.** It is best to adopt a strengths-based approach, examining other areas of your life where you've been able to effectively regulate anxiety and stress. What works for you that you can borrow and bring to testing? How do you manage stress before a sporting event or performance? Debaters, actors, and athletes often have rituals they do to help center themselves before they take the floor. What techniques already work for you? Let's import those and put them to work.
- **Focus on self-care.** How do you nurture and take care of yourself? We all have things that make us feel good and relaxed. Whether it's a warm bath, a favorite meal, soothing music, playing with a pet, or talking with a supportive ally—do things that help you center yourself and calm your mind.

Are We There Yet?

Phew! We covered a lot and we hope you took away a bunch of helpful and actionable ideas. But if you take away only one message from this chapter, we hope that it's to understand that your test scores in no way reflect your self-worth.

All that these tests really do is help colleges predict, a little bit, how ready you are to succeed in their first-year classes. ACT and SAT scores say very little or nothing at all about your creativity, persistence in the face of obstacles, street smarts, interpersonal and communication skills, or whether you are kind or funny or interesting…all the things that matter far, far more over the long haul.

Give these tests their due. Let them work for you. And then never think about them again!

In the Treasure Trove, you'll find:

→ A list of over one thousand accredited colleges and universities that don't use ACT/SAT scores to admit substantial numbers of students into bachelor degree programs

→ *U.S.News & World Report*-ranked schools that don't require the ACT/SAT

→ Khan Academy's free test prep

→ Low-cost test-prep available from the ACT

→ How low-income students can receive free test prep

→ Twenty more techniques for reducing test anxiety

Part III

Essentials before You Apply

Chapter 4

How to Create a Balanced College List

Good news: there are more than four thousand colleges and universities in the United States.

Even better news: most schools accept most students. The national average acceptance rate is higher than sixty percent. (Google "NACAC State of College Admission Report" for proof or check the Treasure Trove for the latest report.) But which of the four thousand is right for you?

Let's find out.

In this chapter, we'll cover:

- How to figure out what you're looking for in a college
- A simple way to organize your college research
- How many schools to apply to
- The two big mistakes students and parents make when considering financial aid
- A three-step process to help you figure out which schools will likely make themselves affordable to you
- What a "balanced" school list looks like (and how to create one)

The following pages contain a three-step process designed to help you whittle over four thousand colleges down to the eight to ten to which you'll ultimately apply.

Just so you know where we're headed: first, you'll need to figure out your personal preferences that you'll use to put together a preliminary list of around twenty schools. Second, from that preliminary list you'll make a new list with only the schools you can afford. And third, you'll eliminate remaining schools until you have a final list of eight to ten that you love.

Think of this process as an inverted pyramid, one that looks like this:

COLLEGE ESSAY GUY'S COLLEGE RESEARCH PYRAMID

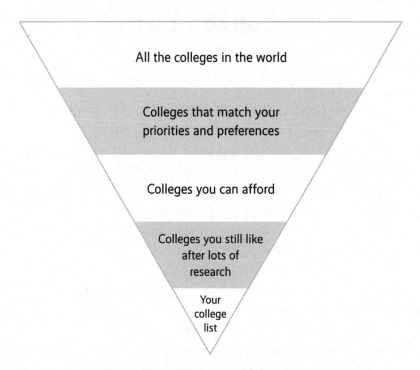

All the colleges in the world

Colleges that match your priorities and preferences

Colleges you can afford

Colleges you still like after lots of research

Your college list

How to Figure Out What You're Looking for in a College

Why should you figure out what you're looking for first? Because you don't want to waste your time on colleges that have something you don't want (like cold weather) or don't have something you do want (like a specific major).

For this section, I sought the advice of a trusted friend and colleague who has spent the past thirty years eating, sleeping, and breathing colleges. He's Dr. Steven Antonoff, former Dean of Admissions and Dean of Students at the University of Denver.

Dr. Antonoff calls himself a "school buff" because, for years, he's planned his vacations around school visits and he even reads about schools while on the treadmill. His book *College Match: A Blueprint for Choosing the Best School for You* is the go-to resource for college list development. I recommend it.

When I interviewed Dr. Antonoff for my podcast, I asked him, "What's the best way for students to spend an hour discovering their college preferences?" He advised going somewhere quiet, like the top of a mountain, and really thinking about two questions: "Who am I?" and "What do I want?"

That could work...if you have a mountain nearby. But if you don't happen to have a mountain nearby, I recommend these:

- **The Self-Survey for the College Bound.** I like the eighty-question "Self-Survey for the College Bound" in Dr. Antonoff's book *College Match*. Get this: if you can't afford the book, Dr. Antonoff offers this resource on his website (see Treasure Trove for link) along with a variety of other resources—for free. These aren't meant to be exhaustive; they're meant to get you started.
- **Corsava Cards.** I love the Corsava website (www.corsava.com), which shows you a set of virtual cards containing college qualities like "access to professors" and "school spirit" that you sort into categories like "must have" and "would be nice."
- **The "Sizing Yourself Up" section at the start of the *Fiske Guide to Colleges*.** If you've already bought the *Fiske Guide to Colleges*, check out the short "Sizing Yourself Up" survey near the start of the book. If you haven't, check it out at your local library, or ask your counselor (it's probably in their office).

But what if you don't have access to these resources? Here's a list of...

Great Things to Consider When Developing Your Preliminary College List

- **Climate.** To be happy, do you need warm weather, easy access to skiing, four seasons, lots of sunshine, low humidity? Be honest with yourself and your body.

- **Location.** Do you want to be near a city, in the countryside, or do you not care?

- **Sociopolitical spectrum.** Do you want your style, values, and opinions to be the norm, or are you okay being on the fringe?

- **Activities.** What are your must-haves in terms of sports, theater/dance/film, and so on?*

- **Distance from home.** How far from home are you willing to travel?

- **School spirit.** Do you love the idea of cheering at football games or not care if you ever see another football game in your life?

- **Institutional type.** Do you want to attend a public or a private institution? A faith-based institution? What about a school that embraces your racial and cultural identity such as a Historically Black College or University (HBCU) or a Tribal College or University (see page 315 for more)? Have you thought about a women's college (see page 361 for more)?

- **College versus university.** Universities offer graduate degrees, whereas colleges primarily serve undergraduates. Universities are usually larger and they often employ master's and doctoral students to teach first- and second-year undergraduate courses. On the flip side, universities may also offer an abundance of undergraduate research opportunities. Which might be better at helping you meet your goals and needs?

- **Parental priorities.** Talk through your preferences with your parents early and often. They'll likely have some strong opinions. Ask them. Then listen.

- **Colleges' unique values**. We know that all colleges value *education*, *challenges*, and *self-knowledge*, but each college was founded on a unique set of values, and, just like you, different institutions have specific priorities that may or may not match with yours. For example, if both you and a school value *justice* or *creativity*, then it might be a school you want to add to your list.

---

* While most colleges say you can do these things, access may be limited. Are you actually good enough to play DIII lacrosse, for example, or should you look for a college with a club team? Or what's the likelihood of undergrads getting a lead role in a main-stage show?

DISCOVERING A COLLEGE'S UNIQUE VALUES

Google any school's mission statement and you might find something similar to the Beloit College mission statement (emphasis mine):

> Beloit College engages the *intelligence, imagination*, and *curiosity* of its students, empowering them to lead fulfilling lives marked by *high achievement, personal responsibility*, and *public contribution* in a *diverse society*. Our emphasis on international and interdisciplinary perspectives, the *integration of knowledge with experience*, and close *collaboration* among peers, professors, and staff equips our students to approach the complex problems of the world ethically and thoughtfully.

Most colleges will be happy to spell out exactly what they value in their mission statement, making it easy to compare to the results of your Values Exercise. But it's not the only way to get a sense for what a college cares about.

You can also learn from their application requirements. If you need to submit only a transcript and test scores, the college is likely one where you will need to be comfortable with *independence* and *self-advocacy*. In contrast, a college that requires supplemental essays, letters of recommendation, and an interview is more likely one where you'll need to be comfortable with *participation* in class discussion and developing *close relationships* with faculty and staff.

Graduation requirements (which can differ wildly among schools) give you another look at a school's values. Generally, schools with less flexible, more standardized course requirements would be a good fit for students who value *structure*, while those that have few requirements to none at all are good for those who value *autonomy* and *flexibility*. Other requirements like community service and studying abroad can tell you that a school values *community* and *helping others* or *adventure* and *curiosity*.

A Quick Plug for Community Colleges

Community college is an often overlooked, yet viable option. Students can complete their first two years of credits before transferring to a larger institution to finish their bachelor's. They generally require only a high school diploma for admission. States like California, Florida, North Carolina, and Washington have well-articulated transfer pathways that end with the same four-year degree. Community colleges are generally more affordable and sometimes have smaller class sizes than universities.

For more resources to help you figure out what you're looking for in a college, the Treasure Trove contains links to more of my favorite resources, including Knowdell Card Sorts and the True Colours Test.

You may be thinking *This is too many resources and I feel overwhelmed! What if I only want to spend like an hour on this right now?*

In my opinion, Corsava offers the most efficient, interactive, and complete resource for this part of the process, so go to www.corsava.com, create a free account, and do the card sort to generate a list of your must-haves and deal breakers.

Have you figured out what you do and don't want using one of the tools listed earlier? Great, time to start searching for schools.

Research Schools (Based on Your Interests and Preferences) and Create Your Preliminary List

This is where you'll create a preliminary list of around twenty schools. How? By using an online platform that matches schools to your preferences.

Many online platforms do this; my favorite is CollegeXpress.com, the online version of Dr. Antonoff's second book, *The College Finder*. You can type in anything from "schools for the free spirit" to "great private colleges for the B student" to generate a list of schools that match each of those descriptions. CollegeXpress is maybe my favorite college admission resource ever. Plus, it's free.*

---

*   Dr. Antonoff is cool with me telling you all this.

STEP 1. EXPLORE COLLEGES ON COLLEGEXPRESS

1. **Go to CollegeXpress.com and create a free account.** Enter either one of your must-have preferences (like "gay-friendly colleges" or "colleges going green") or the name of a school you're interested in applying to. Not sure what to search for? Search for "how to create a great college list" in the Treasure Trove and you'll find a menu of potential search terms.

2. **Click "Lists & Rankings" to see what other lists that school is on.** Say you type in "Northwestern" because you're interested in film. As luck would have it, you see a list called "Colleges with Great Programs in Film and Television." Score! Clicking on that list reveals a few schools whose film programs you've heard of—New York University, University of Southern California, Chapman University. But then maybe you see a few schools you didn't know had great film programs, like Loyola Marymount University, Emerson College, and Columbia College Chicago.

3. **Research those schools as prospective candidates** for your preliminary list of (give or take) twenty schools.

Heads up: You don't have to spend ten to fifteen hours creating your preliminary list because you'll do more research later.

Maybe spend an hour or two creating this initial list. Make sure to keep track of what you discover. Where and how? On your customizable (and free!) College List and Essay Tracker, of course.

The Common Data Set

A great resource for learning about the nuts and bolts of how any school works is the Common Data Set. It allows students and families to compare various aspects of colleges side-by-side, separated into sections A through J and covering just about every statistic you could be looking for.

To find this information, just google "[college name] Common Data Set" and pull the latest version from the school's website. I'll reference specific sections of the Common Data Set throughout the book whenever it's helpful. But for now, if you feel especially curious about a school you're interested in and find the context that statistics can provide helpful, try taking a look at their Common Data Set to see what else you can learn.

STEP 2. CREATE YOUR COLLEGE LIST AND ESSAY TRACKER

First, make a copy of my Sample College List and Essay Tracker spreadsheet, which you'll find in the Treasure Trove.

Next, type your preliminary list of schools on that spreadsheet, dividing them into these categories:

- Wild Card: less than 10 percent chance of getting in
- Reach: low likelihood of acceptance, maybe 10–25 percent chance
- Maybe: in range for your profile, maybe 26–74 percent chance
- Likely: pretty good shot at getting in, more than 75 percent chance*

Pro Tip: Build your list from the ground up.

Most students list schools in this order: Wild Cards (i.e., Super Reaches), Reaches, Maybes… then, begrudgingly, they add a few "Likely" schools. Try doing it the other way around instead. Start with the schools you're likely to get into and that you'd be excited to attend, then build up from there.

Also, think carefully about what you call your "Likely" schools. I've heard some counselors refer to the "Likely" schools as "foundational." I like that. It's so much more positive than "backup." Who wants to go to their backup restaurant or marry their backup person? Language influences how we think about things.

How do you know whether a school is a Wild Card, Reach, Maybe, or Likely? You can and should…

Ask your counselor. They should be able to help you decide which schools to put in which category based on your profile. If you don't have a counselor…

Use an online platform. I recommend www.collegedata.com. It considers your grades, test scores, and a variety of other factors to approximate your chances of getting into certain schools.

Or Google the name of the school and the words "freshman profile." This will tell you, among other things, the average test scores for admitted students.

---

* Don't worry too much about these percentages—they're just rough ways of estimating whether you have a good shot at getting in or not so much.

But these are just guidelines!

I strongly recommend being conservative in your predictions here. If a school is on the border between "Maybe" and "Likely," assume it's a "Maybe." I find that most students don't need to add more "Wild Card" or "Reach" schools to their list; they usually need more "Likely" schools.

Some schools are a reach for pretty much everyone. And often acceptances are based on factors that students can't possibly have any knowledge of. They may want female cello players that year, for example, or students to populate the school's new cognitive modeling major. Or maybe they want more international students because they have parking space issues and they're assuming international students won't bring cars to campus.[†] It's almost impossible to know what these factors will be from year to year, so please don't spend too much time worrying about or trying to guess these factors.

Here's where you'll type these in on your tracker:

WILD CARD (Less than 10% chance of getting in)

[Type school here]	

REACH (Low chance of acceptance, based on my profile)

[Type school here]	
[Type school here]	
[Type school here]	

MAYBE (In range for my profile, but tough to say)

[Type school here]	
[Type school here]	
[Type school here]	

LIKELY (I've got a pretty good shot here)

[Type school here]	
[Type school here]	
[Type school here]	

---

† This is a real example, by the way, that backfired on the college. As soon as the international students arrived in the United States, guess what? Many bought cars.

Feel free to color code the "Likely" schools with green, the "Maybe" schools with yellow, the "Reach" schools in light red and the "Wild Card" schools in purple.* If you've been following along, you should have about twenty. But don't worry, you'll whittle it down. How? By figuring out what you can afford, then diving deep into research, which I'm just about to show you how to do.

Need a break? Take it. Feeling good? Okay, let's talk about money.

How to Figure Out Which Schools You Can Afford

Shout-out to Amanda Miller, a.k.a. The Counselor Lady,
for doing the heavy lifting on this section.

Here are two big mistakes students and parents make when considering how to pay for college:

MISTAKE 1: ASSUMING THEY HAVE TO PAY STICKER PRICE

You know that really huge cost of attendance (COA) number that schools flash on their website that's like a bajillion dollars? Yeah, you can pretty much ignore it for now.

Why? First, a sticker price COA—which includes indirect costs like transportation, books, and social life—sets the cost at the ceiling rather than the floor; it shows the likely maximum a college will cost.

Think of it like going to a car lot. The price on the window is often a beginning point for a downward negotiation. Same thing with college costs, only your grades and test scores take the place of a credit score and your essay replaces your haggling prowess.

Schools with low sticker prices rarely negotiate because they figure you're

---

*   Note that some counselors refer to "maybe" schools as "target" schools, which is great, and some refer to the "likely" schools as "safeties." But I personally don't prefer the term "safety" because who wants to end up at their safety school?

already getting a deal, whereas high-COA schools are more likely to have a lot of wiggle room if they really want a student and have the money to offer.

While $70,000 a year might sound like a lot, the only people who actually pay full price are the ones who can afford it or who don't qualify for scholarships.

MISTAKE 2: WAITING UNTIL THEY'RE ACCEPTED TO A COLLEGE TO BEGIN FIGURING OUT HOW TO PAY FOR IT

Yeah, this usually doesn't work out well for folks. Contrary to popular belief, the most critical step in making college affordable is not applying for tons of scholarships (though they can help). The key to graduating from an excellent-fit college with little-to-no debt is identifying colleges that will lower their price for you.

The best strategy to make college affordable (besides being very, very wealthy) is to apply to multiple schools that are likely financial fits, make sure you meet your colleges' scholarship deadlines (which can be in the fall *before* you know if you've been accepted!), and wait until you receive a financial aid award letter from each college to compare costs and decide.

Seems like common sense, but you'd be surprised how few students actually do this.

So which colleges are financial fits? Great question. Depends on who you are, which we're just about to find out.

(Quick note for international students: you are often subject to different rules when it comes to financial aid, especially need-based aid. Learn more in the chapter on international students on page 306.)

A Three-Step Process to Help You Figure Out Which Schools Will Likely Make Themselves Affordable to You

STEP 1: ESTIMATE YOUR EXPECTED FAMILY CONTRIBUTION (EFC)

In addition to your GPA and test scores (if required), *your EFC is the single* *greatest determining factor of how much money a college will give you.* Why? Because it tells the college how much your family can theoretically afford to pay. (FYI, EFCs are expressed with weird numbers. Example: An EFC of "005400" means your family can afford $5,400 for your first year of college.*) The less you can afford, the more grants the college is allowed to give you.

Side note: Is your family wealthier than most and able to pay full price for college? If so, you can probably skip this step and move down to Step 2. If not, definitely check out the FAFSA4caster step-by-step below.

Now that you know this, you're ready to learn the key formula in financial aid:

Cost of attendance – Expected family contribution = How much money your family needs in order to make the college affordable

COA – EFC = Need

Most colleges do what they can to meet as much of a family's need as possible (especially if they *really* want the student). In fact, some high-sticker-price schools are very generous and meet all needs for every student.

The FAFSA

Each October, seniors fill out the FAFSA (Free Application for Federal Student Aid).[†] Just to make sure you understand how important this is: ***The FAFSA is the key to unlocking financial aid from the federal government, most state scholarship agencies, and most colleges***.

Make note now that you will need to go to fafsa.ed.gov to file your FAFSA submission ASAP in October of your senior year.

---

[*] Financial aid counselors at colleges insist an EFC is an "index number," not a dollar amount. Toe-may-toe, toe-mah-toe.

[†] Note that if you're a high schooler living with parents/guardians, the FAFSA requires all this information from them too.

What goes into the FAFSA?

- Social Security Number or Alien Registration Number
- Tax returns
- Bank statements
- Investment records
- Any other financial information/records of money earned

What comes out of the FAFSA? Your student aid report (SAR), your EFC, and everything that colleges will use to evaluate your financial situation.

But that is (hopefully) for future you (if it's not, get on that right away). For now we're going to use the data that the FAFSA will ask for to figure out which schools you can afford with a fantastic tool called the FAFSA4caster, which will give you a dry run on the FAFSA while calculating your EFC.

How to use the FAFSA4caster to estimate your EFC

1. Grab a parent and tell them you need fifteen minutes of their help to figure out paying for college. (They will be impressed.)
2. Sit down in a comfortable place with your device of choice.
3. Go to studentaid.ed.gov/sa/fafsa/estimate (or google FAFSA4caster and click on the first .gov link) and click on the FAFSA4caster link on the web page.
4. Input your information. Most of the questions are easy (e.g., birthday, address) and nothing is recorded. Having recent tax forms (e.g., W-2s, 1040s) is helpful but not necessary. If your parent doesn't know an answer, don't be afraid to estimate since you can always redo this later with more accurate info.

    Here are some tips for filling out the 4caster:

    a. Anytime it or FAFSA says "you" or "your," it means "the student going to college." This often confuses parents who fill out the form.
    b. The online form uses something called "skip logic," so don't be alarmed when you answer a question and the page keeps changing in response to your answers. It's designed to give you the info you need while asking the fewest possible questions.
    c. Those green question marks to the right of each question are there in case you need clarification. Click them if you get stuck.

d.   Write down the numbers your parent is using to answer all the questions or take a screenshot; you'll need those numbers later when you're calculating financial aid for specific schools in the next step.

e.   Everything after the "which college you want to attend" part is optional. If you keep clicking "Next," you'll still get your EFC.

5.   Hit "Submit." Your EFC will be in teeny tiny print under the word "Difference." **Hold onto that EFC number.** It's a great shortcut for the next step.

STEP 2: USE A NET PRICE CALCULATOR (NPC)

An NPC uses the personal information you provide (again, none of it is recorded) to give you an estimate of how much money you would receive from a particular college upon admission. Every school is federally required to have an NPC on its website.

NPCs are great because they're easy to find, and their results are tailored to each school. To find a school's NPC, either google "[school name] net price calculator" or check out the federal government's NPC directory at collegecost. ed.gov/net-price.

NPCs can vary in reliability. Don't bank on getting the amount projected, as it's a ballpark figure. Generally, the more questions an NPC asks, the more accurate its estimate.

Action item: Go through each of the schools on your preliminary list and use their net price calculator to figure out how much that school is likely to cost you, and make note of the estimated cost for each using your College List and Essay Tracker spreadsheet (the one I mentioned on page 48). Next to that school, type that number into the column that says "How much $ based on NPC." You may need your parent for the first one just to make sure your numbers are right. But they should get easier as you go along.

Some NPCs ask if you know your EFC. You hopefully held onto that EFC number you got from the FAFSA4caster, so you can use this as a shortcut to avoid re-answering all the need-based eligibility questions that the NPC may ask.

EXAMPLE OF A PROBABLY ACCURATE NPC RESULT*

ESTIMATED NET PRICE	
Total Cost of Attendance	$71,337
Redlands Grants & Scholarships University of Redlands gift aid based on academic merit and financial need. Additional awards may be available. The aid amount does not need to be repaid by the student.	- $42,527
Federal Pell Grant Federal grant based on financial need, as determined by the FAFSA. A Pell Grant does not need to be repaid by the student.	- $1,545
Net Price of Attendance The net price of attendance includes both direct costs paid to University of Redlands and an allowance for estimated indirect costs. In 2018, 97% of our first time, full time students who enrolled received some form of financial aid.	$27,265
ESTIMATED BALANCE YOU WILL OWE UNIVERSITY OF REDLANDS	
Direct Costs of Attendance	$65,650
Grants and Scholarships Includes Redlands Grants & Scholarships, Federal Pell Grant	- $44,072
Federal Direct Student Loans Federal loans, which may include subsidized and unsubsidized Direct Loans	- $5,500
Redlands Loan	- $1,500
Estimated Balance You Will Owe University of Redlands	**$14,578**

Notice the difference between "Net Price" and "Estimated Balance"? The net price represents how much the student will end up paying eventually for their first year at this college. This includes the balance the family already paid plus indirect costs like airfare, books, and toilet paper plus loans...but not their interest. The estimated balance represents the first-year "bill" the family has to pay or arrange to pay (via private loans or payment plan) before the student starts.

Circle back to this step if significant changes occur regarding your merit (academic achievement) or your need (your family's financial situation) as these factors can change the results.

STEP 3: IF YOU HAVE IN-STATE SCHOOLS ON YOUR LIST, FIND OUT IF YOU QUALIFY FOR YOUR STATE'S AID PROGRAMS

Note: If none of your schools (including the private ones) are in your home state, skip to the next step. But if even one college is, take a minute to read this part.

---

* It asked a LOT of questions. Good job, University of Redlands!

Because you are a valuable future taxpayer, most states award money to students who choose to stay in their home states. Just like colleges, each state awards money differently. Some states have merit-based programs (good news for those with high GPAs and test scores), while others tend to focus on need-based aid (awesome news for those with low EFCs). Some states simply need you to submit a FAFSA with one school in your home state listed, while others require a more formal sign-up process for eligibility.

Action item: Google "state financial aid programs [name of your state]."* If you want a shortcut, use NASSGAP's Annual Survey (linked in the Treasure Trove) to find out if you qualify for state aid programs and do this:

- Go to the "State Data Check."
- Pick your state and the most recent year.
- Finally, select the "grant and non-grant" table and click "Go."
- Look under the undergraduate column to see need based (grant) and merit based (grant without a need component or non-grant).

Determining exactly how much state aid you'll get is sometimes difficult. Still, knowing if your state might help with college costs is important.

Tuition Exchanges and "Free College"

Some states (particularly those out west) have neighboring state exchange agreements. These allow students to pay the in-state rate at a neighboring state's institution. To see if this applies to you, google "tuition exchange agreements between states" or check out the NASFAA.org site linked in the Treasure Trove.

Some states (such as California and Tennessee) are also moving toward offering free community college to qualified state residents. Google "college promise" or "free college" and your state to see if you might be eligible.

---

*   Look for ".org" or ".gov" websites. Something officially published by the state or a college is most reliable.

Residency for Those with Unconventional Citizenship Statuses

Note to undocumented/DACA students and those with undocumented parents: In-state tuition and state-funded financial aid eligibility varies drastically from state to state. In some states, attending high school for three years and graduating in that state is enough to grant in-state tuition and access to aid. (Yay, Texas!) In other states, you have to jump through additional hoops to (hopefully) gain access, like through North Carolina's Residency Determination Service. In still other states, you may not even be eligible for admission at some state institutions. Don't get discouraged. Do your research ahead of time and you'll find a path to success. Check out uLeadnet.org for the most up-to-date information about your state.

Students who are in the United States on a visa (or are otherwise not U.S. citizens) should talk to a high school or college admission counselor to learn if you qualify for national (unlikely), state (possible), and/or institutional (most likely) aid.

Do you think you qualify? Great! Make note of how this will affect the cost of a school in your list.

Do you feel more knowledgeable now? You should. You now know more about financial aid than some college graduates. That's why you're going to graduate with less debt than they have. :)

How to Make a Balanced College List

There's a joke that a balanced school list takes into account three perspectives that you can chart on a Venn diagram:[†]

- The values of the student: Can I see myself there?
- The values of the school: Can we see you (the student) here?
- The values of the parent/caregiver: Can we afford it?

[†]   Shout-out to Jeff Durso-Finley for inspiring this diagram.

THE VENN DIAGRAM OF COLLEGE FIT

When the priorities of the college, student, and parent match, it's a "fit" school. So how do you go from more than twenty schools to around eight to ten fit schools?

MAKE SURE YOUR LIST IS FINANCIALLY FIT

Action item: Compare the net price calculator estimates for each of the schools on your preliminary list to your EFC generated by the FAFSA4caster. Categorize the results like this:

- NPC estimate price < EFC = Financial Safety (schools you could easily afford)
- NPC estimated price < EFC + $5,000 = Financial Possibility (schools you could reasonably afford with outside scholarships or federal loans)
- NPC estimated price > EFC + $5,000 = Financial Stretch (schools that would require lots of outside scholarships and private/parent loans)

In case this is confusing, here are some examples:

Amanda's Table of Financial Fit	College of Safety	Possibility U	St. Stretch College
Net Price Calculator Estimate	$6,000	$13,000	$17,000
EFC	$10,000	$10,000	$10,000
Difference	–$4,000	$3,000	$7,000
Verdict	**Safety**	**Possibility**	**Stretch**

Next, in the Financial Fit column of your College List and Essay Tracker, mark it:

- "Yes" if it's a financial Safety (you can probably afford it)
- "Maybe" if it's a financial Possibility (you can maybe afford it)
- "Probably Not" if it's a financial Stretch (you probably can't afford it)

This is where you might have to start making tough decisions about what to weed out of your list. A financially fit list will have at least one (but probably two or three) financial Safety schools, two or three Possibilities, and no more than one or two Stretches. So if you find yourself with more than two financial Stretches, the first place to start weeding is likely to figure out which of those are the one or two best, that you're really incredibly excited about, and take the other Stretches off the list.

If you find that you have only one financial Safety (or worse, none at all), you'll need to do more research to find out if there are some more schools that are both good fits and more affordable. Retrace your steps to see if a school that you had glanced at or overlooked before might actually be both affordable and somewhere you really like.

A positive note for you Division I/II sport recruits or scholarship prospects (e.g., music, dance, National Merit): be slightly more optimistic about a financial Stretch becoming a financial Possibility or even Safety. But remember, nothing is certain until it's guaranteed in writing. And you should definitely still do the following…

RESEARCH SCHOLARSHIPS!

Is a particular school you're interested in not looking like a financial fit? Institutional scholarships (i.e., scholarships offered by a school) are a great last resort to possibly tip the scales.

How do you find these?

Action item: Google "[name of college] scholarships." If the college is an out-of-state public university, try "[name of college] nonresident scholarships." Look on the college's website for any scholarships that you might be eligible/allowed to apply for. I mean really look. For like half an hour or more.

Scholarships come in many forms. That's why your high school counselors don't just hand you a list of them. They may be guaranteed (usually based on GPA and test scores and/or state residency), so you can feel comfortable factoring them into a school's financial fitness, but most are determined during the application process and aren't a sure thing. Be sure to read the scholarship policies for each school you're interested in.

The most heartbreaking conversations I've had with students are the ones when they've been accepted to an amazing college, learn it's too expensive, and then realize they could have qualified for big scholarship money from that college if they had only known to apply for the money before they were accepted.
AMANDA MILLER, COLLEGE AND FINANCIAL AID ADVISER

Quick note on scholarships at highly selective institutions: Think of a college that's really, really hard to get into. Yeah, it's probably not going to have many academic merit scholarships. Why? Because all the students getting in likely have ridiculous accolades. Plus, the college can charge whatever it likes and people who can afford it will pay. These institutions tend to be very, very generous to students with high need. So unless you play an instrument (very well), play a sport (very well), or manage to find a weird exception, you likely won't see many merit scholarship options at these schools.

Action item: Write down what you find out next to each college on your spreadsheet tracker. Confused about what you read on the school's website? Call or email the college's financial aid office to ask questions. They will be very happy to talk to you and not your parent. This is not only a very smart idea but also a great opportunity to practice "adulting" for college.

MAKE SURE YOUR LIST IS
ACADEMICALLY FIT

Go back to your College List and Essay Tracker and take a look at the schools you categorized as Likelies, Maybes, Reaches, and Wild Cards. If your list is weighted more toward schools that you have lower chances of getting into, you'll want to start being more selective about which ones you're going to put all the time and effort (and fees) into sending an application. Like with the financial Stretches, if you have more than one Wild Card, try to pick which one is really your dream school and lose the rest.

Also like with the financial Safeties, you'll need a solid foundation of Likelies—at least three. If you have fewer than that, again, retrace your steps to see what other options there might be.

RESEARCH THE REMAINING SCHOOLS ON YOUR PRELIMINARY LIST

This is where you'll dig deep and spend at least a few hours looking into all the schools on your list. You're basically researching the same kinds of things you were before (academics, programs, culture, location, values, etc.), but this time you're looking to see which schools make the final cut.

First, talk to your college counselor! They will be the most likely to know which schools might be a great fit for you. They can also tell you where students from your school and with your profile (scores, grades, extracurriculars) have been accepted in recent years.

Four Tips for Students at Large Public High Schools with Large Student-to-Counselor Ratios (a.k.a. How to Advocate for Yourself)
By college counselor Casey Rowley

1. Be in the know of your school's communication. Essentially, read your emails, check the counseling newsletter, and know what events are going on in your school.
2. Schedule a meeting early in the semester, like way earlier than you think. Counselors will often set a time in the year to meet with all juniors and seniors, but that doesn't mean that's the only time you can meet with them. Email your counselor or stop into the office and ask when you can have a meeting. You'll get more time with them beyond a quick scheduling meeting, and (bonus!) you'll be building rapport for later down the line.
3. Have a résumé and a document handy to help them write a stronger letter of recommendation. Add things like your future goals, any accomplishments,

or past challenges. Don't assume your counselor will know everything you've gone through. Hand them a brag sheet and do just that—brag!

4.   When it comes to requesting transcripts, letters of recommendation, and information like your regional admission counselor contact at a college, your counselor knows the protocols of your school and how to get things done. Ask for what you need and be patient.

Stop into their office to hand them a thank-you note or just to say hi. Not only will you make their day, but you'll also build a relationship that goes beyond the "I have a quick question." You have a counselor in your corner, and as busy as they seem, you'll be amazed by what a little hello or thank-you can do. And yes, this is a life lesson.

For the pro perspective, go to CollegeCountdown.com where you can pay a few bucks for online access to the *Fiske Guide to Colleges*.

For the student perspective, check out Niche.com or Unigo.com where you can read real students' opinions on their schools. And don't just read one or two reviews. Read a bunch of them; you'll get a sense of the school's vibe pretty quickly.

Try Visiting Some Colleges (if Practical)

Now is a good time to consider a college visit or tour, and schools make it easy for you to do this. Just google "[college name] tour" or "[college name] visit" to find out what options they offer.

But this can be expensive if you have to travel far. Or it might be difficult if you or your family have a busy schedule with work or other responsibilities. You definitely do not have to do this. Instead, check out online tours. Simply google or search on YouTube for the name of the school plus "tour," or use virtual tour sites like www.campusreel.org.

Another option to keep in mind is a fly-in program, which is when a college pays for your visit to their campus. You can find these for individual schools by googling "fly-in programs at [name of college]" or find an updated list of fly-in programs in the Treasure Trove.

Ten Tips for College Visits

Special thanks to college counselor Trevor Sturgeon for his contributions to this section.

1. Try to visit when classes are in session so you don't miss out on seeing what campus life is like. Notice the students and how they carry themselves. Do they seem stressed or not so much? (Be sure to take into account the time of the year—if it's Finals Week, for example.)

2. Visit your department of interest (if any). Try to ask your guide or, better yet, students or faculty in the department that look friendly and available some specific questions about the department.

3. Rather than doing just a "building tour" (which is basically you walking around campus looking at different buildings), try to meet with an admission officer. You can usually find out who the admission representative is for your geographical area on the school website or by googling. Email them asking if you can meet while you're there. It's best if the student does this, by the way, and not the parent. If they say yes, bring a few specific questions. This will help you assess the school's fit and help you write your "Why Us?" essay. You'll find a great list of questions to ask in the Treasure Trove.

4. See if the school has an option to stay on campus overnight with a current student. If not, find out if a graduate of your high school attends and ask if they would host you.

5. Eat in the school's cafeteria to get a sense of the vibe. Or try the local food scene in a restaurant close to campus.

6. Drive or take public transportation around the school's town/city to get a feel for the campus surroundings.

7. Explore on your own. Sometimes walking around independently provides observations different from what a guided tour would yield.

8. Read the bulletin boards and posted announcements; they're a quick and easy way to get a sense of what's happening on campus.

9. Talk to random students—you'd be surprised how willing most are to share once they know you're a prospective student.

10. Take pictures and notes while on tours. Especially if you're visiting several colleges in a short period—they will blend together! You may think you'll remember details, but chances are you'll be left thinking, "Wait, where did I see that?" or "Where did they say that?" Take notes during the info sessions too.

PICK TEN SCHOOLS FOR YOUR BALANCED LIST

Why ten? Because your goal is to divide your list like this…

- 1 Wild Card (1–10% chance of acceptance)
- 3 Reach (very low chance of acceptance)
- 3 Maybe (decent chance of acceptance)
- 3 Likely (good or very good chance of acceptance)

…with at least three financially fit schools. Ideally at least one of the financially fit schools will also be a "Likely" school.

Just as important as having a foundation of schools that you will likely be accepted to and can afford without straining your finances is being excited about all of them. Keep searching and researching until you're in love with all ten—yes, even the "Likely" schools—because you can and will. Most schools have a ton to offer, and many (probably more than you think) will connect with your needs, desires, goals, and values. (Tip: If applying to the University of California schools, count them as one. The application and personal insight questions will be the same for all the UC schools to which you apply.)

THE IMPORTANCE OF HAVING A
BALANCED COLLEGE LIST

Most students initially put a bunch of super-selective schools on their list (meaning they have an acceptance rate below ten percent) and not enough schools that are easier to get into.

You might say, "Hey, it's great to dream!" But I can't emphasize how important it is to list schools that you know you can get into—and that you also like. It will relieve SO MUCH STRESS throughout this process.

Why? I tend to see two types of students go through this process:

1. Students who are stressed because they're placing all their happiness in a chance at getting into a school that has less than a ten percent acceptance rate, and
2. Students who are not super stressed because, even though they may be applying to schools with a less than ten percent acceptance rate, they have

a number of schools on their list where they could be happy—and where they have at least a sixty percent chance of acceptance.

Be the second type. All it takes is an open mind and a little research.

Words of Wisdom from an Admission Officer
Beware of "Brand-name-itis"
Adrienne Amador Oddi, Dean of Admission at Trinity College

The media often highlights the same fifty to one hundred schools, and it's very easy to gravitate toward a familiar name. But just because you haven't heard of a school doesn't mean it's not right for you. I hope students (and maybe, more importantly, parents and high school administrators) will keep an open mind in this process. Approaching college decisions with bold individuality allows for the true consideration of unknowns.

We miss a huge opportunity to guide a student through a really thoughtful process when we focus on names and rankings. In focusing on rankings, we take a process that should be very internally driven and flip it to one that is externally driven. Every college and university produces some amazing graduates. Helping students realize that they are in the driver's seat of their lives will give them the freedom to choose a place where they will flourish, even if it's a place that is unfamiliar. This is an exciting time to learn about yourself and to begin to take ownership of building your life. I'd hate for a ranking to lead someone to a place that isn't going to allow them to build the life they want to lead. So students—be bold! Blaze trails! Have the courage to explore the unknown. For some, you may find that the life you want to build is one that starts at a top-ranked institution. For most, you'll find that many colleges will help you build an amazing life.

In the Treasure Trove, you'll find:
→ More resources to help you figure out what you're looking for in a college
→ More resources for finding great colleges
→ A list of college lists you can search for on CollegeXpress (Examples: "gay-friendly colleges" or "colleges going green")
→ Podcast: "Which Schools Are the Most Generous with Financial Aid?"

→ Sample College List and Essay Tracker spreadsheet [Template]

→ A list of great questions to ask on your college visit

→ An updated list of fly-in programs

→ NASSGAP's Annual Survey (to find out if you qualify for state aid programs)

Early Decision and Early Action

Most colleges offer one of two main application options. There's Regular Decision, when the school reviews applications and makes decisions within a certain time frame, or Rolling Admissions, when they review applications and make decisions on a first-come-first-serve rolling basis as they're submitted. But some offer options for applicants who want to join pools of students who get their applications in early—Early Decision and Early Action, with all the pros and cons that come with those admission plans.

So, should you apply early? As counselors, we joke that the answer to every college admission question begins with "It depends…" This feels especially true for this question.

In this chapter, we'll cover:

- Your early application options
- Who should think about Early Decision
- Where Early Action fits in
- How to decide

Your Early Application Options

- **Early Decision (ED):** This is binding, and you can only apply to one school via ED. If you get in, you have to withdraw all your other applications and attend. ED applications are usually due in November, though a few schools have earlier deadlines. Some colleges have two rounds of ED: EDI and EDII (fall and winter).

- **Early Action (EA):** This is nonbinding, so you can apply to several colleges via Early Action. Even if you're accepted, you don't have to attend. EA applications are also usually due in November, but a few schools have earlier deadlines.
- **Restrictive Early Action (REA):** This is also nonbinding, but colleges that offer this don't want you applying to any binding programs at the same time.* Like EA and ED, REA applications are typically due in November.

Note about ED II: The addition of the ED II option (a second round of ED) is a growing trend and basically plays cleanup for all of the students who got dinged by one of the more selective colleges during ED I. More importantly, it also gives students a great opportunity to improve their academic trend, GPA, and test scores and still be able to choose their favorite college and show the strongest level of interest possible. Finally, ED II gives students more time to research, visit colleges, discuss finances with family members, and get recommendations from teachers that might have been harder to wrangle in October.

THE BEST CANDIDATES FOR EARLY DECISION

It's hard to say *in general*. As I said, it depends. On what? Three things.

1. **It depends on you.** If you can check these boxes, you might consider applying for Early Decision:

   ❐ I am totally in love with this college, and I would absolutely attend if accepted.

   ❐ I have done thorough research and can name at least five clear, specific reasons why this college is a perfect match for me.

   ❐ I've visited the campus and know I could be happy there. Or if I haven't visited the campus, I know enough about it to know that I could be happy there.

---

* Important exception: REA means students cannot apply ED/EA to other schools, except to state universities. This exception allows families to hear back from lower-tuition public schools. It also gives students leeway to consider several EA offers.

❐   My grades, test scores, extracurricular activity profile, and the support from my school are so good that I (and my counselor, if I have one) feel I have a reasonable chance of getting in.

OR:

❐   I'm a recruited athlete and the coach loves me and has let me know—either in person or in writing—that I'm an official recruit who will have their full support in the admission process. (And you may even be asked to submit your application through the coach. It's a good idea to have your school counselor contact admissions to make sure that everyone is on the same page—admissions, coach, and student. It's also a good idea to have visited the campus and spent some quality time with your future coach and teammates.)

Here's a flowchart[†] that maps all this out:

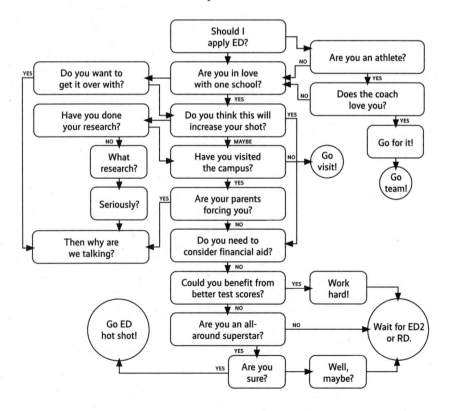

[†]   Shout-out to my friend and colleague Susan Dabbar from Admission Smarts for putting this chart together.

2. **It depends on money.** If you're accepted Early Decision, the college will put together a financial aid package and send your family a bill and that can get, well, complicated. So make sure you can also check this box:

   ☐   The school is a good financial fit, and I'll likely be able to afford to attend regardless of the financial aid package they give me.

3. **It depends on the school.** Some schools value ED more than others. How do we know? Some schools fill a good portion (over half) of their class in the early application rounds. Further, if you compare the Regular Decision acceptance rate to that of Early Decision, some schools have *way* different numbers. For example, the Regular Decision acceptance rate for one school* last year was around ten percent, while their Early Decision acceptance rate was around thirty percent. That's three times higher!

But not every school's ED rate is three times higher than its Regular Decision rate. And wouldn't it be nice to know the statistics for all schools? In fact, wouldn't it be cool if someone assembled a spreadsheet that compared the Early Decision and Regular Decision acceptance rates for hundreds of colleges? Fortunately, someone has. Well, two someones.

In the Treasure Trove, you'll find a spreadsheet compiled by Jennie Kent and Jeff Levy that aggregates the Early Decision and Regular Decision data for over three hundred schools.† That spreadsheet also includes the percentage of the class filled during the Early Decision round.

Words of Wisdom from the Dean

Lee Ann Backlund, Dean of Admission and Financial Aid and Vice President for Enrollment Planning at Sewanee

Students who have done their research, visited an array of schools, and identified their dream school may decide to apply through a binding Early Decision program. While this may be a great option for some, students who need to compare

---

*   To find out which school, check out the chart in the Treasure Trove.

†   I'm not printing it here in the book, as Jeff and Jennie update it each year and I want you to have the most updated copy—so check it out in the Treasure Trove.

financial aid awards should wait to apply in either early action or regular decision rounds. Before making the decision to apply to a school through an Early Decision plan, families should be confident that it makes sense for their pocketbook as well as their futures. There are plenty of tools at your disposal (the most accessible of which will be a school's net price calculator—not a promise, but a good estimate of expected cost), so be sure to speak with the admission officer or financial aid officer at the school before applying under an Early Decision plan.

Know that you will still have great options if you don't apply Early Decision. This is an important commitment, so take your time, spend time on campuses, and be realistic about what you can afford.

What about Early Action?

Applying EA may or may not increase your chances of admission, but it can't hurt unless you need to count senior year grades (to bring up your GPA), achieve higher test scores (because your current scores are just okay), or need more time to write a really great application. If you need more time to do some or all these things, you may want to apply Regular Decision.

Getting an early acceptance in your senior year reduces stress and may shorten your college list. The downside? You may get bad news earlier in your senior year before you get any good news. But this can be important feedback! You may have overestimated your chances of being admitted to the colleges on your list; thus, you may need to make adjustments, and knowing earlier is better than knowing later.

How to Decide

First, go back through your research. Make sure you've completed the college search process on pages 41–50, which means you should at least go through a process of self-discovery to learn what you want and research a bunch of colleges.

Before you decide if you're going to apply to a school early, you'll want to be sure that the potential college is really perfect for you. Make absolutely sure you can check the boxes on page 68. And then you'll also need to run that school's net price calculator (page 54) to make sure you'll be able to afford it, even if they don't give you as good of a financial aid package as other schools might.

Finally, take note of whether the college's ED and Regular Decision acceptance rates differ all that much and whether or not they fill a large percentage of their class via Early Decision relative to other schools. (Sixty percent is definitely a large percentage while ten percent is not.)

TALK TO YOUR COUNSELOR

Your counselor (if you have one) will be able to advise you based on both your academic profile and their knowledge of how students from your school have fared in recent years during early application rounds at the school(s) you're considering. But again, don't base your decision *only* on this information. Weigh your counselor's advice in the context of all the other factors you're weighing and make sure you're clear on how that school will help you explore and expand upon your core values.

In the Treasure Trove, you'll find:

→ "Should You Apply Early Decision or Regular Decision? (And the Chart That Can Help You Decide)"—Podcast with Jennie Kent and Jeff Levy

→ The spreadsheet listing the ED and RD acceptance rates for hundreds of schools

Chapter 6

Demonstrated Interest

*Special thanks to Monica James for her contributions to this chapter**

At this point, you hopefully have a list full of colleges that you love. Probably some of those colleges would be interested in knowing that. This chapter will tell you how (and why) you should let them know.

In this chapter, we'll cover:

- What demonstrated interest is and why it's important
- How colleges track demonstrated interest
- Whether or not you should demonstrate interest
- How to demonstrate interest
- Four steps for building a relationship with a college admission rep

What Demonstrated Interest (DI) Is

Simply put, demonstrated interest is something many colleges and universities use to get insight into how likely a student is to yield (i.e., actually enroll at their college if accepted). Why do they want to know this? Because yield is one of the factors that helps them manage their enrollment numbers and impacts

---

*   In the Treasure Trove, you'll find links to my podcast with Monica James on this topic, plus the longer version of this chapter.

rankings. Very important to them, but not so much to you. But what's very important to you is that, **for schools that track DI, it can make a difference in whether they accept an application.**

A Few Ways That Colleges Track Demonstrated Interest:*

- Interactions with you at college fairs and inquiry card submission (or scan)
- Whether you attend regional information sessions or college rep visits to your high school
- Campus visits you make and campus info sessions/tours you attend
- Whether you apply early (Early Decision or Early Action)
- Your "Why Us?" essay reflecting enthusiasm and thoughtful research on how that particular school fits your interests
- Speaking with alumni or students who may share information about your interest with the admission office
- Your interview with admission reps or alumni
- Whether you attend an overnight program (if available)
- Your contact with admission reps
- Whether you've met with faculty on campus or by phone

What You Should Do about Demonstrated Interest

A few options:

- **Nothing.** That's right. You can just keep getting good grades and participating in the activities and projects you love and keep living your awesome life. *So there is literally nothing that you have to do differently now that you know all of this.* You can still get into a great school without demonstrating interest.

But if you've read this and you're thinking, "Okay, I could probably go to a college fair and maybe reach out to an admission rep, and I could maybe even follow the school on social media," then here's what to do first:

---

* This info is from a presentation given at a recent conference by a few college admission counselors who track demonstrated interest, and which you can find in the Treasure Trove.

- **Make sure you've fully developed your college list.** Why do this first? So you don't stress yourself out trying to demonstrate interest for, like, twenty schools, some of which you may not apply to anyway. But you should have a nice, trim list of eight to ten schools by now (if you don't, go back to page 41).
- **From your list, pick three or four schools you're most excited about and to which you'd like to demonstrate some interest.** This will go further in keeping everything even more manageable, but…
- **(Important!) Make sure that each of these schools actually tracks demonstrated interest, and know that many of the most selective universities do not track it.** How do you find out which schools track demonstrated interest? Google the school's Common Data Set and scroll down to section C7 to find out what the school considers important when making admission decisions.

Should I demonstrate interest if a school does consider demonstrated interest for admission decisions?

If you want to improve your chances of admission, yes.

What if I'm really excited about a school that does not track demonstrated interest?

Still do your research, visit campus (in person or online), and maybe even get to know the admission officer for your area (if there is one). But do so knowing that it isn't likely to score you any demonstrated interest points—or at least that's what the school is reporting publicly.

To simplify: consider demonstrating interest if (a) there's a school you're super excited about attending and (b) that school actually tracks demonstrated interest.

If You Want to Demonstrate Some Interest, Here's When and How to Do It

Okay, with all those qualifiers in place, here are thirteen ways you can demonstrate interest, adapted from Lisa Rubin-Johnson's great article "How Do I Love Thee? Demonstrated Interest and How Colleges Count the Ways."

Thirteen Ways You Can Demonstrate Interest (in Order of the Admission Process)

1. **Get on the school's email list (2 minutes).** Google the school's name and "information request form," then fill out that form.

2. **Open the emails you receive from a school and click on something in the email (3–5 minutes).** That's right: actually read the emails they send you. Do it mostly because, hey, you may learn something! But some schools track open rates and whether you clicked on something in the email. So consider clicking on something of interest, and maybe even spend a few minutes reading the page it sends you to. While you're on the site:

3. **"Click deep" on the school's website (15–30 minutes).** This is my friend Michelle Myers's phrase. It basically means doing research to learn, for example, if the school has a rad program perfect for you. This will not only help you eventually write your "Why Us?" essay (if the school asks for one), but it will also prep you for a potential conversation with your regional rep when you...

4. **Attend a college fair (2–3 hours).** For tips on making the most of a college fair experience, check out College Essay Guy Podcast episode 107 with Maria Furtado and read the accompanying blog post.

5. **Follow the school on social media (5–10 minutes).** Google which social media platforms the school uses, follow or like their pages, and maybe even share or retweet something.

6. **Visit campus (time depends on distance).** This isn't possible for everyone, but if you're within a couple hours from the school, it's a good idea (because if you do live close to the school but never visit, a school might wonder why). Make sure they've got some record you were there by signing up for a tour or meeting with a rep.

7. **Interview (3–4 hours, including preparation and travel).** Some schools have interviews, some don't—you can find out by googling. If they do, then do the interview. An alumni interview is fine; an interview with your regional rep (i.e., the person who will read your application) is better. You can find more tips on interviews on page 267. Note that in that chapter, I begin by asking, "Does the interview matter?" Spoiler alert: for schools that track demonstrated interest, the interview totally matters.

8. **Supplemental essays (time will vary, but you'll have to write these anyway if you're applying).** The big one is the "Why Us?" essay where you

get a chance to show the school why you feel you'd be a great fit for one another. If the school is (actually) your first choice, say that in your "Why Us?" essay. Lots more tips on how to write that essay are on page 196.

9. **Apply Early Action or Early Decision (no extra time).** Check out page 67 for an entire chapter on Early Action and Early Decision.

10. **Submit your application before the deadline (no extra time).** This is especially true for schools that read applications on a rolling basis (in other words, in the order applications are submitted). As Monica James says on the podcast, "Better to be the first oboe player that a reader reads than the sixth!"

11. **Thank-you notes and emails (10–15 minutes).** Hello, life skill. Spend a few minutes following up after an interview or college fair meeting with a little, "Thanks for talking with me!" You can ask a follow-up question if you'd like to keep the conversation going, but don't go crazy with this.

12. **Follow wait-list instructions (10 minutes–2 hours, depending on the school).** If you've been wait-listed by a school, do whatever they tell you—including the optional stuff. They may, for example, ask you to fill out a simple form declaring your interest. Or they may let you submit one more letter—either a recommendation or a brief statement of additional information. (Send the one rec letter, not six, and only include new information if you take the latter option.) The school website will tell you what to do. If you can't find the info, give the school a quick call to ask (and take careful notes).

13. **Contact your regional rep (10–30 minutes).** This person is your main contact point at the school and offers one of the best options for establishing a personal relationship with the decision-makers.

Words of Wisdom from an Admission Officer

Reon Sines-Sheaff, Director of International Admissions at College of Wooster

This is an interesting time in higher education. Technology has encouraged students to apply to a larger number of colleges and at the same time, more colleges now use technology to track students' demonstrated interest. Colleges know that students may have applied to ten or fifteen schools—so how do they figure out if the student is really interested in them? An admission officer sitting at their computer can see if a student has been opening our emails, responding to them, or skipping them. When they read an application, they can easily find out whether a student has completed an interview, attended a high school visit with an admission officer from our school, or has reached out with questions. And many schools ask "Why are you interested in _____ College/University?" This is an important response. Students who know something about the college or have connected with it in some way (even by looking at the program website for their academic interest and mentioning a great program we have) can really add another dimension to their applications and stand out from the crowd.

I work with international students and they often ask if there is a penalty if they can't visit campus or if they're not able to meet me on the road; my answer is certainly not! Easy and free ways to connect include virtual interviews, emailing an admission officer to express interest and ask good questions (questions that are not easily found online), or even simply writing back to say thank you when you receive an email from your admission officer.

Engaging in any way you can certainly bring rewards!

All right, at this point, you might be saying...

This all sounds exhausting and I don't feel like doing it.

Great, then don't! You do *not* have to do any of the thirteen things mentioned earlier. Colleges will still read your application and you will be considered for admission. Assuming you have good grades and test scores, have followed all the directions on the application, and (this is important) have developed a balanced college list, you'll end up at a great school where you can get a great education and find happiness.

But before you decide not to do anything, remember: You don't have to do all thirteen things for all eight to ten schools you're applying to, and you certainly don't have to do them all in one day or even one week. You might just pick a couple of schools that you're certain track demonstrated interest, then pick a few things from the list of thirteen and do those.

Or it might be that you do want to reach out to the school but just aren't sure how. If that's the case...

Build Relationships with College Admission Reps

Why reach out personally? Here's a quick anecdote to show you why. A few years ago I was chatting with a rep at a selective school and a student came up to him and said hello and reintroduced himself. The rep said, "Oh, yeah, I remember you!" and they chatted for, like, a minute and a half, then the student said goodbye. Once the student left, I asked the rep, "What do you think? Good chance of getting in?"

"Oh, he's in," the rep said.

"Really?" I said. "If he's got As?"

"Oh, even Bs. He's a great kid. He was my student ambassador when I visited his school—we'd love to have him."

I don't know if that student ultimately ended up at that school, but his demonstrated interest game was on point.

Four Steps for Building an Authentic Relationship with a College Admission Rep

1. **Search the school's website to find out who your regional rep is.** This is as easy as googling; for example, "Davidson College regional reps."

2. **Email your rep and ask a question you are genuinely interested in.** If, for example, you've looked at the school's website (important if!) and have been unable to find out if your rep will be in your area sometime soon, you might write briefly to say, "Hi! I'm wondering if you might be in the Bay Area (or wherever you live) sometime soon, as I'm excited to apply to your school and I'd love to meet you." Or you might ask something really specific like, "Hi! I'm writing to find out if first-year students enrolled in the School of Speech can easily take advanced courses in Journalism, as I know that they're separate schools. But I'm especially excited to apply to your school because I know it has great programs for both of my interests: Communication Studies and Journalism." Then sign off with a simple "Thank you!" and add your name and your high school's name.

   Pro Tip: I've even seen some students create a simple signature for their emails where they pop in a headshot so reps can attach their name to a face.

3. **Keep the email conversation going (for a little bit).** Not forever, just a

couple emails. How? Ask a question at the end of each email. Careful: this can get annoying after more than two or three, so don't go crazy with this. And make sure you don't email until you have a good and real question. You might, for example, ask if they're going to be in your area visiting other schools and see if they might have time in their schedule to visit your school (make sure to check with your counselor first!). But treat this like you're having an actual, in-person conversation at a college fair. Speaking of which:

4. **If the rep is coming to a college fair near you, go meet them!** Especially if you won't or may not be able to visit the campus. And if you've already met the rep because they visited your school, still go and just say hello.

Wait, is it okay to contact a school directly?

"Yes! Students should always feel comfortable reaching out to the admission office and their assigned regional admission representative with questions. In fact, many schools list their admission team on their website. Students are often also allowed to input their home state or country to see their admission rep's contact info. Additionally, schools that use demonstrated interest in their evaluative process take these outreach efforts into account. Any engagement is an additional point to show a student is really interested. With the development of customer relationship management (CRM) systems, we are able to see that engagement as it is linked to a student record."

—Jamiere Abney, Senior Assistant Dean of Admission and Coordinator of Outreach for Opportunity and Inclusion, Colgate University

"Generally speaking, I feel college admission officers are attracted to this field because of the strong elements of connection and relationship building involved. It's no surprise that 'counselor' is often included in our title or job description. We want to hear from students and help them through the process!"

—Mandy Herrera, Assistant Director of International Admissions at Elon University

---

In the Treasure Trove, you'll find:

→   A huge Wiki list of Common Data Sets

→   Podcast episode 108: "Demonstrated Interest: How to Build Authentic Relationships with Colleges (and Why It's a Good Idea)"

→   Blog post: "Demonstrated Interest: A Brief and Practical How-To Guide"

Part IV

The College Application

Adrian's Brainstorming Exercises

"You can't make a student taller. But you can help them stand up straighter."

UNKNOWN ADMISSION OFFICER

Here's the challenge of the college application: your life represents a series of moments, memories, essences, values, and choices…and the college application asks you to squeeze all that beautiful chaos into a finite set of boxes. But challenges are often engaging, instructive, and gratifying, and making sure you make the most of your application (and your application makes the most of you) might be one of the most interesting challenges in your life so far.

I sadly don't know who said the quote above, but it's brilliant. And while the resources in this chapter (and book!) can't make you taller, they can help you stand up straighter.

In this chapter, we'll cover:

- An example of the brainstorming exercises that will yield content for several parts of the application
- An example of an activities list section

I'm going to share with you the first step that one student, Adrian, took to stand up straighter in his application. Right now, I'll share his brainstorming work. Then when we've reached the end of the process, you'll get to see his completed application. You'll see notes in the margin both Adrian and I made during and after the brainstorming process. Afterward I'll walk you through the same exercises and show you, step-by-step, how to turn them into a great application.

Why am I sharing an example before I teach you how to do this for yourself? Because I want you to see a "before" picture that we can use as a point of reference later. But heads up: You do not have to be like Adrian. Be like you.

Adrian's Essence Objects List

1. Chipped reed(s)
2. Fish Legs ← Adrian: Nickname from my swimming teammates.
3. Tacos (asada and pastor)
4. Toothpaste ← Ethan: This will be in his Stanford short answers.
5. Controllers
6. Scratching pole (a.k.a. my legs)
7. Bookshelf
8. Water polo ball (Blueberry) ← Adrian: This will become the start of my main essay.
9. Goggles tied together ← Ethan: You'll notice that water polo and swimming appear quite a few times in the brainstorming work.
10. Blue heron
11. Full set of dragon balls
12. Broken frying pan ← Adrian: "Experimenting in the kitchen" (ended up in my Stanford roommate essay).
13. Atlas Shrugged
14. Rom coms
15. Curly hair ← Ethan: Represents Adrian's little brother, who will appear in his main essay.
16. Rulers and compasses
17. Clickers
18. Tangled ties and cables ← Adrian: Without a dad I had to teach myself how to tie a tie, an example of the things I picked up on my own. The cables are meant to be a few things I picked up working construction.
19. Dusk/Dawn
20. Origami stars

Adrian's Values Exercise

Top 10

→ Hunger

→ Growth

→ Autonomy

→ Balance

→ Self-discipline

→ Patience

→ Curiosity

→ Leadership

→ Competition

→ Vulnerability

Top 5

→ Autonomy

→ Hunger

→ Balance

→ Curiosity

→ Self-discipline

Top 3

→ Autonomy

→ Balance

→ Hunger

#1

→ Hunger

Adrian's 21 Details

1. I'm a sucker for romantic movies like *The Notebook* and I'm overdue for a rewatching of it.

2. I tend to overlook my victories and accomplishments by hastily setting even higher goals.

3. I used to read so much it became dangerous. I would even read while walking and climbing stairs.

4. As much as I say I love Disney, I've never watched any *Lion King* movie.

5. I have an unexplainable disturbance with Starbucks.

6. Although I play various musical instruments, namely the oboe and saxophone, I cannot sight read.

7. "Jupiter, the Bringer of Jollity" is my favorite planet in Gustav Holst's *The Planets*, second to "Mars, the Bringer of War"

   Ethan: This will connect to Adrian's personal statement.

8. I take being called "normal" as an insult.

9. One of my proudest moments is being accidentally called dad by my younger brother.

10. I prefer to do anything school-related barefoot because I feel shoes and socks block my creativity.

11. After thirteen years of experimenting, I've finally found a haircut that matches me.

12. One of my flaws is that I will care more about others than I do myself.

13. I have an obsession with knowledge, and a passion for math and science.

14. K-pop metal is one of my all-time favorite internet discoveries.

    Ethan: This will end up being a supplemental essay topic for several schools.

15. I have uncontrollable random laughing fits that have gotten me into more trouble than I can remember.

16. I've almost drowned three times, and I didn't learn to swim until I was fourteen, yet my life is now centered in water.

17. I've attempted suicide, but never told anyone. Now I want to help anyone I can going through anything similar.

18. Autocorrect has ruined my spelling.

19. I have a love/hate relationship with pineapple.

20. My biggest obstacle in high school was learning to accept and look for help when I drastically needed it.

21. I've yet to have a pair of glasses last me more than a year.

Adrian's "Everything I Want Colleges to Know About Me" List

1. I was born in Mexico City, Mexico.

   Adrian: This will set up the immigration portion of my main personal statement.

2. My mom, grandma, dad, older brother, and I immigrated to the USA when I was about four years old.

3. My first English word was "tree," and I'll never forget it.

4. I was bullied in elementary school for having trouble speaking English, being behind on math and science, and being weak.

5. My passion for reading was ignited by J. K. Rowling.

6. I started tutoring other kids and neighbors circa fifth grade in math, followed by English soon after (still doing it today but in various other subjects!).

7. My favorite book is *A Solitary Blue* by Cynthia Voigt because of how connected I feel to the protagonist.

8. My dad was arrested and deported when I was six for domestic violence against my family.

    Ethan: This will also end up in his personal statement.

9. Aside from tutoring, my first "real" job was helping put up flyers for a nearby laundromat when I was about eleven years old.

10. I started working construction when I was fourteen to help pay bills at home and cover my own expenses.

    Ethan: This will also end up in his personal statement.

11. After my dad was gone, my older brother and I stepped up and took over various responsibilities at home to make life easier for one another and to help our mom.

    Ethan: This will be in his main statement too.

12. When my little brother was born, my older brother and I took a big part in raising and taking care of him.

13. My grandma was deported when I was about nine years old, leaving just my mom, my brothers, and I in the United States.

14. Being an illegal immigrant has been pretty scary. Growing up, I felt alienated from my classmates, as I was left out of field trips, camping trips, and other free programs because my mom was afraid of anyone finding out we were undocumented.

15. My grades began to drop between eighth grade and the first semester of my high school sophomore year because I felt as an immigrant that college apps would be impossible, and finding a stable job would be even harder.

16. I was planning to drop out my sophomore year and continue working construction to support my family.

17. I've been captain of my high school swim team and water polo team, breaking a swim record and being nominated for the All American in water polo too.

    Ethan: This will go into his Activities List, with contextual notes in his Additional Info section.

18. I revived my school's California Scholarship Federation charter as its president for two years and helped various classmates through their college apps in the process.

    Ethan: This will become a supplemental essay topic of his.

19. I was the first student to pass the AP Physics 1 exam at my school as well as the first student of two to take AP Physics 2 and as of now am the only one at my school to pass the exam.

    Ethan: This will go into his Additional Info section.

20. I had the highest SAT score in my class.

21. I play various instruments, mainly the oboe and tenor saxophone.

22. I was awarded number one male athlete of my high school class as well as student athlete.

Ethan: These will go into his Awards and Honors section.

23. I ran a successful coloring book drive for a children's hospital, collecting nearly 700 coloring books and about 300 packs of colors (crayons and pencils).

24. I have an insatiable hunger for knowledge that only seems to expand as I continue to learn more and more.

Adrian: This will be the ending of my main personal statement.

Ethan: This will end up in his personal statement too.

Adrian's Feelings and Needs Exercise

Challenges	Effects	Feelings	Needed	What I did	What I learned
Family separated twice because of domestic violence	Mom had to take up two jobs Dad was deported Brother and I took bigger responsibilities at home and with our little brother	Confused, yet understanding Anxious Worried Relieved Alone	Order Autonomy Reassurance Growth	Started working to help with bills Took charge of myself and my little brother	I taught myself how to learn To move on Strength Gained purpose
Grandma was deported	Lost a big part of my family Made me realize our position as immigrants	Lost Vulnerable Lonely	Safety Understanding Empathy	Found a way to stay connected with my family across the border Looked to make connection with people going through something similar	Distance can be conquered I was not alone
Being/realizing I am an undocumented immigrant	My grades slipped Lost my drive I couldn't travel far Certain disadvantages like not being able to find work as easily	Disconnected Alone Heartbroken Ashamed Disillusioned	Hope Support Self-acceptance	Researched exactly how my status affected me I've begun to take steps that may lead to me gaining citizenship I sought hope in the endeavors of other undocumented students	Understand what I can and can't do That my status does and will not affect my abilities I can accomplish just as much as anyone else.

Ethan: This will end up in his personal statement too.

Adrian's Activities List (First Draft)

→ **Tutoring**

I tutored neighbors, classmates, and occasionally parents. Material ranged from math to English to science.

→ **Construction/remodeling**

I helped remodel various apartments.

→ **Swim Varsity (9–12) Captain for 11–12**

Participated in School Swim team for all four years. Practice and work out daily, competed at the city level

→ **President of CSF (11–12)**

A statewide organization to honor outstanding high school students

→ **Water Polo (9, 10, 12) Captain for 12**

Participated in the varsity team of Water Polo of Panorama as goalie for all years. Captain for senior year.

→ **Chem Club (12)**

Discuss college level chemistry topics. Ex: stoichiometry, organic chemistry, quantum mechanics, etc. Ran a community water quality lab.

→ **Advanced Band/Orchestra (10)**

First oboe in Advanced Band and Orchestra. Performed at music festivals and competitions.

Adrian's Additional Information Section (First Draft)
Adrian initially left this blank.

Ethan writing again: I *love* reading over these, as I learn in ten minutes what might otherwise take me weeks or months to learn about someone. He completed these over the course of a week as part of the prework that I gave to him. I assign these exercises to all my students before beginning the brainstorming process. And here's a quick rundown of about how long each exercise takes:

- Essence Objects Exercise: 10–12 minutes; 20 if you want to do a thorough job. (Already completed on page 2!)
- Values Exercise: 4–5 minutes (Already completed on page 5!)
- 21 Details Exercise: around 20 minutes

- Everything I Want Colleges to Know about Me Exercise: at least 20 minutes
- Feelings and Needs Exercise: 15 minutes; 20–25 minutes for a more thorough job
- Activities List (first draft): around 20 minutes
- Additional Info (first draft): depends on how much you have to explain

That may sound like a lot of prework, but keep in mind that a thorough job on these exercises will save you tons of time later.

OKAY, IT'S CHOOSE YOUR OWN ADVENTURE TIME...

What you've just read is Adrian's "before" shot. If you want to see how these materials turned into an actual application (a.k.a. the "after" shot), turn to the "Values Scan" chapter on page 277 and check out the final version of Adrian's application.

If, on the other hand, you're ready to get started on your own application, turn the page.

Essential Application Prework*

Your turn.

In the next few pages I'll guide you through the exercises I've used—and still use!—with students. Why do I use these exercises? Because after trying many since 2003, I've found these to be the most efficient, practical, deep, and fun.

In this chapter, we'll cover the:

- 21 Details Exercise
- Everything I Want Colleges to Know About Me Exercise
- Feelings and Needs Exercise
- Preliminary Activities and Awards list

If you want to see what's in the actual Google doc I share prior to a first one-on-one meeting (and download a Google doc version for yourself!), go to the Treasure Trove.

Have you been following along and completed the Essence Objects and Values Exercises already? If so, skip to the third exercise. If not, please do those now.

---

* "Prework" maybe isn't the best description for what you're about to do since the following exercises aren't preparation for your application work, they are the actual work.

ESSENCE OBJECTS EXERCISE

Time: 12–15 minutes

Instructions: Turn to page 2 for this exercise.

VALUES EXERCISE

Time: 5 minutes

Instructions: Turn to page 5 for this exercise.*

21 DETAILS EXERCISE

Time: 15–20 minutes

Instructions:

On a blank sheet of paper (or below), make a list of twenty-one details from your life. These can be interesting facts about you or different, random parts of who you are.

Here's a sample 21 Details written by one of my students. My notes are in the margins.

1. I went to a Jewish private school for the first twelve years of my life and hated it with a passion. It wasn't until after I left that I began to appreciate it, and it also allowed me to meet my very best friend. I wrote a piece on it.

    This detail led to a supplemental essay topic.

2. I have four younger siblings who it took me a long time to appreciate. My little sister, Jenna, is my favorite person in the universe (even when she takes my clothes). I also had two pet birds who flew away when we moved. :(

3. I am annoyingly tall. I never stop growing.

4. I grew up in the mountains. It's a significant part of who I am.

    This ended up in a short supplemental essay.

5. After reading *A Mango-Shaped Space* in third grade, I announced that I had synesthesia and I still use it for all my passwords ($Synesthesia4607#8† is certainly a secure password.)

6. I think my parents are the most amazing people on this earth but

    I love her voice here. let her know that she could bring this tone/ sense of humor to her essays (and she did).

---

*   You'll find videos of me guiding you through the Essence Objects and Values Exercises in the Treasure Trove.

†   This password has been changed, of course.

I cannot stand the sound of them chewing. Like anyone else, I'm okay. My parents? I have to leave the room.

7. I have all of my clothes (seriously, all of them) organized in an app in my phone so that I never repeat outfits.

8. When I was seven, I watched House, MD dissect a brain on TV and a week later announced I wanted to be a surgeon. This has never changed.

9. Everyone associates me with the color sky blue.

10. I really, really enjoy meeting new people (especially if they haven't heard my jokes yet).

11. I constantly get made fun of for being unathletic and for "walking weird." Not my fault!

12. I began drawing in 6th grade on a trip to Israel to meet up with a friend. My parents sent me on the twelve-hour flight alone; I had to find *something* to do.

    a. *Big part of life in 7th–8th grade because I switched schools and didn't have tons of friends, so connected with drawing community on Instagram.*

    b. *Led to stereotypeproject.org.*

13. People come to me to help them write their Instagram captions and for inspirational advice (best of both worlds!).

14. I dyed my hair blonde and chopped it short in 8th grade after being rejected from my top choice high school. It took so long to grow back.

15. I skipped 3rd grade, which is the grade you learn script. Thus, I have the worst handwriting on the planet.

16. I hate wasabi so much. I can handle other spicy things, but wasabi and horseradish freak me out. I can taste it even if it just brushes the other food.

17. If I could never sleep, I would. I think it's a huge waste of time. I almost always wake up naturally before my alarm and can't sleep past 10 a.m. on weekends.

18. Both my parents are from Chicago so I've been there more times than I can count. Chicago is better than New York 100 times.

19. I've walked on fire and I'm a certified scuba diver.

20. When I was little, my dad would go on business trips a lot and catch

These details don't have to make sense. You're brainstorming. Have fun, as she's doing.

She did not include this fact in her "Why NYU?" essay.

flights at 6, 7 a.m. I would always wake up with him at 5 a.m. and
eat breakfast with him.

21. I still visit my 7th grade history teacher who inspired me to be politically active. Mr. Andrews is the coolest.

She wrote a piece on this that made me cry. Twice. But it didn't end up as her personal statement.

See how each detail offers a different peek into her world? It's impossible to capture the entire depth of any human in twenty-five or even 650 words. Yet a few carefully chosen details begin to paint a portrait. Think of these "21 details" as a collage.

Your turn...

MY 21 DETAILS

1.
2.
3.
4.
5.
6.
7.
8.
9.
10.
11.
12.
13.
14.
15.
16.
17.
18.
19.
20.
21.

Once you've written your 21 Details, spend a minute looking for themes or potential crossovers with your Values Exercise. Is there anything that comes up repeatedly? This might serve as a topic for your personal statement or a supplemental essay.

EVERYTHING I WANT COLLEGES TO KNOW ABOUT ME LIST

Time: 15–20 minutes

Instructions:

Make a list of all the things you want colleges to know about you. You can do this either in a bullet point format (organized, easy to read) on a blank sheet of paper (with drawings, get creative) or on a timeline of your life that you draw.

The point of this list is to provide yourself (and your counselor, since this can be a great thing to share to help them before they write your recommendation letter) with a solid list of qualities, values, and cool stuff that will help get you into college. Plus, it generates a list of details and possible topics for your personal statement, supplements, activities list, and additional information section.

Tips for creating a great list:

Have fun. This doesn't have to be a chore. It's a list of everything that's awesome about who you are and what you've done, which can be pretty darn affirming.

Try this on your own so you're not influenced too much by others. If you're still having trouble after trying solo, enlist the help of a parent or friend. You might say, "Hey, I'm trying to make a list of all the reasons why any college should love me as much as you do—can you help?"

Back up general stuff with specific examples. Don't just write, "I can motivate people!" or "I stick with things I'm passionate about!" Provide a specific example to back up your claim—or better yet, both claims! Like the fact that you helped raise debate club membership from nineteen to ninety-six at your school over four years.

Here's an example:

Everything I Want Colleges to Know about Me

Note: this excludes a lot of extracurriculars that will go in the activities list.

1. I am extremely politically active and outspoken.
2. Stereotype Project (stereotypeproject.org)
   a. *March for Our Lives speech and school walkout* ←———————— Love all these examples.
   b. *Student of the month*
   c. *Model UN*

   She's listing something she might do senior year. It's okay to dream here!

3. Working on a children's book?

4. I really like to help people. That's the root of why I do most of the stuff that I do.
   a. *Volunteer in the Dominican Republic* ←———————— Again, great examples.
   b. *Volunteer at Pony Power*
   c. *Volunteer at Tag Teens*
   d. *Math club, peer tutoring*

5. I love art and graphic design.
   a. *Art as a creative outlet from the stress of school, whether it be writing or drawing*
   b. *Art major, 3+ years of study*
   c. *Oil paint is my favorite medium!*
   d. Creativity

   I love this. Don't be afraid to be playful when you create this—remember, it's mostly for your own reference!

6. I love chemistry. So much.
   a. *I DAYDREAM ABOUT MOLECULES*
   b. *AP Chemistry is my favorite class in the world*
   c. *Chemistry family at my school—Dr. Sankar and Ms. Robin—are like my second moms*
   d. *Met most of my best friends through chemistry classes*
   e. *Chemistry inspired me to do research*
   f. *Just the coolest thing in the world*

7. I've wanted to be a doctor since I was 7.
   a. *Mom is a psychologist, used to read us the DSM instead of bedtime stories*
   b. *Got a lab coat and microscope for my 7th birthday*
   c. *JHU center for talented youth summer programs in 7th and 9th grade (summer prior)*

    d.   *Research*

    e.   *House, MD inspired me (I walked around the house with a cane.)*

8.   I am so driven and motivated and passionate about learning.

    a.   *Just a nerd*

    b.   *I love school so much*

9.   Oldest of five, family is incredibly important to me.

    a.   *Stories about breakfast with dad, growing up with all the siblings, etc.*

    b.   *Takes a village*

    c.   *Bombie*

    d.   *Toyin*

This would end up becoming her personal statement topic

10. My Jewish identity is important to who I am.

    a.   *Private school*

    b.   *Temple and community*

    c.   *Conflict in my town with antisemitism, how I overcame it*

This is repeated from her 21 Details, which let me know this was important to her. And it ended up being part of an important supplemental essay that she reused for several schools.

11. I'm outgoing and a leader.

    a.   *I love to make people laugh*

    b.   *Talking to new people makes me so excited*

    c.   *I like working with others and being organized/delegating tasks (Ex: organizing my research team, organizing the walkout)*

    d.   *Trying new things and traveling and adventuring (Ex: Scuba diving)*

    e.   *Having fun is the most important*

12. I am kind and compassionate and down to earth.

    a.   *My friends come to me for advice!*

Your turn...

EVERYTHING I WANT COLLEGES TO KNOW ABOUT ME

1.
2.
3.
4.
5.
6.
7.
8.
9.
10.
11.
12.
13.
14.
15.
16.
17.
18.
19.
20.
21.

FEELINGS AND NEEDS EXERCISE

Time: 15–20 minutes

Instructions:

Take out a blank sheet of paper and turn it sideways (landscape view) and draw seven columns labeled like this:

Challenges	Effects	Feelings	Needs	What I Did	Lessons, Skills, and Values	Future or Career (Optional)

In the **Challenges** column, list any major obstacles you've faced in your life—anything from major health or family issues to experiencing racism or violence.

Spend at least three to four minutes on this first column. The more these challenges affected you, the more productive this exercise can be.

> To watch a video of me guiding you through this exercise, google "College Essay Guy Feelings and Needs Exercise."

In the second column, list the **Effects** (a.k.a. repercussions) that you experienced as a result of each challenge you've listed. How did each challenge impact you?

Important: Don't yet name the emotions you felt as the result of the challenge, as those will go in the next column. Instead, simply list how your world changed due to the item in the first column. Try to isolate the specific external factors that prompted an emotional response. Here's an example: "Moved around a lot growing up" might go in your Challenge column. You might label the effects as "hard to make friends" or "didn't speak the local language."

The purpose of this column is to differentiate your experience of the challenge you named in the first column (e.g., divorce or moving around a lot) from anyone else who might have experienced a similar challenge.

Spend at least three to four minutes on this column. See if you can write down three to four effects for each challenge.

In the third column, name the **Feelings** that each effect caused. You can name the main emotion you felt or several different emotions. If you had difficulty making friends, for example, maybe you felt afraid, isolated, or vulnerable. Maybe some part of you even felt relieved. Don't worry if the feelings you write down contradict. Mixed emotions are normal, and noting them can actually make for a more interesting, nuanced personal statement.

Spend three to four minutes on this column. See if you can list three to four feelings for each challenge you experienced.

And because it can be difficult to think of feelings on the spot, here's a list to give you some ideas:

Delighted	Adventurous	Appreciative
Joyful	Blissful	Moved
Happy	Elated	Touched
Amused	Thankful	Tender

Expansive	Exuberant	Heartbroken
Grateful	Vigorous	Lonely
Excited	Alert	Depressed
Enthusiastic	Focused	Disconnected
Overjoyed	Awake	Detached
Fervent	Clearheaded	Despondent
Giddy	Peaceful	Dejected
Eager	Tranquil	Bored
Ecstatic	Serene	Tired
Thrilled	Calm	Burnt out
Satisfied	Confident	Exhausted
Fulfilled	Secure	Lethargic
Gratified	Safe	Angry
Interested	Hopeful	Furious
Curious	Scared	Rage
Absorbed	Apprehensive	Irate
Healthy	Dread	Resentful
Empowered	Worried	Irritated
Alive	Panicky	Frustrated
Robust	Frightened	Disappointed
Relaxed	Vulnerable	Discouraged
Relieved	Nervous	Disheartened
Rested	Jittery	Impatient
Mellow	Anxious	Shocked
At ease	Restless	Disturbed
Light	Vulnerable	Stunned
Content	Tense	Alarmed
Cheerful	Cranky	Appalled
Glad	Stiff	Concerned
Comfortable	Stressed	Horrified
Pleased	Overwhelmed	Sad
Friendly	Agitated	Grief
Affectionate	Aggravated	Despair
Loving	Hurt	Gloomy
Passionate	Pain	Sullen
Energetic	Agony	Downhearted
Exhilarated	Anguish	Hopeless

Torn	Jealous	Ashamed
Ambivalent	Envious	Contrite
Confused	Bitter	Guilty
Puzzled	Embarrassed	

In the fourth column, write the **Need** that corresponds with each of the feelings you've listed. What do I mean? Consider that each emotion you feel has an underlying need that can help you understand why you feel what you feel (or why you felt what you felt).* Ask yourself what need may have been underneath each feeling you wrote down. Perhaps underneath a feeling of isolation, for example, was a need for connection, or beneath a feeling of vulnerability was a need for safety. Spend a little extra time with this column—this is the heart of this exercise.

Based on the feelings you've listed, what need was or is underneath each one?

And again, because it can be difficult to think of needs (for some of us it's something we rarely think about), here is a list of needs:

Intimacy	Freedom	Support
Empathy	Spontaneity	Collaboration
Connection	Independence	Belonging
Affection	Respect	Community
Warmth	Honor	Consideration
Love	Security	Seen/heard
Understanding	Predictability	Appreciation
Acceptance	Consistency	Forgiveness
Caring	Stability	Purpose
Bonding	Trust	Competence
Compassion	Reassurance	Contribution
Communion	Validation	Efficiency
Divine union	Partnership	Growth
Sexuality	Mutuality	Learning
Autonomy	Friendship	Challenge
Choice	Companionship	Discovery

---

*   *Nonviolent Communication*, which was developed by Marshall Rosenberg, posits that our feelings are the result of needs that either are or aren't getting met. I like this idea and find it useful when I'm trying to understand why I'm experiencing certain emotions.

Order	Humor	Wholeness
Structure	Beauty	Fairness
Clarity	Play	Truth
Focus	Creativity	Peace
Information	Joy	Groundedness
Celebration	Honesty	Hope
Mourning	Integrity	
Aliveness	Authenticity	

For the fifth column, **What I Did**, consider the steps you took to meet the needs you wrote down. Maybe to meet your need for connection you decided to join cross country or the robotics club. Or maybe to meet your need for safety you shared your feelings with your parents or a counselor and that helped you feel better; so you'd write down "talked to a counselor."

I know this is a big question, but ask yourself: "Why did/do I do Activity X?" "What deeper need did/is it meeting for me?" If you're still in-process (i.e., haven't done anything yet to meet those needs), what could you do?

Spend three to four minutes on this column.

In the sixth column, **Lessons, Skills, and Values**, ask yourself: "What did I learn from all this?" "What did that lesson lead to, if anything?" Maybe you joined cross country (what you did) and that taught you to value your health and nutrition (values), which led you to start a blog (outcome). Or maybe joining robotics taught you to code (skill), which led you to create your own board game (outcome).

For ideas of what to put in this column, take a look at the list of values on page 5.

List three to four values you've developed based on each of the actions or activities you've listed in the previous column.

Spend three to four minutes on this. Normally this column ends up being really full.

The final column, **Future or Career**, is optional but can be interesting to consider. Here, write down the name of something you'd like to do in the future. This could be career focused, like "doctor" or "engineer." It can also be broader, like "fight injustice" or "be an amazing mother." Then go back to the Lessons, Skills, and Values column, notice which skills and values will help you in the future, and write those down in the last column.

And that's it. I'll tell you what to do with this on page 146 of the personal statement chapter.

PRELIMINARY ACTIVITIES AND AWARDS LISTS

Time: 15–20 minutes

Instructions:

First, make a list of the extracurricular activities that you're likely to include on your application.

Next, briefly describe, in one or two sentences, your roles and responsibilities. Consider including some of the skills, qualities, and values you've brainstormed in this chapter, as well as any of your activities. We'll revise these descriptions later, so they don't have to be perfect now. This is just a rough draft.

Should I include work and family responsibilities?

In short, absolutely! But don't just take my word for it.

Words of Wisdom from an Admission Officer

Jamiere Abney, Senior Assistant Dean of Admission, Colgate University

We definitely believe work is worth including on the activities list. I encourage students to think about anything they do during their "free time" or time outside of school. Share those things because it allows the admission office a more comprehensive picture of who you are. Particularly when students are working and helping to support family, this might help add context around their academic achievement to help us evaluate specific challenges they've had to navigate, or just the ways they've had to truly manage their time to do well.

Once you've made a list of your activities, briefly describe your roles and responsibilities. Include how long you spent on each one. Here's an example:

Sample Preliminary Activities List

Intern at Department of Cardiovascular Disease (20 hr/wk, 4 wk/yr)
Organized patient diagnosis notes, sterilized tools for surgeries, assisted with
    X-ray analysis.
Vice President, Robotics Club (5 hr/wk, 28 wk/yr)
Elected VP in 10th grade. Recruited club members, organized seminars for
    freshmen, and coordinated team preparation for various competitions.

Korean Compassion: Korean-to-English Letter Translator (2 hr/wk, 8 wk/yr)
Translated letters sent by supporters to impoverished children in Asian and
     African countries.
Art Making (5 hr/wk, 52 wk/yr)
Lifelong artist; exhibited at and organized first teen environmental art show
     at DEWR; encourage creative expression and social consciousness
     through art.
Math Tutor at Sippican Elementary School (2 hr/wk, 12 wk/yr)
Using card games and quizzes to simplify concepts, taught basic math skills
     to third graders.
Finally, make a preliminary list of any awards or honors you've won, like this:

Sample Preliminary Awards/Honors List

2nd place, Novice Debate (among 45 competitors)
Outstanding Taekwondo Student: given by grandmaster for superb skill and
     discipline (1 of 35)
4th place, World Robot Olympiad
Sacramento Bee, Letter to Editor protesting fracking, published by associated
     newspapers
AP Scholar with Distinction

What if I haven't won any awards?

Don't worry. Many schools don't offer awards; many activities are not competitive; and some students don't have the time, money, or resources to compete.
Admission officers understand this based on the context of the applicant (what's
shared in your school report or what you've shared in the additional information
section) and won't hold it against you.

Like I said, don't worry too much about how you draft your list of activities
and awards right now. We're going to get into how you can seriously improve the
way you tell schools about all the awesome stuff you've done outside of class
soon. But if you want to your activities list to be better from the jump, here are
a few questions you can ask yourself. (Note that you'll find a PDF with these
questions in the Treasure Trove.)

Checklist for Reviewing Your Activities and Awards

What I Did (Day-to-Day):

- ❐ Did I list all my tasks or just a few? What did I forget?
- ❐ Did I list tasks I completed that fell slightly outside the scope of my responsibilities?
- ❐ Did I leave out any awards? Any uncommon achievements?

Problems I Solved:

- ❐ Did I consider the internal problems I solved—any personal challenges?
- ❐ Did I name the external problems I solved—for my friends or family? School? Community?
- ❐ Was I tackling a much larger (perhaps global) problem?

Lessons I Learned and Values/Skills I Developed:

- ❐ What were some of the soft skills I learned (patience, communication, etc.)?
- ❐ Did I learn any specific software (Photoshop, Final Cut Pro)? Languages (Spanish, C++)? Survival skills (how to start a fire or clean a fish)?
- ❐ What am I better at now than I was before?
- ❐ What would I have done differently?

Impact I Had (On Self, School, Community and/or Society):

- ❐ Did I consider the impact this had on my family? Friends? School? Who else benefited?
- ❐ What impact did this have on me personally? Did this change my life/perspective? How?

Applications to Other Parts of School/Life:

- ❐ What skills did I develop and what lessons did I learn that will make me a better _____ (tutor, debater, advocate, volunteer, programmer, fill in the blank)? How so?
- ❐ What did I do to build on and take what I learned to the next level?

❐   What surprised me about this experience?
❐   How might I continue this activity during college and beyond?

What's Next?

If you've just worked straight through these exercises, it's time for a break. You might even want to let this stuff marinate in your brain for a few days, and then come back to reevaluate your work. Some students need to spend a good deal of time on these exercises to figure out how they want to structure their application. Keep in mind that these aren't set in stone; you're just writing a first draft.

You may be wondering where all this stuff goes in your application. Don't worry. I'll refer back to these exercises frequently and will let you know what goes where. You've gotten a lot done, so right now, feel free to do something else for at least a few minutes before moving on.

Chapter 9

How to Up-Level Your Activities List in Thirty Minutes (and Why You Should)

What's the activities list again? It's the space on the application where you name and briefly describe your nonacademic pursuits.

What's its purpose? "Extracurricular activities can be a great opportunity to see how an applicant has self-directed their passions and interests," says Jorge Delgado, Associate Director of International Admissions at Brandeis. "There are only so many hours in the day, so seeing how a student has involved themselves outside the academic arena is a great way of understanding their potential fit for a university campus."

In this chapter, we'll cover:

- Why it's worth spending half an hour up-leveling your activities list
- How to develop more and better content for your list
- How values can help you bring much more variety to your list
- Why you should never stretch the truth on your list
- Tips for the Honors and Awards section
- Tons of examples

Why should you spend thirty minutes up-leveling your list? *Your activities list can make a big difference in your application.*

Want proof? Compare these two activities list descriptions:

Art
Created art and organized club

Founder, Art Honors Society
Organized and ran meetings, set up field trips, brainstormed and created
    group art activities, wrote and sent newsletter to members

Most students write a *pretty good* activities list description and then they stop there. But it doesn't take long to up-level an activities list from *pretty good* to *great*. And you can up-level your activities list using three simple, effective steps:

1. **Develop better (and perhaps a bit more) content.** Have you included a wide range of responsibilities? Most students forget to include solving problems, gaining skills, and making tangible (and even quantifiable!) impact.
2. **Use stronger verbs.** Are you describing your activity in the most dynamic way possible? Most students aren't. Why? Because they're using just-okay verbs.
3. **Demonstrate skills and values.** Are you communicating what you learned or how an activity changed you? If not, you may be leaving money on the table.

Here's a quick step-by-step guide:

Three Tools for Up-Leveling Your Activities List

TOOL #1: BEABIES EXERCISE

What's the BEABIES Exercise? Simply the **B**est **E**xtracurricular **A**ctivity **B**rainstorm **I**'ve **E**ver **S**een, and it's going to help you generate better content for your activities list descriptions.

Instructions: Grab a piece of paper and turn it sideways (landscape), and draw five columns with a little space left above them. In that space, write the activity that you want to brainstorm. Label each of the columns from left to right: What I Did, Problems I Solved, Lessons Learned/Skills I Gained, Impact I Had, and How I Applied What I Learned. If you guessed that you're going to fill those columns with your ideas, you guessed right.

Spend five to eight minutes filling out one BEABIES chart *per activity on your list* to start refining the content in your activities list descriptions. You can look back at the list of questions at the end of the Activities List Exercise in the previous chapter to help generate your ideas.

After a few minutes, your chart may look something like this:

The key here is active verbs, which we'll cover very soon.

These problems could be any scale, from personal to school-wide to global.

You can use the Values Exercise for this.

Use numbers and actual quotes to support what you say in this column.

Ask yourself how you applied lessons from the activity *beyond* the activity itself.

Example Activity: Chinese Dance Club				
WHAT I DID	**PROBLEMS I SOLVED/AM WORKING ON**	**LESSONS LEARNED/SKILLS I GAINED**	**IMPACT I HAD**	**HOW I APPLIED WHAT I LEARNED**
Practiced every Sunday morning for 2.5 hours for nine years. Performed at Chinese New Year festivals for nine years. Danced in junior group for four years, senior group for five years, senior small group for three years. Served as club treasurer, managing club-related funds and handling reimbursements. Organized fundraiser at the Chinese Dragon Boat festival that raised over $2,000 for the club. Served as club vice president. Won Honorable Mention at the Chinese School Association in the United States (CSAUS).	Feeling disconnected from Chinese culture and community. Not much connection to relatives in China. Club was struggling to maintain steady funds. Improving technique and artistry in Chinese dancing. Difficulty transitioning to Chinese dancing from ballet. Difficulty articulating ideas and thoughts. Our community lacked Chinese cultural events.	Became more goal oriented. Managed and kept a record of thousands of dollars. Learned: -to articulate and explain my thoughts to younger dancers. -how to handle conflicting interests from group leaders and dancers' parents. -that our surrounding community is actually open to supporting our group. -to express my individuality in a way that I didn't with ballet. -that every movement and pose has its own nuances. -how to choreograph and adapt a dance based on material from past dance groups and videos. -to remain patient and forgiving while teaching.	Grew closer to the values of Chinese culture as there is always a story behind every dance. Relatives in China watched links to my dances, allowing us to connect more on phone calls. Developed a sense of community within the group of dancers and parents. Showed beauty of Chinese culture to local community.	Used teaching skills while tutoring peers in chemistry. Lessons in leadership helped me manage board members in my club. Continued to reach out to my community about other causes I cared deeply about, helping to fund-raise for annual event. Helped me become more expressive and seek other outlets of expression.

This is going to be a lot of content for each extracurricular activity. You aren't going to put all of that into your description for each one, but with more than enough content at the ready, you'll have plenty to work with going forward.

TOOL #2: THE EPIC LIST OF ACTIVITIES LIST VERBS

You probably need stronger verbs. How do I know? I've seen hundreds of activities lists and most need stronger verbs.

Consider this typical description of debate:

Member, Debate
Debated topics, attended tournaments, researched topics

Shall we break that down real quick? *Debated topics* (um, redundant), *attended tournaments* (we assumed?), *researched topics* (I hope so!).

BTW, I am *so* much nicer and less sarcastic in real life—just employing it here to make a point.

Here's a much clearer, more interesting, and varied description:

I lead research and case writing, mentor younger debate students, organize mock debates, host an annual debate tournament. See Add'l Info for Awards.

FRIENDS, LOOK AT THOSE VERBS: "lead" (BOOM), "mentor" (YES), "organize" (SIZZLE), "host" (POP).

That's what I'm talking about. I'm like, "Oh, now I get what debate looks like to you." But wait, what makes a verb stronger?

- A stronger verb…is **more specific**. Example: "taught" is fine, but did you coach, mentor, train, or *demystify*?
- A stronger verb…is **more visual**. Example: "organize" is fine, but did you arrange, catalog, compile, or *systematize*?
- A stronger verb…just **sounds better**. A few examples I like: mediate, publicize, administer, or *plagiarize*. (I'm kidding about plagiarize.)

I know, some of you are probably wondering: "But Ethan, which verbs should I use?"

Oh, sure, wouldn't it be great if I just like GAVE you an epic list of activities list verbs you could choose from like some kind of giant menu? Too good to be true, right?

Behold…

College Essay Guy's Epic List of Activities List Verbs

You'll find a downloadable PDF version of this list with links to more verbs in the Treasure Trove.

Proof You Accomplished Something

achieved	demonstrated	exceeded	reduced	revitalized
attained	earned	expanded	resolved	spearheaded
awarded	eliminated	founded	(problems)	succeeded
completed	enlisted	grew	reached	surpassed
delivered	ensured	improved	rehabilitated	transformed

Creative/Design

adapted	designed	founded	invented	tailored
built	developed	illustrated	originated	wrote
conceptualized	devised	initiated	performed	
constructed	directed	instituted	planned	
created	drafted	integrated	redesigned	
customized	established	introduced	shaped	

Analytical/Research

analyzed	examined	investigated	quantified	supervised
collected	extracted	mapped	recommended	surveyed
confirmed	graphed	organized	researched	systematized
critiqued	identified	oversaw	reviewed	tested
discovered	inspected	planned	scheduled	tracked
documented	interpreted	prioritized	strengthened	
evaluated	interviewed	produced	summarized	

Management/Leadership Skills

campaigned	contacted	coordinated	directed	evaluated
consolidated	converted	developed	established	founded

generated	led	partnered	replaced	supervised
improved	managed	planned	restored	
increased	motivated	prioritized	restructured	
recruited	oversaw	produced	set	

Helping

advocated	cared for	diagnosed	familiarized	rehabilitated
answered	coached	educated	guided	represented
assessed	counseled	expedited	motivated	supported
assisted	demonstrated	facilitated	referred	

Organizing/Detail Oriented

approved	compiled	implemented	prepared	screened
arranged	coordinated	inspected	processed	specified
cataloged	customized	monitored	purchased	systematized
classified	executed	operated	recorded	tabulated
collected	generated	organized	retrieved	

People Skills/Communication

addressed	convinced	edited	lectured	recruited
advertised	corresponded	enlisted	mediated	spoke
arranged	developed	formulated	moderated	translated
authored	directed	influenced	negotiated	wrote
collaborated	discussed	interacted	persuaded	
composed	documented	interpreted	promoted	
contacted	drafted	interviewed	publicized	

Technical Skills/Building Stuff

adapted	designed	operated	replaced
assembled	devised	overhauled	restored
built	engineered	programmed	solved
calculated	fabricated	redesigned	upgraded
computed	integrated	remodeled	
customized	maintained	repaired	

Teaching Skills

adapted	critiqued	evaluated	integrated	trained
advised	demystified	explained	motivated	tutored
clarified	developed	facilitated	persuaded	
coached	enabled	guided	set goals	
communicated	encouraged	informed	supported	
coordinated	enforced	instructed	taught	

Financial/Money Stuff

administered	budgeted	fund-raised	projected
analyzed	calculated	managed	raised
appraised	computed	marketed	researched
balanced	developed	planned	

Important Note about Overdoing Verbs

You want your résumé to be in your own words, to sound like you. Overwriting can make it sound like you hired a professional to write your résumé, which can detract from your application. So unless it's the one and only word that perfectly captures what you did, avoid using "corporate verbs." See examples below. And I'm not going to say "100% DO NOT use these words." At the very least, I am saying, "Proceed with caution."

"Corporate" Verbs I Would Caution against Using on Your Activities List: allocated, apprised, arbitrated, audited, augmented, briefed, dispatched, executed, expedited, familiarized, formalized, forecasted, forged, fostered, interceded, maximized, outpaced, presided, projected, queried, simulated, standardized, stimulated, substantiated, transmitted, validated, yielded

---

Action item: Spend ten minutes comparing the verbs in your activities list to possible replacements you might find as you look through this giant list of verbs. This will seriously up-level your activities list verbs, and thereby your descriptions.

But wait. We're not done yet. Here's the final tool for up-leveling your activities list.

TOOL #3: VALUES SCAN

Remember the Values Exercise? As a reminder, it's on page 5. I'm mentioning it again because you're about to use it to make your activities list EXPLODE with depth and variety.

Pick one of the activities list descriptions you've written and ask of it these three questions:

1. Which values are clearly being revealed in the description?
2. Which values are kind of being revealed, but could probably be revealed more clearly in the description?
3. Which values are not in the description at all yet, but perhaps could be included?

Take this description as an example, written by a student who was secretary of her Red Cross Club:

> *Responsible for taking minutes, updating calendar and active member list, communicating with advisors, acting as a liaison to our local chapter.*

This is a perfectly acceptable activities list description that anyone should feel good about. It has nice details, it uses good verbs. Solid stuff. But even if you're describing your activity well, there are ways you can probe deeper for what it's really saying about you. You can go beyond what you've done with your time and delve more deeply into what you really care about. Now ask those three questions…

1. Which values is this description clearly revealing?
   I see the author values organization ("taking minutes" and "updating calendar"), *responsibility* ("acting as liaison"), and *collaboration* ("communicating with advisors"). Do you see others? Maybe! Either way, this is a good start to the Values Scan.
2. Which values could be revealed more clearly in the description?
   Reading the previous example, I'm curious if the author might demonstrate leadership more clearly. She hints at some responsibilities, but I wonder if she could delete "updating calendar and active member list" in favor of a detail more clearly demonstrating leadership skills.

I might ask the student if she can think of something she did that might demonstrate leadership. (If not, that's okay! This is a process of asking questions and seeing what variety might be possible. But we're not in the business of making stuff up—see warning note that follows.) I'd also wonder if the description could more clearly demonstrate the author's commitment to health—this is the Red Cross, after all—or perhaps social change.

3. Which values are not in the description at all yet, but perhaps could be?

To determine the answer for this student, it helps to know the author. I happen to know one of this author's core values is adaptability. So I asked her: "Did working with the Red Cross help you become more adaptable? If so, how? What detail might show this?"

Once you've written a new draft, hand your activities and awards list to a trusted editor. They should have your Values Exercise nearby for reference so they can assess how well you're demonstrating your values. Here's another example:

Indian tabla, self-taught via YouTube videos; played drums at community meetings for worker rights awareness; helped my sister become proficient.

I see these values:

- *Ambition*: "Self-taught…"
- *Social change*: "Played drums at community meetings for worker rights awareness."
- *Helping others*: "Helped my sister become proficient."

See how that works?

Try to include two to three values per activity. If you can achieve this, just think: your list could demonstrate twenty or even thirty values! That's rad. But don't drive yourself crazy with this. If your activities list shows a nice variety of ten or so values, that's enough. Really.

Activities List Examples That Benefited from Revision

Here are first drafts of descriptions followed by revisions written after using the BEABIES chart, Epic Verbs List, and Values Scan:

Graduate of Harvard U's Public Speaking Course
Learned many different speaking techniques.

We could've guessed this from the title, right? What else might help us understand this activity?

Revision: Obtained confident and powerful public speaking techniques, explored professional speeches, mastered improvised speech, and incorporated theatrical skills.

Mentor, InnerCity Arts Youth Center
Help kids make art projects and teach them things.

What things? What's been the impact?

Revision: Responsible for planning activities and tutoring 9- to 10-year-olds, enhancing their self-esteem, teaching them social skills and respect for others.

Symphony Orchestra III Hired Quartet
I play music outside of school as well.

Great, where?

Revision: Perform professional gigs, from mayor's banquet to Boy Scout ceremonies; often hired to play at community centers, local churches, and hotels.

AYSO Girls Soccer Co-Head Coach
Competed against high school level competition. I play striker and sometimes fill in as goalie.

Cut. Doesn't tell me much.

Cool. Anything else?

Revision: Organize drills, model proper soccer technique for practices, prepare line-up, coach team, send emails to parents.

Yearbook Staff Member
Our yearbook includes photographs of all the students and the events we do throughout the year at our school.

I know what a yearbook is; tell me what you've learned and accomplished!

Revision: Traveled to photograph sporting events, worked with Photoshop and InDesign, mentored new staff members, and helped run a summer workshop for new staff members.

Alzheimer's Family Services Center

Aided those who are suffering from Alzheimer's.

Great. How? What was your impact?

Revision: Taught watercolor classes to Alzheimer's patients; encouraged greater patient engagement and creative expression to mitigate the effects of dementia.

"mitigate"—wowza!

Ryman Arts Program

Developed my artistic skills.

Specifics, please?

Revision: Sketched drawings of still life sets and real-life models with top 100 Southern California high school art students.

Co-President, Foreign Film Club

Watched movies with other students and attended movie theaters around the city.

Unfortunately, this doesn't tell me much about the student or the club.

Revision: Curate range of int'l films and documentaries, facilitate talks on social justice issues, run social media marketing, organized first film festival.

It's fine to use an ampersand if you're trying to save space.

Graphics Editor & Editorial Writer, School Paper

ambiguous. Made backgrounds and wrote articles for our school newspaper, *The Messenger*.

Repeats.

Revision: Designed graphics (backgrounds, typesets, layouts, digital drawings); wrote and proofread peer articles; updated print newspaper to digital format.

Some students prefer commas, other use semicolons; either can work.

Flute—First Chair, Concert Band

Enjoy playing the flute and have played extensively.

Specifics, please!

Revision: 500+ hrs. over 4 yrs. 8 tournaments, 19 concerts. Received Div.1 at 2016 Solo Competition; led early am practices; raised $3k for trip to nat'ls.

Zing.

You can find even more great examples of activities list descriptions in the Treasure Trove.

Nine Tips for Making Your Activities List Awesome

1. **Aim for variety, making sure your verbs aren't redundant.**

Instead of: Instructed, helped, taught children tennis.

Try: Instructed in proper technique while imparting lessons in sportsmanship, health, and integrity.

2. **Use the present tense if it's something you still do.**

You'll be talking about things that you're both currently doing and that you've done before, so it won't sound awkward or sloppy to have both present and past tense in your activities list. It'll be clear.

If you, right now, are giving tours at your boarding school (maybe not *right* right now), then say: I give campus tours and provide info on school history, student activities, and boarding life.

3. **Trim ruthlessly.**

Because the space you're using is so limited, the words you choose are incredibly important. Actually, let me rephrase: Because your space is limited, your word choice is important. One more time: Limited space demands precise wording.

See what I did there? Cut my character count from ninety-two to sixty-one to thirty-seven. In fact, if you're still using complete sentences, stop. No need here.

Instead of: I raised money to donate to a school in India by selling T-shirts and bracelets. After the campaign, I gave a presentation on the project at multiple student assemblies, presenting to over four hundred students overall.

Try: Arranged advertising events, organized fundraisers, and presented to student body at assemblies (400+ students).

4. **State role and organization name in the title so you don't waste characters in the description.**

Instead of: School newspaper, Daily Herald, editor

I am the editor for the school newspaper's International Column, responsible for brainstorming and copyediting articles by underclassmen; managed deadlines; offered layout and design input; liaised with faculty sponsor.

Try:

International Column Editor, Daily Herald

Responsible for brainstorming and copyediting articles by underclassmen; managed deadlines; offered layout & design input; liaised w/ faculty sponsor.

5. **Emphasize tangible, measurable impact.**

Notice, for example, the four hundred students inclusion in the third tip. This comes as a result of asking questions like "Whom did your activity help? How many people? How much money did you raise?"

Instead of: Raised money for children in Africa.

Try: Raised $3,000 to provide three uniforms and scholarships for students attending the Joseph Waweru Home School in Kenya.

6. **Include any responsibilities that demonstrate leadership skills.**

Instead of: I swim on the swim team.

Try: Responsible for leading swim practices, planning fundraising events, assisting in recruiting process.

7. **Describe in more detail when necessary.**

In some cases, a super concise description might not make the impressiveness of the achievement clear. Or if you feel there isn't much to say about the activity, or it was a one-time event, more detail can help bring it to life.

Instead of: Elected class representative.

Try: 1 of 2 student leaders elected by my peers to represent our class of 450.

Or instead of: Tutored students.

Try: Provided support to fourth graders with particularly difficult math concepts.

8. **Avoid extreme language.**

Instead of: to help all those in need (or) to end poverty in the world

Try: to help those in need (or) to fight against global poverty

9. **If your role was simply "member" or "participant," it's okay to just list the activity.**

In other words, instead of: Participant, MLK Day of Service

Try: MLK Day of Service

"Stretching the Truth" on Your Activities List: A Cautionary Tale

I once knew a student who had participated in some wonderful activities. She was a class officer, school club founder, nonprofit volunteer, and former intern. With a near-perfect GPA and test scores, she was applying to some of the most highly selective universities in the world. Once her applications had been submitted, however, her counselor revealed to me that the student had falsified parts of her application. She'd listed a trip she hadn't actually taken, made up a leadership role, and padded her hours.

What happened to her? Initially, she was accepted by several highly selective schools. But when one admission officer noticed application details that didn't line up with her counselor's recommendation letter, they brought it to the counselor's attention. After a little research, the counselor found the same inconsistencies and was professionally obligated to inform the highly selective schools that the student's application contained, for lack of a better word, "alternative facts." (She'd lied.)

When the student was confronted, she claimed she had "stretched the truth" and hadn't technically lied. In this case, however, as far as the counselor and admission officer were concerned, "stretching the truth" and "lying" were pretty much the same thing.

As a result, the student's acceptances to those universities were rescinded. In other words, although she was initially accepted, she was ultimately rejected. Worst of all, it damaged her reputation and relationship with her counselors, her principal, and me.

Please don't lie on your activities list. Don't even stretch the truth. Same goes for your essays too. But you know this.

Activities List FAQs

WHAT IF I DIDN'T DO MUCH FOR THE ACTIVITIES LIST AND I DON'T HAVE MUCH TO SAY?

If you aren't participating in many or any extracurriculars, ask yourself why. And I'm not assuming you should be, I'm really asking…why? Perhaps a better, less confronting way of asking this is: What values have become more important to you than extracurricular activities? Do you have to work and provide childcare for your family, for example? Do you have and enjoy an intense academic load? Or maybe you practice gymnastics eight hours a day. If so, mention this in your additional information section (see page 126), as this will help admission officers see your activities list within the context of your life experiences.

WHAT IF I FEEL LIKE I HAVEN'T DONE "ENOUGH"?

First, don't compare yourself to others! Instead, ask some questions.

Have you remembered everything you've done? Try sitting down with a parent or friend who can help you remember stuff you might've forgotten you did.

How could you explore some things that are important to you, gain some experiences, or learn some new skills in the time left before your application is due?

Heads up: admission officers can usually spot it when a student is loading up activities in twelfth grade just to pad their activities list. That's not quite what I'm talking about doing. If you have a few months before it's time to apply, however, ask yourself, "What can I do that I'd enjoy doing?" But if you've remembered everything and you're submitting your application soon... focus on what you can control. Use the previously discussed resources—the BEABIES, Epic Verbs List, and Values Scan—to describe what you did in a way that's clear and varied.

IS IT BETTER TO HAVE A FEW REALLY STRONG ACTIVITIES (LESS IS MORE) OR SHOULD I LIST EVERYTHING I'VE DONE (MORE IS MORE)?

I find counselors are divided into two camps on this: "less is more" and "more is more." Here's a quick comparison chart:

	POTENTIAL PROS	POTENTIAL CONS
Less is more	You list only your most important endeavors, demonstrating focus and commitment.	You leave off some stuff you did, risking an incomplete portrait of yourself in your application.
More is more	You include everything you've done, demonstrating a wide range of interests and achievements.	Some of your listed activities don't mean a whole lot to you. It may seem as if you're trying too hard to impress.

When I asked Brian Liechti of Warren Wilson College what he prefers, he said, "It depends! I would rather see meaningful, current activities that also show up elsewhere in an essay or a letter of recommendation. This adds weight and validation to what a student includes as an activity and I know it was a more impactful experience. But uncommon activities can add flair and character, especially if those activities are also represented on campus."

In short, the choice is yours.

WHAT IF A MULTIDIMENSIONAL ACTIVITY IS IMPOSSIBLE TO DESCRIBE IN 150 CHARACTERS?

Write a short description in the activities list, then put additional information into the...additional information section (that redundancy was on purpose). Here's an example of such an activity:

Creator, AquaVR
Researched, brainstormed, created three prototypes for virtual reality scuba gear. Recognized statewide. Developing app with Siemens. (See add'l info.)

That little note at the end signals the activity's richness while directing the reader to find out more in the other section (more on this on page 126).

Up-Leveling Your Honors and Awards Section

If it wasn't obvious from the title, this is the place on your application where you list awards you've won. Examples include everything from winning second in the 4 × 100 meter relay at a local track meet to winning a $500 scholarship for a poem you wrote.

In the last chapter you jotted down a list of your awards, and now is your chance to make sure that list is as clear and effective as it can be by following these tips.

Seven Tips for the Honors and Awards Section

1. **List your awards in order of importance.**

   Start with those that mean the most to you personally, then move to those with less personal significance.

   If you're not sure about or can't compare your awards' personal meaning, start with the most widely significant and esteemed. The simplest way is to start with international awards, then go from there to national, state, regional, school, club, and team.

2. **Specify what the award means.**

   Congrats on winning the "Beacon Award"…but I have no idea what that means. Did you win a beacon? Were you the beacon? Say so! Similarly, an "academic excellence" award could mean so many things. Define the bar of excellence in the context of the award.

3. **Emphasize selectivity.**

   Were you the best team out of four teams or four hundred? We won't know unless you tell us.

4. **Explain acronyms.**

   Speaking of things we won't know unless you tell us. Some acronyms (like TEDx and AP) will be familiar to readers, while others like FBLA (Future Business Leaders of America) or regional organizations like CSF (California Scholarship Federation) may be less familiar. When in doubt, spell it out.[*]

5. **Pack multiple awards into one slot (when possible).**

   Just make sure they're somehow connected. Example: SkillsUSA, Best of Show (1st) Interior Design; (1st) Employment Portfolio; (2nd) Web Design Technical

6. **Mention if you won money.**

   Example: TEDx NYC Student Startup Competition Winner: granted $1,500 in seed funding

7. **Let them know if they flew you out to accept the award.**

   Example: Google Young Changemaker winner: all-expenses-paid trip + mentoring @ Google HQ

---

[*]　Totally didn't mean to rhyme there.

Ten Examples of Honors and Awards That Could Have Been Improved—and Then Were!

The examples that follow were revised to add context and specifics.

FBLA Award
Revised version: Won 3rd in nation, Desktop Application Programming (Future Business Leaders of America)

Congressional Award
Revised version: Gold Medalist, The Congressional Award, for 400+ hours public volunteer service

Student of the Month
Revised version: Student of the Month (1 of 350 students chosen) for "positive impact on school culture." Won twice.

Journalism Award
Revised version: Silver Knight Award, Journalism. Given to 1 in entire county; included $2,000 prize.

Science Olympiad
Revised version: 1st in state, Analytical Lab, PA Chemistry Olympics

Debate Awards
Revised version: Debate: (4) 1st place finishes, Dade County Forensic League, 19–3 career policy debate record

Boy Scouts: Various Awards
Revised version: Boy Scouts: 36 merit badges, Silver Buffalo Award (10th) & Distinguished Service Award (11th)

DECA Champion
Revised version: DECA 2× Regional & State Champion and Int'l Finalist out of over 200K members worldwide

Chess Champion

Revised version: 1st place @ Pan American Intercollegiate Team Chess Championship

Dog Breeding Award

Revised version: 4-H Best in Show Project on Dog Breeding

In the Treasure Trove, you'll find:

→   Examples of 100+ activities and descriptions

→   How to create the University of California (UC) Activities List

Chapter 10

How to Write the Additional Information Section

According to Susan Tree, college counselor and former admission officer at Bates College, "We really want to distinguish you from other applicants—please help us!"

At this point, you've already given yourself a good foundation for distinguishing yourself thanks to all the exercises you completed in the "Essential Application Prework" chapter and your up-leveled activities list. This chapter will show you how to provide the reader even more context for your application.

Important: This chapter is not meant to scare you into feeling like you have to put something in the additional information section. You do not have to include anything there. So if you find you don't have anything else to add, that's totally fine! Just give this chapter a quick read to make sure.

In this chapter, we'll cover:

- What the additional information section is
- What you should put into the additional information section
- Examples of how to write that information
- What you should NOT put into the additional information section

Ten Things to Include in the Additional Information Section

On the Common App as well as other applications, this is a section where students can type in extra information they want colleges to know. Keywords: "can" (you aren't required) and "information" (not fluff, filler, or even stories).

Step back and take a look at the information you've already included in your application. What's missing? What might not make sense and need an explanation? You may need help seeing what's missing. Ask someone who knows you (and, ideally, knows the college process) well to offer their editorial perspective.

Words of Wisdom from a Former Admission Officer
Susan Tree, college counselor and former admission officer at Bates College

Reading applications for a research university (after many years as a college counselor), I was shocked to see how many applicants failed to distinguish themselves. Their strong academics and hard-earned personal credentials could come across as predictable and lifeless. Occasionally I came across an additional information section that was like a cold splash of water or an electric shock; it made the student come alive. Two examples that come to mind were a fascinating research project ending in epic failure, and a classically trained singer's out-of-the-box foray into performance art via shape-note singing. Format ranged from research abstract to spoken word and power poetry. What engaged me as a reader was the personality and energy that came through this section of the application; these students seemed to know that in order to understand them, I had to know this dimension of their experience, personality, upbringing, bliss, or adversity. This insight made their applications memorable. It made me believe they had something important to contribute to the university.

Is the additional information section the place to take a risk? Perhaps, if that's who you are. You might use this space to be creative, nerdy, or funny—but make sure it has a purpose and is done well.

What follows are a dozen possibilities for items you might include, written with input from some of my wonderful colleagues on both sides of the college admission desk.

1. IMPORTANT DETAILS ABOUT YOUR ACTIVITIES THAT WOULDN'T FIT IN YOUR ACTIVITIES LIST

Let's say you did a really cool fundraiser that positively affected both the people you were donating to and your local community. And let's say you decided not to write an extracurricular essay on this, either because you wrote about something else or the school didn't request an extracurricular essay. When you look at your activities list description, however, it doesn't capture how incredibly awesome this experience was for everyone. So you might write a short bullet point description in your additional information section that looks like this:

Stand for Haiti Fundraiser

Raised $3,500 to benefit victims of the recent earthquake in Haiti
Proceeds provided housing for displaced persons whose residences were heavily damaged or destroyed
Event also galvanized local community, leading to a second fundraiser, "Hillsboro High for Haiti," to take place next month

Quick tips for writing these descriptions:

- **Be brief.** You're on borrowed time in the additional information section, so give us the condensed version. Imagine your reader is a very important person with a hundred more applications to read before Friday. Because they are and probably do.
- **Be specific and focus on impact.** In this case, how much money did you raise? Whom did it help? How?
- **Put your details in descending order of importance.** The most important stuff should go at the top, since the reader may be skimming.
- **Avoid special formatting.** Formatting like bold and italics may not show up when entered into online forms, so make sure you've emphasized the information you want without those fancy tricks. This goes for your personal statement too.

Or let's say you *did* write a 150–200 word extracurricular essay* for a particular school and you really want other schools to know more about that activity even though they haven't asked for a 150–200 word essay. While you could paste your whole short essay into the additional information section for those other schools, I wouldn't recommend including essays the school didn't request. Instead, create a bullet point version of your essay so the reader can get the information more quickly. How?

Check out this short extracurricular essay:[†]

> The Durham Youth Commission is a teen-led faction of the Durham County government that was created to provide youth input in local politics. To get into the Commission, applicants must submit a thorough description of their extracurricular and academic interests as well as answer questions about what they would like to see accomplished during their time in office. Out of one hundred applicants, I was selected to serve on the commission two years in a row along with about twenty-five other high schoolers attending school in Durham. Along with promoting efforts to combat gun violence during my time serving in the DYC, we also pursued advocacy projects to address mental health challenges and food insecurities. The Commission was regularly updated by various city officials about the nature of their work, including the Mayor of Durham. The DYC also attended several conferences hosted by other city youth councils to build leadership and communication skills as well as encourage active community involvement. I volunteered over sixty hours each term I served on this commission for organizations like Mobile Market, Peace Toys for War Toys, Habitat for Humanity, and Kids Voting. (188 words)

---

*   I cover extracurricular essays in depth on pages 222–240.
†   You'll find the longer version of this essay on page 193.

Here's that essay as a bulleted list:

- The Durham Youth Commission (DYC) is a teen-led faction of the Durham government created to provide youth input in local politics.
- Out of one hundred applicants, I was selected to serve on the commission two years in a row along with about twenty-five other Durham high schoolers.
- Promoted efforts to combat gun violence, mental health challenges, and food insecurities.
- Regularly updated by city officials and Durham Mayor about the nature of their work.
- Attended several conferences hosted by other city youth councils to build leadership skills and encourage active community involvement.
- Volunteered over sixty hours each term for organizations like Mobile Market, Peace Toys for War Toys, Habitat for Humanity, and Kids Voting. (112 words)

See? The bullet point version is shorter and easier to read.

Important: Please don't expand on every single activity in your activities list; there's no need to do that. Check out the "How to Up-Level Your Activities List in Thirty Minutes" chapter (pages 107–125) for tips on how to make the most of your activities list descriptions.

2. HEALTH ISSUES THAT MAY HAVE AFFECTED YOUR HIGH SCHOOL PERFORMANCE

Did open heart surgery keep you from getting the best grades possible in eleventh grade? If so—and if this isn't already in your main statement—say a few words about it. A few tips:

- Mention it **even if your counselor is mentioning it**. Michelle Rasich, a counselor at Rowland Hall Saint Mark's, points out that "Reps have shared that they like reading explanations in the student's own words even if I too am dedicating time to it in my letter." Again, be brief, factual, informative.
- Focus on **information**. Don't tell a story here. Just the facts.
- Focus on **impact**. How did it affect you? Be specific. How many days/ weeks/months did you miss? How'd you make up the work? Did your grades go up afterward? If so, say so. Example: Although my grades dipped

during this time, one year later I'm happy to report that I was able to receive straight As.

- If you choose to discuss **mental health issues**, be sure to run it by your counselor before submitting, as depression and anxiety can often raise more questions than they answer. Admission officers want to make sure their future students have the resources they need on campus. To be clear: I'm not saying you shouldn't mention mental health issues; I'm saying that "if" and "how" are important questions to discuss with your counselor.* If you do not have a counselor and come from a low-income household, you can sign up for one at www.collegeessayguy.com/matchlighters.

3. ANY POTENTIAL RED FLAGS ON YOUR APPLICATION

What might be a red flag? Something in your application that could raise questions in the mind of the admission reader (e.g., a bad grade you received in science, why you dropped two sports last year, or the fact that you want to major in math but didn't take math last year). Anticipate questions the reader may have and offer an explanation that provides context. Did you drop the sports to focus on academics, for example? Or maybe you had a complex schedule conflict.

In terms of length and tone, be as concise as possible and explain rather than complain.

Example: *I dropped soccer and cross country after sophomore year due to chronic back problems. My back healed by junior year and I returned to water polo as an assistant coach, but chose not to return to cross country so I could focus on academics and get a job to help pay bills at home.*

4. CIRCUMSTANCES THAT HAVE MADE IT DIFFICULT FOR YOU TO GET MORE INVOLVED IN EXTRACURRICULAR ACTIVITIES, SUCH AS WORKING TO SUPPORT YOUR FAMILY

I've had students, for example, who have to take two buses plus the Metro to get to school, commuting almost two hours each way. Others have their parents

---

* For more mental health resources, check out the Treasure Trove.

drive them that far. This means extracurriculars have been relatively tough to participate in. But colleges can't know this if you don't tell them.*

Independent counselor Leslie Cohen offers this great advice: "Students need to repeatedly ask themselves, 'If I was reading this application, am I getting enough information to understand the applicant's situation and experiences?' Often students assume what they list is clear, but sometimes it's not. I've had many admission officers say, 'I wanted to know more.'"

Important caveat here! Note that the following details about your family circumstances are important to include in your application somewhere, but I'd recommend trying to work them into your personal statement rather than your additional information section:

- Single-parent household
- Low-income family or large family with many dependents, straining family income
- Non-English language spoken at home
- You'll be the first generation in your family to attend college

How do you know if you should put something in the personal statement or additional information section? The personal statement describes who you are and what you value; your additional info often describes external things that have happened to you.†

Words of Wisdom from an Admission Officer

Meredith McDill, Assistant Director of Admission, Smith College

At Smith College, we view the additional information section of the Common Application as a good place for students to either explain in further detail something we'll read in other parts of the application or tell us something about themselves we won't necessarily see anywhere else in the application. We actually encourage students to use the activities area to list paid jobs and any caretaking

---

* Note that some of this information can be communicated in the counselor recommendation letter, although you aren't likely to know what's in that letter (since counselors don't usually show these to students). If you don't have a counselor, use this section to advocate for yourself.

† Hat tip to my colleague Hollis Bischoff for this distinction.

of younger siblings or older relatives, or tasks relating to household management, etc. Then, if they'd like to emphasize that significant household responsibilities have prevented their involvement in other activities (or other extracurricular activities) in the additional information section, they can.

This section should not be perceived as required. But it should be used when there is a significant circumstance requiring clarification or emphasis, such as coping with learning differences, physical challenges, family crises, or other hardships. Understanding the student's individual context is an important aspect of the unique selection process here in the U.S., as part of our holistic approach to reviewing applications.

5. PHYSICAL OR LEARNING DISABILITIES OR DIFFERENCES

Disabilities should be diagnosed by a health professional. You may consider specifying the diagnosis, when you received it, and how long you've navigated the effects overall.

If you have a diagnosed learning disability, you might include a bit of context to help clarify and describe (but not excuse!) the learning challenge. How has the disability impacted your academic performance and what steps have you taken to navigate your disability? If you are dyslexic, for example, do you use audio books as a work-around? Indicate when the disability was diagnosed and what you have accomplished or navigated since the diagnosis.

Example: *I was diagnosed with ADHD at the end of ninth grade, which helped me understand some of the academic difficulties I'd faced in middle school. Pharmacological treatment, however, led to a complete change in academic performance. Although it sometimes takes me three times as long to comprehend reading material, I've become extremely motivated and self-disciplined and I believe my academic record reflects this. Unfortunately, I do not believe that standardized tests reflect my ability, especially as someone with ADHD, as having more time on a test can be difficult when focusing is the issue.*

Important: Not everyone has to disclose. Ask your counselor what makes sense for your application.

6. FAMILY MEMBER DISABILITY OR
PARENT UNEMPLOYMENT

If a family member is disabled or has been unable to work and this has had an impact on your life or academics, consider including a few sentences of context.

Example: *I would like the admission committee to know that my younger brother has spina bifida and my family and I devote a considerable amount of our free time to his care and trips to the doctor. It also means that my mother has not been able to work outside of our home since he was born.*

Another example: *My mother is a beautiful, warm, and passionate person. Sadly, she also suffers from schizophrenia, which she allows to be treated only periodically with medication. She is rarely able to hold a job for more than a few months at a time, and our family depends on my father's job driving heavy equipment for the city for income as well as insurance. Dad isn't able to take time off on those days or long periods of time when mom needs extra attention. My sister and I have taken over household chores and bill paying to fill in some of the gaps.*

7. UNUSUAL GRADING AND CREDIT SYSTEMS

If your school doesn't use the regular systems of course credits, semesters, and grading on a 4.0 scale, and there isn't an option for indicating this in the application's online forms, you'll need to use the additional information section to make sure this is clear. If you don't, those reviewing your application won't know the academic context of everything they're looking at. This is pretty common at performing arts, religious, or trade schools with a specialized curriculum.

"We have a trimester schedule that is not accommodated by drop-down menus," notes veteran counselor Tara Dowling. "For example—we have numerous two-trimester courses and there are only ten slots. So our students put in 'fake date' indicating that courses are full-year courses. Then they explain in the additional info that the classes are actually two terms long." Would the admission officer know that if you didn't tell them? Probably not.

8. UNUSUAL CLASSES OR ONLINE COURSES

What do I mean by unusual classes? North High School in Newton, MA, once had a class called "The Art of the Graphic Novel." If I was an admissions rep, I'd be curious to know more—wouldn't you? You might include a two- to three-sentence blurb on what that class entailed (course objective, highlights of the reading list, and any special projects). Other weird/awesome high school classes I wish I could've taken include: "Great Books," where students read books like *Ulysses* and (my favorite) *The Brothers Karamazov*; and the "Wise Individualized Senior Experience," in which seniors can avoid senioritis by designing their own ten-week curriculum.

In terms of online courses, not all online classes are created equal. That's why it's important to add context to help the admission officer get an accurate picture. Was it a one-week course that required just a few hours of work? Or was it a rigorous eight-week course that required over ten hours of reading and group work per week, culminating in a final project that you had to sing in front of three hundred people and oh-by-the-way here's a link? Also, maybe say why you took the course(s). Was it because the class wasn't offered at your school? Or did you take it to make room for another class you really wanted to fit into your schedule? Show the reader you were thoughtful in your decision to learn online.

Words of Wisdom from an Admission Officer

Lauren Blalock Sefton, Senior Associate Director of Admission at Rhodes College

Students may use the additional information section to talk about an independent study or research project that may not be accurately or completely reflected on their transcript. This gives us a chance to follow up and learn more about their project, passion, time commitment, and depth of research. For example:

"Arabic classes were discontinued at my school due to the unexpected leave of a teacher as well as low program enrollment between my sophomore and junior academic years. My junior year, a provisional program was set up for remaining students who needed to fulfill language credits as a way of gradually phasing out the Arabic program. Now, to ensure I do not lose the progress I have made in the Arabic language, and to continue to pursue my passion even though it is no longer offered at my school and will no longer appear on my transcripts, I attend private tutoring weekly in the subject."

In other situations, students may use this section to reference traumatic events, like bullying or a serious illness or death of a close family member, which allow us to have greater context when viewing their academic and extracurricular records. In these cases, we sometimes follow up with the student for additional information to have a better understanding of the circumstances. One student referenced a parent's recent job loss, which gave us the chance to follow up with information about the possibility of adjusting financial aid options.

Also, if a student is at a large public high school where the counselor recommendation letter may not be particularly personal, this can be a perfect opportunity for the student to self-advocate:

"Currently I am in a household where there is no access to Wi-Fi and very little financial means. I have been a student who has been private about my circumstances but has also been responsible for many of my personal and family expenses such as paying bills, medical expenses for my sibling, and paying for my own expenses. As much as I wish I could engage more in my extracurricular activities, I cannot because of challenges related to my home's financial status and lack of access to the internet."

Finally, some students provide links to YouTube videos of their band performances, Amazon links to their self-published books, and web links to their Etsy shops and online art blogs. As a reader, I don't always have the time to fully explore these external links, but I try my best to skim through or have the music playing in the background while I'm reading the application. It helps me "get inside the student's head" and better understand their personality.

9. INTERNATIONAL BACCALAUREATE (IB) EXTENDED ESSAY TOPICS

Parke Muth, counselor and former associate dean at the University of Virginia, says, "I suggest that people doing an IB extended essay share the topic and title of the essay and maybe a little more info. So few students do projects like this in secondary school and the topics themselves often say something good about the students."

Example (from my younger brother's actual college application): *For my IB extended essay requirement, I wrote a 4,000-word thesis arguing that French art film director Gaspar Noé breaks the conventions of classical narrative structure as defined by story theorist Robert McKee. My close reading of Noé's film* Irreversible *(2002) seeks to prove that Noé defies McKee's principles of the inciting incident, law of diminishing returns, and balance of high and low pace scenes by Noé's manipulation of the Russian Formalist elements of fabula and syuzhet.*

10. OTHER INFORMATION THAT SIMPLY WON'T FIT ON OTHER PARTS OF THE COMMON APP

"I have students with so many siblings they cannot fit them all on the family page of the Common App," says Kate Coddaire from Cheverus High School. If you have more you need to say but run out of room, put it in the additional information section! (And be sure to let your reader know that that's where they can find it.)

Be aware that it can be easy to misuse this section. To that end, here are…

Five Misuses of the Additional Information Section

1. TURNING IT INTO A SECOND PERSONAL STATEMENT

While some counselors argue that the additional information section is a great place to put a whole essay, I side with those who feel like this section should be reserved for, well, additional information. A bit of an exception is the fifty- to one-hundred-word statements that add factual, succinct context or information.

"When we see that a student has completed the additional information section, we surmise that the student has something to share that could not fit anywhere else in the application," says Patricia Peek, PhD, Dean of Undergraduate Admission at Fordham. "If a student takes the time to complete this section, it should signal that the content is important. This is also a good place to share context about an element, or elements, of the submission that may need explanation (change in grades, extra activities not reflected, or lack of activities, etc.). We do not ask for an extra essay, but even if we did, we would not see this section as a place for another personal statement."

2. BEING OVERLY OBSESSED WITH
ACADEMIC PERFECTION

If you have straight As, or near straight As, and you got a B+ in one class, don't explain that B+. Why? It may backfire, revealing qualities that are not super flattering. It's like when you walk into someone's house and it's in immaculate condition (but it's clear someone has cleaned the place recently) and they're like, "Sorry the place is such a mess…" and you're thinking, "Come on, really?"

3. GIVING EXCUSES

This is the inverse of the red flag item in the previous list. If something happened during high school that might raise a red flag on your application or transcript, of course you'll want to address it, but you won't win any sympathy by attempting to shift blame, give excuses, or complain. Just confidently and matter-of-factly explain what happened.

If you can't give a good explanation for something (e.g., you got a bad grade in math because you didn't like your teacher, you dropped football because you wanted to chill more during the summer), it may be better to not mention it at all. Will the reader wonder about that thing? Maybe. But if you really can't come up with a good reason, not writing anything is better than giving reasons that reflect poorly on your sense of personal responsibility.

4. WRITING AN OVERLY COMPLEX
ABSTRACT FROM A SCIENTIFIC PAPER

Telling the reader that you worked with metastatic malignant neoplasm involving the cervical region of the esophagus may not mean that much without context, and busy admission officers won't be impressed by having to look up what all of that means. If you're going to share information that would usually be communicated in an abstract, consider offering a short explanation that loses the jargon.

A small exception to this rule: you can use a little geeky language to explain the particulars if applying to a highly specialized program. But just a little.

Example: *I contributed to Dr. Li's review article to give an overview of the types of skin diseases typically seen with IBD and their respective pathogenesis, proposed mechanisms, and treatments; my contributions were significant enough to earn me recognition as a second author.*

Notice how succinct, how factual?

On that note, some students provide a link to outside materials such as a scientific abstract or published work. The reader often won't follow that link either because they can't click the link or don't have time. Basically, assume the reader won't click it. Instead, write a short summary of what's in the link.

5. COPYING AND PASTING A RÉSUMÉ THAT REPEATS EVERYTHING YOU'VE ALREADY SAID IN YOUR ACTIVITIES LIST

Why is this bad? Because:

1. It's redundant.
2. Admission readers are reading so much and this wastes their time.
3. It looks insecure, like you're saying, "See what I did? Wait, look again!"
4. It's redundant. (That's a joke, BTW.)

What if I feel like I'm struggling to come up with stuff to add in the additional information section?

It's your call, but if it starts to feel like you're stretching to add random things, then stop, take a breath, and remember what I said at the start: You do not have to use the additional info section.

That's right—leave it blank! In fact, see if you can be really succinct and fit all your information into the areas provided in the activities list descriptions. It's possible! And your college reps will thank you.

Part V

The Personal Statement

How to Write a Personal Statement That Matters

Time for my favorite part of the process. This is the part I've spent most of my time thinking about since 2003.

In this chapter, we'll cover:

- What the personal statement is
- How to use all the exercises you've already done to write your personal statement
- Four types of personal statements
- Narrative structure and montage structure
- How to make your personal statement stand out when you're writing about a common topic
- Lots of examples of great personal statements and what makes them great

The Personal Statement

This is your main essay. Your application centerpiece. The part of your application you're likely to spend the most time on. But of course I'd say that; I'm the College Essay Guy.

The personal statement is likely to be 500–650 words long (so about a page), and many of the colleges you're applying to will require it.* But what's its purpose? Jennifer Blask, Executive Director for International Admissions at the University of Rochester, puts it beautifully: "So much of the college application is a recounting of things past—past grades, old classes, activities the student has participated in over several years. The essay is a chance for the student to share who they are now and what they will bring to our campus communities."

Follow the guidance in this chapter and you'll be able to use this essay for many different schools as well as scholarship applications.

Let's do this.

THE BRAINSTORMING EXERCISES

Here are the six exercises I have every student complete before I meet with them:

- Essence Objects Exercise (page 2)
- Values Exercise (page 5)
- Core Memories Exercise (page 7)
- 21 Details Exercise (page 92)
- Everything I Want Colleges to Know about Me Exercise (page 95)
- Feelings and Needs Exercise (coming up)

If you've been working as you go, you've already completed these. But if you haven't done these yet, make sure you do all of them before moving forward. (You can find a downloadable Google doc with these exercises in the Treasure Trove.) I recommend putting all the content from your exercises in one document to keep things neat.

Don't worry, I don't expect you to have found your personal statement topic yet. If you already have, that's great! But if not, I'll help you find a topic, a structure, and even a path for writing a personal statement that stands out.

---

*   Not all schools will require you to write one; you can find out directly on their website or via the Common App, if the school uses the Common App.

THE STRUCTURE

At the start of the essay process, I ask students two questions:

1. Have you faced significant challenges in your life?
2. Do you know what you want to be or do in the future?

But here's an important qualifier: even if you have faced challenges and/or know what you want to be or do in the future, *you do not have to write about them in your personal statement.*

So a better phrasing for these questions might be:

1. Have you faced significant challenges in your life…and are you interested in potentially writing about those challenges in your personal statement?
2. Do you know what you want to be or do in the future…and are you interested in potentially naming that in your personal statement?

If you're uncertain, don't worry. The next few pages will help you decide. But for the sake of this chapter, answer those first two questions with a gut-level response.

1. Have you faced significant challenges?   Yes   /   No
2. Do you have a vision for your future?   Yes   /   No

Your answers create four potential paths for your personal statement:

Type A	Type B
Student has faced significant challenges (and chooses to write about them) and has a clear vision for their future (and chooses to write about it).	Student has not faced significant challenges (or chooses not to write about them) but has a clear vision for their future (and chooses to write about it).
Type C	**Type D**
Student has faced significant challenges (and chooses to write about them) but does not have a clear vision for their future (or chooses not to write about it).	Student has not faced significant challenges (or chooses not to write about them) and does not have a clear vision for their future (or chooses not to write about it).

At this point, you probably don't know whether you'll write about your challenges or vision for the future. Don't worry, in the coming pages I'll help you figure it out. Read the four types and see which path resonates with you most right now, today.

It's choose your own adventure time. If you choose...

Type A, stay on this page.
Type B, turn to page 154.
Type C, turn to page 162.
Type D, turn to page 167.

Soon I'll introduce you to two structures for these types of essays: **narrative structure**, which works well for describing challenges (Types A and C) and **montage structure**, which works well for essays that aren't about challenges (Types B and D).

Heads up: Some students who are writing about challenges find after reading that they prefer the montage structure to the narrative structure. And some students who are not writing about challenges prefer narrative structure to montage structure. If you're uncertain which type is best for you, read through all four sections. Each is just a few pages long, and you'll learn something different from each path. Often students start down one path, then realize another may be better.

Type A: Student Has Faced Significant Challenges (and Chooses to Write about Them) and Has a Clear Vision for Their Future (and Chooses to Write about It)

If you're interested in writing about challenges, I highly recommend using narrative structure.

NARRATIVE STRUCTURE

This structure has been around as long as we've been telling stories, and you might recognize it from Joseph Campbell's "monomyth" or even from most movies you've seen. Here are its basic elements:

1. Status quo: The starting point of the story. This briefly describes the life or world of the main character.

2. Inciting incident: The event that disrupts the status quo. Often it's the worst thing that could happen to the main character. It gets us to wonder: "Uh-oh…what will they do next?" or "How will they solve this problem?"

3. Raising the stakes/rising action: The building of suspense. The situation becomes more tense, decisions become more important, and our main character has more to lose.

4. Moment of truth: The climax. Often this is when our main character must make a dramatic choice.

5. New status quo: The denouement or falling action. This often tells us why the story matters or what our main character has learned. Throughout this book (and in my first book) I refer to these insights or lessons as the answer to the big "So what?" question.

Now you'll develop your own story using my favorite content-generating exercise for narrative structure, which you've already done! If you haven't completed the Feelings and Needs Exercise, return to the "Essential Application Prework" chapter and do that now (page 98).

(This is a dramatic pause before I tell you the coolest thing about what you just did.)

You may notice that your completed Feelings and Needs chart maps out a potential structure for your personal statement. If you're not seeing it, try turning your paper so that Challenges are at the top of your page and Effects are below them.

Voilà. From top to bottom, you're now looking at a paragraph-by-paragraph outline for a narrative essay.

Okay, this isn't necessarily a *perfect* way to outline an essay. You may not want to spend an entire paragraph describing your feelings, for example, or you may choose to describe your needs in just one sentence. But the sideways Feelings and Needs chart can help you think about how the chronology of your experiences might translate into a personal statement.

Here's an essay that one student wrote after completing this exercise:

THE BIRTH OF SHERE KHAN

Status Quo:
The author is
surrounded by
violence and war.

The narrow alleys of Mardan, Khyber Pakhtunkhwa, Pakistan where I spent the first seven years of my life were infiltrated with the stench of blood and helplessness. I grew up with Geo news channel, with graphic images of amputated limbs and the lifeless corpses of uncles, neighbors, and friends. I grew up with hurried visits to the bazaar, my grandmother in her veil and five-year-old me, outrunning spontaneous bomb blasts. On the open rooftop of our home, where the hustle and bustle of the city were loudest, I grew up listening to calls to prayer, funeral announcements, gunshots. I grew up in the aftermath of 9/11, confused.

Inciting Incident:
She moves to the
United States.

Raise the Stakes:
Rather than find-
ing safety from
war, she is seen
as a villain.

Like the faint scent of mustard oil in my hair, the war followed me to the United States. Here, I was the villain, responsible for causing pain. In the streets, in school, and in Baba's taxi cab, my family and I were equated with the same Taliban who had pillaged our neighborhood and preyed on our loved ones.

War followed me to freshman year of high school when I wanted more than anything to start new and check off to-dos in my bullet journal. Every time news of a terror attack spread, I could hear the whispers, visualize the stares. Instead of mourning victims of horrible crimes, I felt personally responsible, only capable of focusing on my guilt. The war had manifested itself in my racing thoughts and bitten nails when I decided that I couldn't, and wouldn't, let it win.

Moment of Truth:
She decides to
do something
about it.

A mission to uncover parts of me that I'd buried in the war gave birth to a persona: Shere Khan, the tiger king, my radio name. As media head at my high school, I spend most mornings mastering the art of speaking and writing lighthearted puns into serious announcements. Laughter, I've learned, is one of the oldest forms of healing, a survival tactic necessary in war, and peace too.

During sophomore year, I found myself in International Human Rights, a summer course at Cornell University that I attended through a local scholarship. I went into class eager to learn about laws that protect freedom and came out knowledgeable about ratified conventions, the International Court of Justice, and the repercussions of the Srebrenica massacre. To apply our newfound insight, three of my classmates and I founded our own organization dedicated to youth activism and spreading awareness about human rights violations: Fight for Human Rights. Today, we have seven state chapters led by students across the U.S. and a chapter in Turkey too. Although I take pride in being editor of the Golden State's chapter, I enjoy having written articles about topics that aren't limited to violations within California. Addressing and acknowledging social issues everywhere is the first step to preventing war.

Earlier this year, through KQED, a Bay Area broadcasting network, I was involved in a youth takeover program, and I co-hosted a Friday news segment about the Deferred Action for Childhood Arrivals policy, the travel ban, and the vaping epidemic. Within a few weeks, my panel and interview were accessible worldwide, watched by my peers in school, and family thousands of miles away in Pakistan. Although the idea of being so vulnerable initially made me nervous, I soon realized that this vulnerability was essential to my growth.

I never fully escaped war; it's evident in the chills that run down my spine whenever an untimely call reaches us from family members in Pakistan and in the funerals still playing on Geo News. But I'm working toward a war-free life, internally and externally, for me and the individuals who can share in my experiences, for my family, and for the forgotten Pashtun tribes from which I hail. For now, I have everything to be grateful for. War has taught me to recognize the power of representation, to find courage in vulnerability, and best of all, to celebrate humor.

Raise the Stakes (again): She develops a radio persona and becomes an advocate for human rights.

New Status Quo: Though she hasn't fully escaped war, she has learned so much.

(Fun fact: This essay was written by a student in one of my online courses who, as she shared this version with me, called it a "super rough draft." I wish my super rough drafts were this good.)

WHICH SHOULD I USE TO MAP OUT A TYPE A ESSAY? THE FEELINGS AND NEEDS EXERCISE OR NARRATIVE STRUCTURE?

Either can work, actually, because the Feelings and Needs Exercise is designed to create a classic narrative structure sequence of events based on what has happened in your own life.

In "The Birth of Shere Khan" essay you can track both. The elements of narrative structure are highlighted by my notes in the margin, while the elements of the Feelings and Needs Exercise are described next (see also page 98).

But I want you to notice something. It's so important, I'm writing it in bold: **The author doesn't explicitly name every single effect, feeling, or need**. Why not? First, she's working within a 650-word limit. Second, she makes room for her reader's inferences, which can often make a story more powerful. Take a look:

1. Challenge 1: She grows up surrounded by war, which is explicitly stated.
2. Challenge 2: She comes to the United States to find safety, which is implied, but instead of finding safety, she is villainized, which is explicitly stated.
3. Effects: She is ostracized after arriving in the United States. "Every time news of a terror attack spread," she writes, "I could hear the whispers, visualize the stares." Other effects are implied, and we are left to imagine— and feel for ourselves—the kind of impact this might have had on her, and on us.
4. Feelings: Growing up in the aftermath of 9/11 leaves her feeling confused, and after she is shunned, she describes being unable to mourn the victims of horrible crimes, instead feeling "personally responsible, only capable of focusing on [her] guilt." She explicitly names confusion and guilt, but she doesn't name all the things she felt, of course, as there's no need. Here, naming one to two key emotions helps us understand her inner world. If you choose to do the same in your essay, it will help readers understand yours.
5. Needs: As I read this essay, I can imagine the author needed things like safety, order, love, respect, reassurance, connection, and many more. But these are implied by the story events and don't need to be explicitly stated. In fact, spelling these things out might have made the essay sound

weird. Imagine if she'd said, "I needed safety and order" at the end of the first paragraph and "I needed respect, reassurance, and connection" at the end of the second paragraph. That might sound awkward or too obvious, right? While identifying your needs is a great tool for understanding your story (and self) on a deeper level, there's no need to explicitly state them at each juncture.

6. What I did about it: The author developed a radio persona called Shere Khan, attended a summer course on human rights, founded an organization dedicated to youth activism, wrote articles on restrictive blasphemy laws and the forced repatriation of refugees, and probably other things that weren't even mentioned.

7. What I've learned/gained: She found a sense of purpose and discovered "everything [she has] to be grateful for." She writes: "War has taught me to recognize the power of representation, to find courage in vulnerability, and best of all, to celebrate humor."

Important: Notice that the author does not explicitly name the career or major she's intending to pursue in college. Having said that, the essay does make clear her sense of purpose, her interests, and the kind of work she'd like to do in the future. For the Type A essay, give us a sense of your vision, even if you don't name your precise career.

TYPE A ESSAY FAQS

Are there any situations where I may not want to write about my life struggles?

Yes. Sometimes it can be too difficult to discuss them. Or you may be actively dealing with a challenge. If this is the case, reach out to your counselor, a trusted mentor, or if possible, a therapist. If money is an issue (i.e., you feel you can't afford a therapist) and you don't feel comfortable sharing your struggles with your counselor, ask them if they can refer you to a therapist or counselor who works on a sliding scale. Many mental health professionals work with clients at low rates or for free. You may also choose to write about the struggles you've faced without getting into all the details. Saying that you experienced verbal abuse from your father, for example, may be enough; you don't necessarily need to share the specifics.

What about mental health challenges?

Mental health can be very difficult to write about for a few reasons.

- If a student is still very much struggling through the challenges they describe, the admission reader may wonder if the student is ready for college.
- In some cases, the admission officer may feel that a student is ready for college, but their institution may not be adequately equipped to help them thrive.
- Unfortunately, mental health challenges have become so common these days that many students write personal statements about them and so it can be difficult to stand out.*

Here are some questions to ask if you're considering writing about mental health challenges:

- **Do you have any other topics you could write about?** Are there other interesting parts of yourself you would like to share that could reveal important skills, qualities, and values? Or must you write about this challenge? (Remember that you don't need to write about a challenge! The authors of the "My Laptop Stickers" essay on page 159 and the "Home" essay on page 171 were students who faced challenges but chose not to write about them.)
- **Have you truly worked through this?** Are you able to devote the middle third of your essay to describing what you did to overcome the challenge and the final third to describing what you've learned? (You may not know the answers to these questions until you've done some writing. Maybe run your challenge through the Feelings and Needs Exercise to see what surfaces. Even if this doesn't end up being your personal statement topic, you might learn something important about yourself.)
- **If you were an admission officer reading this essay, would you feel like the student writing their story has their situation handled and they are truly ready for college?** (If you're unsure, it's a great idea to have two to

---

* If you are feeling compelled to write about a mental health challenge, consider brainstorming some uncommon connections using the UC Game (page 231).

three folks who have a good understanding of what colleges are looking for read it.)

- **Could your mental health challenge be a brief explanation in the additional info section?** To see if this might work for you, see how briefly you can describe your mental health challenge using factual bullet points. Devote one bullet point to the challenge, another bullet point to what you've done about it, and a final bullet point describing briefly what you've learned.

Important: If you have a counselor, I strongly recommend consulting with them as you decide whether to discuss a mental health challenge in your personal statement. If your counselor is writing a letter on your behalf, some of the information you'd like to share may already be accounted for. Talk to them and find out.[†]

Are there any situations where I may not want to write about my career even if I know what it is?

For sure. Say you're interested in becoming a doctor but you're applying to a medical program with a supplemental prompt asking why you want to become a doctor. If you want to avoid repetition, you might not explicitly mention becoming a doctor at the end of your personal statement. You might describe instead how you've developed qualities that will equip you for a career as a doctor (e.g., creativity or the ability to lead a team).

Type A Step-by-Step Recap:

1. Complete the brainstorming exercises described at the start of this chapter, as these will help no matter which structure you choose. Take special care to complete the Feelings and Needs Exercise, as it will help you outline your essay.
2. Create an outline using narrative structure.
3. Write a first draft.

[†]   For more mental health resources, plus examples of successful essays written by students who struggled with mental health issues, check out the Treasure Trove.

For more Type A (and narrative structure) examples, check out the Treasure Trove.

Type B: Student Has Not Faced Significant Challenges (or Chooses Not to Write about Them) and Does Have a Clear Vision for Their Future (and Chooses to Write about It)

If you are not writing about a challenge, I recommend the montage structure.

A montage is, simply put, a series of moments or story events connected by a common thematic thread.* Well-known examples from movies include the "training" montages from *Mulan*, *Rocky*, or *Footloose*, or the "falling in love" montage from most romantic comedies. Or remember the opening to the Pixar movie *Up*? In just a few minutes, we learn the entire history of Carl and Ellie's relationship. One purpose is to communicate a lot of information fast. Another is to share a lot of different kinds of information. If you want a quick explanation of the core difference between narrative structure and montage structure…

Narrative Structure vs. Montage Structure Explained in Two Sentences

→   In narrative structure, story events connect **chronologically**.

→   In montage structure, story events connect **thematically**.

For the purposes of a Type B essay, your future goal or career is the theme that connects all the parts of your story. The quality of your essay will depend on the strength of the examples and insights that connect your qualities/skills/values to your vision for your future. More on that in just a moment. First, let me walk you through the process.

---

*   In my first book, *College Essay Essentials*, I called this a "focusing lens." I now prefer the term "thematic thread" because I think it's a bit easier to visualize.

STEP 1: WRITE YOUR CAREER
ON A PIECE OF PAPER

Pretty straightforward. Done? Good. We're stacking small wins here.

STEP 2: IMAGINE THE CLICHÉ
VERSION OF YOUR ESSAY

What would the cliché version of your essay focus on?

If you're writing a "Why I want to be an engineer" essay, for example, what three to five common "engineering" values might other students have mentioned in connection with engineering? Use the Values Exercise on page 5 for ideas.

Collaboration? Efficiency? Hands-on work? Probably yes to all three.

Once you've spent two minutes thinking up some common/cliché values, move onto the next step.

STEP 3: NAME QUALITIES/SKILLS/VALUES
THAT WILL SERVE YOU IN THAT CAREER,
BUT START TO THINK OUTSIDE THE BOX

Imagine you're interviewing for a position as a fashion designer and your interviewer asks you what qualities make you right for this position. Oh, and heads up, that imaginary interviewer has already interviewed a hundred people today, so you'd best not roll up with, "because I've always loved clothes" or "because fashion helps me express my creativity." Those might be true, but it's not useful to mention them. Why? Because that's what everyone says.

Many students do the same in their personal statements—they name cliché qualities/skills/values and don't push their reflections much further.

Let me frame it this way:

A **boring personal statement** has a common topic, makes common connections, and uses common language.

A **personal statement that stands out** has an uncommon topic, makes uncommon connections, and uses uncommon language.

For example, a boring personal statement says: I want to be a doctor (common topic) because I'm *empathetic* and I love *helping people* (common connections), and I really want to make the world a better place (common language).

A better personal statement says: I want to run a tech start-up (more uncommon topic) because I value humor, "leading from the battlefield," and stuff that makes me cry (uncommon connections for an essay on this topic), and because my journey to this place took me from being a scrawny twelve-year-old kid to a scrawny twelve-year-old man (uncommon language).*

Important: I'm not saying you should pick a weird career just so it will help you stand out more on your essay.† Be honest. But consider this: the more common your topic is, the more uncommon your connections need to be if you want to stand out.

STEP 4: BRAINSTORM UNCOMMON CONNECTIONS TO YOUR CAREER

If you wrote "chef," for example, push yourself beyond the common value of health and strive for unexpected values. How has cooking taught you about accountability, for example, or social change?

Why do this? We've already read the essay on how cooking helped the author become more aware of his health. An essay on how cooking allowed the author to become more accountable or socially aware would be less common.

And before you beg me for an uncommon values resource, I implore you to use your brilliant brain to dream up these connections. Plus, you aren't looking for uncommon values *in general*; you're looking for values uncommonly *associated with your future career*.

But don't get me wrong. I'm not saying that you shouldn't list *any* common values, since some common values may be an important part of your story! In fact, the great essay examples throughout this book sometimes make use of common connections. I'm simply encouraging you to go beyond the obvious.

Here are some places you can find possible uncommon qualities/skills/values for your future career:

---

*   This essay is on page 177, by the way.

†   A more specific career is more likely to stand out. "Pediatric oncologist," for example, is
     more uncommon than "doctor."

Values Exercise on page 5. This is basically a huge list of qualities/skills/values that could serve you in a future career.

Core Memories Exercise on page 7. Did you do that one? If not, try it!

For others that aren't in this book, check out…

O*NET OnLine. Go to www.onetonline.org and use the "occupation quick search" feature to search for your career. Once you do, a huge list will appear containing knowledge, skills, and abilities needed for your career. This is one of my favorite resources for this exercise.

School websites. Go to a college's website and click on a major or group of majors that interest you. Sometimes they'll briefly summarize a major in terms of what skills it will impart or what jobs it might lead to. Students are often surprised to discover how broadly major-related skills can apply.

Real humans. Ask three people in this profession what unexpected qualities, values, or skills prepared them for their careers. Please don't simply use their answers as your own; allow their replies to inspire your brainstorming process.

Once you've got a list of, say, seven to ten qualities, move on to the next step.

Common or Cliché Topics

Common personal statement topics include: extracurricular activities (sports or musical instruments), service trips to foreign countries (a.k.a. the "mission trip" essay where the author realizes their privilege), sports injuries, family illnesses, deaths, divorce, the "meta" essay (e.g., "It's the night before this is due and I don't know what to write about!"), or someone who inspired you (heads up: this usually ends up being more about them than you).

While I won't say you should *never* write about these topics, if you do decide to write about one of these topics, the degree of difficulty goes way up. What do I mean? Essentially yours has to be one of the best "soccer" essays or "mission trip" essays among the hundreds the admission officer has likely read. So it makes it much more difficult to stand out.

How do you stand out? A cliché is all in how you tell the story. So if you do choose a common topic, I challenge you to make uncommon connections (i.e., offer unexpected narrative turns or connections to values), provide uncommon insights (i.e., say stuff we don't expect you to say), or uncommon language (i.e., phrase things in a way we haven't heard before).

Or explore a different topic. You are infinitely complex and imaginative.

STEP 5: BRAINSTORM EXAMPLES SHOWING HOW YOU'VE DEVELOPED THESE UNCOMMON QUALITIES/SKILLS/VALUES

Help the reader understand which experiences have shaped the qualities you've listed. Why? First, it'll make for a much more interesting story. Second, it'll show that you've truly developed these qualities.

Do this by creating a simple three-column chart:

Qualities/Skills/Values of an Activist	Examples (a.k.a. How I've Developed These Qualities)	Insights (a.k.a. "So What" Moments)
Creative Accepting/open-minded Sense of humor Courageous Entrepreneurial Love the work you do	Designing websites and social media graphics TEDxYouth@Austin Relationship w/ brother Harry Styles (One Direction) Catapult (start-up incubator) Through start-ups/meaningful work	Helped me develop my own style Culture is created, not just consumed in Austin I love my brother I used to internalize my beliefs more, but don't as much now Helped me discover career I hope it's always like this

Once you've written down your qualities, examples, and at least one to two insights, try outlining your essay. To keep things simple, try listing one example and one insight per paragraph. (If that feels too restrictive, feel free to distribute examples and insights differently. I'm offering tracks, but feel free to go off-road.)

Next, ask yourself if these qualities or examples have anything in common. This author, for example, found that many of the qualities/skills/values she wanted to share were represented by the stickers on her laptop.

Here's how this exercise magically* turned into an essay:

---

* It wasn't magic, of course. The author of this essay actually wrote many drafts on an entirely different topic before this idea was born. Once the idea was born, it only took a few drafts for the "My Laptop Stickers" essay to take shape.

MY LAPTOP STICKERS

Great analogy. Sets up the whole essay.

My laptop is like a passport. It is plastered with stickers all over the outside, inside, and bottom. Each sticker is a stamp representing a place I've been, a passion I've pursued, or community I've belonged to. These stickers make for an untraditional first impression at a meeting or presentation, but it's one I'm proud of. Let me take you on a quick tour:

This piques our curiosity: where will we "travel" in this essay?

I'm hooked.

"**We <3 Design**," bottom left corner. Art has been a constant for me for as long as I can remember. Today my primary engagement with art is through design. I've spent entire weekends designing websites and social media graphics for my companies. Design means more to me than just branding and marketing; it gives me the opportunity to experiment with texture, perspective, and contrast, helping me refine my professional style.

Value: *creativity*

This is how she's developed this value.

Insight (a.k.a. an answer to the "so what?" question)

"**Common Threads**," bottom right corner. A rectangular black and red sticker displaying the theme of the 2017 TEDxYouth@Austin event. For years I've been interested in the street artists and musicians in downtown Austin who are so unapologetically themselves. As a result, I've become more open-minded and appreciative of unconventional lifestyles. TED gives me the opportunity to help other youth understand new perspectives by exposing them to the diversity of Austin where culture is created, not just consumed.

Value: *authenticity*

Poop emoji, middle right. My thirteen-year-old brother often sends his messages with the poop emoji 'echo effect,' so whenever I open a new message from him, hundreds of poops elegantly cascade across my screen. He brings out my goofy side, but also helps me think rationally when I am overwhelmed. We don't have the typical "I hate you, don't talk to me" siblinghood (although occasionally it would be nice to get away from him); we're each other's best friends. Or at least he's mine.

Value: *sense of humor*

Here's some more core values

Great insight!

Note that not every part of your essay needs to be "academic"

Value: Awwww... But actually: #*family*

"**Lol ur not Harry Styles**," upper left corner. Bought in seventh grade and transferred from my old laptop, this sticker is torn but persevering with layers of tape. Despite conveying my fangirl-y infatuation with Harry Styles' boy band, One Direction, for me Styles embodies an artist-activist who uses his privilege for the betterment of society. As a $42K donor to the Time's Up Legal Defense Fund, a hair donor to the Little Princess Trust, and promoter of LGBTQ+ equality, he has motivated me to be a more public activist instead of internalizing my beliefs.

Values: *art and activism*

Insight

"Catapult," middle right. This is the logo of a startup incubator where I launched my first company, Threading Twine. I learned that business can provide others access to fundamental human needs, such as economic empower-ment of minorities and education. In my career, I hope to be a corporate advocate for the empowerment of women, creating large-scale impact and deconstructing institu-tional boundaries that obstruct women from working in high-level positions. Working as a women's rights activist will allow me to engage in creating lasting movements for equality, rather than contributing to a cycle that elevates the stances of wealthy individuals.

She clearly names her intended career, with specifics.

Insight

Value: *love the work you do*

"Thank God it's Monday," sneakily nestled in the upper right corner. Although I attempt to love all my stickers equally (haha), this is one of my favorites. I always want my association with work to be positive.

Insight

And there are many others, including the horizontal, yellow stripes of the **Human Rights Campaign**; **"The Team,"** a sticker from the Model G20 Economics Summit where I collaborated with youth from around the globe; and stickers from **"Kode with Klossy,"** a community of girls working to promote women's involvement in underrepresented fields.

A nice mini-mon-tage showing other meaningful parts of her life (and extracurricular activities)

When my computer dies (hopefully not for another few years), it will be like my passport expiring. It'll be difficult leaving these moments and memories behind, but I proba-bly won't want these stickers in my twenties anyway (except Harry Styles, that's never leaving). My next set of stickers will reveal my next set of aspirations. They hold the key to future paths I will navigate, knowledge I will gain, and connections I will make.

One more specific joke, to a) bring us back full circle and b) undercut what might otherwise feel like a some-what common college essay ending.

She comes back to the opening analogy, so it feels like we've come full circle.

TYPE B ESSAY FAQS

Should I mention my career at the start of my essay?

Probably not, as it tends to make the essay sound like a thesis-first English class essay. Instead, save the thesis for the middle, like this author does, or the end.

How do I work in extracurricular activities in a tasteful way (so it doesn't seem like I'm bragging)?

Some counselors caution, with good reason, against naming extracurricular activities/experiences in your personal statement. (It can feel redundant with your activities list.) You actually can mention them, just make sure you do so in context of your essay's theme.

How do I transition between examples so my essay flows well?

The transitions can be some of the toughest sentences to write for this essay type. Fine-tuning them will take some time, so be patient. One exercise I love is called Revising Your Essay in 5 Steps, and it basically works like this:

1. Highlight the first sentence of each of your paragraphs in bold.
2. Read each bold sentence aloud in order. Do they connect to create a short but coherent version of your essay? If not:
3. Rewrite the bold sentences so that they do connect (i.e., flow) together. Once you've done that...
4. Rewrite each paragraph so it flows from those bolded sentences.
5. Read them aloud again. Wash, rinse, repeat until the ideas flow together.

This is a great way to figure out the "bones" (i.e., structure) of your essay. You'll find an example in the Treasure Trove. For more Montage Structure examples, check out the Treasure Trove.

Type B Step-by-Step Recap:

1. Create a chart containing uncommon qualities, examples, and insights.
2. Choose an order for your examples. Consider describing one example per paragraph.
3. Write a first draft.

Type C: Student Has Faced Significant Challenges (and Chooses to Write about Them) but Does Not Have a Clear Vision for Their Future (or Chooses Not to Write about It)

The Type C essay is similar to the Type A essay because it describes challenges you've faced, how you've worked through them, and the lessons you've learned.

In fact, the step-by-step writing process for the Type C essay tracks closely with the Type A essay. So if you haven't already, go back and read about the Type A essay. Once you've done that, return here to the Type C essay to learn about what makes it different.

The important difference between the Type A and Type C essays is the ending. You'll recall that a Type A essay discusses a potential career aspiration, but a Type C essay ending may be a bit more open-ended.

So how do you end it? Instead of communicating your career aspirations, a Type C essay can leave the reader with a very clear sense of your values. Read this sample Type C essay, and then check out how this student used the Feelings and Needs Exercise and narrative structure to write it.

WHAT HAD TO BE DONE

At six years old, I stood locked away in the restroom. I held tightly to a tube of toothpaste because I'd been sent to brush my teeth to distract me from the commotion. Regardless, I knew what was happening: my dad was being put under arrest for domestic abuse. He'd hurt my mom physically and mentally, and my brother José and I had shared the mental strain. It's what had to be done.

Living without a father meant money was tight, mom worked two jobs, and my brother and I took care of each other when she worked. For a brief period of time the quality of our lives slowly started to improve as our soon-to-be stepdad became an integral part of our family. He paid attention to the needs of my mom, my brother, and me. But our prosperity was short-lived as my stepdad's chronic alcoholism became more and more recurrent. When I was eight, my younger brother Fernando's birth complicated things even further. As my stepdad slipped away, my mom continued working, and Fernando's care was left to José and me. I cooked, José cleaned, I dressed Fernando, José put him to bed. We did what we had to do.

As undocumented immigrants and with little to no family around us, we had to rely on each other. Fearing that any disclosure of our status would risk deportation, we kept to ourselves when dealing with any financial and medical issues. I avoided going on certain school trips, and at times I was discouraged to even meet new people. I felt isolated and at times disillusioned; my grades started to slip.

Over time, however, I grew determined to improve the quality of life for my family and myself.

Without a father figure to teach me the things a father could, I became my own teacher. I learned how to fix a bike, how to swim, and even how to talk to girls. I became resourceful, fixing shoes with strips of duct tape, and I even found a job to help pay bills. I became as independent as I could to lessen the time and money mom had to spend raising me.

I also worked to apply myself constructively in other ways. I worked hard and took my grades from Bs and Cs to consecutive straight As. I shattered my school's 100 M breaststroke record, and learned how to play the clarinet, saxophone, and the oboe. Plus, I not only became the first student in my school to pass the AP Physics 1 exam, I'm currently pioneering my school's first AP Physics 2 course ever.

These changes inspired me to help others. I became president of the California Scholarship Federation, providing students with information to prepare them for college, while creating opportunities for my peers to play a bigger part in our community. I began tutoring kids, teens, and adults on a variety of subjects ranging from basic English to home improvement and even calculus. As the captain of the water polo and swim team, I've led practices crafted to individually push my comrades to their limits, and I've counseled friends through circumstances similar to mine. I've done tons, and I can finally say I'm proud of that.

But I'm excited to say that there's so much I have yet to do. I haven't danced the tango, solved a Rubik's Cube, explored how perpetual motion might fuel space exploration, or seen the World Trade Center. And I have yet to see the person that Fernando will become.

I'll do as much as I can from now on. Not because I have to. Because I choose to.

There's so much to love about this essay.

Here's a behind-the-scenes look at how the author wrote this essay so you can figure out how to write yours:

FIRST, THE AUTHOR BRAINSTORMED THE CONTENT OF HIS ESSAY USING THE FEELINGS AND NEEDS EXERCISE

Did you spot the elements of that exercise?* If not, here they are:

- **Challenges:** Domestic abuse, alcoholic stepdad, little brother Fernando's birth, family's undocumented status
- **Effects:** Author and his brother shared the mental strain, father was arrested, funds were tight, mom worked two jobs, brothers took care of one another, they kept to themselves when dealing with financial and

---

* If you search on YouTube for "Feelings and Needs Exercise College Essay Guy," you'll see the author of this essay and me talk through the author's life experiences. I model something called mirroring, or reflective language. This can be especially useful for counselors/caretakers/guides helping students through this process.

medical issues, avoided going on certain school trips, at times author was discouraged from meeting new people, grades started to slip

- **Feelings:**[†] Confused yet understanding, anxious, worried, relieved, alone, lost, vulnerable, lonely, disconnected, heartbroken, ashamed, disillusioned
- **Needs:**[‡] Order, autonomy, reassurance, growth, safety, understanding, empathy, hope, support, self-acceptance
- **What he did about it:** Took care of his youngest brother; became his own teacher; learned how to fix a bike, swim, socialize; found a job to help pay bills; improved his grades; broke a school swimming record; learned to play instruments; became the first student in his school to pass the AP Physics 1 exam; took a leadership role in clubs; and tutored and counseled friends and peers
- **What he learned:** He's proud of what he's done, but wants to do more: dance the tango, solve a Rubik's Cube, explore perpetual motion, see the World Trade Center, see his little brother grow up…and do you notice the value here? Hunger. That was his number one value, by the way. And he ends by saying he'll do these things not because he has to, but because he chooses to. This sounds like autonomy. Another one of his top values.

That's why I love beginning with the Feelings and Needs Exercise. With just fifteen minutes of focused work, you can map out your whole story.

NEXT, THE AUTHOR USED NARRATIVE STRUCTURE TO GIVE SHAPE TO HIS ESSAY

Did you spot the narrative structure elements? If not, here they are:

- **Inciting incident:** While the author is brushing his teeth, his father is arrested for domestic abuse.[§]
- **Status quo:** His father had hurt his mom physically and mentally, and the

---

[†]   These feelings aren't all explicitly stated in the essay, but the author named them in his Feelings and Needs Exercise, which you'll find on page 98.

[‡]   These needs are not explicitly stated in the essay, but the author named them in his Feelings and Needs Exercise.

[§]   Note that the author begins with the Inciting Incident to grab our attention, then provides the Status Quo.

author and his brother had shared the mental strain. "It's what had to be done," he writes.

- **Raising the stakes:** The entire second and third paragraphs describe how living without a father meant money was tight for his family. Things improved for a while after his mother remarried, but his stepdad's chronic alcoholism (raise the stakes) plus a new little brother (raise the stakes again) made things even tougher. As if that wasn't enough, the author raises the stakes even further by revealing that his family was undocumented at the time.
- **Moment of truth:** At his lowest point, he decides to do something about it. "I grew determined to improve the quality of life for my family and myself," he writes, then goes on to tell us all of the amazing things he taught himself, the skills he learned and interests he pursued. It's inspiring.
- **New status quo**: Remember that the initial status quo was the author doing "what had to be done." Not so, by the end of the essay. In the final lines, he writes, "I'll do as much as I can from now on. Not because I have to. Because I choose to."

If This Feels Like It's Too Complicated, That's Okay.

You can use this simple structure to draft a solid Type C essay:

1/3—Challenges I faced and their impact on me
1/3—What I did to work through them
1/3—What I learned through the process

One More Conclusion Technique: Setup and Payoff

Did you notice how the author concluded the opening paragraphs with a variation of the phrase "what had to be done"? (He's setting up for the ending, though you won't know it until you get there.) Then, in the final line, he writes, "Not because I have to. Because I choose to." Why does this work as a final line? We see that he has changed—the person he was at the start is different from who he has become.

This technique is called "setup and payoff." What can you learn from this? Ask yourself: How is the person I am today different from who I was before? Conjure two mental images, one of "who I was" and one of "who I am now."

Imagine opening your story with a description of the first image and ending the story with the second.*

Type C Step-by-Step Recap:

1. As with the Type A essay, complete the brainstorming exercises from the "Essential Application Prework" and "Adrian's Brainstorming Exercises" chapters. Take special care to complete the Feelings and Needs Exercise, as it can be a powerful essay-outlining tool for both Type A and C essays.
2. Create an outline using narrative structure described on page 146.
3. Write a first draft.

You'll find more Type C and narrative structure example essays in the Treasure Trove.

Type D: Student Has Not Faced Significant Challenges (or Chooses Not to Write about Them) and Does Not Have a Clear Vision for Their Future (or Chooses Not to Write about It)

If this type of essay resonates, you may be wondering, "What do I write about?"

Be patient. It may take you longer to find your topic than other students. But resist the temptation to pick the hardest challenge you've been through and work to make it sound worse than it actually was just so you can write a Type A or C essay. Some students do this because they believe writing about a challenge is somehow inherently "better." But it isn't. In fact, you might find that focusing shortsightedly on one experience can sideline other brilliant and beautiful elements of your character that you could express by using the montage structure to provide a wider view of yourself and your life

If you're writing a Type D essay (remember this is a montage structure essay), you'll need two things: a variety of different parts of yourself that you want to show and a concept that ties all these parts of you together.

---

* For another really clear example of this, google "College Essay Guy with Debate Essay."

BEADS ON A THREAD

Here's a metaphor: Imagine that each different part of your personality, beliefs, values, life experience, etc., is a bead and that a select few of those beads will show up in your essay. They're not the kind of beads you'd find on a store-bought bracelet; they're more like the hand-painted beads on a bracelet your little brother made for you.

The theme of your essay is the thread that connects your beads.

Take the "My Laptop Stickers" essay for example. The "beads" are *creativity, open-mindedness, humor, courage*, and *entrepreneurialism*. The "thread" (i.e., the theme that ties everything together) is her laptop stickers. Actually, there's even a second thematic thread you could find: those qualities will also serve her in her women's rights activism. Bonus!

Note that there's a huge range of possible essay threads. Here are some different "thread" examples that have worked well:*

- **Sports** have had a powerful influence on me, from my understanding of history, to numbers, to my relationships, extracurricular activities, and even my career choice.
- **I lived with five different families** as an exchange student, and each one taught me something valuable that I will carry with me to college.
- **Crassulaceae plants**, which can reproduce via stem or leaf fragments, are a great analogy for not only how I make art, but how I choose to live each day.
- **Binary star systems** are a metaphor for my relationship with my parents.
- **I am "trans" in so many ways…**let me describe a few.
- To understand who I am, you must understand **how I cook**.
- **Pranks** have shaped my life in a variety of ways.
- **The number 12** has influenced so much in my life, from my relationship to sports, to how I write, to my self-esteem.

Okay, so if you're on board so far, here's what you need:

First, some stuff to write about (ideally four to ten things) that will make up the "beads" of your essay, and…

---

*   You'll find links to some of these essays, as well as a list of even more thematic threads, in the Treasure Trove.

Second, something to connect all the different "beads" (like a connective theme or thread).

Make sure you've completed the Essential Application Prework Exercises on pages 90–106 to generate tons of content that can be turned into beads. Now let me share an example of how I helped one student find her essay thread, then I'll offer you some exercises to help you find your own.

THE "HOME" ESSAY: A QUICK CASE STUDY

First, take a look at this student's Essence Objects and 21 Details:

My Essence Objects

1. Bojangle's Tailgate Special/Iced Tea
2. Light blue fuzzy blanket
3. A box containing my baby tooth
4. Band-Aid
5. Car keys
6. Gold bracelet from my grandfather
7. Orange, worn Nike Free Run Sneakers
8. Duke basketball game ticket
9. Palestine flag rubber wristband/ISEF Lanyard
10. Friendship bracelet
11. A pair of headphones
12. S'mores
13. Yin-yang symbol
14. Worn, green Governor's School East lanyard

My 21 Details

1. I've been known to have terrible spatial awareness despite being a dancer. Just last week, my shoelace got caught in an escalator and I tripped about twenty people.
2. Zumba and kickboxing are my favorite forms of exercise and I'm hopefully going to become certified to teach Zumba soon.

3. I have misophonia—sometimes I even have to eat dinner in a different room from my family.

4. My go-to drinks are Hi-C and sweet tea.

5. I became a pescatarian this year to avoid fried chicken, and I can honestly get a life's worth of meat out of cod, salmon, tilapia, shrimp, you name it.

6. I collect funky socks—at this point, I have socks with tacos, snowmen, Santa, and even animals wearing glasses.

7. I've gotten different Myers-Briggs personality types every time I took the test. The most recent ones are ENFJ and ENFP.

8. I have no immediate relatives in America besides my mom, dad, and sister.

9. I am a diehard Duke basketball fan, and I can identify all of the Duke basketball fans at my high school on one hand.

10. I love discussing psychology, but sometimes I psychoanalyze.

11. Singing while driving is honestly one of my favorite pastimes.

12. My alarm for school every morning is at 5:42 a.m.

13. I hope to complete a half and full marathon within the next four years, despite not having run a 5K yet.

14. I realized the tooth fairy wasn't real after I lost my second tooth, but I pretended that I still believed in it until I was in 5th grade for the tooth fairy's "gifts."

15. I could eat fruits for every single meal.

16. I don't do well with confrontation.

17. Airports are hands down my favorite place to be, but I hate airplanes.

18. If I'm not busy or working, you can usually find me in my hammock in the backyard.

19. I find that I form the deepest connections with people after 12 a.m.

20. Sometimes, I like TV spoilers.

21. I can't think of something for #21, so let's go with 20 for now.

How This Author Found Her Thematic Thread

When I met with this student for the first time, I began asking questions about her objects and details: "What's up with the Bojangle's Iced Tea? What's meaningful to you about the Governor's School East lanyard? Tell me about your relationship to dance…"

We were *thread finding*—searching for a connection among all the things she listed in her exercises that would allow her to talk about different parts of her life.

Heads up: some people are really good at this—counselors are often great at this—while some folks have a more difficult time. Good news: when you practice the skill of thread finding, you can become better at it rather quickly.

You should also know that sometimes it takes minutes to find a thread and sometimes it can take weeks. With this student, it took less than an hour.

I noticed in our conversation that she kept coming back to things that made her feel comfortable. She also repeated the word "home" several times. When I pointed this out, she asked me, "Do you think I could use 'home' as a thread for my essay?"

"I think you could," I said.

Read her essay below, then I'll share more about how you can find your own thematic thread.

HOME

As I enter the double doors, the smell of freshly rolled biscuits hits me almost instantly. I trace the fan blades as they swing above me, emitting a low, repetitive hum resembling a faint melody. After bringing our usual order, the "Tailgate Special," to the table, my father begins discussing the recent performance of Apple stock with my mother, myself, and my older eleven-year-old sister. Bojangle's, a southern establishment well-known for its fried chicken and reliable fast food, is my family's Friday night restaurant, often accompanied by trips to Eva Perry, the nearby library. With one hand on my breaded chicken and the other on *Nancy Drew: Mystery of Crocodile Island*, I can barely sit still as the thriller unfolds. They're imprisoned! Reptiles! Not the enemy's boat! As I delve into the narrative with a sip of sweet tea, I feel at home.

"Five, six, seven, eight!" As I shout the counts, nineteen dancers grab and begin to spin the tassels attached to their swords while walking heel-to-toe to the next formation of the classical Chinese sword dance. A glance at my notebook reveals a collection of worn pages covered with meticulously planned formations, counts, and movements. Through sharing videos of my performances with my relatives or discovering and choreographing the nuances of certain regional dances and their reflection on the region's distinct culture, I deepen my relationship with my parents, heritage, and community. When I step on stage, the hours I've spent choreographing, creating poses, teaching, and polishing are all worthwhile, and the stage becomes my home.

Set temperature. Calibrate. Integrate. Analyze. Set temperature. Calibrate. Integrate. Analyze. This pulse mimics the beating of my heart, a subtle rhythm that persists each day I come into the lab. Whether I am working under the fume hood with platinum nanoparticles, manipulating raw integration data, or spraying a thin platinum film over pieces of copper, it is in Lab 304 in Hudson Hall that I first feel the distinct sensation, and I'm home. After spending several weeks attempting to synthesize platinum nanoparticles with a diameter between 10 and 16 nm, I finally achieve nanoparticles with a diameter of 14.6 nm after carefully monitoring the sulfuric acid bath. That unmistakable tingling sensation dances up my arm as I scribble into my notebook: I am overcome with a feeling of unbridled joy.

Styled in a T-shirt, shorts, and a worn, dark green lanyard, I sprint across the quad from the elective "Speaking Arabic through the Rassias Method" to "Knitting Nirvana." This afternoon is just one of many at Governor's School East, where I have been transformed from a high school student into a philosopher, a thinker, and an avid learner. While I attend GS at Meredith College for Natural Science, the lessons learned and experiences gained extend far beyond physics concepts, serial dilutions, and toxicity. I learn to trust myself to have difficult yet necessary conversations about the political and economic climate. Governor's School breeds a culture of inclusivity and multidimensionality, and I am transformed from "girl who is hardworking" or "science girl" to someone who indulges in the sciences, debates about psychology and the economy, and loves to swing and salsa dance. As I form a slip knot and cast on, I'm at home.

My home is a dynamic and eclectic entity. Although I've lived in the same house in Cary, North Carolina, for ten years, I have found and carved homes and communities that are filled with and enriched by tradition, artists, researchers, and intellectuals. While I may not always live within a five-mile radius of a Bojangle's or in close proximity to Lab 304, learning to become a more perceptive daughter and sister, to share the beauty of my heritage, and to take risks and redefine scientific and personal expectations will continue to impact my sense of home.

Rad essay, huh?

OTHER WAYS TO FIND A THEMATIC THREAD FOR YOUR TYPE D PERSONAL STATEMENT

In the example you just read, we started with the beads (her Essence Objects and 21 Details) and then we searched for a thread. This is a reliable way to use the exercises you've already done and the beads you already have to find a thematic thread that will connect enough of them to create an essay. If you find it difficult to identify a thematic thread, try these other brainstorming exercises.

BEAD-MAKING EXERCISE

Time: 5–8 minutes

Instructions:

This exercise asks you to start with a thematic thread made from a topic you know well and then create the beads that fit with that thematic thread. Here's how it works:

Step 1: On a blank sheet of paper, make a list of five or six things you know a lot about. For example, I know a lot about...

Words/language	Voices/accents
Games	Self-help books
Productivity	

If you can think of only three or four, that's okay.

Step 2: Read through your list of things you know a lot about and pick one that you think you might like to write an essay about, flip your paper over, and write it at the top of your paper. This is your thread, or a potential thread.

Step 3: Underneath what you wrote down, name five to six values that you could connect to this. These will serve as the beads of your essay. Be sure to review your Values Exercise (page 5) for ideas, and remember that uncommon or otherwise unexpected values can make for a more interesting essay (page 231).

You could even draw a thread connecting your beads, if you want, like this:

Step 4: For each value, write down a specific example, memory, image, or essence object that connects to that value. Check out your Essence Objects (page 2) and Core Memories (page 7) exercises for some possibilities.

My examples/memories/images/essence objects:

Connection: One memory I have is playing "I love" in a circle at camp with twenty friends and strangers. I still marvel at how quickly it helped us bond.

Creativity: After I understand how a game works, I like to try to improve it by tweaking the rules. Two examples come to mind. I remember when I was young trying to find the right amount of money for the Free Parking space in Monopoly, and recently I learned the game Guesstimation is so much better if you add wagers. I see my four-year-old tweaks games too, which drives my wife crazy, as she likes to trust that the rules of the game are there for a reason (which, okay, I kind of get).

Fun/laughter: As I've aged, so much of my life has become planned/programmed, but I can still enjoy losing track of time with board games. Two weeks ago, for example, I laughed so hard I cried while playing Drawful with my friends Lisa, Andy, and Sage.

Family: We played games like charades and Jeopardy when I was young. (My dad was the Game Master who would come up with the categories. As I grew older, I took over the role of Game Master.)

Competition: People don't know this about me because I seem so chill, but I am incredibly competitive. Things I rarely lose at: ping-pong, Tetris, foosball, and cornhole. I've gotten much better over the years at hiding my competitive side, but it's still there.

Knowledge: Can't really think of much on this one—maybe something related to Jeopardy?

This is an actual brainstorm I did using this exercise. Note that I couldn't come up with something for the last one, "knowledge," which is fine. The point is, if you know a thing well, odds are good you'll be able to make a lot of connections to your values. And if you can find a specific example for each value, that can make for interesting paragraphs in your personal statement.

If you're willing to spend a few more minutes, ask "so what?" of each example to see if a specific insight emerges. For examples, check out the "My Laptop Stickers" three-column brainstorming chart on page 158.

And in case you want a formula for what I'm describing, here you go:

value (bead) + example + insight = one paragraph

Once you've written down at least one example (e.g., a memory, image, essence object) and insight (answer to the question "so what?") for each bead (value), you'll probably have enough content for an essay.

FIVE THINGS EXERCISE*

Similar to the Bead-Making Exercise, in this one you'll identify the thread first and then develop the beads.

Step 1: Write down the title of a list of things that are meaningful to you in different ways and include the word "Five" in the title. For example, "Five Pairs of Shoes I've Worn," "Five Houses I've Lived In," "Five Photographs in My Room," "Five Ways Cooking Has Influenced Me," etc. (Spoiler: this is your thematic thread.)

Step 2: Begin by simply naming the five different items in the list. An example of items for the Five Pairs of Shoes list might include high-top tennis shoes,

---

* Special thanks to my colleague Dori Middlebrook for this one.

flip-flops, heels, cleats, and bunny slippers. (Another spoiler: these are your beads.)

Step 3: Add physical details so we can visualize each item on the list.

Step 4: Add more details. Maybe tell a story for each. Pro Tip: Try connecting each of the five to a different value from your Values Exercise (page 5).

Step 5: Expand on each description and start to connect the ideas to develop them into an essay draft.*

THREAD FINDING WITH A PARTNER

Grab someone who knows you well (e.g., a counselor, friend, family member). Share all your brainstorming content with them and ask them to reflect back to you what they're noticing. It can be helpful if they use reflective language and ask lots of questions. An example of a reflective observation is "I'm hearing that _____ has been pretty important in your life...is that right?"† You're hunting together for a thematic thread—something that might connect different parts of your life and self.

THREAD FINDING WITH PHOTOGRAPHS

Pick ten of your favorite photos or social media posts and write a short paragraph on each one. Why'd you pick these photos? What do they say about you? Then ask yourself, "What are some things these photos have in common?" Bonus points: Can you find one thing that connects all of them?

READING LOTS OF MONTAGE EXAMPLE ESSAYS THAT WORK

You'll find some in this book, some in my first book *College Essay Essentials*, and links to more examples in the Treasure Trove. While you may be tempted to steal those thematic threads, don't. Try finding your own. Have the courage to be original. You can do it.

---

* You'll find these example essays in the Treasure Trove under "The Five Things Exercise + Example Essays."

† For an example of how to use reflective language, search YouTube for the phrase "College Essay Guy Feelings and Needs Exercise (How to Review It)."

The Type D essay tends to be tough to do, but it's totally possible and can make for some great results. To prove it, here's another example essay that uses an everyday object as the thematic thread:

MY DESK

Six years ago, a scrawny twelve-year-old kid took his first steps into Home Depot: the epitome of manliness. As he marched through the wood section, his eyes scrolled past the options. Red Oak? No, too ubiquitous. Pine? No, too banal. Mahogany? Perfect, it would nicely complement his walls. As days went on, the final product was almost ready. Ninety-one degree angles had been perfected to ninety. Drawer slides had been lubricated ten times over. Finally, the masterpiece was finished, and the little boy couldn't help but smile. A scrawny twelve-year-old kid had become a scrawny twelve-year-old man. **This desk I sit at has not only seen me through the last six years, but its story and the story of the objects I keep on it provide a foundation for my future pursuits.**

My trustworthy, five-year-old **laptop** sits in the center of the desk. From accompanying me on my ventures to track Null Pointer Errors in my apps to playing classic Billy Joel after a rough day, my laptop is my first-choice vehicle as I drive through a life of curiosity. Whether executing my simulations of stress-analysis tests, teaching me how to make an origami lily, or showing me a TED talk on why people find it difficult to poop away from home, my laptop has allowed me to find different versions of myself. Though I will probably call myself an engineer someday, my heart is in so many different places. I'm a philosopher, a historian, an economist, a black belt in tae kwon do, a tech-y, a farmer, a teacher, an inventor, an entrepreneur, a TED-talk lover, and a sports enthusiast. With each google search, a new world opens.

To my left is a **stack of books**. To earn a coveted top spot in the stack, the "winning" book has to have taught me

His word choice shows us he cares about language

Meticulous...

Thorough...

Here's his thesis, which launches the essay.

I call this geeky language. It shows he knows what he's talking about in just a few words.

Also note the range of labels he's comfortable identifying with.

He's confident enough to use self-effacing humor

He's also smart...

...and he's funny.

The first "bead" on his bracelet—also an essence object!

Notice the wide range of interests that connect back to his laptop.

He's setting up for his ending here so it doesn't feel too random when he references start-ups at the end.

Second "bead" on his bracelet

Values: personal
growth and
vulnerability

a life lesson OR made me cry. Currently, the book on top is *The Way of the Seal* by Mark Divine. Divine's memoir details the training required to become an elite warrior and how

Value: balance

that mentality can be applied to success in all aspects of life (social, mental, physical, and spiritual). Like Divine, I try to avoid a tunnel-vision attitude and consider the implications of my actions on society at large, as a leader and a role model. While running my company, a nonprofit that kindles interest in STEM around the world, I have been particularly

Very brief mention of career that doesn't give away too much.

guided by the principle of leading from the battlefield. This

Values: leadership and humility

mantra of collaborative leadership helps me facilitate many processes, from managing social media to collaborating with potential investors. I'm also reminded to sometimes take a step back in the midst of a crisis and let the universe

Value: perspective

give me the answers.

To the right of the books is **a bead bracelet** identical

Another bead on the thread—and essence object.

to the ones my parents and brother wear. When I look at it, I remember my parents' secret sign language as I stood on the stage of FBLA nationals. One thumbs up means

Values: family, calm, humor

"remember to breathe," two thumbs up means "remember to smile for the photos." Regardless, I forgot to smile for the photo. When I look at the bracelet, I also see my little brother tugging on me, asking me countless questions as I repair my cube-stacking robot. "What's that weird looking spinny thing?" It's obviously a 0.81 lb, 5 mm shaft diameter, 5700 rpm, 35 oz-in stall torque, 22 amp stall current, brushless DC

Here's another example of weaving in brags that don't feel like brags because they're connected to a value (collaborative leadership).

More humor. Also makes us like him.

motor. Duh.

One day you'll find me in a corner office somewhere,

Returns to the essay's central thematic thread: the desk.

running a couple of **different tech startups**, but the desk I'll be sitting at is this same one. I never want to forget that, at heart, I am a confident skinny little nerd unafraid and eager to take my next Home Depot trip.

Returns to Home Depot, which represents building/ creating/learning (all themes in his essay).

TYPE D ESSAY FAQS

What am I looking for again?

You're looking for two things:

1. Parts of yourself that are essential to who you are, a.k.a. your "beads" (e.g., values or "islands of your personality"), and…
2. A theme, or thread, that connects them all.

Your theme could be something mundane or something everyone can relate to, but make sure that it is elastic (i.e., can connect to many different parts of you) and visual, as storytelling is made richer with images.

This is hard! I'm not finding it yet and I want to give up. What should I do?

Don't give up, at least not yet. Remember, be patient. This takes time. If you need inspiration, or assurance that you're on the right track, check out Elizabeth Gilbert's TED Talk, "Your Elusive Creative Genius."

In the Treasure Trove, you'll find:
→ A variety of sample montage and narrative structure essays
→ Four Qualities of a Great Personal Statement (i.e., The Great College Essay Test)

Part VI

The Supplemental Essays

Chapter 12

Creating Your Supplemental Essay Tracker

Supplemental essays feature a variety of prompts designed to help colleges dig deeper into who you are, what matters to you, and what you can bring to their school. When you're applying to eight to ten schools, these essays can add up, which is why...

In this chapter, we'll cover:

- Organizing the essays you'll need to write in your College List and Essay Tracker
- How spending twenty minutes doing this now will save you twenty hours in the long run

For this chapter to make sense, you'll need a list of colleges that you're likely to apply to and your own College List and Essay Tracker. If you don't yet have either of those, read the chapter "How to Create a Balanced College List" (page 41) and then come back here, because I'm about to ask you to look up all your supplemental essays and copy/paste them into that handy spreadsheet. And here's how you're going to do it:

Step 1: Go to the College List and Essay Tracker spreadsheet and click on the tab at the bottom that says "Essay Tracker."

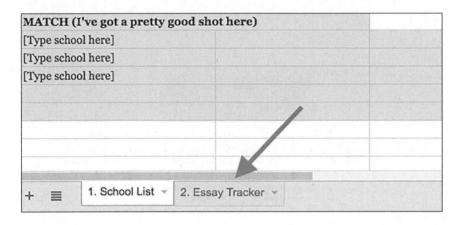

BTW: If you don't have this spreadsheet, you'll find a template in the Treasure Trove.

Step 2: Find the supplemental essay prompts for each school using one of these methods.[*]

- **Common App or Coalition App.** This is a reliable way to find up-to-date information on supplemental essay prompts; however, some prompts are a bit tricky to find (e.g., some are listed in an additional questions section) and not every school is on one of these platforms.
- **Individual school websites.** If the prompts aren't on the Common App or Coalition App, this way is slow but reliable. Schools tend to post prompts on their sites around the same time they publish them to the Common App.
- **A third-party medium.** In the Treasure Trove, you'll find my favorite software for looking up essay prompts.

Step 3: Copy and paste the prompts and word limits into your Essay Tracker. It'll look something like this:

School	Essays Required	Word Limit	Topic Chosen
Common App	Main statement	650	
	Common App Activities List	150 chars per	
	Add'l info, if needed	650	

---

[*]   Note that supplemental essay prompts are usually released around August, so if you're looking them up before then, make sure you aren't looking at the previous year's prompts.

School	Essays Required	Word Limit	Topic Chosen
Northwestern (Sample)	Other parts of your application give us a sense for how you might contribute to Northwestern. But we also want to consider how Northwestern will contribute to your interests and goals. In 300 words or less, help us understand what aspects of Northwestern appeal most to you, and how you'll make use of specific resources and opportunities here.	300	
USC (Sample)	1. Please respond to one of the prompts below. USC believes that one learns best when interacting with people of different backgrounds, experiences, and perspectives. Tell us about a time you were exposed to a new idea or when your beliefs were challenged by another point of view. Describe something outside of your intended academic focus about which you are interested in learning. What is something about yourself that is essential to understanding you?	250	
	2. Describe how you plan to pursue your academic interests at USC. Please feel free to address your first- and second-choice major selections.	250	
	3. Answer all: Describe yourself in three words.	25 characters each	
	What is your favorite snack?	100 characters	
	Favorite app/website	100 characters	
	Best movie of all time	100 characters	

At this point, some students freak out because they see how many essays they'll need to write. Don't worry. In the following chapter I'll show you how to identify when and where you can write a Super Essay™† that will cover multiple prompts and significantly cut down your workload.

In the Treasure Trove, you'll find:

→   My favorite third-party software for collecting supplemental essays

→   A College List + Essay Tracker spreadsheet [Template]

---

†   I'm joking with the trademark symbol here. It's just to show you this approach is *super* legit. ;)

The Super Essay (Combining Essay Prompts to Write Better Essays in Less Time)

One of the most daunting aspects of applying to college is the sheer number of essays you have to—wait, get to!—write.

What do I mean? Say you're applying to eight to ten schools. While not every school has supplemental essays, some have up to five essays you'll need to write in addition to your personal statement. Quick math tells us that could end up being several dozen supplemental essay prompts. But guess what?

You totally don't have to write several dozen essays.

In fact, you may end up writing fewer than ten. Why? I've developed a pretty simple, step-by-step process designed to help you see which supplemental essay prompts can overlap. Follow my lead and it may not only save you dozens of hours of writing, it may also improve the quality of those essays.

In this chapter, we'll cover:

- A relatively quick and totally free way to figure out which of your essay topics overlap
- How to write a Super Essay that will work for multiple prompts
- Two sample Super Essays
- How to expand the elasticity of your topic using the Best Extracurricular Activities Exercise I've Ever Seen (BEABIES)

The Overlapping Game

Writing an essay that works for several prompts leads to essays that have much more *elasticity* (i.e., they can stretch to fit multiple prompts), which often means they'll have more depth and variety.

For example, a single essay you write about your improv comedy troupe could probably work for both of the following prompts (emphasis is mine):

(University of Michigan) Everyone belongs to many different communities and/or groups defined by (among other things) shared geography, religion, ethnicity, income, cuisine, interest, race, ideology, or intellectual heritage. **Choose one of the communities to which you belong, and describe that community and your place within it.**

Duke University seeks a talented, engaged student body that embodies the wide range of human experience; we believe that the diversity of our students makes our community stronger. **If you'd like to share a perspective you bring or experiences you've had to help us understand you better**—perhaps related to a community you belong to, your sexual orientation or gender identity, or your family or cultural background—**we encourage you to do so**. Real people are reading your application, and we want to do our best to understand and appreciate the real people applying to Duke.

And if your essay answers both prompts, it'll probably be a better essay.

But it doesn't just have to be two essay prompts. The more prompts you find that your topic could work for, the more time you'll save and the better your essay might be. Take this prompt, for example:

(Stanford University) Tell us about something that is meaningful to you and why.

You could use the same improv comedy troupe essay to answer that prompt too, right? Plus, now Stanford will not only learn why improv comedy is meaningful to you (from their own prompt), but also how it has created a community for you (from the Michigan prompt) AND how it has equipped you with a unique perspective (from the Duke prompt).

Here's a Venn Diagram to help illustrate this:

> **Wait, is it okay to do this?**
>
> Yes! As long as the student removes all references to other schools before they submit it again…Nothing is worse than reading a great essay addressed to another school. —*Brian Liechti, Warren Wilson College*

How to Plan Your Super Essays

STEP 1: COLLECT ALL YOUR COLLEGE ESSAY PROMPTS IN YOUR ESSAY TRACKER

If you completed the exercise on pages 183–185 you've already done this. If not, be sure to do that and come back after you've completed the exercise.

STEP 2: CREATE YOUR ACTIVITIES LIST

If you completed the exercise on page 103, you've already done this. If not, be sure to do that too and come back after you've completed the exercise.

STEP 3: CHOOSE TWO TO FOUR ROCK STAR ACHIEVEMENTS OR PASSION PROJECTS OF YOURS

A rock star achievement is anything you've done that's especially (for lack of a better word) impressive. These might include:

- Starting or leading a project or club that makes a tangible impact on people's lives
- Performing independent research, maybe with a teacher or professor, and publishing your findings
- Creating a product or service that makes people's lives easier

A passion project is something that you've put lots of time, effort, thought, and emotional investment into because of your own drive to do something you thought was interesting or important. If it's also a rock star achievement, then that's awesome! You'll definitely want to include that in your list here, but it doesn't need to be an achievement. It just needs to be something that shows your drive and what matters to you. Some possible passion projects might include:

- Developing a mobile puzzle game
- Participating in a citizen-science initiative cataloging butterfly species
- Writing and illustrating your own sci-fi graphic novel

STEP 4: IDENTIFY YOUR SUPER TOPICS

A super topic is something (often an activity) that can potentially work as the topic for a super essay covering multiple essay prompts (e.g., the improv comedy troupe topic). And, if you've completed the step above, hopefully you have in mind a couple options.

How do you know what else might be a super topic? It could be something you've spent a lot of time doing but that is not featured in your personal statement, like the "Durham Youth Commission" essay (see page 193). Or it could be something a little unusual that might help you stand out, like the hiking essay (see page 192). Before moving ahead, spend a minute or two brainstorming a couple ideas for potential topics.

Once you have one to four potential super topics in mind, it's time for...

STEP 5: THE OVERLAPPING GAME

In the topics column of your essay tracker, note which topic(s) might work for which prompt. For example, say you picked "hiking" as a potential super topic. And say your list of supplemental essay prompts looks like this:

> In the space available, discuss the significance to you of the school or summer activity in which you have been most involved. (1/2 page)
>
> Briefly describe a nonacademic pursuit (such as service to community or family, a club or sport, or work) that best illustrates who you are and why it is important to you. (250 words)
>
> Please briefly elaborate on one of your extracurricular activities or work experiences. (150 words)
>
> Everyone belongs to many different communities and/or groups defined by (among other things) shared geography, religion, ethnicity, income, cuisine, interest, race, ideology, or intellectual heritage. Choose one of the communities to which you belong, and describe that community and your place within it. (250 words)
>
> We're seeking a talented, engaged student body that embodies the wide range of human experience; we believe that the diversity of our students makes our community stronger. If you'd like to share a perspective you bring or experiences you've had to help us understand you better...we encourage you to do so.* (250 words)

Ask yourself, for which of these topics could "hiking" potentially work? It can work for them all, of course, and I'll show you how in the example that follows.

But first a heads-up: you don't want to go overboard with this and try to overlap ALL your prompts, as that could get messy. Be creative, but know that you'll have to write at least a few different essays.

---

* To keep things organized, try color coding your different super topics. To see an example of this, check out www.tinyurl.com/adrianessaytracker or look in the Treasure Trove.

STEP 6: COMPLETE THE BEABIES EXERCISE

What's that again? Simply the **B**est **E**xtracurricular **A**ctivity **B**rainstorm **I**'ve **E**ver **S**een. On page 108 you'll find the full set of instructions for this exercise and a list of twenty-five questions that will not only help you with your activities list but will also help you brainstorm super essay content. Here's an example:

Activity: Hiking				
What I Did	**Problems I Solved**	**Lessons Learned/Skills I Gained**	**Impact I Had**	**How I Applied What I Learned**
Arranged and led Historical Trail hikes Provided first-hand perspectives on what it felt like to sleep at Valley Forge in the winter Told stories to scout mates about the history that surrounded us Mentored scouts on how to orienteer and conserve the environment around us (Leave no trace) Maintained trail we adopted	Helped preserve the environment, specifically a trail we adopted Applied the lessons of biology to conservation Mentored new scouts who were unfamiliar with hiking and the dangers/joys that come with it The disconnect that one Cub Scout (Louis) felt after leaving his video games	The beauty of the outdoors The joy of mentoring others The value of disconnecting from technology	Spread the importance of preserving history through stories among peers Mentored peers in developing scouting skills and appreciation of preserving the environment Helped Louis connect more closely with nature	Connected w/ history class even more Made me a better (academic) tutor Taught me how other seemingly unrelated subjects (ex: music w/ science) could be connected

Okay, your turn.

Choose a potential super topic and spend ten to fifteen minutes filling out a BEABIES chart. By the end you should have enough content for a super essay. You can create it on your own, if you like, or click the "BEABIES Exercise Downloadable Template + Examples" link in the Treasure Trove. There you'll find a blank chart plus two BEABIES examples.

Do this now.

STEP 7: BRAINSTORM YOUR SUPER ESSAY, THEN WRITE IT

Finally, here's an example of a super essay about hiking:

HIKING

By starting with an academic subject, this essay could answer a prompt asking about an academic subject that inspires him.

I'm a history nerd, to the point where I would be that guy reading history textbooks for fun. However, reading about history can only go so far. Through Boy Scouts, I have been able to arrange and lead Historical Trail hikes, giving myself and my troop firsthand perspectives on what it felt like to sleep at Valley Forge in the winter, or what the walk up Breed's Hill along Boston's Freedom Trail is really like.

I call this "curiosity with legs": he goes from reading about history to experiencing it firsthand.

Naturally, I became the troop "storyteller" along these hikes, adding my own tidbits of information such as pointing out Eisenhower's five-star general flag waving from his personal putting green in Gettysburg or how Spuyten Duyvil was perhaps named following one of the first reported shark attacks in America.

These details are great because they show us what it might be like on one of his historical hikes. Also great for covering a "summer activity" prompt.

This paragraph shows not only his commitment to the environment, but also some of the skills he's developed through Boy Scouts, and the details came directly from his BEABIES.

Organizing these historical hikes has also given me the opportunity to teach younger Scouts about various Scouting skills, from orienteering (using a map and compass) to conservation principles like Leave-No-Trace. My troop engages in trail maintenance projects, and we actively monitor a trail we adopted from the NY/NJ Trail Conference.

I especially relished the opportunity to apply what I had learned in AP Biology toward actually helping preserve the environment. It is one thing to learn about pollution, global warming, and invasive species in a classroom; it is another thing entirely to see the biodiversity of an ecosystem quickly succumb to man-made pressures.

This is from the final column of his BEABIES (my favorite column) and demonstrates the importance of these hikes.

Here's a great example of impact (column 4 of the BEABIES).

Finally, hiking with the Boy Scouts has given me the chance to help others experience the beauty of the outdoors. On a recent hike, a new Scout, Louis, confided in me how disconnected he felt away from his video games. I stayed with Louis for the remainder of the hike and pointed out everything from milkweed stalks to coyote scat. After the hike, Louis was exhausted but had a glimmer of excitement toward the environment around him and could even tell the difference between poison ivy and Virginia creeper. Louis is currently one of my troop's most active younger Scouts.

The conclusion, which feels both surprising and inevitable, brings the whole essay together.

When I'm hiking, I'm not merely a hiker; I'm a historian, a conservationist, and a teacher all in one.

Can you see how this essay could work for a wide variety of prompts? Turn back to the prompts on page 190 to see what I mean.

Here's another one of my favorite super essays, written by a student who used the process I outlined earlier. You'll see how her essay could have worked for any of the prompts mentioned in the Venn diagram on page 188 or the start of a "Why Us?" essay (read more about those on page 196).

DURHAM YOUTH COMMISSION

When I joined the Durham Youth Commission, I met David. David told me his cousin's body had been stuffed into the trunk of a car after he was killed in a gang fight. After that, my notion of normal would never be the same.

Besides being a fantastic hook (which it is), this opening would allow the student to use this for a prompt asking the author to reflect on engagement with someone who is very different from her.

Drawing its nearly thirty members from a spectrum of public, charter, and private high schools, the DYC is a group of motivated students chosen to represent youth interests within the Durham County government. To say it is diverse would be an understatement. It is a melting pot of ideologies, skins, socioeconomic classes, faiths, and educations that is nearly unparalleled in Durham.

This paragraph would allow this essay to work for a prompt asking the author to reflect on a community she's a part of.

When I first heard stories like David's, I only saw the ways in which our lives seemed to be going in thirty different directions. However, I soon realized that the members of the DYC never let those differences become an obstacle to understanding. Even now, our experiences are like an elaborate network of roads: weaving, bumping, and diverging in unexpected ways. The DYC became an outlet for us to bring our individual experiences into a shared space of empathy.

This was taken from the Lessons Learned column of the BEABIES.

David recounted heartbreaking stories about boys

who are brutally punished for being in the wrong place at the wrong time. DYC supervisor Crystal Alexander told me about girls who get ten-day school suspensions for simply stepping on another student's sneakers. Witnessa educated us about "food deserts," where people never know when their next meal will be. And I talked about being born in Tokyo, moving to North Carolina, and living in London for a year, finding a way to call each place home. How my family's blending of Jewish tradition and Chinese culture— bagels and lox on weekends and dumplings every Lunar New Year—bridges distinct worlds. Honest discourse takes place at every meeting, adding new facets to my knowledge of the local community.

My experience in this dynamic space of affirmation and engagement has shaped me into a more thoughtful person and listener. We learn from each other and use our differences to come up with multifaceted solutions for issues facing twenty-first century youth. It is that motivation to solve real problems through cooperation and tolerance that I hope to bring with me to college. After joining the DYC, I felt my life's frame of reference double in size. I want to continue this effort and be the woman, friend, classmate, and student who both expands perspectives and takes action after hearing people's stories.

Macalester has a genuine devotion to increasing multiculturalism, promoting diversity, and broadening students' worldviews. Whether it be through the SPEAK Series, nearly thirty organizations promoting on-campus diversity, over ninety study-abroad programs, or a multitude of course partnerships with Twin Cities businesses, Macalester is the ideal place for me to continue the growth I've started in the DYC. Reconciling disparate lifestyles and backgrounds has prepared me to become a compassionate leader at Macalester, a place where I can both expand perspectives and take collaborative action.

These two paragraphs directly answer both prompts listed earlier, showing us not only what she's learned, but what unique perspective she might bring to a campus.

This paragraph was added for a particular school (Macalaster), which asked how her background, experiences, or outlook might add to the campus community, academically and personally.

Check out that final paragraph again. Can you see how the author transitions from discussing what she has learned from her involvement with the Durham Youth Commission into describing why she might be a good fit for a particular school? The author does this by making sure some of her values (diversity, compassion, collaboration) are clear in the first half of the essay, then naming a few specific ways those values might manifest themselves on campus. And, while this might work well for a prompt that asks some version of "What would you contribute to our campus?" I wouldn't necessarily advocate for this strategy on all your "Why Us?" essays (which you're going to read about in just a moment). What would I recommend instead?

Turn the page.

In the Treasure Trove, you'll find:

→ An example essay tracker with potential (color coded!) super topics

→ BEABIES Exercise Downloadable Template + Examples

Chapter 14

How to Write the "Why Us?" Essay

The purpose of the "Why Us?" or "Why this college?" essay is to demonstrate—through specific details and examples—why you and a school are a great match. In some cases, the "Why Us?" essay is an important way to demonstrate interest (see page 76).

In this chapter, we'll cover:

- Five common mistakes students make on the "Why Us?" essay
- How to write your "Why Us?" essay
- How to find all the resources you need to learn about a particular school
- The top-secret three-word trick to finding specific info for your "Why Us?" essay
- Three approaches to the "Why Us?" essay
- How to write a "Why Us?" essay if you don't know what you want to study
- Three ways to make sure your "Why Us?" essay is doing its job

Five Common Mistakes Students Make on the "Why Us?" Essay

MISTAKE #1: WRITING ABOUT THE SCHOOL'S SIZE, LOCATION, REPUTATION, WEATHER, OR RANKING

Why shouldn't you do this? Because that's what many other students are writing about, and you don't want to blend in. Take a hint from Emory University, whose "Why Us?" prompt used to read:

> Many students decide to apply to Emory University based on our size, location, reputation, and yes, the weather. Besides these valid reasons as a possible college choice, why is Emory University a particularly good match for you?

Or check out Georgia Tech's prompt:

> Beyond rankings, location, and athletics, why are you interested in attending Georgia Tech?

Clearly their admission readers are tired of reading about those things.

On a related note, find out the school's common traditions (throwing toast on the field at Penn, for example, or painting the rock at Northwestern) and then *don't write about those things*. Why? Everyone and their brother already has.

MISTAKE #2: SIMPLY USING EMOTIONAL LANGUAGE TO DEMONSTRATE FIT

Telling the school that you walked onto campus and "it just felt right" (a) is something else a lot of students say and (b) doesn't help the reader understand how you are a good match for the school. And for that matter, neither does the statement, "I can see myself rooting for the Wildcats at MetLife Stadium on Sundays."

MISTAKE #3: SCREWING UP THE MASCOT, STADIUM, TEAM COLORS, OR NAMES OF ANY IMPORTANT PEOPLE OR PLACES ON CAMPUS

This is one of the quickest ways to show you're a crappy researcher. In the example in mistake #2, for example, the Wildcats play neither at MetLife Stadium nor on Sundays.* Also, the "I can see myself in [insert school colors here]" is a cliché of the "Why Us?" essay. Avoid it too.

MISTAKE #4: PARROTING THE BROCHURES OR WEBSITE LANGUAGE

It could be that the person reading your essay and evaluating your application actually wrote the words you're copying and pasting. "On the one hand, it shows that a student has actually researched us and I appreciate that," says Brian Liechti of Warren Wilson College. "On the other, as one of those people who wrote the words you're copying, I'd rather see evidence of how what I wrote resonated with you—do we share values?† What stood out or spoke to you in that brochure or on that web page? That's what I really want to see."

MISTAKE #5: THINKING OF THIS AS ONLY A "WHY THEM?" ESSAY

The school knows it's awesome. "You probably don't need to tell us about the beautiful Nott Memorial," says Nicole Buenzli of Union College. "I pass the Nott every day, it's on every brochure we create, and we all know it has sixteen sides!"

Instead, think of this as a "Why are we perfect for each other?" essay.

In fact, imagine you're on a date and the person sitting across from you leans in to ask, "So, why do you like me?" Don't just say, "Because you're hot," or "My auntie says a relationship with you will improve my job prospects." When it comes to the "us" in "Why Us?" think of it this way:

"Us" ≠ the school by itself

---

*   And based on their home record these days, neither do the Giants. But I digress.

†   Yes, he actually said "values," and no, I did not pay him to say that.

"Us" = the school + you

In order to prove you and the school are destined to be together, make connections between the two of you. Here's a step-by-step guide for doing just that.

How to Write Your Essay

STEP 1: DO YOUR RESEARCH

How? Much like you did when you were creating your college list.

"Click deep" on the school's website.‡

Spend serious time on the school's online catalog/course schedule and look for not only majors and minors, but also specific programs, courses, activities, and opportunities that set this school apart from all the others you're applying to.

Read reviews from experts.

Here are some good college guide books:

> *The Fiske Guide to Colleges* (Edward B. Fiske)§
> *Colleges That Change Lives* (Loren Pope)
> *The Best 384 Colleges* (Princeton Review)

Read student reviews.

Students sometimes say things that experts don't or won't say. Both Niche. com and Unigo.com have real student reviews. Read a bunch so you can get a sense of the campus vibe and aren't skewed by just one or two opinions. I

---

‡   Shout-out to my counselor friend Michelle Myers for this term.

§   This is my top choice, as it has long been one of the best resources for researching schools. You'll likely find one in your counselor's office or at your local library, or you can purchase a searchable version online.

particularly like the Unigo question, "What's the stereotype of the students at this school?" and "Is the stereotype true?" Note that if the "stereotype" comments contradict one another (one student says "hippie school," another says "nerdy," and another says "jocks and frat boys"), that could be a sign it's actually a pretty diverse school.

Take real and virtual tours.

It's hard to really know a campus without seeing it. And if you can, do it. But if you can't visit in person, check out:

> www.campusreel.org
> www.campustours.com
> www.youniversitytv.com
> www.youtube.com (search "[school name] online tour")
> Tours on individual school websites. Take at least five online tours so you can compare schools.

Contact the admission office, and if possible, talk to your local rep.

Most colleges have representatives for particular regions of the country (and the world). You can talk to them. And they're really nice! A few reasons why this is a good idea:

It's a fantastic way to find out about a school. In fact, there are people who get paid to answer your questions. (My best friend was one of them.) Don't be afraid. They won't be mad at you; they'll be happy you asked.

Your conversation may help you write your essay. If you learn something meaningful on the call, you may be able to write in your essay, "When I spoke to so-and-so in the Admission Office, she told me..."

At some schools, the person you speak to on the phone may be the one who reads your application. And how cool will it be when they're reading your app and they think, "Oh, I remember this student! They were so nice."

Pro Tip: Definitely have a few specific questions in mind before you call, and try not to ask about anything you could google in five minutes. Don't ask, for example, if the school has a Biology major (spoiler: it does!). Ask instead how easy it is for nonmajors to take advanced musical theater classes or what sets their Engineering program apart from other schools' (assuming you've already googled these things and can't find the answers).

Get in touch with a current student.

Try putting out the word on social media: "Anyone know a current or former student at Purdue?" Ask that person for fifteen minutes of their time. Then ask a short set of questions that you've prepared beforehand. Ideally these are questions that will help you write your "Why Us?" essay and will be interesting, specific, and open-ended. Don't just ask, "So, what's it like there?" (too general) or "Did you like it?" (close-ended question). Ask open-ended questions that will be fun for them to answer like:

> "What was the most mind-blowing class you took and why?"
> "What surprised you about [this particular] college?"
> "What do most people not know about [insert school]?"

The more interesting your questions are, the more interesting the answers will be.*

My favorite way to find specific info for a "Why Us?" essay:

Find a syllabus.

That's it. Research high and low, search the deepest darkest depths of Google (or better yet, ask someone who attends the school), and find a syllabus for a class you may take at that school.

Why does this help? Imagine you're trying to articulate why you'd take a certain class. What better way than to peruse the language the professor is using in the part of the syllabus that says "What I hope you will learn from this class"?

Take this course description, for example, excerpted from a syllabus by Dr. Frank Anderson at the University of Michigan:

> This course provides a comprehensive introduction to the field of

---

* Also a life lesson.

reproductive health, both in the United States and from a global perspective. The course will introduce students to cross-cutting themes including (1) historical discourses on reproductive health; (2) the social ecology of reproductive risks (e.g., gender, race, sexuality); (3) the relevance of physical anatomy to reproductive risks; (4) life course perspectives; (5) human rights frameworks; and (6) application to health behavior and health education assessments and interventions. Additional (more specific) topics in reproductive health will be addressed including maternal morbidity, contraceptive use, pregnancy, STI care, HIV, abortion care, and violence against women.

You can show off your research skills by mentioning in your essay you found a syllabus:

"When I read Professor Anderson's syllabus for his class covering reproductive health, I was intrigued by the possibility of exploring the history of public policy regarding contraceptives and religiously affiliated healthcare providers…"

STEP 2: ORGANIZE YOUR RESEARCH

College Essay Guy's "Why Us?" Essay Research Chart

Grab a piece of paper for each school on your college list that requires a "Why Us?" essay and write the name of each school at the top of its own page. Then draw a line down the middle of each page to make two columns and label them "What I want from college" and "What this college offers." It'll look something like this:

WHAT I WANT FROM COLLEGE		WHAT THIS COLLEGE OFFERS	HOW I'LL CONTRIBUTE / ENGAGE
Generally	**Niche**	**Majors:** Marketing Management Entrepreneurship	**What I've done so far:** Taken advanced math courses to get ahead Joined DECA club to immerse myself into the world of marketing
Academics: Business **Interests:** Violin Literary magazine	**Academics:** Marketing Management Entrepreneurship **Interests:** Folk music Editing	**Institutes:** College of Business Administration Center for Entrepreneurship **Classes:** FNCE 3410, INBA 3810, MGMT 3610, MRKT 3510 **Organizations:** Country dance club Student literary journal	**What I will do on campus:** Join faculty mentorship program in Center for Entrepreneurship Copy edit literary journal Play violin for country dance club

This will help you make use of all your research. Find at least ten specific connections between the school and your own interests and needs.

Note that you might have multiple interests and needs that connect to one detail about the school or vice versa. Definitely include all of those—this doesn't need to be a one-to-one ratio, and having multiple details per connection can lead to an essay that's more fun to write and to read.

Pro Tip: Remember that the "Why Us?" essay is another opportunity to share a few more of your skills/talents/interests/passions. So look back at your "Everything I Want Colleges to Know about Me" list (page 95) and ask yourself: Are all these values/qualities somewhere else in my application? If not, where could I weave them into my "Why Us?" essay?

STEP 3: PICK ONE OF THREE APPROACHES

Important: There is no "best" approach, and students are accepted to wonderful schools every year with each of these strategies.

Approach #1: The Basic, Solid "Why Us?" Essay That Includes a Bunch of Reasons Why You're a Match

How it works: Translate your Extremely Advanced "Why Us?" Essay Research Chart into an essay by turning your connections—details about what you want and what the college has that connect with each other—into clear reasons why you are a match. Here's a simple formula:

(At least one school-related detail) + (At least one
connection back to you) = a great "Why Us?" sentence

How many is "a bunch"? Make sure you have ten to fifteen connections. While you may not ultimately name all the connections in your final version, having this many will give you plenty to choose from when you start your draft.*

Here's an outline for a basic, solid "Why Us?" essay:

1. Thesis that names the academic area(s) you want to pursue and maybe charts the path of the essay†
2. Main connection #1 with three to four specific details
3. Main connection #2 with three to four specific details
4. Main connection #3 with three to four specific details
5. An ending that maybe discusses what you'll give back to the school and the world at large

The "Why Michigan?" essay is an example of a basic, solid "Why Us?" essay that includes a bunch of reasons that came from detailed connections between the student's needs and the school's offerings.

WHY MICHIGAN?

Prompt: *Describe the unique qualities that attract you to the specific undergraduate College or School (including preferred admission and dual degree programs) to which you are applying at the University of Michigan. How would that curriculum support your interests?* (500 word limit)

Here are the three things he'll discuss in each of the next three paragraphs (note how each, which I've marked in bold, corresponds to the paragraphs that follow). This sentence is his thesis and provides a map for the essay.

Mark Twain was a steamboat pilot. Agatha Christie was a nurse. Robert Frost was a light bulb filament changer. The best writers do not only write beautifully, but also integrate their personal experiences and knowledge outside the world of literature. By combining the study of **literature, media,**

This short hook draws us in.

---

*   An exception here is the 100-word "Why Us?" essays. For those, I'd recommend Approach #2.

†   Don't know what you want to study? I'll cover that approach on page 218.

and perhaps law,‡ I believe the University of Michigan will provide the education necessary for me to evolve as a journalist.

A journalist cannot reach the peak of his craft if his **knowledge of literature and critical-thinking skills** are weak, which is why I'm excited to explore what the Department of English has to offer. I look forward to courses such as Academic Argumentation and Professional Writing, as I believe these will provide me with a firm basis in journalistic writing technique and improve my abilities to write analytically and develop well-supported arguments. Furthermore, the Professional Writing course will teach me how to write in a concise, straightforward style, a skill vital to a journalist.

At the College of Literature, Science, and the Arts, I will be able to apply the skills learned in class with **media studies** in and beyond the classroom. The Honors Program provides an opportunity for independent research into the field of mass media, which will allow for intensive group studies and in-depth research opportunities, and the superb networking opportunity provides the chance to meet and engage with prominent figures in media-related studies, which will provide a deeper insight and knowledge into the field. Outside the classroom, I can see myself writing scripts for the student-run television station WOLV-TV or composing headlines for *The Michigan Daily*.

And although journalism is the path I'm currently on, I want to remain open to other opportunities I may encounter at UM. The **Pre-Law** Advising Program is interesting because I want to explore the intricacies of law and policies that govern this world. I believe that the judicial role of a lawyer is closely related to the expository skills of a writer, and I look forward to exploring this new field of study that wasn't offered in my high school education.

Next he names specific courses he'll take, and even includes the course codes from the school website (fine, but not always necessary).

Then he goes on to say why these courses will help him specifically.

This is the media studies paragraph, and again the topic sentence makes clear what's to come.

Same formula as before: he names a specific offering at the school...

Then he moves from inside the class to outside the class and gives two more school-related reasons that relate to his major.

Connection to his intended major.

This is the literature and critical thinking paragraph, and this topic sentence makes clear what's coming.

A third example followed by one more specific reason that (bonus points!) is *different* from the reasons named in the previous sentence.

...followed by specific reasons why these are perfect for him (a.k.a. how they'll serve him as a journalist).

This is the law paragraph, which he sets up with two sentences. Works.

This is a great example of the "salt" technique, which I explain in the next section.

---

‡ I'm bolding school-specific connections in these essays so you can spot them more easily, but you shouldn't do this in your final draft.

But all these are what UM has to offer me. I realize that, as a member of the UM community, **I'll want to give back as well**. The various volunteer programs offered by Volunteers Involved Every Week appeals to me, as does the possibility of volunteering at the Boys and Girls Club of Southern Michigan, as I have previous experience with elementary school teaching. And as an international student, I know the pains of learning English as a second language. I believe I can contribute to the ESL teaching program either at UM or abroad, and see this as an opportunity to have an impact not only at UM, but in Washtenaw County and beyond. (466 words)

More specific opportunities followed by specific connections to the author's own life.

How's that for a cool segue? (Don't steal this; find your own segue.) Another great topic sentence.

He even looked up the county the school is in. (Again, don't steal this; let it inspire you.)

Four Things I Love about the "Why Michigan?" Essay

1. **The short hook.** Many students devote too many words to their "Why Us?" opening when a short one will do. This essay's hook is just forty words long and works well. Does your "Why Us?" even need a hook? Nope. If you use this first approach, get to the main argument as fast as you can.

2. **The clear thesis that provides a path for the essay.** This will probably take you back to AP English class essays where you were asked to make your argument explicit at the start and then provide evidence to support it. That's what you're doing in a "Why Us?" essay, and your argument is that you and the school are a perfect match.

3. **The three main connections with three to four bits of supporting evidence per paragraph.** I recommend finding three main connections as it keeps your essay organized, is easy to adapt for different length "Why Us?" essays, and provides "buckets" for your research. (Buckets = the themed paragraphs you'll "fill" with research.)

4. **The way he sprinkles "salt" into his essay.** Remember where the author notes that he "look[s] forward to exploring [law at Michigan, as it] wasn't offered in [his] high school education"? I call this sprinkling "salt" into your "Why Us?" essay. Why? Consider this analogy: salt makes one thirsty, and by mentioning opportunities you haven't had access to, you let the reader know that you're thirsty for something the school has to offer.

Here's another example that follows the basic structure of the "Why Michigan?" essay, but it's slightly more specific.

WHY UPENN?

Prompt: *How will you explore your intellectual and academic interests at the University of Pennsylvania? Please answer this question given the specific undergraduate school to which you are applying.* (Word limit: 650)*

Here's his two-sentence thesis that names his goal, the school, his intended major, and a few words on why. No hook here, which is fine.

I want to be a catalyst when I grow up, someone who sparks growth while also trying to sustain the environment through improved efficiency. At UPenn, I look forward to pursuing a major in Mechanical Engineering and exploring interdisciplinary programs, as I believe that sustainability can be a viable solution to preserve Earth's resources.

Here's a really specific academic offering at the school that is in his intended major and that connects to him in a really specific way.

At the **GRASP laboratory**, I hope to work at the **Haptics Lab** under **Professor Katherine Kuchenbecker** to devise an integrated haptic-responsive camera trap. I believe that the use of teleoperation (in camera traps) in wildlife censuses and studies can be a potential game changer in a geologically diverse country like India. I also feel that haptics interfaces can catalyze the process of discovering and studying unexplored biodiversity hot spots like the Western Ghats and the high-rising Himalayas. Besides this, I would also really get a chance to perfect my butterfly stroke through stroke rehabilitation at the Haptics Lab!

FYI: The details here connect back to his personal statement, which was about his experience as a wildlife photographer. He also uses some jargon (a.k.a. "geeky language") so we can tell he knows what he's talking about.

Here he names two more really specific academic offerings in his intended major and connects them to product design, another interest he mentioned in his personal statement and which he reiterates in the next paragraph.

In addition, hands-on project courses like **Machine Design** and **Manufacturing and Product Design** will help me in developing, testing, and prototyping product permutations, and through *ISAC Program* 2018, I would love to advocate for a course called Environmentally Sustainable Product Design, as I feel that a product's longevity in a market is directly related to its environmental sustainability.

This is a great insight that helps the reader understand his "why."

I believe that little sparks of innovation can turn into

---

*   This is an old prompt for Penn, by the way, so don't write for this one. This is a good reminder, though, to check your Common App for updated prompts—and not just for Penn but for all your supplemental essays! See page 219 for an example of this.

He takes a
brief moment
to mention an
achievement, but
then in the same
sentence...

developed businesses if given the right acceleration and, having already negotiated a deal with the software company Everlution Software Ltd. for my eco-friendly innovation "Water Wave," I look forward to using the opportunities at **IGEL** to turn my innovations into sustainable technological ventures. After accompanying my father to joint-venture meetings across Europe, I have picked up certain technical aspects of negotiations such as the influence of "EBITDA," the use of intercultural body language to change mindsets, and the long-drawn-out process of due diligence. Courses like **Engineering Negotiations** will advance my skills in the subtle art of negotiation and develop my thinking in high-pressure situations.

...he connects his
achievement to
an opportunity
at the school
and how it will
help him do even
more.

Here's something
academic
that's not in his
intended major,
which brings
in some variety
by showing us
another of his
interests.

I look forward to contributing in unconventional ways. Through **Penn's policy of Climate Action 2.0**, I'd love to help increase the efficiency of alternative energy machinery through responsive auto-sensors and I would also contribute to the establishing of wildlife corridors at UPenn by conducting case studies at the Morris Arboretum with the help of the **Penn Green Fund.** I also look forward to engaging in bird photography and ornithology by being an active member of the **Penn Birding Club** and potentially conducting fall bird censuses to illuminate for students the birdlife that nestles in the university. I hope to photograph and document each and every one of the 104 species **(Morris Arboretum Checklist)** of birds at UPenn. Furthermore, courses like **Documentary Strategies** and **Photographic Thinking** will help me better integrate critical thought into my photos and construct out-of-the-box documentaries to put into perspective environmental sustainability at UPenn. Also, contributing photo essays to the **Penn Sustainability Review** will allow me to depict the need for a change beyond words.

Environment/sustainability is the
theme for this
paragraph, and
he names both
extracurricular
and academic
opportunities for
exploring this
interest at Penn.

Here's his
miscellaneous
extracurriculars
paragraph (2–3
things that
demonstrate
social/nonacademic fit).

UPenn will also help me pursue a multitude of activities at its various clubs such as **Penn Cricket Club; PennNaatak,** where I hope to spark my flair for **Marathi Drama;** and **men's club basketball** (I was all state for three years!).

As I move with a redefined pace toward the goal of

global sustainability, I am reminded of the UPenn ideology of addressing the most challenging questions and problems of our time by integrating and combining different disciplines and perspectives. Through my stay at UPenn, I hope to do just that.

Closing, which is somewhat general but works fine.

Here's the outline for the "Why UPenn" essay (which you can adapt for your own essay):

1. Intro/Thesis (say what you want to study and why)
2. Really specific academic offering at the school that is in your intended major/concentration (this should connect to you in a really specific way)
3. A second really specific academic offering that is also in your intended major/concentration (and that also connects back to you)
4. Something academic that's not in your intended major/concentration (this keeps the focus on academics, but also brings in some variety)
5. Best/most important extracurricular offering (that connects to you in a really specific way)
6. Miscellaneous extracurriculars paragraph (two to three things to demonstrate social/nonacademic fit)
7. Closing (this can be short and is unnecessary in shorter "Why Us?" essays)

Note that the these two essays are roughly half about the school and half about the student, which is a nice balance. The following is an example essay that uses a similar structure (thesis followed by main reasons), but is more like three-fourths about the school and one-fourth about the student. This isn't "wrong," it's just a slightly different approach.

WHY TUFTS?

Prompt: *Which aspects of Tufts' curriculum or undergraduate experience prompt your application? In short: "Why Tufts?"* (200 word limit)

He begins with a clear thesis.

In addition to providing a strong foundation in economics, Tufts provides me the opportunity to further explore global health care policy through an International Relations

Here he doesn't say why he'd take these courses, as he decided to list more reasons (in the next sentences) instead. That's a trade-off you may have to make: more school-specific reasons or more "why me."

Program that leverages the strengths of eighteen related departments and programs. I'm also keen to continue my study of the Chinese language through Tufts' Chinese Department, studying with Professor Mingquan Wang and perhaps study abroad at Zhejiang University in Hangzhou, China, to receive the full immersion experience. Tufts' Experimental College intrigues me as I can take unconventional courses such as Game Strategy (EXP-0029-S) and Rising Tide: Climate Change, Vulnerability, and Adaptation (EXP-0021-F). Further, Tufts' urban backdrop provides me the opportunity to play league cricket year-round to train for my bid to become the first Jumbo on the US National Cricket Team, while studying abroad at Oxford would provide me with not only global economic perspectives, but also the opportunity to continue my pursuit of cricket in its birthplace. Visiting Tufts, my mother's alma mater, I felt I was at home in Singapore. Its strengths in Chinese, Econ, and International Relations, combined with its beautiful suburban campus, academic rigor, and global reach have confirmed that Tufts is the place for me.

This sentence clearly connects Tufts' offerings to the author's interest.

His main statement and activities list discussed his love for cricket, so no need here.

He lists two reasons for Oxford here, although it would have been even better if he'd named a Tufts-specific connection to or program at Oxford.

He could have perhaps cut this last sentence and used the words to expand on the "why me" for the Experimental College courses (third sentence), but this ties things up nicely.

I call this the "fire hose" approach because it packs fourteen reasons into 196 words. The author offers the reader a sense that he has clearly done his research and knows how he might make use of the school's offerings, which is the goal of the solid, basic "Why Us?" essay.[*]

But how do you make the school feel really special? Like this:

Approach #2: The "3–5 Unique Offerings" Strategy

How it works: Find three to five opportunities *that are particular to the school* (i.e., available at no other school, or at least no other school you're applying to) and connect each one back to you.

This is my favorite approach, as focusing on fewer reasons allows you the

---

[*]   Here's a trick: Switch out "eighteen" in "eighteen related departments and programs," change the names of the Chinese professor and University, name two different interesting courses, cut the "alma mater" line and voilà! Suddenly this is an essay for another school.

chance to share more about yourself and your interests (i.e., "why you"). But it can be more difficult to write because, frankly, it can be hard to find specifics that truly set a school apart from other schools.[†] But it's possible to find these unique offerings by digging further into research to compare schools, and I believe it's worth trying, especially for your top-choice school(s).

As an example, notice how the author of this next essay names four unique offerings that connect him to Cornell University (I've labeled them). Plus, we learn a little more about the author's interests than we do from the previous essays.

WHY CORNELL?

Prompt: *Students in Arts and Sciences embrace the opportunity to delve into their academic interests, discover new realms of intellectual inquiry, and chart their own path through the College. Tell us why the depth, breadth, and flexibility of our curriculum are ideally suited to exploring the areas of study that excite you.* (Word limit: 650)

Whenever I have time on my hands, I hook myself up to my EEG and analyze my brain waves. Or if I am feeling slightly less adventurous, I am reading about the latest neuroscience trends in ScienceDirect or NCBI PubMed. I want to spend my life studying, understanding, and helping to fix the human brain.

Short hook (40 words).

Clear thesis.

I bought my EEG online two years ago for about $150 and have used it to compare the beneficial effects of both circadian and non-circadian sleep on the brain by analyzing the number of clear peaks in a three-minute interval of a theta wave. But just counting the peaks is not the best way to measure the benefits. I look forward to gaining a deeper understanding of the fundamentals of neurophysiology (as well as working with better equipment) in courses like Principles of Neurophysiology. As someone who has long

---

[†] Pro Tip: Ask admission reps what sets their school (or the department you're applying to) apart from other schools.

been passionate about neurotechnology, I appreciate that Cornell is unique in offering classes devoted specifically to the field.

The first time he notes what makes Cornell unique.

I would also like to be able to contribute my experiences with neurotechnology to support the cutting edge research in Cornell's brand-new NeuroNex Hub. I would love to work with Dr. Chris Xu in expanding the current three-photon microscope to be applied on various animal models. I also look forward to helping Dr. Chris Schaffer, whose research on deep neural activity is not being done anywhere else in the world. I freak out at the possibility of helping him develop a tool to look at multiple brain areas at the same time.

The second time he notes what makes Cornell unique.

Though I have long aspired to study at Cornell, when I visited and sat in on Neurobiology and Behavior II, it made me all the more determined. I found Professor Christiane Linster's presentation on synaptic plasticity absolutely riveting. Her animations of neurotransmitters crossing a synapse and new synapses forming in neuron clusters kept her students engaged in a way I have not seen in any other classrooms. I want to go to Cornell because of teachers like her.

The third time he notes what makes Cornell unique.

During my visit I also enjoyed talking with Kacey about her experiences in the college scholars program. I loved that she had studied the effects of circus and gymnastic performances, like Cirque Du Soleil, on therapy for children with neurological disabilities. I am very excited by the idea of combining neuroscience with something like the effects of learning a classical language on developing brains. Many studies have shown the plethora of positive effects of being bilingual, but not much research has been done on classical languages. I have been studying Latin for over seven years, and I have experienced firsthand the positive effects. I spend hours every day breaking down complex sentences such as those in Virgil's *Aeneid,* and so have extended this approach to problem solving to other aspects of my life like my neuroscience research. This is the program I would create for my college scholars project.

He does a great job of weaving connections between the school's offerings and his own interests.

Cornell is also the only university I am interested in that

offers a speaking course in Latin: Conversational Latin. For the past six years, I have rarely had to translate more than a few sentences at a time from English to Latin, never truly experiencing the unique grammatical features of Latin, such as intricate wordplay by Catullus in his Odes, that drew me so much to this language. I would love to supplement my knowledge by being able to formulate my thoughts in Latin and actively immerse myself in the language. I am really excited about learning the language as it was meant to be learned, as well as the new perspective it will provide me on Latin rhetorical artifacts.

The fourth time he notes what makes Cornell unique. He clarifies that this is not unique among all universities, but among those he's applying to, which is fine.

As a kid who loves inventing, enjoys interactive learning, and wants to speak a dead language, I know Cornell is where I want to be. I wonder if my roommate will mind if I bring my EEG?

He ends with a quick callback to the opening and brings in a little humor.

This essay is similar to the Approach #1 essay examples in that the author begins with a short intro and solid thesis, and then weaves back and forth between what he wants and what the school offers.

But this essay is different in that the four (much fewer) examples that name how the school is unique give us a *really* clear sense of how Cornell is a great fit for this student. Also, we know this essay was written specifically for the school because it would be much more difficult (than the "Why Tufts" essay, for example) to switch out the variables and use this for another school. Finally, while the "Why Michigan?" and "Why UPenn?" examples go for breadth, discussing many different reasons, the "Why Cornell?" example discusses fewer reasons but with more depth.

Approach #3: The "One Value" Strategy

How it works: Identify one core value that links you to the school and tell a story.

This approach can be difficult but might be good for schools that have shorter "Why Us?" essays* and seem to be asking for this type of response,

---

* I wouldn't recommend this approach for longer "Why Us?" essays (500–650 words), as I think it's too hard to do. For longer essays I'd recommend Approach #2 (if possible) or #1.

or for students who feel approaches #1 and #2 might blend in with other applicant essays too easily, and they are willing to take a risk.

Why is this a risky approach? First, you're foregoing listing a bunch of reasons that connect you to the school, which some admission officers like to see. Second, if your reader is skimming (as many are), or your story isn't well told, or the central theme or value isn't clear, or the insight doesn't make the reader feel something…the essay may not work.

That's a lot of ifs! But it can work, and here's an example essay that, I think, does.*

WHY BOWDOIN?

Prompt: *Bowdoin students and alumni often cite world-class faculty and opportunities for intellectual engagement, the College's commitment to the Common Good, and the special quality of life on the coast of Maine as important aspects of the Bowdoin experience.*

Reflecting on your own interests and experiences, please comment on one of the following:

1. Intellectual engagement

2. The Common Good

3. Connection to place

(Word limit: 250)

Wait a second, this doesn't sound like your typical "Why us" essay…

On the first dawn of the summer, I found myself in a familiar place: sitting awkwardly in the back of a crowded bus full of rowdy twelve year olds. But this time around, I wasn't the shy, new kid at school, a position I knew all too well. I was the teacher, implementing a middle school aquatic ecology curriculum I'd developed the year before.

---

*   Heads-up: If you skim this essay, you may not get it. :)

As New Jersey's Passaic River appeared on the horizon, I tightened the red laces on my Merrell hiking boots and checked my bag: clipboards, lesson plans, and a new water testing kit.

This is subtle, but he's already communicating core values with these details. Can you spot them?

For the entire day, I watched as twenty-five young minds tested the Passaic River's water. Using the river as a natural learning laboratory, I taught them about pollution and industrialization, urban design, and remediation strategies.

This is the turning point of the essay, explaining all that's come before and setting up for his thesis in his final paragraph.

These specifics show us how well he knows what he's teaching.

That summer, through my work in environmental education, I discovered the power of place. I realized that in a changing world, places really are the best storytellers. By tracking the Passaic's pollution levels, we toured the tales of its waters, beginning with its use by the Lenape Native Americans, to its unjust usurpation by European hegemons, to the Vietnam War, during which tons of Agent Orange were dumped recklessly.

This almost sounds like a college-level course studying the intersection of history, politics, and the environment.

This is beautifully crafted. Wow.

At Bowdoin, I'll encounter this again. I find myself doing the very thing I was teaching: investigating the rich stories behind a place. As part of my major in Earth and Oceanographic Science, I blissfully get lost on Orr's Island, researching everything from the historical ecology to the changing geography of the Maine coastline. And I can't wait.

I love this final sentence. It's powerful; I can feel his enthusiasm.

Note here that a thesis at the end works well.

Why does this essay work? This author checks a few "Why Us?" boxes by focusing on specifics, showing us he's done his research, and clearly answering the prompt. But want to know the main thing that sets this essay apart?

The author found a deep connection between one of the school's core values and one of his own.

I know this flies in the face of the "provide a whole bunch of specific reasons" for your essay that I mentioned in Approach #1. Instead, the author found one really good reason: both he and Bowdoin are deeply committed to investigating *place*. This focus was particularly apropos for this student, as he planned to major in Environmental Science. And as you read this essay, you sense that it couldn't have been written for another prompt. (Even though this student did reuse some of the language in this essay for a short extracurricular essay, which goes to show how reusable even very specific essays can be. Read the chapter on the Super Essay on page 186 for more.)

Because he used a value as the central theme, this essay is primarily about the author. Check out that word count: the essay is 258 words long, but he doesn't even mention the school until word 202. This works because he stays connected to the central themes, which are nature and storytelling. In fact, if we don't get a sense of the central themes in the first 200 words of your essay, we might wonder, "Where is this going?" Instead, though, we feel as we read this essay that the author is taking us somewhere. He's a guide we trust. So we relax.

Approach #3 in Three Steps

1. **Find a way in which you and the school are deeply aligned.** Hint: It's probably a value. It'll take some research, and it may be easier to do this with a smaller liberal arts school (like Bowdoin) that has a particular character. Reed College, for example, is proud to call its students "Reedies"—even going so far as to call them a particular species—so for Reed, you might figure out what being a "Reedie" means to you, then demonstrate why you are without a doubt one of them.

2. **Take your time crafting the essay.** What do I mean? I believe a great "Why Us?" essay is similar to a great personal statement in that it should demonstrate:

   a.   Core values

   b.   Insight (a.k.a. important and interesting connections, a.k.a. "so what" moments)

   c.   Craft (it should be obvious, in other words, that the author has revised the essay over several drafts and knows the purpose of each paragraph, sentence, and word)

And because the Bowdoin essay primarily focuses on one important and interesting connection (connection to place), I believe that craft becomes a lot more important. In other words, this essay would be much less awesome if it were much less beautiful.

What do I mean by beautiful? Read it aloud. Note phrases like, "Using the river as a natural learning laboratory" and "places really are the best storytellers." The writer even makes water testing kits sound like exciting tools of a real-life adventurer, as essential to the author as an explorer's compass (and when I read this essay I'm convinced they are)!

How do you get to this point? I think you have to really love the thing you're writing about. I also think (if I'm being honest) that you have to love to write, or at least to convince yourself you do. This approach takes time. But it's worth it. Why? I believe this is the type of essay that, particularly at a small liberal arts college, can truly make a difference. I have only anecdotal evidence—stories from a few admission officers—to prove it, but in some cases I believe essays like this have tipped the scales in favor of a particular student.

3. **Find a way to be vulnerable.** This part is perhaps the most difficult, but most crucial. I mentioned earlier that a great "Why Us?" essay should demonstrate important and interesting questions and craft. But there's a third quality that I think a great personal statement should have and that a "Why Us?" essay can, in rare instances, demonstrate. That quality is vulnerability.

How does the Bowdoin essay above show vulnerability? He lets his geekiness show. (My definition of "geek," by the way, is someone with a lot of knowledge in a particular area that's not conventionally popular.) He does this by writing about what he loves without apology.

Why is this vulnerable? Because in doing so, he risks public ridicule. (I mean, *water testing*? Come on…) But he pulls it off because he doesn't go too far or include too much jargon. Why is this important? He draws us in rather than pushes us away. And we've all met both kinds of geeks: the kind that draws us in and the kind that alienates us. Be the draw-us-in kind.

THE HYBRID APPROACH

Could you create a hybrid approach by focusing on a central theme but still list a few reasons? Yup!

If you go with this approach, ideally you would find offerings unique to the school (as in the "Why Cornell?" essay). But if you can't, just find reasons that are as specific as possible and connect them back to you (as in the "Why Michigan?" and "Why UPenn?" essays).

Here's an example of an essay that uses the hybrid approach.

WHY SWARTHMORE?

This sets up the central theme of the essay.

The human body's greatest asset is its ears. They come pimpled, freckled, mushed, bent, rounded, and pointed. But, despite their differences, they share a single purpose: to listen.

Here's the broader theme (and a value!), which will allow the author to discuss many parts of the school + herself.

Swarthmore is all about ears. It not only understands the importance of empathetic and open dialogue, but also the ways in which listening can be the first step toward bridging deeply entrenched ideological divides. Whether I'm learning from guest lecturers at the Center for Innovation and Leadership, engaging in dialogue at the Global Health Forum, or exploring my sexuality through the Intercultural Center, I know I'd be at a place that values collaboration, honest discourse, ethical leadership, and creativity invested in the public good. Everything at Swarthmore is about putting those cartilage appendages on the sides of your head to good use.

Notice how the author highlights the values she shares with the school.

Returning to the focusing lens at the start of each paragraph helps keep the essay focused. It also helps that she's ending the sentence with the connecting thread ("listening").

And shows her sense of humor! Yes, it's possible even in a "Why Us?" essay.

As a person drawn to audio and visual storytelling, my life has been defined by listening. At Swarthmore, I would continue to foster the quality relationships I've created and the love I've spread by inviting people to share their stories on my podcasts. Majoring in Film & Media Studies or English Literature, broadcasting at WSRN, and writing for *The Review* is the next chapter in my life of listening. I would creatively explore how narratives have been told in the past and can be redefined digitally for a new generation of ears. Swarthmore knows that global change starts with an honest conversation. I want to be pioneering new networks of connection. I want to be starting those conversations.

I love that she ends her final sentences with "I," as this brings it back to her. Plus she highlights two of the core values (connection, communication) at the heart of the essay.

Notice how these are variables that could be switched out for the radio station and newspaper at another school.

How to Write a "Why Us?" Essay if You Don't Know What You Want to Study

Good news: you can still write a great "Why Us?" even if you have no idea what you want to be when you grow up.

Consider including a thesis that either names your two to three areas of interest or states that you're unsure what you want to study. In that thesis, consider saying what you do want and including the name of the school. (Example: "I'm interested in X, Y, and Z, and I believe there's no other place for me to explore these areas than the University of Wisconsin-Madison.")

You can also begin with a nice hook to not only show your creativity but also perhaps distract from the fact that you have no idea what you want to be when you grow up (and oh by the way, it's totally fine to not know).

Here's a great example to illustrate these points (emphasis mine):

WHY JOHNS HOPKINS?*

Prompt: *Johns Hopkins University was founded in 1876 on a spirit of exploration and discovery. As a result, students can pursue a multidimensional undergraduate experience both in and outside of the classroom. Given the opportunities at Hopkins, please discuss your current interests (academic, extracurricular, personal passions, summer experiences, etc.) and how you will build upon them here. (500 words)*

Dear 2016 Ariana,

It's 2026. I have just returned from the G20 summit after delivering the annual report on demographic transition and population stability. Throughout your seventeen years of life, you have been barraged with choices: Which airline seat to choose? Is the answer B or C? Is "the dress" blue/black or white/gold? But you will soon make a choice that will allow you to harness your knowledge and apply it to reality. The choice to go to Johns Hopkins.

By now, you have lived in India, the UK, and the USA: multicultural exposure that shaped your worldview. You are confused as to what you want exactly, but deep down you

A lovely (short) hook that also sets up her ending.

Great example of using the "Why Us?" to share information that wasn't in the personal statement.

Great thesis that admits she doesn't know what she wants to study but still says what she wants and names the school.

---

*   Heads-up that JHU no longer has a "Why Us?" or may not when you apply. (I'm still including it because it illustrates a few important concepts.) But this is another reminder to check your Common App for updated prompts.

strive for a synergy of ideas and fields. That can and will be found at Hopkins.

Particularly, the **JHU Humanities** Center will provide you with a flexible approach toward interdisciplinary study: important, as you value the need to explore before settling on a choice. You will find this at **Homewood**, but also globally through study at the **Sciences Po campus, Paris,** which outlines the interconnectedness between areas such as law, finance, and urban policy.

In Model United Nations, you built skills in collaboration, working with students across the country to embody pluralism and reach consensus. At Hopkins, you will enhance these skills and your knowledge of international relations in **Professors Moss and Hanchards's class, Diaspora, Nation, Race, & Politics.** The discussions, which range from political sociology and human rights to the fall of late nineteenth century empires, will give you greater insight into how history determines our understanding of today's geopolitical challenges.

And although you stuck your toe in the ocean of government and politics through your internship in Senator Glazer's office, JHU provides an immersive dive into this field through their **International Studies Program,** with opportunities at the **Nanjing Center, China, and the Nitze School in Washington, DC.**

On a local level, you will be able to extend your political service when you run for **JHU Student Government Association,** where you will continue to represent diverse viewpoints and provide a forum for recognition and discussion.

You will also have the opportunity to continue your work with **the Red Cross,** giving back to the Baltimore community by joining the **JHU and the Chesapeake Regional chapters**. And by joining the **Public Health Student Forum,** you will gain access to speakers who have worked in these fields all their life, like **Former Director of the Peace Corps, Dr. Jody Olsen, and Dr. Richard Benjamin, Chief Medical Officer of the Red Cross.**

Pro Tip: If you mention study abroad, say specifically where and why.

Core value: exploration!

More core values

This is a solid example of (a) something the school offers and (b) what specifically she hopes to gain/learn.

Here's another solid example that, for variety, lists her interest first before connecting that to how the school will help her explore that interest.

The simple structure repeats here by naming (a) an experience/interest she has pursued, followed by (b) how she'll expand on that experience/interest at JHU.

Here she uses another specific example to expand on the central themes of the essay (and her core values) of diversity and synergy.

All your life experiences, from building community to understanding behavior in order to enact decisions, have stemmed from One. Single. Choice. Without Johns Hopkins, you would not have become an expert on global policy change, speaking at events like the G20 emporium.

This was a placeholder for her, and while she doesn't name a specific major, this phrase helps pull the essay elements together.

Yes, the world has changed dramatically in the past ten years. But Hopkins recognizes this fluidity, and paired with you, Ariana, will propel the importance of integrative study.

Love the ending. Brings us full circle back to the start, plus shows her sense of humor.

Love,

Future Ariana

PS: The dress is white/gold.

Do you notice how, in the end, this approach isn't all that different from Approaches #1 and #2? The main difference is her thesis, which instead of naming a major, simply states that she's unsure what she wants to study. We're cool with it, though, especially because she still includes lots of reasons and connects each back to herself.

Three Ways to Make Sure Your "Why Us?" Essay Is Doing Its Job

1. **Scan your essay for capital letters.** Why? Because chances are, capital letters mean you've included something specific that the school offers. In fact…
2. **Highlight in bold your reasons for wanting to attend.** I've done this in the "Why Johns Hopkins?" essay. Once you've done this, and if you're using Approach #1 or #2, see if you can trim anywhere to make room for more reasons. (Don't actually submit the essay with the bold text, though.)
3. **Make sure that each time you mention something about the school you connect it back to yourself.** Simply check each mention of the school and see if you've explained why this is important—not just in general, but to you.

In the Treasure Trove, you'll find:

→ A basic downloadable "Why Us?" essay chart

→ Article: "Your Annual Reminder to Ignore the *U.S.News & World Report* College Rankings"

Chapter 15

How to Write the Extracurricular Activity Essay

The Extracurricular Activity Essay is another great chance for you to show schools what you've accomplished and to make sure they know what values and experiences you're going to bring to campus.

In this chapter, we'll cover:

- The narrative approach (via the Elon Musk Exercise)
- The montage approach (via the Uncommon Connections Exercise)
- How to stand out on your extracurricular essay if your topic and achievements are common
- Seven tips for the 150-word extracurricular essay
- Five more 150-word extracurricular essays I love

The prompts for these essays ask you to describe, in detail, some of the things you've done outside of class that you're most proud of or involved in. So they might look something like this:

> *Briefly discuss the significance to you of the school or summer activity in which you have been most involved.*
> *Please briefly elaborate on one of your extracurricular activities or work experiences.*

If you could only do one of the activities you have listed in the Activities section of your Common Application, which one would you keep doing? Why?

Note that some prompts won't mention the word "activity," but they could be answered with a description of your involvement in an extracurricular activity. These prompts might include:

Describe an example of your leadership experience in which you have positively influenced others, helped resolve disputes, or contributed to group efforts over time.

Every person has a creative side, and it can be expressed in many ways: problem solving, original and innovative thinking, and artistically, to name a few. Describe how you express your creative side.

What have you done to make your school or your community a better place?

When it comes to your extracurricular activity essay, it works much like the narrative structure and montage structure essays from the "Personal Statement" chapter (page 143). They're alike in that you'll either describe a challenge/problem or series of challenges/problems you've encountered, or you'll create a montage of uncommon connections to your values.

The Narrative Extracurricular Essay (a.k.a. the Elon Musk Exercise)

This approach works particularly well for an extracurricular essay about overcoming a challenge, volunteering, community service, or social issues.

This structure was inspired by an article written by Andy Raskin that analyzes a pitch Elon Musk gave for his signature home energy storage solution. Here's Raskin's take on Musk's pitch:

Musk's delivery isn't stellar. He's self-conscious and fidgety. But at the end, his audience cheers. For a battery. That's because Musk does five things right that you should emulate in every pitch you ever make to anybody.

While reading Raskin's article I realized (because I'm the College Essay Guy and this is where my brain is half the time) Musk's approach could easily be applied to a wide range of extracurricular essay topics, so I adapted the structure, added a sixth step, and created an approach that will help you map out a challenges-based extracurricular essay in about ten minutes. Here's how it works:

Step 1: Identify the problem. Describe the challenge you were (or are currently) facing. The problem could be something global, like an environmental issue, or something more local, like a lack of creative opportunities in your high school.

Step 2: Raise the stakes. Help us understand: Why was (or is) overcoming this challenge important? What might happen if this problem went (or goes) unchecked?

Step 3: Describe what you did. Tell us the specific things you (or you and your team) did to solve the problem.

Step 4: Clarify your role. Describe your particular involvement. Why were (or are) you crucial to the project or club's success?

Step 5: Share the impact you had, lessons you learned, or values you gained. Provide specific evidence that gives us a sense that your work mattered. I'll show you some ways to do this in a minute.

Think that's too much to do in one essay? Behold:

THE CATALYZING
CREATIVITY CLUB

Prompt: *What have you done to make your school or your community a better place?* (350 words)

I live in the suburb of Los Angeles, California, known to its residents as the bubble. It has the perfect weather, location, and schools. As amazing as it sounds, however, growing up in La Cañada Flintridge has its drawbacks: the community pressures adolescents to achieve success through mainly academic means. While this approach isn't necessarily wrong, it can be difficult, particularly in my high school, to thrive in a creative and imaginative way.

The Problem: It's hard, in this student's community, to thrive in a creative way.

The Vision: A community where students can thrive creatively.

Sophomore year, my friends and I began to wonder, What if the teenagers of La Cañada had greater opportunities to express themselves. To pursue their creativity. To follow their dreams.

That's when we decided to start the Catalyzing Creativity Club. Founded two years ago, the Catalyzing Creativity Club (C3, for short) provides students in our community the opportunity to pursue their passion and aspirations outside the classroom.

This single sentence serves as a kind of mission statement, succinctly defining the Who, What, and Where of the club (specifics come in the next paragraph).

Some of our opportunities include: a yearly music festival for our community's young aspiring musicians that showcases local talent to the masses and scouts; a technology expo, which allows students to be rewarded with funding and demonstrate their coding abilities to prospective companies; recording sessions for aspiring musicians, photo-publishing competitions, and a variety of guest speakers ranging from nineteen-year-old college seniors to millionaire entrepreneurs. In addition, we have a blog for aspiring writers to publish their work and are holding a shoe drive for underprivileged athletes.

What they (as a team) specifically did

As vice president of finances for C3, I work to ensure we can fund these activities. I handle our bank account, fundraising, and organize the event planning. Moreover, I make sure that C3's activities and finances are approved by and follow the guidelines of my high school. This role is crucial, as we work to achieve nonprofit status.

Clarifying his particular role

Even though C3 is only a few years old, I believe it is already making an impact in the community. As we grow and the opportunities we provide become more popular, our hope is to inspire our peers to follow their dreams and burst the La Cañada Flintridge bubble.

Ideally this would have included one or two details describing impact.

Brief Notes and Analysis:

- Check out how the third paragraph is basically a straightforward listing of the club's accomplishments. This was pulled directly from the bullet points of his BEABIES exercise (page 108). It works.
- Notice how specific he gets in the fourth paragraph where he clarifies why he was essential to the club's success. Doing this helps us understand that he was more than just a passive participant who showed up to meetings.
- Another potential use of your extracurricular essay is to expand on something you mentioned only briefly in your personal statement. In this case, the author mentioned in his personal statement that he's "a numbers guy," and the fourth paragraph in this essay expands on why numbers are meaningful to him.

Here's another wonderful example that uses this structure:

EARTHQUAKES

Prompt: *What have you done to make your school or your community a better place?* (350 words)

The problem: earthquakes

Last year, nearly 600 earthquakes hit my hometown of Reno in a "swarm." Although the magnitudes of these quakes ranged from 2.5 to 3.7, the constant fear and anxiety of impending doom rose in the community. A disaster is unprecedented and unpredictable, and in our community, we always acknowledged their occurrence elsewhere but never fully admitted that a large-scale catastrophe may happen at our doorstep.

Raise the stakes part 1: This could lead to a large-scale catastrophe...

Recognizing this unspoken apathy, I decided to take a step beyond my school club and get involved in the community chapter of the Reno Red Cross Disaster Cycle Services team. As I was learning the basics of preparedness (i.e., general earthquake and fire safety drills), I realized that if disaster was to strike, the majority of people in my community could not confidently say that they are prepared. As part of the DCS committee, it is my goal to increase the confidence of as many youth and families as possible.

What she did about it

A clear, succinct description of her "Why."

Raise the stakes part 2...the community may not be prepared to handle such a catastrophe.

During my training, I accompanied volunteers during the Home Fire Preparedness Campaign, where we installed and updated smoke alarms and detectors in over thirty low-income households in the Reno area, free of charge. I began teaching the "Pillowcase Project" in local elementary schools, leading workshops in and instilling the importance of disaster preparedness for the youngest of children.

These specifics expand on what she did.

Representing DCS on the Youth Executive Board for our local chapter, I also led a Youth in Disaster Services Seminar, where we trained young adults in CPR Certification as well as basic Shelter Fundamentals.

Through my work with the Red Cross, and in my interactions with survivors and rescuers who assisted during Hurricane Katrina, I've come to discover how teaching even just small preparedness procedures to individuals can help save entire communities.

Here's the personal impact on the author vis-à-vis a lesson she learned.

The impact of disaster services reverberates throughout our communities, both at home and internationally. It is a selfless, necessary job in which youth, as the future generation of an ever-changing disaster-prone world, must take urgent action.

Raise the stakes (a.k.a. "Why now?")

Brief Notes and Analysis:

- As you can see, this structure can work for either local, more personal problems (as described in the "Catalyzing Creativity Club" essay) or larger-scale problems (as described in the "Earthquakes" essay).

- These two examples are similar in that the middle includes specific, straightforward details pulled directly from the What I Did column of the BEABIES.

- The elements of this structure can be used in whatever order makes sense for your story. In this essay, for example, the author chose to conclude with a Why now/Raise the stakes moment to provide a call to action that creates a sense of urgency and helps us understand the importance of her work. This puts the focus not on the author, but on the value of the work she's doing. And that's something people want in a leader.

A STEP-BY-STEP GUIDE TO BRAINSTORMING AND WRITING AN EXTRACURRICULAR ESSAY BASED ON A CHALLENGE

Step 1: Complete the BEABIES exercise (page 108).

The more time you spend working on this chart, the easier it'll be to write your extracurricular essay.* Students who spend ten minutes on this exercise will have an outline; students who spend twenty minutes or more will have all the content they need to write their essay.

Step 2: Start drafting with a central problem as the hook.

Decide which problem you want to use to start your essay, and then start writing. Some more examples from past students:

> *Our campus was divided into separate social groups...*
> *Our music program was at risk of being shut down...*
> *We didn't have adequate sports equipment...*
> *A hurricane had recently flooded our nearby town and we wanted to help...*
> *Maternal mortality rates were extremely high in the community where we were working...*

Draw us in. Get us to wonder how one might solve this problem.

Step 3: Raise the stakes.

After the problem is established, your essay should help us understand why this problem was/is important to solve. What were/are the consequences we would face if the problem wasn't solved? Why did/do we need to act right then/now?

Step 4: Tell us what you did/are doing about it.

This content will come directly from the first column of your BEABIES exercise. As I've said, if you spend some quality time thinking about your bullet points, you'll have all the content you need for this section.

---

*   And if you're working on the University of California Personal Insight Questions, completing this chart will basically write the essay for you (in the sense that it'll give you all the content you need).

Step 5: Tell us why you were/are crucial to the project or club's success.

Many students skip this step, but it can be useful in helping us understand your particular gifts, skills, and strengths. Consider:

> Did you draw on knowledge you'd gained elsewhere (like your musical talents or your love of research)?
>
> Did you learn to do something brand new for this project (like coding, for example, or how to ask local business owners for donations)?
>
> What was your special talent that qualified you to be there? Were you the visionary, inspiring the team to dream bigger? Or the team parent, sending reminder texts and making sure everyone was eating enough?

Step 6: Show us the impact.

While this is perhaps the most important part of the extracurricular essay, many students struggle to articulate the impact of their work. And it's no surprise—even nonprofits and large organizations struggle to articulate the impact of their work. Here are some ways to think about impact:

> **Numbers.** Example: "In the past year, club membership has tripled" or "We raised over $1,200 to buy new books for the library!"
>
> **Anecdotal evidence of impact or quotations.** Example: "We've received numerous requests to return next year" or "Last week, a first-year student named Elena wrote me an email to say, 'Thank you for making a difference in my life.'"
>
> **Personal impact** (on you, the author) in the form of lessons learned, skills gained. Example: "I have come to better understand the pervasive, damaging effects of white supremacy culture."
>
> **Relevance to other areas of your life.** Example: "The facilitation skills I learned through my work with the Gay-Straight Alliance helped me communicate more effectively with my soccer teammates."

Once you've brainstormed these elements, you should have everything you need to write your essay.

FAQS FOR EXTRACURRICULAR ACTIVITY ESSAYS BASED ON CHALLENGES

How do I know if my challenge is a "good" challenge?

If it's clear, specific, and compelling, then it's probably a good one. Try asking yourself, "Would this make an interesting news segment or documentary short?" And if you find your challenge/problem isn't compelling enough on its own, that's what the "raise the stakes" part is for—tell us why it matters.

Do I have to include every single element of the Elon Musk structure in order for the essay to work?

Not necessarily. Note, for example, how the "Catalyzing Creativity Club" essay doesn't include a "raise the stakes" moment. Use the elements that make sense for your story; don't use the ones that don't.

Do I have to focus my extracurricular essay on a challenge?

Absolutely not! Here's how to write your essay if you have NOT faced a challenge related to your extracurricular activity (or don't want to feature one in your essay).

The Montage Extracurricular Essay (a.k.a. The Uncommon Connections Approach)

Remember (from page 155), the difference between a boring essay and a stand-out essay is this:

- A **boring personal statement** chooses a common topic, makes common connections, and uses common language.
- A **stand-out personal statement** chooses an uncommon topic, makes uncommon connections, and uses uncommon language.

By "uncommon connections" I mean the values people don't normally or immediately associate with the activity you've named. Another word I use for uncommon connections is "insights."

And I know what you're thinking: *What if I don't play an obscure instrument or my most important extracurricular activity and achievements are somewhat common?*

If you have no uncommon topic or achievements, it's all the more important to make uncommon connections related to your values. With a common topic and common connections (i.e., basketball taught me hard work and discipline), you'll likely blend in. Instead, you want to generate insights others won't have thought of. And we can do that using a reimagined version of the step-by-step process used to create a Type B montage structure personal statement.

THE UNCOMMON CONNECTIONS GAME*

First, let's pick a cliché topic that you might use for an essay. The more cliché the better. Football, you say? A mission trip? Awesome, let's do both.

Step 1: Brainstorm the cliché version of your essay.

First, tell me what the typical football or mission trip essay will focus on. How? Take a look at that Values Exercise on page 5 and list some cliché values that you think the typical essay would focus on.

Cliché values for football would be *teamwork, responsibility, hard work*, etc.

Cliché values for a mission trip would be *helping others, hard work, passion*, etc.

Step 2: Come up with three to four uncommon values.

Next, brainstorm values that might not normally be associated with football or a mission trip.

Uncommon values for football might be *resourcefulness, healthy boundaries, critical thinking*, etc.

Uncommon values for a mission trip might be *serenity, accountability, practicality*, etc.

If you can find a connection to an uncommon value, you can find two; if you can find two, you can find three; and if you can find three, then you have enough content for a 350-word essay.

---

*   I offer a version of this exercise on page 155, but the application for this type of essay is different, so I'm describing it here again in a slightly different way.

Step 3: Tie the values to specific examples from your life.

Describe one specific example of how you've developed or explored that uncommon value through that activity...and maybe even applied it to other areas of your life.

Example: Football has made me a better reader.

"As a cornerback, I meticulously and systematically scan the offense, looking for nuances in formation before the quarterback snaps the ball, all in a matter of seconds. It's not unlike annotating a novel. Finding the subtle complexities in my rival teams' spread offense has not only led me to intercepting a pass, but has given me the skills to fully digest, for example, Dostoevsky's *Crime and Punishment*, where the smallest, and at first glance, almost unnoticeable details, add to an intricate story that I wouldn't appreciate in the same way had I not been able to notice those details in the first place."

See how that makes for a more interesting football essay? Uncommon Value (critical thinking) + Application Elsewhere (English class) = Win.

Do this with a few more of your uncommon values. Once you have a list of three to four uncommon values and examples of how they've manifested in your life, you can move on to the next step.

Step 4: Decide on an order for your details and write a draft.

I recommend chronological order, as it'll make transitions easier. Then try a draft. It doesn't have to be perfect the first time, just get something down on paper.

Check out the next example for which the author wrote about the extracurricular activity of playing the santur (an ancient Persian instrument) and brainstormed these values: *beauty, culture, social change, family, helping others, language*.

SANTUR

I love how short and simple this hook is.

Do re fa mi, re do fa mi, re do sol fa mi re mi re. Have I completely lost it? Should I be locked up in a mental hospital chained to a chair? No. Then what are these utterances coming from my mouth? Music.

He introduces the topic right away, which helps ground the essay.

I have devoted thousands of hours of my life to playing

Eliminates any potential confusion by explaining right away.

the santur, a classical Persian instrument that originated in the Middle East. Some people think I'm strange: a Persian redheaded Jewish teenager obsessed with an ancient musical instrument. But they don't see what I see. My santur is King David's lyre: it can soothe, enrapture, mesmerize.

I love this sentence because it sets him apart from other students, plus shows he's confident enough to use self-deprecating humor.

Nice metaphor (uncommon language)

Value/uncommon connection: culture and heritage

The santur also allows me to connect to my culture and Persian heritage, and to visit Iran of the past, a culture rich in artistic tradition. Sometimes I imagine performing for the king in the Hanging Gardens of Babylon, the santur sounds echoing through the Seven Hills of Jerusalem.

Another uncommon connection (music = social change), plus uncommon language

Today, some Americans view Iran as a land of terrorists, but when I play, the innocent of Iran, the educated, the artists, the innovators, come to life. Iran is not a country of savages; it's *Kubla Khan's* fountain, an abundant source of knowledge and creativity.

More uncommon language

Finally, the santur represents one of my remaining links to my grandfather. In the last few years of his life, Baba Joon did not know me as his grandson. Alzheimer's slowly took over his brain, and eventually he could not recognize me. Baba Joon grew up with the music of the santur and my father plays it in his car every day, so when I play, the music connects all three generations.

Another uncommon connection (family) and it's expressed in an uncommon way.

Uncommon achievement

In December I'll be releasing my first album, a collection of classical Persian pieces. Proceeds from the album will go toward Alzheimer's research, as I hope to play some small part in finding a cure for the disease. My teacher is one of only a handful of santur teachers from Iran, and I sometimes wonder if the santur will soon become extinct, like the seven thousand endangered languages which may soon be gone.

Uncommon connection (cultural music = endangered language)

Not if I have anything to say about it.

For another essay written using this uncommon connections technique, check out the "Hiking" essay on page 192.

But you might be wondering: "Do I have to use uncommon connections? Can't I just tell the reader about what I've done and learned?"

You can! In fact, here's an essay that does just that.

THE STRAIGHTFORWARD (BUT SPECIFIC!) SWITCH-SIDE POLICY DEBATE ESSAY

Value: *diverse intellectual perspectives*

Through switch-side policy debate, I not only discuss a multitude of competing ideas, but also argue from both sides of widely disputed issues. By equipping me with Protagoras' antilogic and Dissoi Logoi, switch-side policy debate has provided me with a forum to cultivate a diversity of intellectual perspectives that has informed my own intellectual growth.

Value: *leadership*

Value: *teaching/ helping others*

I strive to give others the same opportunity for intellectual stimulation. Over the past two years, I have helped expand my debate team from a struggling club of fifteen to a force of over one hundred debaters, leading my team to place first in our debate league. As team president, I teach new debaters fundamentals in communication theory while facilitating formal and informal debates. Playing a dual role as instructor and competitor has allowed me to establish debate as a lasting forum for discussing ideas at my school.

Value: *openness*

Value: *courage*

Value: *curiosity with legs*

Value: *managerial and communication skills*

Values: *environmental awareness and taking action*

Values: *approaching problems critically and clearly articulating complex ideas*

The lessons I learned as both a leader and debater have helped me to succeed beyond my debate circles. Inside the classroom, I possess the openness to consider the views of others and the courage to voice my own opinions. Having been elected to student office four times, I have used these skills to sell my ideas to the student body and earn its vote. More importantly, debate has taught me how to transform these ideas into concrete actions. As the current ASB vice president, I have used the managerial and communication skills I developed as a debater to spearhead a school-wide sustainability campaign that spanned issues concerning water scarcity, ecology, and campus beautification.

Value: *career*

Similarly, the lessons I learned in debate will be instrumental in my future work as an entrepreneur and engineer, both of which require the capacity to approach problems critically and clearly articulate complex ideas. Continuing to develop these skills will be crucial if I am to become a competitive member in the future marketplace of ideas.

Brief Notes and Analysis:

- This essay uses the "fire hose" approach. It's a straightforward account of this student's accomplishments and the lessons he has learned. Does it feel too braggy? Maybe not, as I really appreciate how he connects each accomplishment ("Having been elected to student office four times...") to lessons he's learned through debate ("...I have used these skills to sell my ideas to the student body and earn its vote").

- I also appreciate how this essay weaves together different parts of his application, describing both his role in the classroom and his work in student government. In this sense, debate ends up being a thematic thread that connects many parts of his life.

- One thing that I think prevents his essay from sounding cliché is the specificity of his language throughout the essay.

The 150-Word Extracurricular Activity Essay

The short extracurricular essay can be tricky, as it asks you to communicate a lot of information in just a few words. Here's a great example, followed by some tips:

JOURNALISM

VIOLENCE IN EGYPT ESCALATES. FINANCIAL CRISIS LEAVES EUROPE IN TURMOIL. My quest to become a journalist began by writing for the international column of my school newspaper, *The Log*. My specialty is international affairs; I'm the messenger who delivers news from different continents to the doorsteps of my community. Late-night editing, researching, and rewriting is customary, but seeing my articles in print makes it all worthwhile. I'm the editor for this section, responsible for brainstorming ideas and catching mistakes. Each spell-check I make, each sentence I type out, and each article I polish will remain within the pages of *The Log*. Leading a heated after-school brainstorming session, watching my abstract thoughts materialize on-screen, holding the freshly printed articles in my hand—I write for this joyous process of creation. One day I'll look back, knowing this is where I began developing the scrutiny, precision, and rigor necessary to become a writer.

SEVEN TIPS FOR THE 150-WORD EXTRACURRICULAR ESSAY

Tip 1: Value content (information) over form (poetry).
Space is limited here, so make sure the reader understands what you've done and what you've learned. Notice how in the "Journalism" essay a lot of the content probably came from the first column of the BEABIES (i.e., What I Did).

Tip 2: Use active verbs to give a clear sense of what you've done.
Check out the active verbs in the essay: writing, delivering, editing, researching, rewriting, brainstorming, catching, polishing, leading, holding, knowing. You can use the Epic Verbs List on page 111 for ideas.

Tip 3: Consider telling us in one good, clear sentence what the activity meant to you.
Examples:

> "I'm the messenger who delivers news from different continents to the doorsteps of my community."
> "I write for this joyous process of creation."
> "One day I'll look back, knowing that this is where I began to develop the scrutiny, precision and rigor necessary to become a writer."

Tip 4: You can "show" a little but not too much.
You've probably heard that it's better to "show" things to your reader through descriptions, events, conversations, etc., rather than just tell them what you want them to know. And sometimes it is! But there isn't much room for that in a short essay.

This essay shows a little bit in the first line: "VIOLENCE IN EGYPT ESCALATES. FINANCIAL CRISIS LEAVES EUROPE IN TURMOIL." And later, "Leading a heated after-school brainstorming session, watching my abstract thoughts materialize on-screen, holding the freshly printed articles in my hand..."

The first one grabs our attention; the second paints a clear and dynamic picture. Keep 'em short!

Heads up: This essay uses the montage approach and does not name a specific problem. If, however, you're using the Elon Musk structure from page 233 and want to adapt it for the 150-word essay...

Tip 5: Consider starting your short essay with the "problem."

In fact, probably name the problem in the first sentence. Then in the second sentence, say what you did about it. See the Hospital Internship essay on the next page.

Tip 6: Don't forget to include specific impact even if it's brief.

This is a great place for results that can be quantified or quickly expressed in a one-sentence explanation.

Tip 7: Write it long first, then cut it.

The author of the "Journalism" essay started with 250–300 words, then trimmed ruthlessly. In my experience, this tends to be easier than writing a very short version and then trying to figure out what to add.

FIVE MORE 150-WORD EXTRACURRICULAR ESSAYS I LOVE

PHOTOGRAPHY

Developer, one minute; stop bath, thirty seconds; fixer, two minutes. Under the red beam of safelights, a new photo comes to life, a carefully crafted compilation of dark shadows, light skies, and all the grays in between.

I like this hook. It's short, cinematic, evocative.

I've spent many hours exploring photography using film cameras, pinhole cameras, plastic cameras, Polaroids, digital cameras, and disposables. I scour antique stores for old cameras to experiment with and learn from. As a result of my passion for photography, I have become one of my school's photographers, responsible for documenting school events and teaching younger students darkroom

Here's the "What I've Done" from her BEABIES exercise.

Here's the "How I've Applied What I've Learned" from her BEABIES.

techniques. Making decisions in the darkroom about contrast filters and apertures has made me more confident in my ability to make choices quickly. I also use my photography to advance social justice causes by drawing attention to issues such as unattainable standards for women's bodies. (139 words)

ACTIVISM

These three words show us how long the author's been committed to this cause.

Rather than wait until the end of the essay, she shares the impact here in the second sentence—and it works.

In eighth grade, I created an art piece addressing a stereotype I had faced and posted it online, encouraging my friends to do the same and hashtag it #StereotypeProject. The drawing snowballed into a viral movement, gathering the attention of over 1,000 youth artists worldwide, each contributing their own stories and drawings. The Stereotype Project has since grown, extending into local schools and calling on the next generation to stand strong against the biases they face due to race, gender, sexual orientation, mental illness, and more. In a time of increasing youth activism and reminders of the potential we have as young revolutionaries, the Stereotype Project is a channel for creative expression, unity, and a means of imparting a positive impact on the world. Our website continues to be live and accept submissions: stereotypeproject.org. (136 words)

Here she explains in one sentence the purpose of the project.

In case you're wondering: No, the admission reader probably will not look at the website—but feel free to include it, since it's nice to know you created one.

HOSPITAL INTERNSHIP

Here's a narrative essay that employs the Elon Musk structure and addresses not one but two problems.

Problem #2

Upon applying to Irvine Regional Hospital, I was told there were no spaces for junior volunteers. After securing additional recommendations, however, I reapplied and was finally accepted and assigned front desk duties, where I delivered flowers, transported biopsy samples to labs, directed visitors, and answered nurse requests. Unfortunately, the hospital was shut down due to lack of funds, and hundreds of workers became unemployed, including me. It was distressing to experience the effects of a declining economy. When Kaiser Permanente opened, my

Problem #1

What he did about it

applications were also initially rejected. But by requesting an interview, I proved my qualifications from past experiences and was specially assigned to medical surgery instead of the gift shop. I answered patients' requests, administered patient surveys, organized wound documentations, filed records, delivered blood and urine samples, assisted nurses with check-ups, stocked supply carts, updated dietary needs with doctors, and discharged patients safely. (146 words)

What he did about it

SUMMER JOB

Yes, work counts as an extracurricular activity!

Regular Dog: $1.49. Jimmy's Famous: $1.89. Twenty-five cents for cheese. Bologna's out. Milkshake machine's broken. Refill sweet tea.

Love this opening. Grabs our attention.

As cashier at Jimmy's Hot Dogs, I was everything but the cook. After day one, my hair stood straight and old southern ladies sympathetically asked, "Oh honey, is it your first shift?" I wanted to cry.

Love her tone here. So human. She shows it's possible to be vulnerable in a 150-word essay.

But an hour before closing, Nondas, the cook, checked the register. He smiled and said, "Luci Lou, you the best." Stress forgotten, we danced around the kitchen in celebration, talking about his brothers in Greece, World Cup soccer, and grilled fish.

This is a setup for the ending, but you won't know this on a first read.

After that, I didn't feel alone. I had Nondas. I had the regulars. And I had the southern ladies to back me up. Jimmy's taught me to value the people that make a job worthwhile. To focus on the positive when there's soccer to be watched and perfectly grilled fish to be eaten. (150 words)

What she learned

This pays off the setup at the end of her previous paragraph.

SPORTS

Sports is a common extracurricular topic, so it's all the more important to seek and name uncommon connections and achievements.

Two years ago I won the Coach's Award without ever stepping on the volleyball court. How? Sophomore year, a stress fracture prevented me from practicing, but I came to every practice and game to encourage and laugh with my teammates. At the end of the year, I won the award based on my positivity.

Another great opening. Note each of these hooks is one sentence long.

The problem

What they did about it

Another problem

What they did
about it

The subsequent year, I transferred schools and tried out for volleyball. Due to MHSAA rules, I couldn't play because of the transfer, but I could practice. I never missed one, worked hard, and acted as team manager. So guess what happened? I won the Coach's Award again, this time from a different coach. Again, without ever having set foot on the court.

While I'm not sure I'll play DI or DII sports, I know for sure that one of my favorite activities ever is being positive and I plan to continue it at Michigan.

Obviously you don't have to name the school, but you can!

In the Treasure Trove, you'll find:
→   The Uncommon Connections (UC) game

Chapter 16

How to Write the "Why Major?" Essay

Can you skip this chapter?

Heads up: the "Why Major?" essay applies to only certain schools. How do you know if you need to write it? Look at the required supplemental essays listed on the essay tracker you created on page 183. If your schools don't ask for a "Why Major?" essay, skip this chapter.

In this chapter, we'll cover:

- What a "Why Major?" essay prompt looks like
- A brief, step-by-step guide to writing your "Why Major?" essay
- Three "Why Major?" essay examples
- What to do if you're unsure of your major or choosing "Undecided" on your application
- How to write your "Why Major?" essay using a thematic thread

What does a "Why Major?" essay prompt look like? Like this:

Why are you drawn to the area(s) of study you indicated earlier in this application? (You may share with us a skill or concept that you found challenging and rewarding to learn, or any experiences beyond course-work that may have broadened your interest.)

Or this:

As of this moment, what academic areas seem to fit your interests or goals most comfortably? Please indicate up to three from the list provided. Why do these areas appeal to you?

In short: Why do you want to study what you want to study?

Writing Your "Why Major?" Essay

Step 1: Imagine a mini-movie of the moments that led you to your interest and create a simple bullet point outline:

Why Biology?

- Elementary school: Getting my first dinosaur toy and reading dinosaur books
- Middle school: Visiting museums, seeing water under a microscope
- High school: Doing online research, getting internship where we analyzed brainwaves and dissected a stingray

Step 2: Put your moments (a.k.a. the "scenes" of your mini-movie) in chronological order, as it'll help you see how your interests developed. It also makes it easier to write transitions.

Pro Tip: If you're writing a shorter essay (e.g., 100–150 words), try writing one scene per sentence. If you're writing a medium-length essay (e.g., 250–300 words), try one scene per short paragraph.

Step 3: Decide if you want to include a specific thesis that explicitly states your central argument—in this case what you want to study and why. This thesis can be at the beginning, middle, or end of your essay.

Three "Why Major?" Essay Examples

WHY ELECTRICAL ENGINEERING?

My decision to major in Electrical Engineering was inspired by my desire to improve security through technology. When I lived in Mexico, my father's restaurant security system lacked the ability to protect our property from robbers, who would break in multiple times a year. Thanks to the influence of my cousin, who now studies Autonomous Systems, I developed an interest in electrical engineering. I am inspired to not only improve my father's security system, but contribute to security innovations for larger companies and perhaps, one day, national security. (88 words)

This is a short essay that puts the thesis at the beginning. Here's the outline:

Why Electrical Engineering?

- Thesis: I want to improve security through technology.
- Robbers broke into dad's restaurant
- Cousin taught me about Autonomous Systems
- In the future: Work with large companies or on national security

WHY GENDER AND SEXUALITY STUDIES?

My interest in Gender and Sexuality Studies was sparked in my eighth grade Civics class when we studied topics pertaining to sexual equality. I went into the class knowing I believed women had a right to make choices for their own bodies and that view remained the same, but I discovered the complexity of abortion debates. I challenged myself by thinking about the disparity between actual and potential personhood and the moral rights of unconscious lives. If pregnancy had the same consequences for men as it does women, how might the debate be different? Would this debate even exist?

A year later, I shadowed an OB/GYN at a nearby hospital. On my first shift, I watched an incarcerated woman receive a postpartum exam after giving birth in her cell toilet with just Advil, and the issues discussed in Civics suddenly became urgent and real.

My school projects have often focused on reproductive rights. I've spent numerous hours delving into summaries of Supreme Court cases on abortion and contraception, and am even known as the "Tampon Fairy" at school because I frequently restock the school bathrooms with tampons and condoms.

I'm interested in exploring how Gender and Sexuality Studies connect to Public Health and Reproductive Biology, as well as Public Policy and Law. The interdisciplinary nature of this major will allow me to investigate many other areas of study and create a more nuanced understanding of how this particular field interacts with our world and society. (245 words)

This is a medium-length example with the thesis at the end. Here's the outline.

Why Gender and Sexuality Studies?

- Eighth grade Civics class conversations
- Shadowing OB/GYN at a nearby hospital and seeing woman receive postpartum exam
- Being the school "tampon fairy" (restocking school bathrooms with tampons and condoms)
- School projects on reproductive rights
- Thesis: name my major and briefly say why.

WHY NEUROSCIENCE?

Imagine all the stars in the universe. The brain has a thousand times the number of synapses, making neurological errors a near certainty. I learned this fact firsthand as a fourteen-year-old, when I suffered from sleepless nights because of an uncomfortable, indescribable feeling in my leg. It took months of appointments and tests to be told it was a condition called cortical dysplasia. Even after the diagnosis, there is no cure.

I am lucky. My condition does not severely affect my quality of life. However, I know this is not the case for everyone. After this experience, I took AP Biology and attended a neuroscience program, which reinforced the subject as my future calling. One of the most impactful lectures discussed the plight of healthcare in developing nations. Newborns with extreme neurological deficits are common, but finding treatments is not. Without prenatal care, this is becoming a growing epidemic, leaving millions of children helpless.

With a degree in neuroscience, I will gain a strong understanding of neural tube development and neuronal migration in infants. I will then become a neurologist, specializing in pediatric care. I hope to work for humanitarian organizations, such as Doctors Without Borders, in Africa, where HIV and polio are rampant, as are numerous other diseases.

Imagine the stars once more. From across the world, I will look at the same stars in the future as I help children secure the ability to not only look at the stars, but do much more. (248 words)

This is a medium-length essay that uses a hook to grab our attention, noted in the outline below.

Why Neuroscience?

- Hook: Connect number of stars to number of connections in brain (and maybe mention cortical dysplasia)
- AP Bio + neuroscience program, learning about healthcare in developing nations
- Thesis: I will use neuroscience to help children.
- Return to opening (stars) and look to future

How to Write Your "Why Major?" Essay Using a Thematic Thread

Another option for the "Why Major?" essay is to identify a thematic thread and use it to tie together the "scenes" in the "movie" of your essay.

The following example establishes in the first paragraph the thematic thread of *storytelling*. The second paragraph then explains how her particular major would take her storytelling to the next level. Take a look.

WHY LITERARY ARTS OR MODERN CULTURE AND MEDIA?

My whole life, storytelling has shaped me. When I lived in London, my parents would read me *The Lion King* every night until I'd memorized the whole book. In elementary school, I would curl up in my bed, warm lamplight making my room golden, listening to my dad bring to life classics like *Wilderness Champion* and *Tom Sawyer*. Later, I found audio storytelling, laughing hysterically at *Wait Wait Don't Tell Me* on the car ride to school and connecting to a radio network of humanity through *This American Life*. It wasn't long before I got hooked on visual narratives, mesmerized by the cinematic intensity of *Whiplash* and the whimsical world of *Moonrise Kingdom*, alternate realities I could explore as if they were my own. By high school, I was creating my own array of stories through satirical school newspaper articles, analysis of mise-en-scène in film class, podcasting, and my own locally broadcasted radio series.

A concentration in the Literary Arts or Modern Culture and Media is the next step in my life of storytelling. The dynamic world of connection and vulnerability a well-told story can create is what continues to fascinate me. At Brown, I would explore how engaging narratives have been told in the past and can be innovated in the future through new digital platforms. Whether researching radio's historical impact on public opinion during World War II or the Vietnam War, developing screenplays, producing my own documentary, or learning from Writers-in-Residence, I hope to pioneer networks of connection. (250 words)

Here's the outline:

Part 1: Establish storytelling as thematic thread

- Mom and Dad reading me *The Lion King* before bed
- Dad reading me *Wilderness Champion* and *Tom Sawyer*
- Audio storytelling: *Wait Wait Don't Tell Me*, *This American Life*
- Visual storytelling: *Whiplash*, *Moonrise Kingdom*
- Creating my own stories: school newspaper articles, film class analysis, podcasting, local radio series

Part 2: Why Literary Arts or Modern Culture and Media

- Next step in my journey
- Values: connection and vulnerability
- Explore history of storytelling (past) + digital platforms (future)
- Ways I might do this: studying impact of radio during wars, writing screenplays, producing a documentary, or learning from Writers-in-Residence
- End on the theme of "connection" to tie things together

"WHY MAJOR?" ESSAY FAQS

What if I'm not sure of my major or I'm choosing "undecided" on my application?

If you're choosing "undecided" on your application, that's okay! Even if you're unsure of your major, you might still research and select one to three areas of interest and describe how you became interested in each. If possible, connect them to each other using one value or other aspect of yourself.

What if a school asks me to describe my interest in several possible majors?

If writing a short essay (100–150 words), perhaps describe one interest per sentence. If writing a medium-length essay (200–250 words), try describing one interest per paragraph.

Here's a short example written by a student who listed on his application the following areas of interest: Computer Science and Mathematics, Computer Science and Psychology, Electrical Engineering, and Computer Science.

> Having attended college Physics classes every Saturday for a year, I've embraced the wisdom from centuries-old mathematics and the vast potential of computers, a realization I can honor by pursuing Computer Science and Mathematics. Much of my interest in AI lies in its basis in the human brain, which I can pursue in a Psychology concentration. And Electrical Engineering allows me to connect the virtual world with the physical, as I currently do in robotics. Yale will fuel my interdisciplinary interests that stem from my curiosity about connections between the materials and systems in the world around me. (98 words)

Final note: While this may feel straightforward, that's okay. Prioritize content over poetry when writing a short "Why Major?" essay.

Chapter 17

The Dos and Don'ts of the Short Answers

DO think of your short answers as an advent calendar.

Consider that each of your short answers, no matter how short, is a tiny window into your soul. Make sure the reader finds something inside that's awesome and different from the window before. Can you do that in fifteen words? You can!

DO use all the space allotted to explain your answer.

You're often given space for thirteen words for an answer that could easily be one or two words. So use it up! In other words, answer the question "Why?" even if the prompt doesn't ask you to. Do this because your core values may be hard to express in one to two words.

Here's a question: *What's your favorite food?*

If you just say "tacos," what does this reveal about you? Maybe that you live in Austin, or…? A better answer might be, "My abuela's birria tacos—the recipe has been passed down for generations." This answer reveals connections to family, culture, and even goats!*

Another question: *Who is your role model?*

---

* That's what birria is, by the way: goat.

Answer: *Louis Zamperini*

The admission officer might read that and think, "Great, no idea who that is."

Don't make your readers google your answer. They won't. Instead, expand just a bit: *Olympic athlete Louis Zamperini, who survived Japanese prison camps and overcame severe alcoholism.*

DON'T make the short reason you provide (or any of your answers) super obvious.

Question: What's your favorite website?

Obvious answer: *Instagram (social media photo-sharing site)*

Yup. That's…pretty much what Instagram is. Thanks for telling me zero about you.

Another question: *What historical moment or event do you wish you could have witnessed?*

Obvious answer: *The Big Bang. It was the beginning of our universe and it would have been amazing to see that.*

Yup, that's…what that was. (Also, FYI, many students write "The Big Bang" for this question.)

Better answer: *I want to watch George Washington go shopping. I have an obsession with presidential trivia, and the ivory-gummed general is far and away my favorite. Great leaders aren't necessarily defined by their moments under pressure; sometimes tiny decisions are most telling—like knickers or pantaloons.*

DO get specific.

Question: What inspires you?

Nonspecific answer: *Documentaries. They are my favorite source of inspiration.* (Side note: Don't. Sound. Like. A robot…Using contractions like "they're" is fine.)

Better answer: *Documentaries. "Forks Over Knives" made me go vegan; "Born into Brothels" inspired my Gold Award.*

DON'T, for your favorite quote, say something that you'd find on one of those "Success" posters or a Hallmark card.

Cheesy examples include: "Life is what you make of it," or "Always follow your dreams," or "Life is like a dream and dreams are like life are dreams dreams life life dreams." (You get the idea. Pretty much anything with "life" or "dreams.")

DON'T use common or obvious adjectives on the "3–5 words to describe you" question.

Again, they don't tell us much, and you can probably guess what the most common adjectives are: *adventurous, friendly, outgoing, compassionate, passionate, empathetic…*

DON'T use adjectives that repeat info already clear on your application.

Examples: *motivated, hardworking, determined*. Yup. You and every other student with a great GPA. Which reminds me…

DO make sure your adjectives are interesting and demonstrate variety.

In the previous example, they all basically mean the same thing. So make sure they reveal something interesting about you.

Tell me who you'd rather meet, someone who is "passionate, persistent, and extroverted" or an "ardent, Panglossian visionary?" Or maybe the "gregarious horse-whispering philosopher queen?"*

DON'T worry so much about pissing off people.

I'm doing that in this chapter, using sarcasm and phrases like "pissing off people."

Let me clarify: Students often ask me, "Is [this] okay? Is [that] okay? I

---

*   I have questions for that last girl.

don't want them to think that I'm too [blank]." Oh, you mean you don't want them to think that you have a personality?

I encourage students to take (calculated) risks on these. To push boundaries. To be, I don't know, funny? Human? Compare, for example, the following answers:

Question: What's something you can't live without?

Play-it-safe answer: *My family.* Me: *Zzzzzz.*

Better answer: *The Tony Stark-made arc reactor in my chest.* Me: *YESSS, LOVE IT.*

DON'T check your humor at the door.

If you're funny in life, feel free to be funny in your short answers. If you're not funny, no need to start now.

Irony is one of the best ways to demonstrate intelligence and sensitivity to nuance. Check out these examples:

Question: *What are the two qualities you most admire in other people?*
Answer: *Spock's logic & Kirk's passion*

Question: *What are you most proud of?*
Answer: *Only crying once during* The Notebook *(maybe twice)*

Question: *Who or what inspires you?*
Answer: *Shia LaBeouf yelling "Just Do It"*

Question: *What do you wish you were better at being or doing?*
Answer: *Dancing—especially like Drake, "Hotline Bling" style*

Question: *Most freshmen live in suites of four to six students. What would you contribute to the dynamic of your suite?*
Answer: *A Magical Mystery Tour of Beatles keyboard songs*

You totally want to meet this guy, right? Make the reader totally want to meet you.

DO offer a variety of things you're interested in.

If you love science and wrote a supplemental essay about science, don't answer with twenty journals, websites, or publications you've read on...science.

Show your interest not in astrophysics but also literature, philosophy, *Star Trek*, programming, and *Godfather 1* and *2* (but not *3*.)

In short, use the other parts of your application to show you are hard-working and responsible. Once you've done that, you can have a little fun here.

In the Treasure Trove, you'll find:

→   More short answer examples (with notes on why they're great)

Part VII

The Other Parts of the Application Process

Chapter 18

How to Get Great Letters of Recommendation

Written with Alexis Allison

The letter of recommendation is the one part of the application that students *don't* have to write. *Cue the Hallelujah chorus.*

But wait! Before you celebrate, know this: you still have to know how to ask for one.

The art of persuasion relies on good strategy. That's how you convince your parents to un-ground you. Or how you get your teacher to throw out that homework assignment over spring break. A good strategy can also help you get a *crème-de-la-crème* letter of recommendation for college.

Don't worry. "Strategy" is this chapter's middle name.

In this chapter, we'll cover:

- Why you need letters of recommendation for college
- Who should write your letters of recommendation
- The difference between the counselor and teacher recommendations
- When to ask for letters of recommendation
- How to set yourself up for a great recommendation letter
- How to ask for a letter of recommendation
- How to follow up (the very same day you ask)
- One really important thing you can't forget to do

In the spirit of this topic, we've gathered advice from a number of experts. You can read about them at the end of this chapter.

Teachers and counselors: the Treasure Trove contains a step-by-step guide on How to Write a Great Letter of Recommendation + Samples.

Why You Need Letters of Recommendation for College

Why bother? Because some colleges consider letters of rec pretty darn important. When colleges are comparing you and another student with the same stats (GPA, class rank, test scores, extracurricular activities), your essay and letters of recommendation make you stand apart.

Words of Wisdom from an Admission Officer

Heath Einstein, Dean of Admission at TCU

Letters of recommendation can be a powerful tool for admission officers to understand the role a student plays in the classroom and the community. The former is found in letters written by teachers and the latter in letters offered by a counselor. The best letters breathe life into a student's application, providing a window into personalities and characteristics. A teacher can help colleges understand how a student hasn't just earned a strong grade, but has been a classroom leader, helping peers achieve greater understanding of concepts. A counselor sheds light on the impact a student has had on the high school or greater community.

These letters tell a story, threading activities, passions, and future goals. For these reasons, students are best served by requesting letters from teachers who know them well, eschewing the inclination to pursue only teachers in classes where the highest grades were earned. Some of the best letters come from teachers who can speak to the persistence demonstrated in earning that hard B.

Who Should Write Your Letters of Recommendation?

The three main categories of letters of recommendation are those from your school counselor, your teachers, and other recommenders (don't worry, I'll get more specific shortly).

But all your recommenders should ideally have two things in common:

1. They know you.[*]
2. They like you.

If you don't think any of your teachers, counselors, or other possible recommenders know you well, start getting to know them. How? Pop in to see them when you know their day hits a lull. Or schedule an appointment. Show curiosity about who your recommenders are as real people. Ask questions about class, work, life…a two-way conversation will give them a different insight into who you are.

But let's talk about how the letters will differ among…

Your counselor. The purpose of the counselor letter is to help admission officers see you in the context of your school and community, or to illuminate any hardships you may have endured (familial, learning differences, etc.). As school counselor and former Assistant Dean of Admission at Stanford Martin Walsh says, the counselor letter "backlights" a student's application.

Your teachers. By contrast, the role of the teacher letter is to spotlight your participation in their class. The letter might give insights into things like: how your brain works, what your intellectual and creative capacity is, how consistent your work ethic is from day-to-day, what your commitment to learning looks like, how you work with your peers, and how your peers respond to you.

When deciding which teachers to ask for recommendations, add two more things to the general criteria I mentioned earlier (they know you and like you). Consider those who…

---

[*]   And I don't mean they "know" you as in they can connect your face to your name; I mean they really know you. Another way of looking at it is this: a recommender can only help a college get to know you as much as the recommender knows you.

- Taught you a core subject (English, math, science, social studies)
- Taught you recently (junior year is prime)

Important note: Some colleges and certain programs require or recommend that students submit recommendations from teachers in certain subject areas. Be sure you double-check that.

Pro Tip: If you need more than one teacher recommendation, pick teachers who know about your different strengths and can highlight them.

Other people. Don't forget about other people in your life like your coach, boss, volunteer coordinator, priest, rabbi, etc. These people may need a little more guidance on writing the letter because they may not be accustomed to writing recommendation letters to colleges. But don't miss an opportunity to have someone write a letter about all the awesome things you do outside school.

WHAT'S THE DIFFERENCE BETWEEN THE COUNSELOR AND TEACHER RECOMMENDATIONS?

A counselor's letter describes:

- The student's abilities in context, over time—how do they fit within the school's overall demographics, curriculum, test scores?
- Special circumstances beyond the classroom that impact the student

A teacher's letter describes:

- The impact this student has on the classroom
- The "mind" of the student
- The student's personality, work ethic, and social conduct

WHAT IF I CAN'T FIND A RECOMMENDER WHO MEETS ALL THE CRITERIA?

Prioritize in this order: first, someone who actually likes you. Then someone who knows you well. And for teachers, someone who taught you recently, then someone who taught you a core subject.

When to Ask for a Letter of Recommendation

Ask in advance. I mean way in advance—like, end-of-junior-year-in-advance, if possible. Three weeks before the application deadline should be your minimum, and even that's pushing it. Martin Walsh, former Assistant Dean of Admission at Stanford, recommends a ninety-day heads-up.

A rule of thumb: the more time you give your teachers, the more they will love you and the better your letter will turn out.* Some teachers will write them on a first-come-first-serve basis and cap the number of letters that they'll write, so don't procrastinate.

How to Ask for Letters of Recommendation for College

Actually ask. Don't just add the name of your teacher, counselor, or boss to your Common Application. Actually speak to them.

Ask in person. An email ask should be a last resort. If one of you has moved, making an in-person request impossible, opt for the phone call first, email second, then texting as a last resort.

Make one-on-one requests. Once I had two students who were friends walk up to me together to ask for their letters of recommendation, so I felt obligated to tell them both yes—how awkward would it have been if I'd told one yes and one no?

Time it right. You know how you wait until your parents are in a good mood before you ask them for something? Do that with your recommenders, too. Don't ask your teachers during class. Don't ask your counselors during lunch. (They're humans. They eat.) Don't ask your priest on Sunday after mass or your boss on the busiest day of the week. You get the idea.

Handle the print submissions. While this is not the norm, some schools still want you to snail mail your rec letters. If that's the case, it's your responsibility to provide your teacher with a stamped envelope addressed to the admission office of the relevant college. Make sure

---

*   And heads-up that teachers may retire or take maternity leave or something else between your junior and senior years, so asking junior year gives them the chance to tell you this and give you their contact info.

to let your snail mail writers know that your full name and birth date should be clearly stated at the top of the page, so the letter makes it into your file. You may also do this for Other Recommenders.

Many teachers and counselors will have created a questionnaire for you to fill out when you ask for their recommendation. Do it! If they don't have one, use or adapt the Letter of Recommendation questionnaire in the Treasure Trove. Make your own copy of the document, fill it out, and either email it to them or print it and deliver in person.

When it's time to ask, here's how to do it: Schedule a brief meeting with your recommender in advance, or wait until all the students have left the classroom at the end of the day (when asking your teacher, cautiously approach them, as you would a wild animal). Here's some sample dialogue (with stage directions):

You: "Ms. Smith, do you have five minutes to talk?" (This is key. You're inviting her into the conversation, while also giving her a quick out if she needs one.)

Ms. Smith: "Sure, Ralph. What's up?"

You: "Well, I'm in the throes of applying to college. I've got some deadlines in about three months, so I'm trying to be proactive and organized before all hell breaks loose. (She'll love you for thinking ahead.) Of all the teachers I've had, I think you know me the best, and I'm wondering: Would you be willing and able to write me a strong letter of recommendation?" (The word "strong" gives teachers a polite out if they feel like they don't know you well enough or don't have time to take on your letter.)

Ms. Smith: "Oh Ralph, I thought you'd never ask." (She probably won't say this, but hey.)

You: "Really? That would be wonderful/epic/lit. Tonight I'll email you all the relevant information—my résumé, my list of colleges and their deadlines, and some bullet points with stuff I've done in class. (More info on this follow-up email to come.) Is there anything else you'd like from me?"

Ms. Smith: "Wow, no, I think that about covers it. Thanks, Ralph."

You: "Thank you, Ms. Smith!" (Turns away, nearing the door. Stops as if remembering something, turns back toward Ms. Smith with a winning smile.)

You: "Oh, Ms. Smith! I almost forgot to ask …what's your favorite coffee shop?"

Ms. Smith: "Oh heavens. Starbucks, I think. Why?"

You: "No reason! Have a great day!" (Skips out the door and immediately jots "Starbucks—Ms. Smith" into notes app. Now you'll remember to put a Starbucks gift card into the thank-you note you write her when all this is over.)

And that's how it's done! Although you should totally switch out Starbucks with your local coffee shop, if you have one.

How to Follow Up (the Same Day You Ask)

Once you've had That Conversation, you need to do one more thing *the very same day*: **Write your recommender a follow-up email.** The human brain is like a very smart bowl of spaghetti: if you don't put your conversation down in writing, it might get lost in a thick vat of garlic and marinara. For this follow-up email, you'll need these things:

- A heart of gratitude. Seriously.
- If you didn't already/recently give it to them, the Letter of Recommendation questionnaire that either they gave you or that you downloaded from the Treasure Trove. Be detailed. Your recommender will love you for it.
- An up-to-date professional résumé. Don't have a résumé? Find a how-to guide in the Treasure Trove.
- A list of the colleges that will need your letter of recommendation along

with each college's application deadline. (This part is in the questionnaire so you don't forget!)

- A brief paragraph about what you hope to study and any relevant life dreams (also in the questionnaire).
- (Optional: for teacher recommenders) A project or paper you're especially proud of from their class.

Here's a good example:

SUBJECT: Letter of recommendation follow-up (Deadline: Nov. 15)
BODY:

Dear Ms. Smith,

I hope this email finds you well.

First of all, thank you. It means a lot that you're writing a letter for me. To smooth the process, I've included my current résumé, as well as the attached questionnaire to remind you of all my amazing qualities (he-he). Otherwise, here's what you need to know in brief:

I'm applying to Florida Atlantic, Rice, and Temple.*

All three schools have a deadline of [date here].

I hope to study education regardless of where I end up, but Rice is my No. 1 because I'm hoping for the Rice-UT Public Health Scholars Program.

My dream job: Community college professor (we talked about this last week).

That's it! Again, thank you, thank you for doing this for me. Please let me know if there's anything else you need, or if you have any follow-up questions. If it's okay with you, I'll probably send a check-in email maybe a week or two before the deadline to make sure all is well.

In the meantime, I hope you have a beautiful day!

Sincerely,
Ralph Figueroa

---

*   Easter egg: Can you spot what these schools have in common?

PEER LETTERS OF RECOMMENDATION

A few schools ask for a peer letter of recommendation, as they want to understand who you are from a different perspective. Consider whom you might ask: a teammate, coworker, camp friend, lab partner, or coleader of a club? Choose someone who can speak to what a great addition you would make to a campus community.

HOMESCHOOLERS

Yes, you will need letters of recommendation too! See page 309 for more.

DISCIPLINARY HISTORY

We all make mistakes. If you have a disciplinary violation on your high school record, your counselor will need to explain the situation on your school report form, and you'll also need to address it on your own application. Even though it's awkward, talk to your counselor about the situation and how to address it so that you're both on the same page.

And finally, here's…

ONE REALLY IMPORTANT THING
YOU CAN'T FORGET TO DO

Don't forget to say thank you. These rec letters—especially the good ones—can take three hours to write. And the thing is, teachers and other recommenders don't have to write these letters. They don't get paid for them. They write them because they care about you. At the very least, write a thank-you email or note.

And in the spring, let them know where you're heading in the fall. It's a little thing, but it means a lot to them. To us.

In the Treasure Trove, you'll find:
→ Letter of recommendation questionnaire
→ How to write a letter of recommendation: Counselor's Guide + Samples
→ Writing a recommendation letter for a student: Teacher's Guide + Samples

Quick shout-out to some of the experts consulted for this chapter, as well as the guides for counselors and teachers (in the Treasure Trove):

Chris Reeves, school counselor and member of the NACAC Board of
  Directors
Trevor Rusert, Director of College Counseling at Chadwick International
Michelle Rasich, Director of College Counseling at Rowland Hall
Kati Sweaney, Senior Assistant Dean of Admission at Reed College
Sara Urquidez, Executive Director of Academic Success Program
Martin Walsh, school counselor and former Assistant Dean of Admission
  at Stanford
Michelle McAnaney, educational consultant and founder of The College
  Spy

How to Do the College Interview

*Special thanks to Monica James for her contributions to this chapter**

Not a whole lot of schools require interviews, but very many offer them and will even recommend that prospective students have one. Sitting down for an interview can be stressful and nerve-racking, but it can also be fun and extremely helpful for both showing a college that they want to have you on their campus and for getting to know the school yourself.

In this chapter, we'll cover:

- The types of interviews colleges offer
- How much interviews matter
- Whether you should interview
- A brief step-by-step guide to preparing for your interview
- Nineteen college interview questions you might be asked

What Types of Interviews Do Colleges Offer?

Colleges will offer you either an informational interview or an evaluative interview.

---

* Check out my podcast with Monica James in the Treasure Trove.

An informational interview is usually done by an alumnus or a current college student, and its purpose is to give you an opportunity to ask questions and learn more about the college. Colleges also use these interviews as a gauge for your interest (learn more about demonstrated interest on page 73).

Evaluative interviews are usually done by an admission officer. They're meant to evaluate whether or not you're a good match for their school based on what you're looking for.

Do Interviews Matter?

Sometimes. In most cases your interview will not be the deciding factor. Having said that, if you're on the bubble (which is admission-speak for not-a-clear-admit and not-a-clear-deny), the fact that you even did an interview could make a slight difference. But some colleges care more about interviews than others. To find out how much a school cares, check out Section C7 of a school's Common Data Set.

Should You Interview?

I'd say you should do it unless you have a really good reason not to. Not only is it a great way to score demonstrated interest points, but it's also an opportunity to show the college your sense of humor, your ability to ask great questions, and your ability to prepare.

Words of Wisdom from an Admission Officer

Paul Sweet, Associate Director of Admission, Babson College

The college interview not only gives the prospective student the opportunity to add a personal side to the application but also the college a chance to highlight specific aspects of the school to the applicant. Both students and colleges are concerned with fit so the college interview can be a helpful tool in determining it.

A Brief Step-by-Step Guide to Preparing for Your Interview

STEP 1: WRITE OR TYPE THE ANSWERS TO THESE THREE QUESTIONS

What interests you besides academics? What do you want to study and why? Why do you want to attend this school?

Good news if you're reading this in December or January: you've probably already answered these in your supplemental essays—yay! If not, you've got a little more work to do.

Once you've answered these questions, spend a few minutes reviewing the brainstorming work you completed on pages 91–106, especially these exercises:

- Values
- Core Memories
- 21 Details
- Everything I Want Colleges to Know about Me
- Feelings and Needs
- Also, your activities list will provide a menu of potential interview topics. And while that may sound like a lot, remember this:

You do not have to memorize all this stuff for your interview.
Why? You're about to simplify things. A lot.

STEP 2: DEVELOP YOUR MESSAGE BOX

What's a message box? It's basically a PR term for the three to four points you definitely want to cover no matter what the interviewer asks.

Say you've worked in your dad's restaurant since the eighth grade, learning the ins and outs of the business while helping support your family. Notice how that could apply to typical interview questions like, *What do you do besides school? What's the largest challenge you've faced and how did you resolve it?* or *What makes you unique?*

Here's how to develop your own message box: First, review the material mentioned in Step 1. Then pick three to four details/experiences/memories/

values that you think you'd like to talk about in your interview. And voilà. That's your message box.

STEP 3: PRACTICE PIVOTING TO YOUR MESSAGE BOX WITH A VALUES-BASED TRANSITION

How? Find someone you're comfortable with and sit with that person in a quiet space where you won't be interrupted. Have them ask you a random question from the following list, then try to answer their question while pivoting to something in your message box.

Example: Let's say one of the things in your message box is the robotics team you started at your school. One cool thing about it is that even though it started out with just two members, now it's grown to twelve and you even placed second in a recent competition.

And say you're asked a question like, "What's your favorite subject?" You might say, for instance, "I love my math and computer programming classes. To me, there's nothing more exciting than trying to solve tough problems—especially when you're working with others and learning how they think. That's part of why I started my school's Robotics Club…"

See what I did there? I used a value as a segue. Two values, actually: *solving problems* and *collaboration*.

But let's say your favorite subject has nothing to do with robotics. Can a values-based transition still work? Totally. You could give an answer like this:

Right now my favorite subject is art. I'm not like a professional or anything but I love trying to figure out ways to communicate what I'm feeling, whether it's through painting or sculpture. And the process of creating something, getting feedback, and then tweaking it actually reminds me a lot of how coding works, except in coding the feedback sometimes comes a lot faster because most of the time either something works or it doesn't. But I really love that process of creative problem solving and getting feedback…I think that's part of why I decided to start a Robotics Club at my school.

See what we're doing here? You're not simply answering the question you were asked. You're answering the question you *wish* you were asked. You'll get better at this with practice, and once you've done this a few times, you'll be connecting your Robotics Club to everything from reading to social life to "the one thing you'd change about your school if you could." But don't feel like you have to memorize your answers. There's no need to say it exactly the same way in the real interview—in fact, you probably don't want to. It'll sound all weird.

STEP 4: INVENT A FEW GREAT QUESTIONS TO ASK YOUR INTERVIEWER (I.E., FLIP THE SCRIPT)

Here's the part students don't often prepare enough for, but I think it's one of the best ways to make a great impression. Why? Asking great questions allows the interviewer to talk about themselves, which can be nice as it turns an interview into a conversation. Plus, your questions can show them you've done your research.

Here are some quick tips on asking great questions:

- **Make sure your answer isn't easily googleable.** "What is your student-to-faculty ratio?" for example, is not a great question to ask your interviewer.
- **Ask questions that require more than a one-word answer.** "Did you like college?" is a yes/no question, whereas "What do you wish you'd known before going to college?" invites more reflection.
- **Build a connection.** Don't be afraid to ask the interviewer personal questions about what he or she likes and dislikes about their alma mater. Remember, people love to share their experiences, and if you can get them to talk about what interests them, you can build a connection around that. To this end…
- **Ask questions that the interviewer might have fun answering.** Example: "What's one of the best days you ever spent in college?"
- **Be prepared for your interviewer to turn your question back on you.** If you ask a question about campus diversity, for example, your interviewer may ask you, "What does diversity mean to you?" or "Why is diversity important to you?" So be ready.
- **If you haven't yet written and submitted your "Why Us?" statement, ask questions that will let your interviewer help you write it.** How? Ask them what they feel sets their school apart from other schools. Or what professor they wished they'd studied with.

You don't need to have eight to ten questions ready. Three or four good ones will do. You'll find sample questions to ask your college interviewer in the Treasure Trove.

Nineteen College Interview Questions You Might Be Asked

1. What subject areas are you most interested in?
2. Tell me about your current extracurriculars.
3. What have you done during the last few summers?
4. What would you do with a year off between high school and college?
5. What are your personal strengths?
6. What are your weaknesses?
7. Tell me about a challenge you've overcome.
8. What three words best describe you?*
9. What characteristics do you admire in your teachers?
10. What do your friends say about you?
11. Have you worked in a job or internship? If so, what surprised you? What did you learn about yourself?
12. If you could meet anyone, dead or alive, who would it be?
13. What would you change about yourself?
14. What's your favorite book and why?
15. What kind of community service do you do?
16. What are you most proud of?
17. What would you do with a free day? Academic or otherwise?
18. What qualities do you look for in friends?
19. How do you want to be remembered?

Five Quick Tips for a Video or Phone Interview

1. Be sure you've got the right software downloaded and practice with it.
2. If you're using your phone for a video call, find a way to prop it up so you don't have to hold it in your hand.
3. Be aware of lighting. If it's daytime, try sitting near a window so the light

---

*   Do you see how your prework exercises might help you answer some of these questions? Go back and look at your 21 Details and Everything I Want Colleges to Know about Me Exercises.

hits your face (but not so you're backlit). If it's at night, spend two to three minutes setting up some decent lighting (maybe just move a lamp) so the interviewer can see your face.

4. Be aware where you're looking. If you look directly into your computer camera it'll feel to them like you're making eye contact. It feels weird, so you don't have to keep doing this, but doing so occasionally can increase the feeling of connectedness.

5. For a phone interview, try standing up. This energizes your voice.

Interview FAQs

WHAT SHOULD I WEAR TO MY INTERVIEW?

You don't have to dress up, but you don't want to look sloppy. Jeans are fine as long as they're not torn and you wear a nice shirt. Oh, and no strong perfume or cologne. Some folks are allergic.

SHOULD I BRING A RÉSUMÉ?

Yes. While your interviewer may not ask for a résumé, it can be useful for them, as interviewers can learn a lot about you in a thirty-second scan and it can provide some great talking points. Keep in mind that the majority of interviewers will not have access to your application. Also, if your interviewer has many interviews scheduled that day, having a résumé handy can help them remember you when they're writing their report later.

HOW ARE SCHOLARSHIP
INTERVIEWS DIFFERENT?

While initial screenings are pretty much identical to regular admission interviews, scholarship interviews sometimes have a weekend component where you'll attend seminars and social events and maybe do more interviews. Assume during those weekends that there is never a time when you aren't being evaluated. Sometimes you'll be put in groups, for example, and asked to solve problems. Or you may have dinner with students and it might feel really casual. It is! But also—and I know this may sound weird—you're being watched. Don't try to impress; try to connect. How? Ask them specific questions about their lives that you genuinely want to know the answer to. In short, stay curious.

One Final Tip

Take control of the interview, when appropriate. Students often tell me that the interview went "fine" but felt frustrated that they weren't asked certain questions. If you feel like there are parts of yourself you'd like to include, pivot to your Message Box!

In the Treasure Trove, you'll find a link to my ultimate guide, which includes:

→ A downloadable interview guidebook you can use to prepare your answers

→ Sample Questions to Ask Your College Interviewer

→ 160+ College Interview Questions

Part VIII

How to Make Sure Your Application Is Doing Its Job

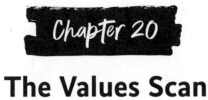

The Values Scan

What's the job of your college application? To show the skills, qualities, interests, and values you'll bring with you to college.

How to make sure your application is doing its job is in the title of this chapter: the Values Scan.

This is the process I've used with my one-on-one students for years. It's a great way to either build confidence (if the application is revealing a lot)* or reveal gaps (if it isn't). It's fast too.

The Four Values Scan Steps

STEP 1: CREATE AN "ALMOST DONE" DOCUMENT.

Copy and paste into a single document your personal statement, activities list, additional info, and supplemental essays. Then label the document with your name and the words "Almost Done." You'll see an example of what this looks like in step 4.

---

* This can be especially useful for students who are perfectionistic and just need to be shown all the ways their application is revealing who they are.

You'll also want to have your Values Exercise (page 5) available along with your Everything I Want Colleges to Know about Me Exercise (page 95).

STEP 2: READ THROUGH YOUR APPLICATION AND SCAN IT FOR VALUES.

This means simply making a note of each value you're communicating right next to where you're communicating it using the document's comment feature. As you work through each section, ask these three questions:

1. Which of my values are being communicated really clearly in my application?
2. Which of my values could be made clearer?
3. Which values are missing, but could or should show up in my application?

Feel free to make revisions before the next step.

STEP 3: SHARE YOUR "ALMOST DONE" DOCUMENT WITH SOMEONE YOU TRUST AND WHO KNOWS YOU WELL.

When you do, ask them the same three questions from step 2. See if they agree with your assessments. Take what each person says with a grain of salt; don't feel obligated to revise everything they suggest. While outside opinions are valuable, don't forget this is your application.[*]

STEP 4: MAKE SURE EACH ITEM FROM YOUR "EVERYTHING I WANT COLLEGES TO KNOW ABOUT ME" EXERCISE IS COMING THROUGH IN YOUR APPLICATION.

If not, could this be something worth including in your additional information section?

Once you've done these four steps, you should have a pretty clear sense of all the qualities your application is revealing.

---

[*]   For more on the dangers of getting feedback from too many people, check out the Treasure Trove.

The following is a great example of a completed Values Scan. In fact, this is the "after" photo of the application prework that you saw in chapter 7.

ADRIAN'S "ALMOST DONE" DOCUMENT

MAIN PERSONAL STATEMENT

At six years old, I stood locked away in the restroom. I held tightly to a tube of toothpaste because I'd been sent to brush my teeth to distract me from the commotion. Regardless, I knew what was happening: my dad was being put under arrest for domestic abuse. He'd hurt my mom physically and mentally, and my brother José and I had shared the mental strain. It's what had to be done.

Living without a father meant money was tight, mom worked two jobs, and my brother and I took care of each other when she worked. For a brief period of time the quality of our lives slowly started to improve as our soon-to-be stepdad became an integral part of our family. He paid attention to the needs of my mom, my brother, and me. But our prosperity was short-lived as my stepdad's chronic alcoholism became more and more recurrent. When I was eight, my younger brother Fernando's birth complicated things even further. As my stepdad slipped away, my mom continued working, and Fernando's care was left to José and me. I cooked, José cleaned, I dressed Fernando, José put him to bed. We did what we had to do. *hard work, family*

As undocumented immigrants and with little to no family around us, we had to rely on each other. Fearing that any disclosure of our status would risk deportation, we kept to ourselves when dealing with any financial and medical issues. I avoided going on certain school trips, and at times I was discouraged to even meet new people. I felt isolated and at times disillusioned; my grades started to slip.

Over time, however, I grew determined to improve the quality of life for my family and myself.

adapt-ability/ resourceful-ness

Without a father figure to teach me the things a father could, I became my own teacher. I learned how to fix a bike, how to swim, and even how to talk to girls. I became resourceful, fixing shoes with strips of duct tape, and I even found a job to help pay bills. I became as independent as I could to lessen the time and money mom had to spend raising me.

autonomy, indepen-dence, problem-solving, social skills, humor

family

I also worked to apply myself constructively in other ways. I worked hard and took my grades from Bs and Cs to consecutive straight As. I shattered my school's 100 M breaststroke record and learned how to play the clarinet, saxophone, and the oboe. Plus, I not only became the first student in my school to pass the AP Physics 1 exam, I'm currently pioneering my school's first AP Physics 2 course ever.

grit, ath-letic and musical talent, uncommon achieve-ments

These changes inspired me to help others. I became president of the California Scholarship Federation, providing students with information to prepare them for college while creating opportunities for my peers to play a bigger part in our community. I began tutoring kids, teens, and adults on a variety of subjects ranging from basic English to home improvement and even calculus. As the captain of the water polo and swim team, I've led practices crafted to individually push my comrades to their limits, and I've counseled friends through circumstances similar to mine. I've done tons, and I can finally say I'm proud of that.

leadership

knowledge, helping others

empower-ing others

leadership, counseling/ mentoring

vulnerability

But I'm excited to say that there's so much I have yet to do. I haven't danced the tango, solved a Rubik's Cube, explored how perpetual motion might fuel space exploration, or seen the World Trade Center. And I have yet to see the person that Fernando will become.

optimism

family

I'll do as much as I can from now on. Not because I have to. Because I choose to.

autonomy

You might notice a couple grammatical and spelling errors. These were part of the application he submitted to Stanford. I don't want to make a big deal of it, but I do want to signal that these applications are imperfect at times.

ACTIVITIES AND AWARDS LIST

organization

President, California Scholarship Federation (CSF)
Planned meetings, recruited members, advocated for college readiness, provided information on college applications; part of a statewide honors society.

social justice, knowledge, achievement/ excellence

Captain of the Varsity Swim Team
I lead practice routines to individually match needs of my comrades. Motivate teammates to push themselves to their limits. Rigorous solo training over summer.

sensitivity, emotional intelligence, leadership

hard work

communication, collaboration, responsibility, knowledge, real-world experience

Social Media Account Manager
Edit documents, run various social media pages, research new methods to promote growth of online traffic and convert traffic into sales or potential customers.

Water Polo Varsity (9, 10, 12) Captain for 12
Play as goalie, participate in fundraisers, lead practices, lead during games alongside our coach, prepare/clean up pool on game days.

leadership, athletic abilities

science, leadership, environmental awareness/ engagement

Chemistry Club (12)
Discuss college-level chemistry on topics that include: stoichiometry, organic chemistry, and quantum mechanics. Ran a community water quality lab.

Providing Academic Support to K–12 Students
Topics have included: simple math, calculus, APUSH, AP Chemistry, English, physics, and computer-integrated operations.

helping others, knowledge

Advanced Band/Orchestra (10)

musical talent

First oboe in Advanced Band and Orchestra. Performed at LAUSD Arts Festival, Received superior rating at LAUSD "Let's Celebrate" Festival.

hard work, helping others, knowledge

Construction and Remodeling
Helped local residents in repairing, renovating, and maintaining apartments. Duties include demolition, painting, landscaping, and installing floors.

leadership, organization

Engineering club (11)
Brainstormed and planned out an event to showcase our HS's science department to Local Middle School Students.

nutrition/ health, organization, helping others

Wrestling Varsity (11)
Learned to maintain weight, wrestled at 152 LBs. Participated and planned fundraisers. Taught basic wrestling skills to beginners.

ADDITIONAL INFO

(11) Could not finish wrestling season
Mom and older brother were in a car accident.
Responsibilities at home stacked up and I was also working at the time to pay bills, so I was unable to stay for practice.

(11) Water Polo: Could not get a team going
leadership, helping others
Returned from summer without coach or lifeguard
Worked with swim coach to find a lifeguard and coach
By the time we had them in place, we had to forfeit the season

(11–12) Summer Courses
Tried to take college courses during the summer but I could not afford the classes and there was an issue regarding my residency.

(10) Learned oboe to play in Advanced Band and Orchestra during second semester of sophomore year

Although I was in the Beginning Instruments (Advanced Band conflicted with Swimming during 6th period), I practiced the advanced music on my own and performed with the advanced section.

AP Physics I

I was the first student at my school to ever pass the AP Physics I exam. *intelligence, leadership*

There were two issues during the test: (1) the test began late because the previous test (AP Spanish) ran long and (2) during the AP Physics I exam, the fire alarms went off and continued for about an hour (the second half of the test). Unfortunately, this was the only time the test was offered and I was nonetheless proud of my score.

Calculus BC Explanation

After taking Calculus AB in my junior year I wanted to take Calculus BC in my senior year. Unfortunately, my teacher felt he wouldn't be able to teach the class, and he lacked the knowledge/training to teach it. Instead I took up a second science, AP Physics II, during my senior year. I am one of the first students to take this course at my school.

Swimming

I've swam on a county team. During the summer I would practice at a park about twelve miles away, and travel either the same or farther to compete. Competed at LA84. Most Valuable Swimmer, scored most points at swim meets, shattered school record in 100M breaststroke, and qualified for city section on multiple occasions.

Student Athlete of the Year, Varsity Wrestling

Given to the student with the highest GPA on the wrestling team. Courseload was also the most rigorous on the team, *athletic leadership, excellence academic leadership, excellence* → and I earned straight As.

Highest SAT Score in My Class
Scored a 1910 on old SAT (570 CR, 730 Math, 610 WR), which was the highest overall test score in my grade.

athletic and academic leadership/ excellence → Nominated for the USA All-American Award, Water Polo
Recognizes outstanding athletes that have exemplary performance and sportsmanship. Requires athlete maintain a GPA of 3.5 or more.

athletic achievement → League Champions Water Polo
Went undefeated in our league for the Fall Water Polo Season of 2013. Played as goalie. Required excellent team coordination.

STANFORD SUPPLEMENTAL QUESTIONS*

Briefly elaborate on one of your extracurricular activities or work experiences. (150-word limit)

Our school's CSF chapter was originally founded as an honor's society designed to help students find scholarship opportunities. But two years ago the club's engagement was at an all-time low. I saw an opportunity to make a difference, so I ran for president of the club and won. *recognizing needs (leadership)*

organization, communication → As president, I ran membership drives, presented the organization in different classrooms, and reached out to students during lunch, growing membership from fifteen to almost seventy. At the time, members were concerned that our school lacked adequate college preparation, so I turned *helping others, creativity, bravery, ambition* → the club's attention to preparing students for college. We created presentations focusing on requirements for state

---

*   Note that while I'm using the Stanford prompts as an example, the values scan will apply for any school.

(Note: many
students
in his high
school are
first-gen or
low-income)

*social
change*

universities, brought in guest speakers, and created opportunities for students to become more involved in our community through fundraisers like car washes and toy giveaways.
    Our aim has become clear: to help students get to the
college of their dreams.

**Name your favorite books, authors, films, and/or artists.
(50-word limit)**

*Note the
variety.*

*Books: A Solitary Blue, House of the Scorpion, Harry Potter
Series, Heart of Darkness, This Is for the Mara Salvatrucha:
Inside the MS-13*
Films: The Butterfly Effect, Hitchhiker's Guide to the Galaxy
Documentaries: The World According to Monsanto
*Artists: Avenged Sevenfold, The Strokes, Paul Halley, George
Gershwin, Weezer, The Architects*

**What newspapers, magazines, and/or websites do you
enjoy? (50-word limit)**

*global
awareness*

Websites: BBC World News, StoryVault, Crunchyroll

**What is the most significant challenge that society faces
today? (50-word limit)**

*care,
presence,
slowing
down*

We're going too fast. Society emphasizes fast cars, fast service, fast food, and of course fast communication. But if we
go too fast, we miss out on the opportunity to think through
decisions before making them. Particularly at this point
in history, it's imperative we think through our decisions
meticulously.

How did you spend your last two summers? (50-word limit)

Swimming training at El Cariso, where I ended up competing for my county, working construction.

What were your favorite events (e.g., performances, exhibits, competitions, conferences) in recent years? (50-word limit)

athletic excellence, social change, family

200 yard individual medley

100 yard backstroke

Chicano Youth Leadership Conference

My little brother's drill team recital

What historical moment or event do you wish you could have witnessed? (50-word limit)

heart

The Christmas truce of World War 1914 on the Western Front. An act of humanity amidst war and turmoil; just thinking about it leaves me speechless.

What five words best describe you? (10-word limit)

Again, note the variety.

Busy, geeky, introspective, assiduous, Fish.

Stanford students possess an intellectual vitality. Reflect on an idea or experience that has been important to your intellectual development. (250-word limit)

knowledge, vulnerability

While most students and even some adults cower in fear at the utterance of the word "calculus," I quake with excitement.

Want to know how fast that falling object is accelerating? You can derive it with calculus. Need to know the rate of decay for an unstable compound? Just take the derivative. Need to find the volume of a peculiar shape? There's a chance a simple integral can help you out. You get the point.

It's simple: One plus one is two, two times two is four, the derivative of x is one, and the integral of one is x plus c. Calculus, like any other form of math, is the language of logic.

I've reached a point where my life has begun to revolve

around math. When I can, I drop in on my old math teach- *helping others*
er's class to tutor students in precalculus or calculus. I've
spent nights discussing weird equations, all sorts of problems, and different applications of mathematical concepts *family*
with my older brother.

I've also started to seek ways to apply math to the rest of
my life, and it's become a part of my philosophy. Everything *insight*
scattered in the world and universe is bound together by
an underlying force. I believe we can represent this force
through math, just as Euler attempted to in his famous
equation: $e^{i\pi} + 1 = 0$ by combining four fundamental constants into one beautiful identity.

I haven't decided on my major yet, but you can bet it'll
be math heavy.

**Virtually all of Stanford's undergraduates live on
campus. Write a note to your future roommate that
reveals something about you or that will help your
roommate—and us—know you better. (250-word limit)**

Hi Roommate!

I am extrovertly introverted, but definitely not the other *humor*
way around. That means I tend to keep to myself while I work,
but when I need a break, I look for ways to indulge myself
in the company of others. In fact, after my morning run a
couple days ago at the park near my house, I was delighted
to meet an older gentleman who will soon be a father. We
had an insightful conversation over the state of the nation.

At home, whether I'm experimenting in the kitchen,
organizing my work area, or studying a mind-boggling
concept, know that there will be music playing—anything
from pop to country, metal to classic, and even K-pop. If *music*
you're not a fan, don't worry I have these awesome headphones that light up, by the way.

I should mention that I prefer a neat room (I call it "mod- *organization,*
ernistic decor") to keep things organized and simple. *simplicity*

connection Most of all, I have an undeniable passion for deep, pensive, lively conversations on a myriad of topics. It's these conversations that keep my point of view and mind from becoming static. I expect to learn just as much from my classes as I will from the diverse student body at Stanford, especially you.

What matters to you, and why? (250-word limit)

helping others, family Five years ago I took up a demolition job from a couple of neighbors so that I could help my mom pay bills around the house. I did a good enough job the first time that my neighbors told me that, if I wanted, I could continue working with them on other construction projects.

It has been a demanding job and I made numerous mistakes at first, like using the wrong tools for different tasks or the wrong size screw. On occasion, I was scolded for my *perseverance* mistakes and I felt incompetent, as I wasn't able to complete tasks as fast as my coworkers. There were even days that I considered quitting, but I stuck with it.

Since then, I've built, repaired, and remodeled numer-*uncommon* ous homes for family, friends, neighbors, and even strang-*knowledge* ers. I've removed and replaced carpets; broken down walls as well as driveways; installed cabinets, lights, both wood and tile flooring; and painted room after room.

Working in construction has made me feel like a bigger part of society because I'm shaping the buildings and offices my community uses. Although I don't make the choices in design, my workmanship is reflected in every job I've done. Because of this, my most memorable projects are those that I've taken on by myself.

But this is not what I will do the rest of my life.

family, helping others What matters to me is supporting my family. But there are other ways I can help. Getting a degree is the next step.

Why Do a Values Scan?

A Values Scan can build your confidence. If you've followed the advice in these chapters, your application will reveal a wide range of skills, qualities, interests, and—of course—values. You can submit your application knowing you're showing many parts of yourself.

On the other hand…

This exercise can also illuminate where more work needs to be done. Maybe one of your extracurricular essays isn't revealing much about you. Or maybe you find that the same value is coming through repeatedly in every part of your application, so you may decide to make a few small changes in order to show a wider range of values. As I suggested at the start of this chapter, consider revising based on these questions:

Which of my values could be made clearer?

Which values are missing but could or should show up in my application?

Final Check

Before you submit, notice if certain schools are getting parts of you that other schools aren't. Could it be, for example, that School A is getting a much better sense of you than School B because School A has more supplemental essays? If so, you might consider a bullet-point summary of a particular supplemental essay for School A in the additional info section for School B. For an example of how to do these summaries, see the "Durham Youth Commission" essay on page 129. But as I've said before, don't overdo this. Be judicious.

Once you've completed these checks, it may be time to submit.

!!!

In the Treasure Trove, you'll find:

→   A short video on the dangers of getting feedback from too many people

Part IX

More Resources for More Students

A Quick Word on This Section

Many of this book's recommendations apply to most students. Some students, however, have unique questions to consider, hence this section. And because I'm trying to keep it to the "essentials," these sections will not be comprehensive. My goal here is to provide basic information and share resources where you can explore further. If you're not finding answers that address your specific context for applying, don't stop here. The Treasure Trove contains lots of resources, from tips on the artist's statement to how to write a transfer essay.

Chapter 21

Artists

This chapter was primarily written by Laura Young, Director of Enrollment Management at the UCLA School of the Arts and Architecture because she talks about this stuff pretty much all day every day. But I've got firsthand experience creating art in both the liberal arts and conservatory environments,* so this topic is close to my heart too.

Laura was my guest on the College Essay Guy podcast episode 113, "Debunking the Myth of the Starving Artist." I'll share more about the episode at the end of this chapter.

Majoring in the Arts

So you want to major in the arts? Awesome. Creativity is an amazing superpower and it's in high demand across industries. Unfortunately, timeworn, centuries-old cultural messages (and the media) have given us tropes like the "starving artist" and tell us to believe that the only way for an artist to be successful is to be famous.

But you know what? There are plenty of successful working artists out

---

* I majored in Performance Studies at Northwestern, then received an MFA in Acting from UC Irvine.

in the world leading normal lives that include family life, travel, hobbies, etc. Many just aren't immediately visible to you. Take a look at the credits in a movie, for instance. All those special effects people, dialect coaches, composers, stunt doubles, set dressers, costume designers are non-famous artists making a living by putting their talents to work.

WHY IS ART-MAKING IMPORTANT?

The arts are essential to a meaningful life. Sometimes creativity is in your face, like an amazing new musician or an A-list actor. More often it's a subtle experience, like restaurant lighting that's just bright enough for you to see your friend across the table, but low enough to feel private. Or a floral arrangement that looks both elegant and organic. Or a building that makes you want to walk inside. The arts invite us to look at the world differently, to consider other perspectives, and to feel like someone else out there understands you.

Part of what an artist can do is communicate an idea or share an experience that helps us feel less alone. In an increasingly commodified world, knowing how to create an individualized experience is and will continue to be an incredibly important—and robot-proof—skill.

WHAT KINDS OF MARKETABLE SKILLS CAN ART-MAKING HELP YOU DEVELOP?

There are many, but a few include:

- Critical thinking: Artists are trained to drill down into ideas, to think about different perspectives and approaches after most people have stopped.
- Empathy: When an artist wants to communicate ideas, it can be helpful to deeply inhabit the experiences of others—something artists practice all the time.
- Project management: Many artists can see both details and the big picture. This skill helps a person work alone without supervision, collaborate as part of a team, or lead a group of people toward a common goal.

In short, the arts are essential, valuable, and a perfectly valid college major.

WHAT ARE MY OPTIONS WHEN IT COMES TO STUDYING ART IN COLLEGE?

Liberal arts colleges and universities. These schools can be public or private and offer a full range of majors in addition to the arts. If you want to double major or minor in a non-arts area, you can. If you want the full college experience with student groups, athletics, Greek life, and traditions like undie runs, you got it. If you come in as an arts major and then decide you'd rather study microbiology, you can switch your major without switching schools. Some liberal arts colleges and universities offer professional programs for the arts with more rigorous arts curricula and separate admission requirements. But you can get the best of both worlds: high-quality, intimate arts programs with all the benefits of a college experience.

Visual and/or performing arts schools. The majority of these institutions are private with a few public exceptions, and all degree majors are in creative areas. If you came from a high school where artists were in the minority, you'll get the experience of being surrounded by your people at these schools. In most cases, you'll still be expected to complete academic courses, but the classes are typically smaller and the content may be tailored to artists.

Conservatories. Most arts programs are looking for potential from a prospective student, but conservatory programs seek a high level of polish. Conservatories seek to preserve and perfect the art of dance, theater, or music. Beyond baccalaureate and advanced degrees, they sometimes offer artist diplomas, a specialized program for extremely high-level performers.

Community colleges. If you want more time to explore your options, a clean academic slate from high school, to save money to transfer later—or if you aren't interested in a baccalaureate degree—community colleges can support you in lots of ways. Some campuses offer stronger arts programs than others, which is important if you want to transfer smoothly to a four-year school. You'll want to work with your destination institution to prepare (more on this in the transfer chapter on page 353) and be sure to ask your community college counselor for guidance.

Vocational schools. These are for students who prioritize gaining technical experience targeted at entering the workforce (usually in areas like film editing, special effects, makeup, sound engineering, etc.). Heads up: credits offered at these schools are sometimes proprietary, meaning that credits may not transfer and you may have to start from square one.

VALUES-BASED QUESTIONS FOR
ARTISTS TO CONSIDER

How large of a community am I seeking?

Some people feel invigorated by a bigger campus where they can come into contact with lots of people studying a variety of topics. Others feel more engaged on smaller, more intimate campuses. The student body at an art school may be as small as a few hundred people.

How important to me is mentorship?

Ask about the student-to-instructor ratio in your studio areas.* Music majors sometimes have one-on-one lessons with their faculty, which is about as intimate as you can get! Especially ask when looking at arts programs on university campuses. Classes outside of the arts in university art programs might have bigger class sizes, while the arts classes will often be smaller to facilitate relationship building and critique. So if you're looking into universities, be sure to ask about class size in your intended major.

Will the resources and facilities support
my creative development?

If you're a sculptor looking to pour bronze, for example, ask if the school has a foundry. And do ask about research resources; not everything is on the internet, so things like slide libraries, music archives, and print collections are still extremely relevant to you as a young artist.

How important to the school are your
grades in non-arts-related classes?

Some schools care more about the non-arts portion of your application than others. More conservative schools may even overlook the many different rigors of making art—including the academic and intellectual labor behind your

---

*   I know I told you in the Interview chapter not to ask this, but this is an exception, as the
      answer may be different for specific arts disciplines.

process—by excluding your work from their definition of "academic." Look into how much weight your artistic portfolio carries in the admission decision, relative to other kinds of academic performance, and who is involved in the selection process (faculty, admission counselors, and so on).

How to Crush Your Audition

By Chris Andersson, former Director of Admissions for the Drama department at NYU Tisch School of the Arts and founder of NothingButDrama.com

Find material you love. If you can't wait to get in that room and share your monologue, song, design project, or director's notebook with your evaluator, then that's the material you should present. Loving your material will make the artistic review so much more enjoyable for both you and your evaluator. Remember, you're sharing something you love with people who love it, too. It's a win-win!

Organize like crazy. Performing arts schools often have many more program-specific requirements—so many it can be hard to remember them all. Start a spreadsheet to track things like:

- When prescreen submissions are due (if required)
- When and where auditions are offered
- How long monologues and songs need to be and what parameters they must meet
- Whether the school requires a dance call
- What must be included in a directing, design, or stage management portfolio
- Whether the artistic review includes a conversation component

Then double-check all the information. The clearer you are on which tasks need to be done by when, the more relaxed you'll be throughout the process.

Research, research, research. Knowledge is power, right? Research will help you better understand specific programs and drama school as a whole. It will help you clarify exactly what kind of program you're looking for and where you might thrive. Learn about the department's mission, curriculum, faculty, production season, student experience—anything you can find.

Your research will also serve you in the artistic review if interviewers ask why you're interested in their program. You'll be able to answer precisely why you love their department, which is almost always impressive to the evaluator, and maybe even come up with some great questions for them.*

Have fun! Here's a trick: look at your fellow applicants not as competition but as future colleagues. Talk to people. Make new friends. You just might end up in the same program! Keeping a positive attitude will serve you well by making the application experience more pleasant. Having said that…

Take solo time when you need it. If you're someone who needs some private time before your audition, find a corner or a hallway, away from the crowd, where you can focus and concentrate on what you need to do. You'll feel better and more confident when you go into the audition room. You can socialize once you come out!

How to Create a Great Art Portfolio

*By Clara Lieu, Adjunct Professor at the Rhode Island
School of Design & Partner at Artprof.org*

Give yourself time to prepare your art portfolio. Preparing a portfolio for college admission is not a casual undertaking; it's common for high school students to underestimate how much time and labor is involved. For most students it takes several months, even up to a year to create a portfolio.

Create more artwork than what the application requires. Even if the portfolio requires fifteen artworks, aim to create thirty to forty artworks. The quality of your work will progress tremendously and you'll have many more pieces to choose from.

Pay attention to different prompts and requirements among schools. For example, one art school has a sketchbook requirement, while others provide a different required prompt every year on top of the portfolio.

Draw from life. The vast majority of high school students draw exclusively from photos they find online, which causes them to develop all sorts of bad

---

*   When Yale Drama asked me (Ethan) at my final audition if I had any questions for them about their program, I was like, "Nope!" Cue awkward silence. Cut to me not getting into Yale Drama.

drawing habits. Drawing from life is more challenging and time-consuming, but you'll reap tremendous rewards from the experience and develop excellent drawing habits.

Include a wide variety of subject matter in your work. Admission officers don't want to see a portfolio of twenty self-portraits. The most common subjects are things like figures, self-portraits, still lifes, landscapes, interior spaces, and architectural spaces. But there are so many other subjects you could address such as character design, abstraction, industrial design, editorial illustration, architecture, typography, urban sketching, political art, poster design, book covers, and more!

Prioritize your best work over what represents your intended major. Many students worry that having no artworks in their intended major will work against them when, in fact, it doesn't at all. You could have every intention of majoring in architecture, not have a single architectural model in your portfolio, and still be a really strong candidate.

Avoid clichés in your artwork. Take the initiative to create artworks that demonstrate your thinking process and push beyond clichés. For example, if you are given a prompt called "time," many students will respond with an image of a watch, clock, or hourglass. Throw those out and find an uncommon connection.

Express your own point of view. Aim to express an opinion, a narrative, a mood, an emotion, etc., in your artworks. Show intellectual or emotional engagement with your subject matter beyond visual eye candy or a mindless technical exercise. Choose themes and subjects that excite you and show why.

Include a sketchbook spread. It's a good idea to include an image or two of a sketchbook spread in your portfolio. It's an opportunity for you to demonstrate your thinking, sketching, and brainstorming process in its raw, unedited form.

Present your artwork professionally. Neat presentation is really important; this means no dirty fingerprints, no ripped edges, no tape hanging off the side, etc. The same drawing presented neatly versus messily can make or break the impression your artwork gives.

Bring your artwork to full completion. Many portfolio pieces by high school students are only about half finished, and they have big problems like glaringly empty backgrounds and a lack of refinement and detail. Sometimes the difference really is one extra hour of work to fill in those gaps.

Include drawings in traditional media. You might have fifteen digital paintings displaying impressive technical skill, but none of that will matter if you have poor drawings in traditional media. Drawing is not about just copying a photograph as accurately as possible. What can you express through drawing that a camera can't reproduce?

Create using a wide range of media. This is your chance to show you are skilled in more than one medium. Many people equate drawing with a pencil, but so many more drawing media are out there: crayons, conte crayons, markers, soft pastels, oil pastels, etc. Include drawings, photography, paintings, sculptures, mixed media, collages, digital media, animation, printmaking, clay, video, installation, and more.

Use high-quality photographs of your artwork. A poor photograph is distracting and can really make or break an admission officer's initial reaction to the piece. Shooting high-quality photographs is time-consuming and requires lots of advance planning. Don't leave this task until the last minute!

Get feedback from an art teacher or professional artist. Many students don't seek out feedback and help on their portfolios. All artists, even professionals, can get stuck in their own heads, and feedback from outside viewers can be an extremely valuable part of art-making that can help you progress as an artist.

Attend National Portfolio Day. National Portfolio Day is basically a college fair where representatives from art schools and colleges with art programs are available to critique your portfolio in person. Go in the fall of your junior year just to get a feel for things, then go again during the fall of your senior year. Be ready for very long lines and huge crowds, especially at the top schools. Brace yourself for the possibility of harsh words, rushed comments, and reviews that last for only a few minutes. But don't be discouraged if you get a tough critique or a rude comment!

For more from Laura, check out my podcast episode 113, where we discuss:

- Data that proves art degrees are important
- The freedom that working a side job gives to self-employed artists
- How to know if art school is for you
- What your ability to take feedback says about you
- Clichés to avoid using in your art school application
- How parents can best support their child wanting to attend art school

In the Treasure Trove, you'll find:

→   How to prepare an art portfolio for art school admission

→   How to light and photograph 2-D and 3-D artwork

→   Tips for writing your artist statement

→   Ask the Art Prof articles

→   Art school portfolio video critiques

→   Pro development videos and tips for artists

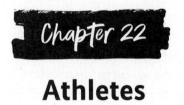

Athletes

Written by David Stoeckel and Katie Andersen (The Student-Athlete Advisors)

My co-authors on this chapter, David Stoeckel and Katie Andersen, are former college athletes with over three decades of combined experience advising college-bound student-athletes. Here are some of the questions they get asked all the time:

Can I realistically play my sport at the college level?

Statistics show that about three to twelve percent of high school athletes will compete at the NCAA level, depending on their sport. Don't underestimate the power of your athletic abilities, though, especially if you've played your sport for at least as long as your high school career and had good coaching. You may be surprised to learn how many college athletic recruiting opportunities await you.

When should I start my athletic recruiting process?

Many college coaches are looking for tenth grade recruits, so try introducing yourself to recruiters by the middle of sophomore year. If you wait longer, you may still get recruited but you'll likely have missed a few opportunities.

Will college coaches discover me or should I do something in order to get recruited?

This is mostly on you. If you're not proactive in your initial recruiting efforts, coaches will never make the effort to evaluate you simply because they won't know who you are. You can introduce yourself to college coaches by sending them an introductory email and attaching your Student-Athlete Profile. (You can find an example in the Treasure Trove.)

How do college coaches gauge my athletic ability and decide if I'm a good athletic fit for their program?

A quality video is usually the single most valuable recruiting tool a high school athlete can have, especially if you're trying to reach coaches who may never see you play in person. Some tips for recruiting videos: put your best clips first, use spot shadows, record in HD, don't worry too much about music, and keep it around three to five minutes. Oh, and recruiters must be able to quickly find your jersey number and be able to clearly see you as you showcase your abilities. Two other ways recruiters evaluate athletes include ID camps and showcase tournaments.

What are ID camps and showcase tournaments?

ID camps are generally sponsored by an individual school or a private organization. They provide individual recruits the opportunity to display their skills while giving coaches the opportunity to "identify" and evaluate top prospective recruits for their programs.

Showcase tournaments usually involve entire teams, and like ID camps, they offer college coaches the chance to scout prospective recruits.

Important: When you participate in one of these events, it's essential to email your list of coaches two to three weeks prior to the competition, and possibly send a friendly and short reminder email the weekend before. That way they'll be sure to know you're participating in the event.

Pro Tip: Don't forget to tell coaches the dates and times of your games, your field number, your uniform colors, your jersey number, and your position.

How should I identify and contact realistic "Likely" schools that are a good match with my grades, test scores, and athletic ability?

Begin with the process described in the "How to Create a Balanced College List" chapter (pages 41–66). Student-athletes should also look into these questions:

What are my feelings about playing college sports?

How much playing time should I anticipate during my freshman year?

How likely am I to play NCAA Division I, II, or III?

How realistic is it for me to earn an athletic scholarship?

Also, it's a good idea to seek the input of both your counselor and your high school and club team coaches. They may suggest schools that aren't yet on your radar. Create a recruiting list of at least sixty* schools that generally meet your academic profile and athletic recruiting goals.

Do coaches use social media for athletic recruiting?

Absolutely! Instagram, Facebook, and Twitter are among the most popular tools for student-athletes to showcase their talents and tell their stories. It should be no surprise that college coaches use these as an easy way to stay updated on a potential recruit's recent successes. It also allows them to research a student-athlete's character, personality, and interests. Keep in mind that college coaches evaluate the consistency of your email and phone conversations with your social media presence to make sure you represent your authentic self.

Will visiting a college help me get recruited, and if so, when should I plan to visit?

Visiting campus won't necessarily improve your chances, but it tells the coach that you have a sincere interest in their school. Beyond that, it can give you an opportunity to check out the athletic facilities, watch the team practice, or even meet some of the team. Make these visits around this schedule:

---

* Why so many schools? An average athlete receives responses from only fifteen to twenty percent of the coaches they email introductions to (you'll find an example email in the Treasure Trove). Initiating this step as soon as possible increases your chances of hearing back from college coaches. The *NCAA Guide for the College-Bound Student-Athlete* details the specific dates when coaches initiate communications with prospective recruits.

Division I: starting August 1 before junior year

Division II: starting June 15 after sophomore year

Division III: any time

Before you make a visit, do your research to find out if you're a match for their program and focus on schools where the coaches have expressed a strong positive interest in you.

What are the NCAA recruiting rules?

The NCAA establishes and enforces strict rules on when and where college coaches can actively recruit you (i.e., when coaches can speak with you on the phone, in person, or on their campus). Every high school athlete should know these rules. To find them, download the *NCAA Guide for the College-Bound Student-Athlete* (www.NCAAPublications.com). These rules are reviewed and updated each year (usually around June), so it's important to stay in touch with your college advisor and check the NCAA website (www.NCAA.org). Pay special attention to the pages regarding recruiting rules.

If a college coach wants me to be on their team, can they help me get accepted to their university?

Maybe. College admission officers take many factors into account, and sports ability is just one aspect of your application. At Division I and II schools, recruited athletes may receive support in the college admission process, while coaches at Division III schools have less influence over the admission process.

In the Treasure Trove, you'll find links to:
→ College priorities analysis (PDF)
→ Student-athlete profile example (PDF)
→ Example email template
→ NCAA general recruiting rules timeline (May 2019 new rules)
→ Student-athletes "Do-It-Yourself Guide"
→ *NCAA Guide for the College-Bound Student-Athlete* (www.NCAAPublications.com)
→ Athletic recruiting advisors across the United States

Chapter 23

International Students

Written with Joan Liu (UWC South East Asia) and
David Hawkins (The University Guy)

Much of this book will apply to international students.* But there are a few important differences you, as an international student, will need to understand about the process.

Financial Aid Essentials for International Students

- **Find your local EducationUSA office.** EducationUSA is a U.S. Department of State network of over 425 international student advising centers in more than 175 countries. These offices offer free, accurate, legitimate information on U.S. universities and available financial aid and scholarships.
- **Find out if you're eligible for the largest scholarships at public universities.** Some are indeed available for international students, but to find them you'll want to consider schools that are not flagship institutions. Be aware of deadlines and look for these hidden gems.
- **Focus on schools that are need-aware and meet full need.** Many U.S. universities are need-blind for U.S. citizens, but need-aware (they factor a student's financial need into their admission decisions) for noncitizen

---

* By "international" student here I mean either you don't hold a U.S. passport or you do but your high school education has taken place wholly or partly outside of the United States.

students seeking financial aid. Read the fine print and dig into each school's Common Data Set.

- **Be prepared to fund-raise.** Seek sponsorship or support from your community or relatives even if you get a financial aid package or merit scholarship that covers tuition, room, and board in full. Hidden costs such as flights, health insurance, and personal expenses are not covered by these packages. In order to get the I-20 allowing you to travel to the United States, you'll need to prove your bank account contains enough to cover the full cost of attendance.
- **Explore need- and merit-based financial aid.** The amount of this aid available to international students is limited. As a starting point, Jeff Levy and Jennie Kent's spreadsheet[†] lists the average annual financial aid awarded to international students at over three hundred U.S. colleges and universities. It also details the percentage of international students who receive aid. Remember, just because a college gives financial aid to international students doesn't mean they will cover the full cost of attendance.
- **Keep more affordable options in mind.** Look outside the United States at programs in Canada, Europe, Asia, SE Asia, and Africa that may have a smaller price tag. A growing number of accredited universities model themselves after U.S. institutions. The number of branch campuses to consider outside the United States is also increasing. Don't overlook the opportunities available to you at community colleges, which are typically significantly cheaper than a four-year college. Transfer pathways into four-year colleges open once you complete the two-year associate's degree. So starting at a community college can be a wise move if you are cost conscious.

Testing Essentials for International Students

- Different parts of the world will have different levels of access to test centers for the ACT or the SAT, and there may not be the same level of choice. If the nearest SAT center is in your city but the nearest ACT center is a flight away, the ACT may not be your best option. U.S. testing and registration dates differ from international test dates, so don't miss out; make sure you are looking at the correct information on the ACT and SAT websites. Also, if you need accommodations (e.g., extra time, access

---

[†] Find this in the Treasure Trove or by googling "College Essay Guy Podcast Which Schools Are the Most Generous with Financial Aid? (International Version)."

to a computer, rest breaks), bear in mind you may have to travel a long way to find a test center willing to provide these arrangements.

- Given that many international high school students must take exams in order to graduate, lots of U.S. universities waive SAT or ACT scores for international applicants. When you look for test-optional or test-flexible colleges, see if this applies to international applicants, as many colleges require SAT or ACT from domestic students but not from international students.*

- Depending on your school system and the requirements of the universities you're applying to, you may need to take an additional test to prove your English fluency. TOEFL and IELTS are the two main tests traditionally accepted, but others such as the Duolingo English Test are also acceptable. Find the English language requirements pages on college admissions websites.

A Few More Essential Tips

- U.S. universities send admission officers around the world to recruit students, visit international high schools, and attend university fairs. EducationUSA has advising centers around the world where you can find guidance and connect with visiting universities.†

- If you attend a high school that doesn't teach in English, you may have a hard time getting the materials for your application.‡ You might also need to send your documents through a credential evaluator who can translate and provide an official report to the universities you're applying to.§

- At some point in the application process, you'll need to provide proof of finances to a university. Most will ask you to do this when you have chosen to enroll, but a small number will ask you to prove this when you apply. Check the required documents section for international applicants on each college's admission website to find out.

In the Treasure Trove, you'll find:
→ A podcast with more advice for international students

---

*   See the Treasure Trove for links to a database of test-optional schools.

†   Find a link that allows you to search for your nearest center in the Treasure Trove.

‡   Find a link to sample school documents to share with your high school in the Treasure Trove.

§   The Treasure Trove also contains list of evaluators.

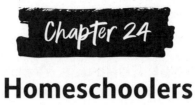

Homeschoolers

Written by Lisa David (Fearless Homeschoolers), with special thanks to counselors Laura Kazan and Rebecca Orlowski[¶]

Are you someone who veered off the path and decided to homeschool? If so, you're one of almost two million students in the United States choosing to learn in a way that is personalized and purposeful. Now that you're working on your application, your out-of-the-box experience may feel like it has to be stuffed into a box so that colleges can make sense of it.

You may be worried that you haven't been doing enough to prepare for college, or wonder if colleges will take your homeschool education seriously. You might not even be sure what colleges want from homeschoolers.

Some good news is that, in many ways, this process is no different from a traditional student's application. You're expected to demonstrate your readiness and fit for college.

But unlike traditional students who have guidance counselors and resources set up to support their journey, homeschoolers often have to do the work themselves. Here's what the main differences look like…

- **The homeschool parent acts as the guidance counselor.** Your parent is responsible for submitting your transcript and supporting homeschool documents to colleges.
- **Some schools have additional requirements for homeschoolers.** These may include extra testing, a graded essay, lab reports, and interviews.

¶   Rebecca was my guest on podcast episode 212—you'll find a link in the Treasure Trove.

It's important that you know what these requirements are as early as possible.

- **You and your parent work together to tell your homeschool story.** Be prepared to collaborate!

What Colleges Want from Homeschoolers

Each school is different in what they require from homeschool applicants, but what all of them need is a collection of indicators that your unconventional education has prepared you for entering the world of higher education.

- **Evidence of a quality education.** You can show this through your grades and test scores. Your parent can do this with thorough homeschool documentation.
- **Evidence that you took advantage of homeschooling's freedom and flexibility.** Make sure they understand the extent to which you created your own education.
- **Evidence of socialization.** Yes, the stigma still exists. Get involved in a community. Take classes outside your home.
- **Evidence of your core values.** What matters most to you? How can you show that through your academics, your extracurriculars, your personal life?

How to Prepare for College as a Homeschooler

Take college prep courses.

One of the best reasons to homeschool high school is the freedom to pick and choose the best classes and instructors and formats for you. Take online courses, community college classes, or homeschool co-op classes. Hire a tutor. Audit university classes. Design your own course. The choice is yours!

Consider testing.

Before ninth grade, take a peek at some college requirements for homeschoolers. If AP or Subject Tests are in your plan, schedule those exams after the corresponding course.

Homeschoolers have three options when taking APs: take an online AP course (and exam), get your own AP syllabus approved by CollegeBoard, or self-study for the AP exam without an official AP course.

Note: Only CollegeBoard-approved courses can be designated as AP on the homeschool transcript.

Another note: Test-optional schools may not be test-optional for homeschoolers, and this varies by college. Be proactive about researching this, and if you can't find the information on the school website, call school admission officers and ask.

Follow your interests.

You've heard it before. Do the things you love, go deeply into your passions, and take advantage of the extraordinary freedom and flexibility that homeschooling has given you!

Nurture relationships.

It's important for homeschoolers to proactively seek out and connect with academic teachers during high school. Many colleges require at least two teacher recommendations, and you want these to come from teachers who can speak deeply and sincerely about who you are beyond academics.

Learn your state requirements.

Be sure you're meeting your state requirements for homeschool graduation. This information can easily be found on your state's Department of Education website. Know what these are before ninth grade!

The Documentation You'll Need as a Homeschooler

Your Transcript

This is a one-page document that lists your courses, credits, and GPA. A grading key explains the grading and weighting system used. Test scores are often put on the transcript unless you're applying test-optional.

Course Descriptions

These provide much-needed context and are commonly between ten and twenty pages. Include the course description, methods of evaluation, materials used, teacher/provider name, credit amount, and grade.

A School Profile

This is a brief look at your homeschool. Begin with the history and philosophy of your homeschool. Follow with brief descriptions of outside course providers, explanations for grading and credit, and state requirements for homeschoolers. Provide neighborhood demographics if they add context to your story. The school profile is usually not more than two pages.

A Counselor Letter of Recommendation

In this case, the counselor is your parent/guardian. It addresses your academics, your extracurriculars, and your character in a way that balances professionalism with the personal insight only a parent can provide.

College Bound Homeschoolers' FAQs

Is homeschooling a hook in college admissions?

Despite the myths, colleges aren't actively recruiting homeschoolers, and homeschooling doesn't give you an edge in the admissions process. But homeschool applicants have a unique opportunity to use their story to highlight their values.

Let's say for example that innovation, diversity, and social change are your core values. You might design your own science fiction and gender course and list that on your transcript. Do an independent study on diversity in robotics and elaborate on it in your course descriptions. Create a podcast on the benefits of machine learning and have your parent highlight that in their letter of recommendation. Your core values directly affect how you make decisions about your education, and colleges can see those values in action when you demonstrate in your application how you've spent your time homeschooling.

Will colleges take your homeschool seriously?

They will! But you need to show colleges that you take your education seriously. Do that by backing up strong homeschool grades with Dual Enrollment classes, AP exams, Subject Tests, admissions interviews, and compelling letters of recommendation. And support your passions with deep dives into extracurriculars, competitions or contests, summer programs, and research. And along the way, create thorough homeschool documents. Admission officers know how traditional students compare within the context of their school as they'll be familiar with the student profile of that particular school. With a homeschool situation, however, they're missing that context. So the more information you provide the schools, the better.

Can homeschoolers get into selective schools?

Absolutely! Prepare yourself in the same way as a traditional schooler. How?

- Take four or more years of each major subject, including foreign language.
- Demonstrate rigor.
- Maintain a high GPA and test scores.
- Participate in extracurriculars that show depth and commitment and have a significant impact on a certain community.
- Provide excellent teacher letters of recommendation.
- Demonstrate intellectual curiosity, initiative, leadership, and social awareness, and as your passions and interests strengthen and deepen throughout high school, create opportunities that nurture these qualities.[*]

---

[*] You'll find ideas in the chapter on self-directed learning (page 343).

What's the parent's role as the homeschool guidance counselor?

Think of it this way: as the applicant, your job is to tell the story of who you are. As the guidance counselor, your parent's job is to tell the story of your homeschool. How?

- Keep track of your grades and course descriptions throughout high school.
- Know each college's homeschool requirements. These can be found on most websites, but it's a good idea to call admissions for confirmation.
- Find out who your admission officer is. Some schools have specific reps assigned to homeschoolers. Others have a regional rep. They'll be happy to answer any questions you have regarding the process.
- Create counselor accounts for applications. And be prepared for questions that aren't applicable to homeschoolers. Just answer in a way that feels right.
- Create homeschool documents to submit with the counselor report: transcript, course descriptions, school profile, and counselor letter of recommendation.

Should my personal statement be all about homeschooling?

Nope. While homeschooling can be mentioned in the essay, it shouldn't be the focus. If you want to explain the reasons you chose to homeschool, use the additional information section of the application. Use the personal statement to write about something that isn't yet in your application.

In the Treasure Trove, you'll find:
→   An example of a homeschool transcript
→   Sample homeschool course descriptions

Chapter 25

Students Interested in Historically Black Colleges and Universities (HBCUs) and Tribal Colleges and Universities (TCUs)

Written by Charlotte West (education reporter), Jamiere Abney (Colgate University), Jamon Pulliam (Viewpoint School), and Nikki Pitre (Center for Native American Youth)

More and more students from Generation Z—the most racially and ethnically diverse generation—are going to college. Even though the number of students of color might be higher than ever, if you identify as a racial or ethnic minority, you may want to think about a few things.

What kind of college will offer the right fit in terms of the support you might want as a student of color? Do you want to attend a Minority Serving Institution such as a Historically Black College or University (HBCU) or a tribal college? What factors should you consider if you want to attend a predominantly white institution?

Minority Serving Institutions (MSIs)

Minority Serving Institutions are colleges and universities whose missions serve students from minority backgrounds. A number of MSIs exist in the United States, including 102 Historically Black Colleges and Universities (HBCUs) and thirty-seven Tribal Colleges and Universities (TCUs). Hispanic students make up at least a quarter of all undergrads at Hispanic-Serving Institutions

(HSIs). The 274 HSIs enroll around forty percent of all Hispanic-American students.* And Asian American, Native American, and Pacific Islander Serving Institutions are considered those whose undergraduate enrollment is made up of at least ten percent students from those groups.

MSIs play an important role in educating a large number of minority and low-income students. Not only do they celebrate students' cultures, they are often more diverse, more affordable, offer more academic support for minority students, and have higher graduation rates.

PREDOMINANTLY WHITE INSTITUTIONS (PWIs)

Through the obstacles I've faced as a minority at a predominantly white institution, I've gotten a chance to truly embrace my ethnicity and bond with other people of my race who have gone through similar experiences. Becoming involved with organizations on campus that cater to minority students has definitely provided a sense of inclusion that I would have otherwise struggled to feel. Being a part of the small percentage of African Americans in my university's student body has allowed me to not only form genuine friendships, but has also helped me learn more about myself.

Kristen Adaway, University of Georgia

Creating a relationship with my favorite professor in the Lakota language course, who also taught the Introduction to Native History course, motivated and inspired me to learn while giving me the confidence to stay in college, despite the challenges. Embracing my Native identity was the key to completing my first year of college and will continue to help me navigate other challenges I may experience. My advice to all of the young, strong, and resilient Native students who will be pursuing higher education is to embrace and appreciate your identity, culture, and heritage. Find the resources available to you, and do not be afraid to speak up for the things you know are right.

Foster Cournoyer Hogan (Rosebud Sioux Tribe), Stanford University

---

*   "Minority Serving Institutions Program," U.S. Department of the Interior. doi.gov/pmb/eeo/doi-minority-serving-institutions-program.

If your home community's majority population is made of ethnic or racial minorities, you may want to consider a few things when looking at PWIs. A PWI can be a real culture shock with regard to seeing significantly fewer people who look like those in your home community. While this change is significant, it may not be a reason to completely write off a PWI.

Some Questions to Ask about a PWI

- Do they have explicit plans and missions regarding diversity, equity, and inclusion?
- Do they offer cultural resource centers, such as a diversity office or center for students of color? These centers can provide some respite from the challenges a minority in a predominantly white community might face.
- Does their counseling center employ counselors of color? Do they offer in-person or remote emotional support? Do they offer group sessions?
- Does the school employ faculty and staff of color? Are these people visible on campus and available as resources?
- Does the student body lead any ethnic and cultural affinity organizations where you can find support and kinship?
- Does the college's admission process account for race?

Ultimately, you have to decide whether a PWI feels like a comfortable fit. Prejudice, privilege, and microaggressions can (and likely do) still exist at schools that dedicate resources to equity and inclusion. But these resources signal that a school is working toward a more inclusive culture; it suggests that they recognize—and are trying to alleviate—the burden students of color face to represent their race when addressing institutionalized racism. Asking about a school's diversity and inclusion initiatives and affirmative action policies, or even reaching out to the professionals in these roles, can provide you and your family some peace of mind as to the support for your experience at a PWI.

Historically Black Colleges and Universities

The first HBCU, now called Cheyney University of Pennsylvania, was founded in 1837 to train teachers of African descent. Cheyney is now just one of roughly one hundred HBCUs in the United States. Many were founded post-Civil War to allow African Americans access to higher education, which they had previously been denied, and since then, they've defined one of the cores of African American achievement in U.S. history, cultivating leaders and visionaries like W.E.B. DuBois, Ida B. Wells, Booker T. Washington, and Martin Luther King, Jr.

Fast-forward 150 years and many students may wonder how HBCUs are still relevant today. Well, HBCUs comprise three percent of America's institutions of higher education but enroll sixteen percent of all African American students and award almost a quarter of all bachelor's degrees earned by black students.[*]

WHY YOU SHOULD CONSIDER AN HBCU

- **Diversity.** HBCUs offer a deep dive into diversity within the black diaspora. Yes, the majority of the students are black, but students from a wide range of socioeconomic, religious, and family backgrounds hail from all over the nation and world. Being part of a community like this can expand your idea of what it means to be black.
- **History.** Many HBCUs were founded by former slaves or with the help of former slaves. To walk on the grounds that many of those people built with their hands gives a true sense of appreciation of where black people have been—and where they're going.
- **A sense of belonging.** HBCUs provide a space where the majority of students and teachers look like you. Attending an institution you know was built for you and that tailors experiences to black students can give you an incomparable sense of belonging.
- **Relationship-oriented culture.** Going to an HBCU will foster some of the strongest relationships you could ever imagine. Some of the ways people grow their sense of pride and forge family bonds with their HBCU classmates include attending cafeteria-themed days like "Fried Chicken Wednesday", "Soul Food Thursday", or "Fish Friday"; joining Black Greek-Letter Organizations, which were created by black students to build social access like the fraternal organizations that historically denied

---

[*]   "Minority Serving Institutions Program," U.S. Department of the Interior. doi.gov/pmb/
       eeo/doi-minority-serving-institutions-program.

them membership; and participating in many other activities, like football games and school bands.

These are just some of the unique elements of the HBCU experience.

Beyoncé's Coachella performance (and her concert film, *Homecoming*, about that performance) has increased the visibility of HBCUs, showcasing many of the cultural assets of HBCUs. By highlighting even a portion of the HBCU world, many people took away a powerful message: the HBCU experience is black and beautiful, and one worth experiencing for yourself.

Take it from Queen B, who said, "I grew up in Houston, Texas, visiting Prairie View. We rehearsed at TSU [Texas Southern University] for many years in Third Ward and *I always dreamed of going to an HBCU.*" Ultimately, you have to decide what experience works best for you, but the multilayered HBCU option is worth exploring because you can gain a unique experience that fosters an understanding of and appreciation for who black people are.

Tribal Colleges and Universities

Tribal colleges were created by Native American tribes to address the fact that the U.S. government failed to include their people within the traditional public higher education system. They chartered and created their own colleges, which are now fully accredited by the Higher Learning Commission.

Most are tribally chartered, meaning they are created and approved by tribal councils, they are located on Native American reservations, and they operate many programs relevant to the local community. The thirty-seven that currently operate in the United States offer certificates and degrees ranging from associate's degrees to graduate degrees.

What unique perspectives and experiences does a tribal college or university offer?

Nikki Pitre, a member of the Coeur d'Alene Tribe who has dedicated her career to helping Native American students succeed in education, says many Native American students who struggled at a large university due to an absent sense of belonging were later successful at tribal colleges. "Tribal colleges are culturally immersive and cater to a young person's mind, body, and spirit. There is a stronger sense of belonging and a core sense of identity that you're able to really hone in on at a tribal college—and that you're not going to get at a mainstream university."

WHY YOU SHOULD CONSIDER A TRIBAL COLLEGE OR UNIVERSITY

- Tribal colleges offer a smaller student-teacher ratio, greater support for students who have children, and the opportunity to study in your native languages.
- Many also have partnerships with four-year public universities that allow students to transfer, earn dual credit, or collaborate on research.
- Students attending tribal colleges and universities are eligible to receive federal financial aid, including Pell grants.

"There are a lot of accommodations for students," says Pitre. "That personal touch they receive regardless of their financial background, regardless if they're Native or non-Native—you just don't get [that] at any other institution of higher education."

QUESTIONS FOR NATIVE AMERICAN STUDENTS TO ASK ABOUT NON-TRIBAL INSTITUTIONS

The American Indian College Fund published a guide, *Native Pathways*, for Native American students thinking about applying to college. It is amazing. The authors include a list of several questions to think about:

- Does the college have a Native American resource center?
- How many Native American students attend this school? How many do they admit per year?
- Do they employ Native faculty and staff?
- How does the college support or engage with local tribes or Native organizations?
- Do they recognize the tribal land they are located on?
- Can I smudge on campus?

- Does the college provide opportunities for me to give back to Native communities?
- Do they provide specific funding for Native American students?

MORE RESOURCES FOR NATIVE AMERICAN STUDENTS

Check out the American Indian College Fund's (AICF) website (see link in the Treasure Trove) for a map of all thirty-seven tribal colleges and universities in the United States. AICF provides information about scholarship and transfer pathways. The American Indian Higher Education Consortium also lists resources for Native American students on its website, aihec.org.

Finally, check out the nonprofit organization College Horizons. It "supports the higher education of Native American students by providing college and graduate admissions workshops to American Indian, Alaska Native, and Native Hawaiian students/participants from across the nation."[*]

In the Treasure Trove, you'll find links to:
→ More information on Minority Serving Institutions
→ Penn Center for Minority Serving Institutions
→ Hispanic Association of Colleges and Universities (HACU)
→ Asian American and Native American Pacific Islander-Serving Institutions (AANAPISI)
→ National Association for Equal Opportunity in Higher Education (NAFEO)
→ HBCU Clearinghouse for LGBTQ Inclusion
→ American Indian College Fund (AICF) website
→ Native Pathways—A College-Going Guidebook
→ Center for Native American Youth
→ The American Indian Higher Education Consortium
→ College Horizons
→ National Indian Education Association
→ Advancing Chicanos/Hispanics & Native Americans in Science
→ American Indian Science and Engineering Society

---

[*]   "About Our Organization," College Horizons. collegehorizons.org/about.

Chapter 26

First-Generation and Low-Income Students

Written by Charlotte West (education reporter), with thanks to Matt Rubinoff (Strive for College) and Jamiere Abney (Colgate University)

Something that I realized over the course of my college career is that low-income, first-gen students have to overcome so many obstacles to get to the same place that other students have sort of had their mind set on their entire lives. For a lot of my peers, their parents have been telling them their whole lives that they're gonna go to the University of Michigan. Their teachers and college counselors and everyone were telling them what to do and how to get there and helping them along. A lot of my first-gen, low-income peers had to figure a lot of things out for themselves and they had to navigate this process that was not designed with them in mind. We should take a lot of pride in that because the fact that we did not have this path set out for us but still chose to forge it for ourselves is incredible.

LAUREN SCHANDEVEL, UNIVERSITY OF MICHIGAN

What does it mean to be a first-generation student?

Being "first-gen" means you'll be the first in your family to attend college. If this is the case, you may not be able to ask your parents about navigating the college application process and you might be the one explaining things like financial aid to them. "It doesn't stop there," notes Amanda Miller, the counselor and expert who helped write the financial aid sections of this book. "Once on campus, speed bumps continue to pop up. My sister had no idea how many 'credit hours' would be a good idea, so she signed up for twenty-one credit hours her first semester. (That's a LOT.) That lesson almost prompted her to quit before she realized others weren't taking nearly as many classes. These easily preventable setbacks can make the whole college experience a bit more daunting for first-gens."

Around a third of all college freshmen are first-gen, according to the National Center for Education Statistics.[*] Intersectionality here is important too. Many, but certainly not all, first-generation students are also low-income and are students of color.

Who qualifies as a low-income student?

The most common way colleges and universities define low-income students is by Pell grant eligibility. Pell grants fund students who have exceptional financial need and have not earned a bachelor's degree or higher, and about a third of all undergraduates receive Pell grants.[†] Because they are grants and not loans, you don't have to pay them back. Google "Pell eligible" or look it up in the Common Data Set, section B, for the school you're interested in to see how many students receive these grants.

Students who aren't eligible for Pell grants can still struggle to cover the cost of higher education. Research shows a widening gap between financial aid and rising costs of living, especially in cities with expensive housing markets. (Check out researcher Sara Goldrick-Rab's book, *Paying the Price: College Costs, Financial Aid, and the Betrayal of the American Dream*, for more about this.[‡])

The Experience of Applying for College as a First-Generation, Low-Income Student

Lauren Schandevel, a recent graduate of the University of Michigan, created "The Being Not Rich Guide" for low-income students at her school. These

---

[*]   "Home," First Generation Foundation. firstgenerationfoundation.org.

[†]   "Trends in Higher Education," CollegeBoard. trends.collegeboard.org/student-aid/ figures-tables/undergraduate-enrollment-and-percentage-receiving-pell-grants-over-time.

[‡]   You can also hear more from Sara Goldrick-Rab on the College Essay Guy podcast—link is in the Treasure Trove.

student-generated, crowd-sourced guides are springing up at campuses across the country.*

Lauren says she didn't ask anyone for help when she applied to college. "It ended up sort of shooting me in the foot because I didn't know a lot about the programs that I was applying to. So when I applied to Columbia University, I applied to their journalism school because I didn't know the difference between undergraduate and graduate programs. I didn't know that I was applying to the wrong programs. Having someone who knew the nuances of higher education would have been very helpful in that process," she says.

She didn't contact the admission officers for any of the programs she was applying to because she was afraid they would think she wasn't a serious student or that she hadn't done her research. Many first-generation students express this fear. "I wish I had gone in knowing my own strengths as a first-gen, low-income student because I feel like that identity was something I had to develop over time and by junior and senior year," she says.

YOU DON'T KNOW WHAT YOU DON'T KNOW UNTIL YOU GET THERE

The experience of being a first-generation and/or low-income college student can feel, for some, like culture shock. Mai Mizuno, a student at USC, described it like this during a panel discussion at Real College, a conference organized by the Temple University Center for College, Community, and Justice: "You're walking into these spaces and you're realizing that the world is not as you thought it was back in the fields of Kansas. And you're realizing that social capital matters, who you know matters. And you see other people who are able to just sit back on their heels and not worry about working X hours a week like you do so you can pay for food, for housing, for tuition on top of your courses."

Professors and staff might make assumptions about who is in their classrooms, and students might not be aware of all the unspoken values, norms, and expectations on campus.

---

*   You'll find a link to the guide in the Treasure Trove, as well as (you guessed it!) a podcast
     with Lauren Schandevel.

ONE-ON-ONE MENTORSHIP FOR FIRST-GEN AND LOW-INCOME STUDENTS

Strive for College, a leading college accessibility advocate, produces the *I'm First! Guide to College* specifically for first-gen students, has an extensive mentor network, and partners with the Common App to provide one-on-one support to thousands of first-gen students each year. To sign up, go to www.ustrive.com or opt-in via your Common App account.[†]

Another option for free one-on-one mentorship is the Matchlighters Program I set up. Experienced college counselors provide one-on-one help to low-income students in completing their college essays and applications. I started the program after a student emailed me to let me know that she was a first-gen, low-income, high-achieving student who just needed someone to "light a little match." Little did she know she would be an important match in my life and the lives of many others; the program pairs hundreds of students with counselors each year. To sign up for free help, go to www.collegeessayguy.com/matchlighters. Counselors can sign up to be mentors at that link as well.

Questions to Ask When Applying to College as a First-Gen or Low-Income Student

Matt Rubinoff, Chief Strategy Officer for Strive for College, shared with me some good questions to ask during your college search:

- Does the college offer scholarships for first-generation college students?
- What financial aid opportunities are available for low-income students?
- Does the college host a visit program or open house, or offer a fly-in program for students like me?
- Does the school have a conditional admission program that might take a chance on me?
- Does the college offer an orientation or summer bridge experience that will help me acclimate to college life?

[†]   For more on Strive for College's partnership with the Common App, plus its partnership to provide test prep to low-income students, check out the Treasure Trove.

- What attention is given to first-year students to ensure a successful transition to college?
- Are there peer mentoring opportunities to help me connect with upperclass students on campus?
- What academic advising and personal counseling resources exist on campus?
- Does the school have a support office or student organizations to help first-generation or multicultural students find community?

You'll find many more resources at www.imfirst.org, including:

- Video testimonials from first-gen students and graduates
- A blog written by current first-gen college students who chronicle their college experiences and give advice to future first-gens
- Info on how to get the *I'm First! Guide to College*—the only college guidebook designed uniquely for first-gen college-bound students.

Seven Tips for First-Generation and/or Low-Income Students

1. **Look for colleges that have need-blind admissions**, but be aware that not all need-blind policies are created equal. Need-blind admissions don't consider financial need in their decisions, but they won't necessarily offer loan-free financial aid. Some colleges guarantee all students full loan-free financial aid. Check with the specific colleges on your list to get a detailed picture of the financial aid they might offer you.
2. **Look for colleges that offer programming for first-generation and low-income students.** These might be mentorship programs, orientation programs, or a dedicated office that offers resources to these students.* (See the Treasure Trove for more.)
3. **Don't be afraid to ask about support for first-generation students** if you don't understand something about the college application process, or if something seems weird once you get on campus. Admission officers and other college staff want to help, but they may not know you're struggling!

---

* The *I'm First! Guide to College* is full of these—ask your counselor to order it or buy it yourself! It's worth it.

4. **Know you're not alone.** Many first-generation and low-income students are afraid to talk about their experiences. But around one-third of all college students are first generation and/or low income.

5. **Ask the admission office if there are application fee waivers** for first-generation and low-income students. There probably are, and this can help alleviate or remove the financial burden of submitting many applications.

6. **Find your people before moving onto campus.** Look online or call your admission officer (who will likely direct you to student services) to identify five different offices or people on campus you can turn to when you hit a speed bump. These "free" services might include Residence Life, Professors and Academic Advisors, a Student Success Center, Career Services, an LGBTQ+/Diversity Center, or the Counseling Office. Because these services are built into your tuition, it's silly not to use them.

7. **Your experience as a first-generation or low-income student can be a powerful personal statement topic.** Counselor Amanda Miller notes, "It doesn't need to be your entire essay, but don't be afraid to share how your experiences—including being first in your family to attend college or being low income—have shaped how you've grown and gained perspective and focus. That's precisely the sort of thing colleges want to know about you!" You can also describe significant responsibilities—like working to help support your family or caring for younger siblings—in the additional information section.

Words of Wisdom from an Admission Dean

Patricia Peek, Dean of Undergraduate Admission at Fordham University

Students are not always able to participate in sports, student government, or other activities because their responsibilities at home preclude doing so. However, students often don't realize that taking care of siblings, working part-time, and similar commitments can demonstrate a high level of leadership, service, and a sense of responsibility. Students should list these in the activities list section and expand in the additional information section if needed.

Fly-in Programs

Special thanks to Jamiere Abney (Colgate University)
for his contributions to this section

Fly-in travel subsidy programs are another prominent example of a school's commitment to diversity and inclusion that many prospective students experience. These programs, usually hosted through admission offices, invite you to campus, typically overnight, to see if the campus environment is the right fit for you.

WHO IS ELIGIBLE

Institutions actively seek students from traditionally underrepresented communities. Students from disadvantaged socioeconomic backgrounds and students whose parents didn't attend a four-year college or university are also encouraged to take advantage of these programs. Students are usually invited for fly-in programs during their senior year. But note that some programs are available only to already admitted candidates. Eligibility varies from place to place, so always consult the admission office for clarification.

Students need only contact a college's admission office to receive this information. In some cases they are invited to apply by submitting an essay, transcripts, and test scores. In other cases, fly-in programs invite eligible students to RSVP on a first-come, first-serve basis.

ADVICE FOR STUDENTS UNABLE
TO VISIT CAMPUS

If you can't fit a visit to your dream school into your schedule (as a fly-in or otherwise), don't fret. Here are some tips:

- Use a virtual, online tour if the college/university has one.[*]
- Reach out to admission staff and alumni in your area. Admission officers travel far to promote their colleges to students, counselors, and families. Many colleges ask regional alumni to attend events or meet with students

---

[*]   See links in Treasure Trove for great online tour websites.

for one-on-one interviews. These are great opportunities to hear from people who have actually attended a school of interest. Also, some colleges require these interviews; make sure you know if this is the case!

- Visit similar schools in your own backyard. Maybe you can't visit the private liberal arts college across the country, but you probably can check one out an hour away. Use nearby colleges to get a feel for different types of academic environments. This can help you and your family save time and money.

Advice for College-Bound Students from Rural Areas

Andrew Moe, Ed.D., Associate Dean of Admissions and Director of Access, Swarthmore College

Students coming from rural areas and small towns add dimensions of diversity that are often absent from college campuses, especially selective institutions. I recommend that students from rural places talk about what it's like to grow up and attend school in their communities. Highlight the types of co-curricular experiences they have that may be different from others. Of course, this might have to do with farming and agricultural work if that's prominent in their community, but students may also spend time at their family's small business or engage in hobbies that are more common in rural spaces. My advice to students: be authentic and think about what makes you different from other students applying to that institution.

Students from rural areas or small towns make significant, and different, contributions to the classroom experience than their urban and suburban peers. Think about a discussion about healthcare access in a college seminar. For students growing up in large cities, they might point to lack of access to preventive healthcare in low-income neighborhoods as a chief concern. Students in rural areas may have a completely different perspective. Perhaps they are an hour or more away from an emergency room facility. Those worldviews must be present in our classrooms, and colleges must seek out these perspectives in the admission process.

In the Treasure Trove, you'll find links to:

→   "The Being Not Rich Guide" and a podcast with Lauren Schandevel

→   Podcast with Sara Goldrick-Rab, author of *Paying the Price: College Costs, Financial Aid, and the Betrayal of the American Dream* (also a link to the Temple University Hope Center for College, Community, and Justice)

→   www.striveforcollege.org and www.imfirst.org

→   The Matchlighters Program (free one-on-one help with college essays and the college list for low-income students: www.collegeessayguy.com/matchlighters)

→   The *I'm First! Guide to College*

→   College Greenlight's List of Fly-ins and Diversity Programs

Undocumented Students

Written with Dr. Aliza Gilbert (Highland Park High School)

Veteran counselor Dr. Aliza Gilbert, PhD, is regarded by many as a leading advocate for undocumented youth. Her doctoral research examines how schools support or fail to support undocumented students.

What Does It Mean to Be Undocumented?

The National Immigration Law Center defines an "undocumented" person as a foreign national who entered the United States without inspection or with fraudulent documents, or entered legally as a nonimmigrant but remained in the United States without authorization, thereby violating the terms of their status.

In other words, you are undocumented if you live in the United Students but are not a citizen or legal permanent resident, or your visa is expired. Federal law does not explicitly prohibit an undocumented person from attending college, but undocumented students, including those protected by Deferred Action for Childhood Arrivals (DACA), are ineligible to receive federal aid. In most states, undocumented students are ineligible to receive state aid and often must pay out-of-state tuition costs at public universities. Some states also prohibit or restrict undocumented students' access to public universities.

But by no means does this mean that you can't have access to a quality education in the United States. The following tips can help you navigate this process.

Nine Tips for College-Bound Undocumented Students

1. **Identify a trusted ally, teacher, advisor, or mentor** at your school who can help you navigate the admission and financial aid process.[*]

2. **Find out if you are in a state that offers in-state tuition and/or state aid to qualified undocumented students.** You'll find a link to state-by-state information in the Treasure Trove.

3. **Develop a broad list of colleges** and consider schools for which your profile is at the top of their applicant pool. This will increase your chances of significant merit awards.

4. **Directly ask each college on your list if they give undocumented students institutional scholarships and grant aid.** If they do, it's important to get on the admission counselor's radar. This person can tell you the financial forms required in lieu of the FAFSA to be eligible for institutional grants and scholarships.

5. **Identify an admission counselor or staff member at each of your prospective colleges who has the following**: experience with undocumented students, a solid working knowledge of the challenges and situations you might face, and the willingness and capability to support you through your education at their school.

6. **Remember, you do not have to share your status if you don't want to!** But if you do, decide *how* to reveal your status in the essays.[†]

7. **Explore all scholarship sites and online resources to see which are open to non-U.S. residents.** Leave no stone unturned! Some sites we recommend: Dreamers Roadmap, My Undocumented Life, Immigrants Rising, Illinois Association for College Admission Counseling, MALDEF (some of these scholarships require citizenship but many do not), The Dream.US, and Golden Door Scholars. Many of these organizations also have a Facebook page where they post additional scholarships. Also, download the DACA Scholars App on your phone. Finally, remember to think locally and explore community-based scholarships.

---

[*]   If you don't know of someone locally, you can find one at www.collegeessayguy.com/matchlighters.

[†]   See "Should I Come Out as Undocumented in My Personal Statement?" in the Treasure Trove.

8. **Consider air travel restrictions** that might impact your ability to travel home if you're exploring colleges out of state.

9. **Think about college as a four-year investment.** You might qualify for more scholarships as a first-year student than as a transfer student. Starting at a community college, while cheaper initially, might be more expensive in the long run.

In the Treasure Trove, you'll find links to:

→ "Should I Come Out as Undocumented in My Personal Statement?" (Blog, Part 1)

→ "How to Come Out as Undocumented in Your Personal Statement" (Blog, Part 2)

→ "15 Ways to Advocate for Undocumented Youth" (Blog)

→ "Life as an Undocumented Student at Harvard" (Podcast)

→ "How to Advocate for Undocumented Students" (Podcast)

For a great example of an undocumented student's application, check out the "Values Scan" chapter that begins on page 277.

Students with Learning Differences

*Written by Marybeth Kravets, co-author of The K&W Guide
to Colleges for Students with Learning Differences*

College-bound students with learning differences are not labels, but individuals. As I (Marybeth) like to say, "Labels are for jelly jars." Having a learning difference means you've navigated the rigorous academic landscape, developed compensatory learning strategies, and are heading into this journey like all other college-bound students.

Some values many college-bound students with learning differences share include *pride* in their accomplishments; *insight* into how their learning difference has shaped them; *articulation* of their learning difference; and *acceptance, patience*, and *commitment*.

Still, high school is different for many students with learning differences. That's why you'll need to research whether colleges that meet all the standard criteria also offer the right level of support. To this end, here are…

A Few Important Considerations during High School

What accommodations do you use in high school? What accommodations are officially stated on your Individualized Education Plan (IEP) or #504 Plan? Do they match? Do they include every accommodation that is appropriate?

Regarding those resources, keep a couple important pieces of information in mind. The IEP is terminated upon high school graduation, but colleges do use a #504 plan for securing accommodations/services at college.

Homework and classroom accommodations could include:

- Teacher's notes
- Note takers
- Separating large assignments or projects into chunks
- Preferential seating
- Use of a calculator
- Use of a computer
- Access to audiobooks
- Weekly check-ins
- Clarification of directions
- Breaks as needed

Testing accommodations might include:

- Extended time on tests and exams
- Test-taking locations with reduced distractions
- Use of a calculator
- Use of a computer
- Testing across multiple days
- Small group testing
- Clarification of directions
- Breaks as needed
- Scribe programs
- Oral examinations
- Spell-checker programs

Furthermore, when was your most recent psycho-educational evaluation done? Most colleges won't grant accommodations unless you were evaluated within the last three years at age sixteen or older.

Assessments might include:

- Woodcock-Johnson Cognitive Battery

- WAIS (Wechsler Adult Intelligence Scale)
- Nelson-Denny Reading Test
- TOWL (Test of Written Language)
- KAIT (Kaufman Adolescent and Adult Intelligence Test)

Questions Students with Learning Differences Should Ask When Creating Their College List

- Is the college "test optional" or does it require an ACT/SAT score for admission?*
- Are course waivers or substitutions available if I have appropriate documentation?
- What kinds of support does the college offer? Do they provide a structured program with a fee for services, or only what colleges are required by law to provide?
- Who is the staff providing this support? Are they certified in learning differences?
- What is the route into my intended major? Will I be directly admitted as a first-year student in that major, or am I not allowed to declare my major until the end of my second year? Is the major GPA driven?
- How are professors notified that a student is eligible for accommodations? More importantly, are professors instructed on teaching to students who learn differently?

Should you self-disclose your learning differences in your college application?
It's important to discuss this with your counselor, if you have one, to make sure you're on the same page. You might look at your high school transcript to see if any courses reveal you were in a resource room or enrolled in a learning strategies class. If so, disclose. Does your transcript show a weakness in a specific discipline like math or science? If so, you might disclose the reason for the struggles. If you made awesome progress in high school and learned the strategies to successfully navigate through your learning differences, maybe contrast where you were before with where you are now. Bottom line: it can be great to disclose and show your pride and ability to deal with setbacks or obstacles.

---

* See the Treasure Trove for links to a database of test-optional schools.

If you have trouble finding information about disability services on the college's website, this may be a sign the college sees disability support on campus as relatively unimportant. Talk to your high school counselor, high school special education case manager or department chair, or the college's disability office.

Keep in mind, students over eighteen years old have to sign a FERPA waiver to allow their parent/guardian permission to talk to disability services.

Ten Essential Tips for Students with Learning Differences

1. Be sure to take a copy of your current #504 Plan and/or your most recent psycho-educational testing to request accommodations in college. Keep these electronically somewhere so you always have access to them.
2. Knowing the accommodations you received in high school is important in order to match these requirements in college.
3. Know what accommodations federal law mandates colleges provide by federal law and what is "not required" by law.
4. Tutoring is not a mandated service. Ask about your professors' office hours. Know the process for signing up for a tutor where tutoring is offered. Ask if there is a limit on how often you can seek the help of a tutor.
5. Be familiar with all the resources on campus such as the Writing Center, Technology Center, Tutoring Center, and Counseling and Health Services.
6. Find out if you are eligible for professor's notes and how to access them.
7. Ask in advance about an "official" date to drop courses in college without the penalty of a grade. Put that date in your calendar. (That's a good idea for all students, incidentally.)
8. Meet your professors before class to discuss their process for securing your accommodations. Where do you take your tests with extended time, for example? Do you have to ask in advance of each quiz or test?
9. Know that being a self-advocate is one of the most important skills for success in both college and life. Do you seek help when needed? Do you ask for clarification of assignments? Do you reach out in advance of deadlines to ask for an extension of an assignment?
10. Learn to articulate your learning difference. In fact, write the description down and practice telling your story. Make sure you understand the impact of the learning difference so you can "teach the teacher." If you

meet resistance from a professor, don't just clam up; take your concerns to the Office of Disability Services. You have a diagnosis that allows for specific accommodations, and knowing your intended college can meet your needs is really important.

Keep the macro goal in neon lights and remember that getting into a college is just the beginning. Speak with confidence and pride; live bravely and take reasonable risks. You got this.

In the Treasure Trove, you'll find:

→ Standardized testing resources and information for students with learning differences

→ The *K&W Guide to Colleges for Students with Learning Differences,* 14th edition, the premier resource guide with information about college admission, services, programs, and accommodations at colleges in the United States

→ Choices: a postsecondary planning night for college-bound students with learning differences

→ National Center for Learning Disabilities: learn the laws and policies in the United States

→ CHADD: provides information for adults and families dealing with attention deficit hyperactivity disorder

→ A resource outlining the obligations colleges and universities must meet in all institutional programs and activities to provide access to students with disabilities

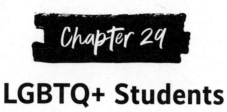

LGBTQ+ Students

Written with education reporter Charlotte West

As if it wasn't hard enough to find a college that's the right fit for your academic and personal interests, you might have additional questions about finding an inclusive campus if you identify as LGBTQ+. You might be wondering about everything from housing options to whether or not you should come out in your personal statement.

Where to Begin

Check out Campus Pride, a nonprofit working to create safer college environments for LGBTQ+ students. They publish the Campus Pride Index, a national list of LGBTQ-friendly colleges and universities.

They also run the HBCU LGBTQ Clearinghouse, which reviews LGBTQ-inclusive policies, programs, and practices at Historically Black Colleges and Universities. The Trans Policy Clearinghouse landing page has a list of resources where you can find which women's colleges welcome transgender students. You can also see which schools provide options to live in gender-inclusive housing, which allow students to change their name and gender on campus records, and which cover transition-related medical expenses under student health insurance.

Where to Avoid

Campus Pride also maintains a Shame List, which identifies the "absolute worst campuses for LGBTQ youth" in the United States. The colleges and universities on the Shame List openly discriminate against LGBTQ+ youth or have a track record of anti-LGBTQ+ actions, programs, and practices.

Where to Learn What You Need to Know

Check out an institution's website and reach out to college reps if you can't find answers to your questions. "Perhaps the most helpful question is the direct one," says Wes Waggoner, Associate Vice President for Enrollment Management at Southern Methodist University (SMU). "Ask, 'What resources and opportunities does this university have that particularly support LGBTQ+ students?'"

Waggoner also suggests asking the admission office to put you in touch with a current student who identifies as LGBTQ+ to ask about life on campus. SMU, for instance, has a resource center and a student senator dedicated to representing LGBTQ students.

Andrew Moe, Associate Dean of Admissions at Swarthmore, agrees. "While students should view an institution's website and publications to ensure LGBTQ+ students and community are represented and celebrated, they should also ask tough questions," says Moe. "That's our job—to answer questions of prospective students and families, so use us as a resource."

Tips for Students Who Identify as LGBTQ+

- **Dig through the university's website, starting with its anti-discrimination statement.** "Find out: Does the school's nondiscrimination policy include sexual orientation and gender identity?" asks Wagonner. "This is a good first check. Does the campus have an active LGBTQ+ student group? Does that group sponsor events for LGBTQ+ students? Is there an LGBTQ+ resource center on campus?"
- **Pay attention to the details.** Check whether university representatives include their pronouns in their email signatures. "If you do a campus

visit, look for posters advertising organizations and events oriented toward LGBTQ+ students," says Kaelie Lund, Assistant Dean of Admissions at Carleton College. "If the school has an office dedicated to supporting queer students, see if it is student run or if paid staff members oversee that office. That can give you additional insight into how the school you are interested in supports queer students," she says.

- **Ask about housing options and living-learning communities for LGBTQ+ students.** Some universities have gender-neutral, gender-inclusive, or all-gender residence halls. University of California Santa Cruz (UCSC) has trans-inclusive housing for transgender and gender-nonconforming students. UC Berkeley offers a living-learning community called Unity House welcoming students who identify as LGBTQ+. Residents also take an academic seminar together organized by the Gender Studies Department.

- **Look for scholarships specific to LGBTQ+ students.** Campus Pride has a national database of scholarships for LGBTQ+ students. The Point Foundation offers scholarships for community college and university students who identify as LGBTQ+. If your parents are unwilling to support you because of your sexual orientation or gender expression, talk to the financial aid office about what options are available. "I recommend students open a dialogue with admission and financial aid officers to ensure they know their options if family members are less than supportive," Moe says.

- **Know that you decide whether or not you write about your sexual orientation or gender expression in your college essay.** You might not be ready to share something so personal, and that's okay. It can also be a powerful experience to use your personal statement as an opportunity to process and reflect. As is the case for all students, the most helpful essays are ones in which you communicate what is important to you (yup, your values!) and how they will contribute to a campus community. "Students should not feel like they have to talk about their sexual orientation or gender identity in the main essay," says Waggoner, "but it can be powerful if done well."

In the Treasure Trove, you'll find links to:

→   Campus Pride

→   HBCU LGBTQ Clearinghouse

→   Trans Policy Clearinghouse

→   A database of scholarships for LGBTQ+ students from Campus Pride and
      another from the Point Foundation

→   Blog post: "Should I Come Out in My College Essay? If So, How?"

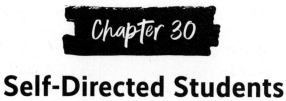

Self-Directed Students

Written with Blake Boles, author of The Art of Self-Directed Learning:
23 Tips for Giving Yourself an Unconventional Education

"Self-directed learning involves exploring what you want without regard to arbitrary standards and requirements," says homeschooling expert Becca Orlowski. "And while a learner's self-directed path can intersect with standards and requirements, it doesn't always."*

For the College Essay Guy podcast episode 214, I interviewed self-directed learning expert Blake Boles and I asked him, "What do self-directed learners care about?" Like me, Blake is big on values, so he named these three: genuine choice (autonomy), building real skills (mastery), and community and purpose (relatedness).

And while self-directed learning is often associated with homeschoolers, it can be useful for almost anyone. In his book (and on our podcast), Blake offers these tips for those who have carved or plan to carve their own educational path:

Five Tips for Self-Directed Learners
From *The Art of Self-Directed Learning: 23 Tips for Giving Yourself an Unconventional Education*

1. **Attitude is your most precious resource.** Rather than "I can't," try using the phrase, "I could if I…" Ask yourself, "What information or resources do I need to make this happen?"

---

* Becca Orlowski was also a guest on the College Essay Guy podcast; link in the Treasure Trove.

2. **Google everything.** The internet is the most powerful tool in human history. Research, create, build, or promote anything your imagination can dream up.

3. **Email strangers.** You may be surprised at how many interesting people will be willing to respond. Feeling shy? In the Treasure Trove you'll find two tips and examples from Blake.

4. **Find your nerd clan.** Who's into the things you're into? Yes, even the weird things. (It's those things that often make for the most interesting college essays.)

5. **Create an awesome digital paper trail.** Consider that your future employers, romantic partners, and maybe even your kids will google you. As Blake says, "Start filling the internet with your creations and leave a [digital] trail worth following."

Essential Resources for Self-Directed Learning

- BlakeBoles.com includes: *Off-Trail Learning* (Blake's podcast), books, articles, and YouTube videos
- Radical education books: John Taylor Gatto, Grace Llewellyn, Peter Gray, Kerry McDonald
- Less radical books: *The Self-Driven Child*
- Blogs: Will Richardson, Penelope Trunk
- College books: *Excellent Sheep, The Case Against Education*
- Parenting: *The Nurture Assumption*
- Websites: Alliance for Self-Directed Education (Tipping Points blog)
- Summer camps: Not Back to School Camp, Camp Stomping Ground
- UnschoolAdventures.com

Warning: Spending too much time with these materials may have you wondering: Is college right for me anyway? And that's a great question to ask. Pull on that thread and watch what happens.

How to Develop a Self-Directed Project Based on Your Values

Written with Lauren Calahan (LEAP4change)

AN ESTABLISHED PROJECT VS. A SELF-DIRECTED PROJECT

These two may sound the same, but they're actually very different from each other. How?

An established project is generally designed by others and already up and running (so you join it as opposed to create it). Examples include:

- In-school opportunities such as fundraising for a club, beautifying your campus, or tutoring
- Opportunities outside your school such as working in a soup kitchen, volunteering at a hospital or animal shelter, playing music at the local senior center, or paying money to volunteer in a developing country[*]

A self-directed project is initiated by you, is rooted in your own vision, is led by you (either independently or with other decision-makers), and measures its success by the work and outreach that you do personally. Examples include:

- Starting a garden or composting program at your home or in your community
- Petitioning your school board to provide more healthy food options in your school cafeteria
- Creating a career day panel to speak to students about their paths
- Planning a history field trip to document headstones in a cemetery for your local historical society

While joining an established project can be great, it's worth at least considering a self-directed project for a few reasons.

You'll learn a ton about yourself. Building a project on your own will

---

[*]   For great volunteering ideas, check out www.DoSomething.org.

teach you to work outside your comfort zone, discover your weaknesses, develop new strengths, become more emotionally intelligent, and develop your confidence.

You'll become a more confident leader who possesses entrepreneurial skills, like how to create a clear vision, build a team, hold others (and yourself) accountable, assess your decisions, admit mistakes, fail, and get back up to reach your goals in a new way.

Your project may help you stand out on your college application.[*] There aren't many students that have what it takes to organize, lead, and complete a project. So it's easy to look impressive as a student who has done that.

Values Check

For full-time high school students, self-directed projects sometimes require more work and responsibility than an existing project or organization. Higher-stakes challenges can lead to more personal growth opportunities and a stand-out project to feature on your college application. But a self-directed project isn't for everyone.

Here are some good values-based questions to consider when deciding whether a self-directed project is right for you:

→ Do you prefer the safety that comes with having someone else lead you, or not so much?

→ Do you like taking control of weekend plans, or are you fine doing whatever the group wants?

→ Are you more comfortable offering your gifts in a supporting role or when you're leading? And which do you prefer in the context of volunteer work?

→ Are you the kind of person who spends lots of time thinking idealistically about the future?

→ Taking into account your other current commitments and interests, do you have the time to develop an additional project?

If this feels like a checklist for "Are you an entrepreneur?" you're right. The kind of project we're about to describe is an entrepreneurial venture. If you don't already possess entrepreneurial qualities and you want to, this might be a great opportunity.

---

* This reason is listed last because "getting into college" isn't the best reason for developing a self-directed project.

A Step-by-Step Guide to Developing a Self-Directed Project Based on What You Care About

STEP 1: CONNECT WITH WHAT YOU CARE ABOUT

Over the years, Lauren, my co-author for this section, and I have found that students whose projects don't closely connect to their values tend to burn out faster than those whose projects clearly connect. But students who take time to develop a project that's deeply connected to their values have a much better chance of actually getting stuff done and loving the process.

But how do you connect with your values? Complete the Core Memories Exercise on page 7, if you haven't already. It's a wonderful way of reconnecting with what you care about.

STEP 2: CONNECT YOUR VALUES TO A PROBLEM THAT IS EITHER LOCAL, GLOBAL, OR BOTH

Imagine for a moment you have a magic wand. If you could wave it, and the world would be different, what would you change? Spend a minute thinking about this.

Consider: What causes suffering (for you personally)? What suffering (by other people) do you react to the strongest? What makes you most afraid for the future? What would you like to be different in the world?

Now ask yourself: *To make that image a reality, where would I need to start?*

For inspiration, here are two examples of self-directed solutions designed by students like you that address local problems:

- One student was tired of seeing all the discarded water bottles around his high school campus, so he and his Environmental Club members presented speeches to the Board of Education, raised $2,500 through their GoFundMe campaign, and had water fountains installed. Their efforts kept thousands of plastic bottles out of landfills over the course of two years.
- Another student was bullied terribly so she developed an app called "Sit With Us" that helps new students find peers willing to share their lunch table. It not only helped transform her school community but surpassed 100,000 downloads.

And here are two examples of students who developed self-directed solutions to address global problems:

- A team of over twenty students in Connecticut and Uganda identified poverty, education, and leadership as three areas where they could reduce the achievement gap in their shared communities. As a result, they helped start a student-run tutoring group as well as LEAP Kumazima, a nonprofit that promotes leadership through soccer.
- Another group of students decided to empower women through education, health, and social justice. Through their partnership, they built night schools in India to ensure that the young women can simultaneously do their chores, become educated, learn more about their health, and build a more supportive community free from human trafficking.

STEP 3: WRITE YOUR VISION STATEMENT

A vision statement is an inspiring assertion that reflects your core values and describes the world as you'd like it to be. Why write one? A vision statement can motivate your team, help you as you work to attract new partners, and help you focus your efforts (by helping you decide what your project will and will not be doing).

But don't worry, it doesn't need to be several paragraphs or a page. In fact, it should be short, maybe ten to twenty words long.

Vision Statement Examples from Large Organizations

We envision a world where all people—even in the most remote areas of the globe—hold the power to create opportunity for themselves and others.

KIVA

A world where everyone has a decent place to live.

HABITAT FOR HUMANITY

A world without Alzheimer's disease.

ALZHEIMER'S ASSOCIATION

Equality for everyone.
HUMAN RIGHTS CAMPAIGN

But vision statements don't always have to be super epic or global. If the problem you're dealing with is more specific, your vision statement might sound more like these:

We envision a Lincoln High School where all students are able to creatively express themselves and follow their dreams.

We envision a Sunset High School where every member of the student body has access to clean and delicious drinking water.

We envision a Westminster Academy where every student has access to the resources they need to get the education they deserve.

(You get the idea.)

Action item: Spend five to ten minutes drafting a vision statement. In fact, write it here:

And yes, I realize it may take you more than five to ten minutes to write your vision; I'm just asking you to get started. And if you need a little more direction, try to make it fit these criteria: *future focused, values based, present tense, simple language, inspirational.*

Whether or not you've finished your vision statement (and let's be real, it could take you some time to fully articulate it), let's talk about how to…

STEP 4: CREATE YOUR ONE SHEET

A one sheet is basically a piece of marketing you'll use to attract potential partners. It should provide a clear sense of what you're doing and how you might partner together. It should also be professional so your potential partner sees how serious you are about this project.

How do you create your one sheet? First, answer the W5H questions:

1. WHOM do you need for success?
2. WHAT do you need for success?
3. WHEN do you plan to start your project?
4. WHERE will you build your project?
5. WHY are you building your project in the first place?
6. HOW will you build your project?

Next, use the answers to the W5H questions to create an inspiring one sheet based on one of the one sheet examples that you can find in the Treasure Trove.

STEP 5: BUILD YOUR TEAM

For some people and projects, independent work is better. But many of the great self-directed student projects I've seen involved a team.

If you feel like you'd enjoy working with others on your self-directed project, you'll get to benefit from a lot of the best reasons to work with a team, such as the project getting done more efficiently and with more diverse perspectives. Not to mention going through the whole process will teach you a ton about how to delegate tasks, hold yourself and others accountable to goals, and inspire others to collaborate. And team projects tend to make dynamic stories in college application material.*

Ask these five questions of anyone you're considering partnering with on a project:

1. Is this person great at something that I'm not great at?
2. Is this person someone I want to spend hours with?
3. Is this person someone I look up to?
4. Does this person have the same bar of excellence that I do?
5. Is this person a reliable communicator?

If you have good answers to most or all of those questions, they're probably going to be a great partner.

---

* Again, notice I'm putting this one last because there are so many other great reasons (besides just getting into college) to develop your collaboration skills.

STEP 6: COLLABORATE WITH YOUR TEAM TO WRITE YOUR MISSION STATEMENT

Vision statements and mission statements are often confused. Whereas your vision statement defines your vision for the future (hoped for state), the mission statement is a shared statement of purpose that defines your present and how you will achieve your vision together with your partners.

Heads up: Although this is a short statement, every single word matters. So it may take some time.

Mission Statement Examples

To accelerate the world's transition to sustainable energy.
TESLA

Greenpeace is an independent campaigning organization, which uses non-violent, creative confrontation to expose global environmental problems, and to force the solutions which are essential to a green and peaceful future.

To help bring creative projects to life.
KICKSTARTER

LEAP4change coaches, educates, and empowers youth to become culturally competent, emotionally intelligent, entrepreneurial leaders committed to making a positive impact on our world...together.

As with a vision statement, your mission could be project specific:

Our mission is to provide clean drinking water to the students at Westminster Academy.

The mission of our Eco Club is to protect and improve our environment, both locally and globally.

The mission of our project is to leverage music in a variety of world cultures to connect students, inspire knowledge, and build compassion in the young leaders of Drug Fighters School in Kibera and Ampark and Fieldston in the Bronx.

Action item: Work with your new team to craft your collaborative mission statement. Write yours here:

STEP 7: MAKE YOUR PROJECT HAPPEN

Time to create your action plan. You'll find a sample action plan in the Treasure Trove.

STEP 8: HOW TO WRITE ABOUT YOUR PROJECT IN YOUR COLLEGE APPLICATION

Learn how to write an Extracurricular Activity Essay on page 222.

A Final Word about Not Letting This Stress You Out

Remember, this may not be for everyone. If you're short on time, overcommitted, would rather join an existing project or organization, or are working with other limitations, *you do not have to do all this.*

You can get into a great college without creating a self-directed project. Many students do every year.

In the Treasure Trove, you'll find:

→ Blake Boles's "Tips on Emailing to Request a Letter of Recommendation" or "Connecting with an Interesting Stranger"

→ More tips on writing a great mission statement

→ Two one sheet examples

→ Tips for learning what type of leader you are

→ Sample one-week plan [Template]

→ Checklist for conversations with potential partners (and what to do when someone says "no")

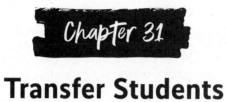

Transfer Students

Special thanks to Dan Nannini (Santa Monica College), Sunday Salter (LA Pierce College), Deborah Wong (UCLA), Whitney Enwemeka (formerly at USC), and Susan Dabbar (Admission Smarts) for their contributions

There are two kinds of transfer: unplanned and planned.

Say you're accepted to a four-year college and you initially think, "Yes! This is the place for me!" Then a year goes by and you realize that it's absolutely not the place for you and you actually want to leave. It happens more often than you might think. I'd call that an unplanned transfer.

On the other hand, maybe in high school you decide to save some money and earn some credits by taking classes at a community college with an eye toward eventually transferring to a four-year university. I'd call this a planned transfer.

This chapter will address both.

The Eleven Commandments of Transfer*

The following tips (ahem, commandments) apply to both planned and unplanned transfers.

---

* The "Commandments of Transfer" format was inspired by a presentation given by Dan Nannini (Santa Monica College), Sunday Salter (LA Pierce College), and Deborah Wong (UCLA). I think it's fun.

IF THOU MIGHT BE PLANNING TO TRANSFER, THOU SHALT...

1. Observe admission requirements and keep them sacred.

How can you find out what they are? Google "[school name] transfer admission requirements." Some guidelines:

- Research to see if an articulation agreement exists between the school you want to transfer from and the school you want to transfer to.
- Contact the transfer advisor at the schools you're interested in to ask if they limit transfer credits. Ask if there are other limitations—some schools, for example, don't want to take students for a particular major. Others may take students in the fall but not in the spring.
- Some universities have an online database that includes all coursework they have previously granted credit for. You can find these with a quick google search or call to a transfer counselor.
- Save your syllabi from previous college courses you've taken; some institutions might require you to submit these.

What's an "articulation agreement" and why is it important?
Articulation basically outlines which specific courses a university will accept from another institution. In other words:

X course at one institution = Y course at another institution

Courses fall into one of three categories: major requirement, general education requirement, or elective requirements. Actually, there's a fourth category: nontransferable courses.

Some schools have worked out the details of which courses will count for all (or most) of their courses. This articulation agreement is nice because you can know more easily which of your credits will transfer.

---

2. Choose and prepare for your major.

Must you pick a major? It depends on the school. Private institutions might let you delay the decision a bit, whereas University of California schools, which accept over seventeen thousand transfer students per year, require a major.

It also depends on whether the major or the school is more important to you. Say you want to study film and you're only interested in the most well-known film schools. If you *really* want to attend these schools more than you want to study film, you might have a better chance of getting in if you apply with a different major. (You can still meet film students and create with them!) If, on the other hand, you want to transfer only because of their film schools and you'd rather stay closer to home in Delaware if you aren't accepted, then hey, go for it!

But picking a major is a good idea. "For one thing, *not* picking a major can potentially be expensive," notes Dan Nannini, transfer coordinator at Santa Monica College for the past seventeen years. "If you've just spent 70K on one year's tuition at a private university, for example, you may want to focus on classes that fulfill a particular major so you can graduate in four years. That way your family doesn't have to pay for five or six years of college."

Completing major requirements can also make you a more attractive candidate for admission. And the sooner, the better! A student who has completed their courses earlier in the year—in the fall, for example—is more attractive to a school than a student who still has courses to complete—say, in the spring.

3. Keep up your GPA.

You've got to keep your grades up even if you're already dreaming about the school you'll transfer to. So make it happen.

4. Mind your test scores.

Heads-up that the closer you are to high school, the more your standardized test scores will count (if they're required as part of the application). Transferring as a junior can push these scores further back in the rearview mirror.

5. Engage In campus activities.

It'll be important to show the school you're transferring to how you'll contribute to campus life once you arrive. The best way to do that? Contribute right now, right where you are—make the most of your current resources and opportunities. (It'll also give you more to write about on the essay.)

6. Interact with your professors and make sure they know you.

Why? For one, it up-levels your academic experience. More practically speaking, you may need them—depending on the school you're transferring to—to write you a recommendation letter.

7. Make your summers count.

Whether you work, volunteer, or create a project on your own, it's important to show colleges how you engage with the world.

8. If possible, visit the campus.

If this is a planned transfer, make sure this is where you want to be. If it's unplanned, make sure you don't make the same mistake twice.

9. Double-check your requirements.

Each school is different, so make sure you double-check these. And yes, I know that this was commandment #1. We're reemphasizing it here to make a point.

10. Apply to multiple schools.

In the "How to Create a Balanced College List" chapter, I mention having a range of "Reach," "Maybe" and "Likely" schools—probably two or three of each. The same applies here. Pro Tip: Find out how many transfers each school takes. Stanford, for example, takes fewer than 100 transfer students per year, whereas UCLA takes more than 3,000.

11. Write a great essay.

For a *very* complete guide on how to write a great transfer essay, check out the Treasure Trove.

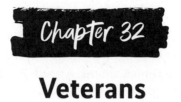

Chapter 32

Veterans

Written with Bob Dannenhold (Collegeology/Application Navigation)

As a veteran, you are entering higher education with a set of life experiences, perspectives, and benefits like no other. College is full of fantastic opportunities for you to take advantage of, and this chapter will help you do that.

The Post-9/11 GI Bill

The Post-9/11 GI Bill made more than two million service members eligible for the most generous veterans' education entitlement program since World War II. But unlike the original GI Bill, the amount of support a veteran receives varies, depending on both the location of the school, college, or university (relative to where the vet resides), and the type of degree being pursued.

HOW THE POST-9/11 GI BILL CAN HELP PAY FOR COLLEGE

- The Post-9/11 GI Bill pays all public school in-state tuition fees; private and international school costs up to $17,500 annually; and the cost of taking the SAT, GMAT, LSAT, or any other required standardized tests.
- Most veterans are entitled to thirty-six months of eligibility, or forty-eight months if they are utilizing more than one program.

- In addition, the Yellow Ribbon Program can help cover out-of-state fees, some private school fees (if they are a participating school), and other costs above the $17,500 cap.

- All of these benefits are transferable to other qualified family members, including eligible dependents such as spouses and children. You have to request to transfer unused GI Bill benefits to eligible dependents while serving as an active member of the Armed Forces. A family member who is enrolled in the Defense Eligibility Enrollment Reporting System (DEERS) is eligible to receive benefits at the time of transfer. You can find more information at www.tricare.mil/deers.

Benefits for state universities are calculated based on the cost of the highest in-state tuition for residents, including fees. If you are not a resident of that state, the difference may be waived, or Yellow Ribbon funding may cover the difference. All qualifying vets get full compensation for all public school in-state tuition and fees.

These benefits for private and public schools and universities apply to both graduate and undergraduate degrees, and vocational/technical programs. But it is important to check in advance about what is specifically covered.

QUESTIONS TO ASK ABOUT YOUR VETERANS BENEFITS

When deciding which college is right for you, here are a few questions you need to ask the Department of Veterans Affairs or the schools you're interested in to understand which benefits you are entitled to and any special considerations you might need to keep in mind:

- Which Post-9/11 GI Bill tier or payment rate am I eligible for?
- Which benefit offers the greatest compensation to me?
- Is the type of education or training I'm seeking covered?
- Am I using other education benefits that may be altered by my decision?
- Will I need to take online or distance learning credits?
- Is there a deadline for completing the degree or training?
- Am I eligible for a Transfer of Entitlement, and is this a consideration for me?
- Do I have entitlement remaining under another VA education program?

Ten Tips for Veterans Applying to College

1. Understanding what benefits are available to you is an important first step. A good place to find the answers is the U.S. Department of Veterans Affairs Education phone line, which will connect you with a helpful person who is ready to spend as much time as it takes to answer every question you have: 1-888-442-4551.

2. College is a new experience. You will return from service with an impressive cache of skills and experiences, but especially if you went straight into the military from high school, navigating the college application process can be unfamiliar territory. Don't be afraid to ask for help if you feel lost.

3. You might need to shift your mindset. You need to start thinking of yourself in terms of your strengths and abilities as a student and approach the world as someone who is inquisitive and questioning rather than someone who is always obedient.

4. Before you apply to college, consider first getting involved with either volunteering or a low-stress job. Doing so will give you a chance to experience new people and new responsibilities without the pressures of college. It also might give you something new to write about in your personal statement.

5. Loved ones can be an important source of support during the college admissions process. Involve your spouse or partner, or even a close friend, when working on identifying your goals for higher education. Invite them to come on campus visits or meetings with admission officers.

6. If you are anxious about taking standardized tests like the ACT and SAT, call the admission office to see if they are willing to waive the requirement for returning veterans. You also might check out test-optional schools (see page 23 for more information).

7. The on-campus veterans resource center at your university can be an important source of information and support. When applying, reach out to connect with current students who have served. The university may also have staff that can answer questions about benefits eligibility.

8. You might be able to use your military training toward college credit. An increasing number of colleges now award military students credit toward degrees based on training, coursework, and occupational specialty. Depending on the degree the service member is seeking, credit may be

awarded for use toward an associate's or bachelor's degree program. This is coordinated by The American Council on Education.

9. Your experience in the military can make an excellent topic for your personal statement. Think about where you were intellectually and emotionally when you joined the armed forces, where you are now, how your military experience has possibly influenced you, and where you want to go in the future.

10. Enrolling in college is another transition, just like transitioning to being home. You might have spent years learning about the military but may have had only one week of "civilian transition training" to unlearn it. You'll find a link in the Treasure Trove to resources that have helped many veterans with readjustment issues.

In the Treasure Trove, you'll find links to:

→   The website for Education Benefits

→   Yellow Ribbon Program

→   Student Veterans of America

→   American Council on Education, which coordinates college credit for military service

→   A *Transfer Guide: Understanding Your Military Transcript and ACE Credit Recommendations*

→   Information on the Joint Services transcript

→   Service 2 School

→   Housing allowance

→   VA Benefit Comparison Chart (Click on GI Bill comparison tool)

→   GI Bill Benefits from the American Council on Education

Chapter 33

Students Interested in Women's Colleges

Written with Aimee Kahn-Foss, Director of Admission, and Rachel West, Associate Director of Admission, at Agnes Scott College

As someone who made the decision to attend a women's college, I didn't choose my college because it was a women's college. I chose my college because I loved the location, the beautiful campus, the study abroad opportunities, and the feeling that the institution would give me an education very different than what I saw at traditional universities. I did not realize the importance of the women's college aspect until I was actually there as a student, but it was truly what made the institution and opportunities so unique. The depth of the classroom conversations, the push and support of the faculty, and the incredible women I called my friends and classmates who also chose a nontraditional college because they wanted to do things differently as well. My experience was transformative. I became a better student and a better person.

AIMEE KAHN-FOSS, AGNES SCOTT COLLEGE ALUMNI

The Unique Opportunities and Perspectives of Women's Colleges

One of the most common questions we get asked by students, parents, and college counselors is "Why a women's college?" It's an important question in determining fit, but it's also a little bit of a difficult question to answer. Just like all colleges and universities, women's colleges have their own DNA.

Institutions vary greatly in terms of campus locations, student characteristics, opportunities, and atmosphere. Some students know they want to attend a women's college early on, while other students realize this later in high school or apply to both coed schools and women's colleges because they like characteristics of each.

Women's colleges were originally created in the United States to give women access to higher education during a time when educating women went against the status quo. This changed in the 1960s and '70s when many colleges and universities began offering admission to women. But black women, indigenous women, and women of other demographics continued to be excluded from higher education until the '60s and '70s—even from most women's colleges. HBCU women's colleges, like Spelman College and Bennett College (see page 315 for more information on HBCUs), were created to serve these women. Since the early 2000s, women's colleges as a whole (thirty-seven in total) have become some of the most diverse and inclusive institutions in the United States. Recently, interest and enrollment in women's colleges has resurged, proving their continued relevance and necessity in our higher education landscape.

Why You Should Apply to a Women's College

- **You seek small, personal communities where forming real relationships with your professors is easy.** Women's colleges tend to be smaller liberal arts colleges where more students live on campus for all four years of their experience. Women's college students also report higher rates of interaction with their professors than their coeducational counterparts.*

- **You thrive in environments where students with many different perspectives learn from one another.** Women's colleges typically enroll a more racially and ethnically diverse population of students than coeducational institutions.† They also enroll students from a wide variety of economic backgrounds, consistently ranking high on social mobility.

- **You seek a college experience with a global focus.** Many women's colleges focus heavily on intercultural awareness and study abroad programs. For example: all first-year students at Agnes Scott College participate in the SUMMIT curriculum where they go on a cultural study abroad tour; St. Mary's College has a great Intercultural Leadership program.

---

*   Casey Near and Sara Kratzok, *Why a Women's College?* (New York: Collegewise, 2014), 20.

†   Linda J. Sax, PhD, *Who Attends a Women's College?* (Los Angeles: UCLA, 2015), viii.

- **You seek opportunities to grow as a leader.** Many women's colleges have specific programs to help students grow in their leadership skills, like Barnard College's Young Women's Leadership Institute and Salem College's Leadership Salem. And students observe women in top positions. Ninety percent of women's college presidents are women, for example, and fifty-five percent of faculty are women. Finally, women's college graduates move on to strong leadership positions in their fields. Women's college graduates make up two percent of the college graduate population, yet more than twenty percent of women in Congress and a third of women on Fortune 1000 boards graduated from women's colleges.[‡]

- **You are a woman who wants more equitable access to working in a STEM field.** It's no secret that STEM fields suffer from a lower number of women in leadership positions. But women's colleges are doing their part to equalize the numbers. Students at women's colleges are one-and-a-half times more likely to major in the STEM fields than women at coeducational institutions.[§] Women's college faculty are also more likely than faculty at any other type of institution to involve undergraduate students in STEM research.[¶]

- **You seek a safe space for LGBTQ+ students.** Women's colleges historically have been sources of safety for marginalized groups, originally founded as spaces of education for women at a time when they didn't have higher education options. Now, many women's colleges have strong policies around gender and sexual identity, considering all applicants who identify as women. Many transgender, gender neutral, and genderqueer students find safe communities at women's colleges too.

- **You want to feel prepared for the real world after college.** Women's college graduates are well prepared for their next steps, whatever those might be. Graduates of women's colleges were more likely than all other college graduates to graduate in four years or less. They were also more likely than all other college alumni to complete a graduate or professional degree.[**] Students also graduate from women's colleges with a strong sense of self and confidence in their own abilities. Women's college alumnae are more

---

[‡] Near and Kratzok, *Why a Women's College?* 19.

[§] Near and Kratzok, *Why a Women's College?* 19.

[¶] Linda J. Sax, PhD, *Who Teaches at Women's Colleges?* (Los Angeles: UCLA, 2014), iii.

[**] Susan Lennon, *What Matters in College After College* (Decatur, GA: 2012) 33.

likely to report that they are prepared for their first job, more likely to say they have the communication and leadership skills employers want, and more likely to report higher levels of self-confidence than their coeducational counterparts.*

SO WHO IS A GOOD FIT FOR
A WOMEN'S COLLEGE?

That's another question that's hard to answer because women's colleges are not a monolith; each of the thirty-seven institutions has their own specialties and definitions of "fit." Broadly speaking, if some or most of the previous list fits your higher educational goals, a women's college might be a good place for you.

Often we say that the best fit for a women's college is someone who is not afraid to tell their friends that they are applying to one. It takes a certain amount of courage, rebellious spirit, and individuality to be willing to say to your peers that you are applying for a nontraditional college experience. If that sounds like you, we encourage you to consider the idea. Dig into the women's colleges and see if one feels like the right place for you.

In the Treasure Trove, you'll find links to:

→ Women's College Coalition—Read more about the thirty-seven women's colleges in the United States

→ Campus Pride's list of women's colleges that admit transgender students

---

* "Get the Facts," Women's College Coalition. womenscolleges.org/discover/parents.

Part X

After You Apply

How to Write a Great Letter of Continued Interest

So you've been wait-listed or deferred. Darn. But wait—all is not lost! You may have another chance to make your case. And that, my friends, is what this chapter is all about.

In this chapter we'll cover:

- What a letter of continued interest (LOCI) is
- When you should send a LOCI
- What you should include in a LOCI
- A great example letter

What is a letter of continued interest (LOCI)?

A letter of continued interest is an email you send to an admission office, typically after you've been deferred or placed on their wait-list. It lets the college know you're still interested in attending and why.

Should I send one to every school?

Not necessarily. When you're deferred or placed on a waiting list, follow the directions the college provides for what they want you to do next. If they specifically ask you not to send a letter, don't! But many colleges will invite you to update your application with a letter describing your new achievements and why you are still interested in attending. If you're unsure, just email back to ask, "May I send a letter of continued interest?" Sometimes all they want is for you to check a box on a form they provide.

Words of Wisdom from an Admission Officer

Ed Devine, West Coast Regional Director of Admissions, Lafayette College

If you're placed on the wait-list (WL), the first thing to consider is if you want to prolong the decision process. Assess how that wait-list school stacks up against the other schools you've been admitted to. If you feel a deep connection to that school, a few more weeks of uncertainty may be worth it. But you'll need to express your continued interest to the WL school. Many schools will ask students via survey or email whether they want to be an active member of the wait-list. While it's imperative to respond in the school's requested format, you can often send an additional letter. Strategy is key, though. Your high school counselor may be able to help you formulate one. If you have a connection with your admission counselor, this is a good time to reconnect. Ask the admission officer to recommend what you might do to show interest. Some schools allow WL students to provide further information (e.g., updated grades, new recommendation letters, a refreshed "Why Us?" essay, a video response, or maybe even a meeting with the admission officer). Do not overdo your response; observe requirements and be discerning about what you include. Looking into the school's WL history can reveal helpful insights. For example: How many WL students were accepted in the previous year? When June arrives, you may need to let go of your WL school. Developing connections with schools that admitted you can help you transition to college. You'll want to earnestly prepare for this next step in your life. Connect virtually with classmates, get to know your new city/home, and read the materials your Student Life Office and professors send.

What should I include in a letter of continued interest?

New information. The school has made a preliminary decision that your application is a "maybe," which means you're a competitive applicant but you didn't quite make the cut. New information is the best way to turn that "maybe" into a "yes."

Here's an example of a great LOCI:

Dear Ms. Veronica Lauren,

My name is Zola Avery, and I'm a hopeful Yalie from Bergen County, New Jersey. Though deferred from the Early Action pool, I remain absolutely convinced that Yale is the school for me. I'd like to thank the admissions department for reevaluating my materials.

Thank them for reevaluating your materials and reaffirm that X school is the place for you. If they're your first choice, say so!

This past weekend, I got the opportunity to spend some time up in New Haven for the Yale University Model United Nations Conference (YMUN), serving as part of the United Nations International Strategy for Disaster Reduction Committee (UNISDR) and debating rising sea levels and volcanic eruptions. Speaking with current Yale students made me realize more than ever before that I was with my people—warm, incredibly funny, artistic in their own way, and unabashedly inquisitive. This weekend, I was where I belong.

Consider including two to three brief "Why Us?" details describing why you and the school are a great match.

I would also like to take this time to briefly tell the admissions department about a few things that have happened since I submitted my Early Action application. First, I wrote, illustrated, and published a children's book centered around gender inclusivity in STEM fields, with all proceeds going toward supporting curriculum development and outreach for the Stereotype Project, an organization I've been running for the past four years that focuses on combating stereotypes through art. I've attached PDF copies of my book *Mika and the Microscope*, along with some other information, but you should be receiving a copy in the mail soon. I very much believe the magic of reading is magnified when the book is in its physical form (and I think my brother and sister, five and nine, would definitely agree).

Offer new information such as updates on extracurricular activities, any awards won, projects you've begun, or improved GPA or standardized test scores (if applicable).

Secondly, I'd like to add the following honors to my admissions file:

- Best Delegate, Yale University Model United Nations Conference
- Outstanding Delegate, Bronx Science High School Model United Nations Conference

Include any
info on a
campus visit,
if you've made
one, and what
specifically you
loved.

- Member of the Andrea Rubino Sheridan Chapter of National
  Honor Society

My whole life I have worked to draw connections and bridge the gap between science, social justice, and art. Whether wandering through the Yale Art Museum, bringing together feuding nations as part of YMUN, or listening to Dr. Woo-Kyoung Ahn speak about causal learning and the relationship between genetic explanations and psychopathology, I know that no community will help me flourish quite like Yale's would. I know that there is nowhere else I'd rather create the future.

Again, thank you for taking the time to reevaluate my application. Please let me know if there's anything else I can provide.

Thank the
reader again
and sign off.

Sincerely,

Zola Avery

Will a letter of continued interest really help?

Maybe. It depends on how the school uses its wait-list and what they're looking to add to the first-year class. Colleges might use the wait-list to achieve gender balance, beef up enrollment in certain academic programs, or add certain talents. For schools that track demonstrated interest, the LOCI may matter a bit more. Some schools may not even go to their wait-list in a given year, as they'll fill their class through the early and regular decision rounds. Having said that, ask yourself, "Will I regret it if I don't write a letter?" If so, it may be worth a shot—you never know. And *definitely* write a letter if they ask you to and you're still interested.

Where and to whom should I send my letter?

The school will likely tell you where to send your LOCI in your wait-list or deferral notice. There may be a form to fill out—if so, use that!—if not, send your letter to the person who sent you the original notice. If you're unsure, email or call the admission office and ask.

Read the wait-list letter carefully, follow the directions, and if need-based aid is a deal breaker, make sure you are clear on whether or not it will be available.

Chapter 35

How Senioritis Can Earn You a "Fear of God" Letter

Think you're safe if you're already accepted into a college? Guess again.

Slacking off your senior year and letting your grades slip may mean the college you thought you'd call home withdraws their offer. Sometimes this comes in the form of a "fear of God" letter, like this one from Texas Christian University that was quoted on the *New York Times* Choice blog:

Dear Joe:

We recently received your final high school transcript. While your overall academic background continues to demonstrate the potential for success, we are concerned with your performance during the senior year, particularly in calculus. University studies are rigorous and we need to know that you are prepared to meet T.C.U.'s academic challenges. With this in mind, I ask that you submit to me, as soon as possible but no later than July 31, 2012, a written statement detailing the reasons surrounding your senior year performance.

Joe, please understand that your admission to T.C.U. is in jeopardy. If I do not hear from you by the above date, I will assume you are no longer interested in T.C.U. and will begin the process of rescinding your admission.

Please realize that your personal and academic successes are very important to us. I look forward to hearing from you.

Sincerely,

Raymond A. Brown

Dean

Does it sound like I'm trying to scare you? I am. Why? Because I really want you to make it to college. Oh, and one more thing.

It almost happened to me.

True story: In my senior year, I was way more interested in drama and debate than math. So when 5th period rolled around I would ask Ms. Turino to let me miss class "just for today" if I promised to make up the work. Ms. Turino was pretty lenient and there must have been more than a few "just for todays" because my March progress report didn't show a C in her class, or a D. No. I had an F...actually, 0.69 on a 4.0 scale.

I almost cried. My dreams of strolling through the Art Institute, devouring Giordano's deep dish pizza, and studying with world-renowned theater artists suddenly vanished. Poof.

So things got real, fast.

"What can I do?" I asked her, my voice probably cracking.

"Nothing. It's too late."

"Seriously?"

"Sorry. You haven't been here."

I left class that day a little broken. And then I got to work.

First, I begged Ms. Turino to let me make up my assignments, to let me prove to her I wasn't a slacker. Eventually, she agreed to let me make up some of the work. (In retrospect, this was incredibly kind of her and though I thanked her then, I'd like to thank her here, again.) I completed extra credit assignments, studied harder than ever before, and got As on the rest of my tests.

I escaped precalculus my senior year with a C. I still feared, up until the last moment, that I'd get the "fear of God" letter from Northwestern. Fortunately, I didn't. But looking back at how much I gained there, it would have been devastating.

What am I saying to you? Avoid the devastation.

If you're reading this in the spring of your senior year and you're in danger of failing (or getting anything other than As and Bs), here are some tips.

How to Avoid Getting the "Fear of God" Letter Your Senior Year

1. If you can't find your grades online, check in with your teachers or guidance counselor ASAP to check the status of your current grades.
2. (Teachers will cringe reading this, but I'll say it anyway…) If you don't like what you see/hear, ask your teacher(s) what you can do to bring your grade(s) up. Do this in an apologetic way and without an ounce of entitlement or expectation that they will show you mercy. They do not owe you this.
3. Create a to-do list that actually works.
4. Try a one-week social media fast.

How Parents and Teachers Can Help Motivate a Student with Senioritis

1. Copy and paste the "fear of God" letter above into a blank MSWord doc.
2. Google image search the college where your student has been accepted and put a logo from the college into the header of the doc.
3. Change the name "Joe" to your son/daughter/student's name.
4. Print it out and tape it on a door, laptop, or somewhere they're bound to see it.
5. Hide and wait.

In the Treasure Trove, you'll find:
→   How to create the simplest, best to-do list ever

Part XI

After You're Accepted

Financial Aid Awards, and How to Write a Financial Aid Award Appeal Letter

Written with Amanda Miller (The Counselor Lady) and Jodi Okun (financial aid consultant at Occidental College and Pitzer College and author of Secrets of a Financial Aid Pro)

In this chapter, we'll cover:

- What a financial aid award letter is and why it's important
- How to find your award letters if you don't already know where they are
- How to read what's on your award letters and compare across schools (using a handy tool) to determine how affordable each college will be
- Some last important tips about college affordability
- How to write a financial aid appeal letter (if you need to)

You're in! Congratulations. You're in that sweet spot between the joy of acceptance and the reality of the college workload. Soak it in.

Ever since you received your acceptance you've been bombarded by your schools asking you to "submit your deposit." And while you definitely do not want to miss the **May 1 deposit deadline** (seriously, they will give away your spot), you generally don't need to commit to a school any earlier than May

1—and you definitely don't want to commit before you've got all the facts about financial aid.*

> Don't commit to a college before you've read (and understand!) all your financial aid award letters!

So how do you figure out how much the schools you were accepted to are actually going to cost?

STEP 1: FIND YOUR FINANCIAL AID AWARD LETTER

By April of your senior year, each college granting you admission and applied financial aid will send you a document called your Financial Aid Award Letter. This will arrive via email or snail mail. If you're unsure how to find it, call the college's financial aid office to ask how they sent it. Better yet, ask them to guide you to it electronically while you're on the phone. Yay self-advocacy!

Pro Tip: Anytime you speak with your college's financial aid office, keep a record. Include the name of the person with whom you spoke, the date, and what they said to you. Most of the time you won't need this, but it's better to have insurance against bureaucratic kerfuffles just in case.

> **WARNING!**
> Did the financial aid office say they don't have an award letter ready for you because they're missing important financial documents or because you've been selected for "verification"? Yikes! This needs to be resolved ASAP so you know how much you're getting in time to decide before May 1!! Stop what you're doing and get on this, like, right now.

---

*   Notable exceptions are those who applied Early Decision and athletes who've signed National Letters of Intent. Once you're in, that's where you go. Also, beware about earlier housing deposit deadlines. (These are set by residence life, not the admission office.) Many colleges will extend this deadline if you ask them, though. And any deposit made before May 1 should be refundable if you ask for a refund on or before May 1. #OpenLineOfCommunication.

STEP 2: FILL OUT AMANDA MILLER'S AWARD LETTER ANALYZER

Almost every award letter looks different, which can make it difficult to compare across schools or even understand what the letter is actually saying. This is why a tool like the Analyzer is super helpful. You'll find a copy here with line-by-line guiding tips on how to fill it out. You can also find a downloadable copy in the Treasure Trove.

	College Name	College Name	College Name
Tuition & Fees			
Room & Board			
Total Direct Costs			

GIFT AID

	College Name	College Name	College Name
Pell Grant			
State Grant			
Institutional Scholarships			
Institutional Grants			
Other Grants/Scholarships			
Total Gift Aid *Money that is free to you.*			

LOANS

	College Name	College Name	College Name
Subsidized Federal Loan			
Unsubsidized Federal Loan			
Other Loans			
Total Loans *Borrowed money that must be repaid later.*			

	College Name	College Name	College Name
Total Billed Costs (Total Direct Costs—Gift Aid) *Total amount you will pay the college now and later for this year of college.*			
Estimated Bill Costs (Total Billed Costs—Loans) *Amount you will need to pay before the end of this year of college.*			

	College Name	College Name	College Name
Amount of Parent PLUS Loan Offered on Award Letter			
My College Expenses (Books + Cell Phone + Travel...) Average is $2,000–$3,000/year			
Total Work-Study Can be used to pay college expenses if offered. This money must be earned.			

Useful for college and good practice for filling out tax forms! #Adulting

How to Fill Out Your Award Letter Analyzer

Cost Section

Tuitions and fees. Tuition is a given, though it may not appear on your award letter. If it doesn't, look it up for the upcoming school year. (Tuition generally increases a little every year.) Fees cover all those "free" amenities on campus: "free" athletic tickets, "free" gym, "free" tech support, "free" counseling center, "free" concerts, etc. There can also be extra lab fees for STEM classes. One fee you can generally get taken off is the health insurance fee, as long as you submit proof you are on your parents' insurance plan. Also, optional add-ons like parking stickers are usually not included.

Room and board. These costs can have some flexibility. If you live in a suite or have a single room, your housing will be more expensive. Most colleges require those who live on campus to have a meal plan. My advice is to downgrade from the unlimited meal plan as soon as possible. No one needs that much food unless they are an athlete, only eat in the dining hall, or wake up every morning before class to eat a giant stack of pancakes.

Pro Tip: Many schools will let you apply for a resident advisor (RA) position after your first year. This can not only reduce housing costs, but in some cases, you can sometimes make money for living there. Consider becoming an RA if you enjoy organizing ice cream socials and don't mind politely policing other forms of recreation.

Total Direct Costs. Add your Tuition & Fees and Room & Board lines. This is how much your first year will cost before financial aid. (Gasp!) Colleges may completely omit cost information on the award letter. Or they may provide an exhaustive list, including indirect costs like travel (read: airfare/gas money to get there), personal expenses (movie tickets, deodorant, etc.), and books and supplies. While you do have to pay for those indirect costs, they will not be billed directly by the college.

Gift Aid Section

Pell grant. A Pell grant is a free federal grant you received because you filled out the FAFSA and you qualified for the grant. If you check your FAFSA Student Aid Report (SAR), you will either see Pell grant with its amount listed or you will only see the standard federal loan.

State scholarships/grants. These can be a little tricky to figure out, but don't sweat it. If the award letter says something about a "grant" or "scholarship" with the name of your state attached to it, it probably goes here. Again, the link to find out about your state's aid program is in the Treasure Trove. If you think you're eligible for something that's not on your award letter, check with your college's financial aid office. They may be waiting on the state for final numbers but can likely give you a solid estimate.

Institutional scholarships/grants. Scholarships are the free money you're receiving from the college because you're awesome and they want your awesomeness at their school. Grants are the free money you're receiving from the college because they want to help you make their school more affordable. (We mostly see these from private colleges.) Either way, it's free money!

Other scholarships. Did you apply for and win any of those local scholarships through your high school? Or an online scholarship? Employers, unions, fraternal organizations, and community organizations are the most common sources of "outside" scholarships. Record all those outside scholarships and any other type of free funding you will receive outside your family here.

Beware: Some colleges deduct outside scholarship dollars from your institutional aid! Be sure to ask your financial aid office if your outside scholarships will "stack" on top of the aid they've already given you.

Total gift aid. Add all your gift aid and put that amount here. Don't sweat whether you got the right things on the right lines within this category. The total will be the same. What is important to know is how you received the money and how to make sure you get the money again next year.*

Loans Section

Subsidized/unsubsidized federal loans. Everyone who fills out a FAFSA is offered the option of taking out unsubsidized federal student loans. What can differ is whether or not you are offered a subsidized loan.

A *subsidized* loan is a loan that the federal government pays the interest on while you're in college (and for a few months thereafter).

An *unsubsidized* loan is a loan that accrues interest (gets bigger) while you're in college.

The maximum loan (of both types together) a student can take out for their first year is $5,500. The maximum allowed increases each year. These loans are also typically "deferred" loans, which means you don't have to make payments on them until you're done with school. This includes graduate school, medical school, etc.

Other loans. Only a small percentage of student borrowers arrange for outside private loans from a bank or other institution because they tend to have higher interest rates and require a cosigner. Before getting an outside loan, check the lender's interest rate against the federal rate.

Total loans. Add all your loans.

---

* That's right. Don't assume it will be the same each of your four years. Make sure by talking about any questions you have with your college's financial aid office. You'll be amazed how much heartache and confusion this will save later!

Pro Tip: Loans aren't automatically dispersed. You can refuse them and pay the amount out-of-pocket instead. If you do decide to take out any federal loans, you'll need to do two things:

Complete Entrance Counseling: an online module to make sure you understand how loans work

Sign a Master Promissory Note: a binding legal document saying that you, the student, will pay back this money after you graduate.

You can complete both of these steps on the federal government's student loans website, conveniently named studentloans.gov.

Bill Section

Now for some math. Don't worry. This is calculator active.

Total billed costs. This is how much you will eventually pay (with interest if you're taking a loan) for your first year at this college. Multiply by four and you'll get a ballpark of how much your college degree will cost at this school.[†] It's calculated like this:

Total Direct Costs − Total Gift Aid = Total Billed Costs

Estimated bill. This is how much you have to pay (or arrange to pay) before the end of your first year of college. Typically, it's split into two payments: one due in August and one due in December/January. It's calculated like this:

Total Billed Costs − Loans = Estimated Bill

Families can set up monthly payment plans starting in the summer. Talk to your college's financial aid office to investigate this option by no later than June 30 before you start.

[†] Bear in mind, tuition tends to increase every year, and the percent of need met can decrease after first year for a number of reasons, including not meeting Satisfactory Academic Progress (SAP) and a regressive policy that some colleges practice called "bait and switch."

Bonus equation: Divide your Total Billed Costs by ten. That's how many hours you'd have to work a $10/hour job to pay for this one year. So don't skip class!

Some Odds and Ends

PLUS loans. These are federal loans that parents can apply for to help them pay for their child's college expenses. Most parents with decent credit are eligible; however, just because it's listed on an award letter doesn't mean the money's guaranteed.

The dangerous aspects of these loans are twofold. First, eligible parents can borrow enough to cover the cost of attendance minus your gift aid and student loans, but this is likely way more than you could possibly need to pay the bill. Second, the interest rate is higher than that of a student loan. These factors combined can get families into a lot of trouble if they don't have a clearly defined plan to repay the money. While these options may be okay for a little assistance, hopefully this book has helped you find a college that doesn't place a heavy financial burden on you and your family.

My college expenses. Your college includes things like books, personal expenses, and transportation when they calculate the cost of attendance. Just because your college doesn't charge you for these things directly doesn't mean they don't cost money. Each college usually provides an estimate of these expenses, but these estimates may be way off for your situation. Add for yourself (and maybe ask for parent advice about) how much you will need to budget for the following:

A new laptop/device and its accessories

Books and materials like pens, notebooks, etc.

Gas/airfare to get from your home to campus at least four times

Spending money

Toiletries (deodorant, shampoo, Tylenol, Band-Aids, and all those other items stocked under your bathroom sink)

Dorm room furnishings (a powerstrip, a light, a rug, those weird-sized sheets)

Add all these expenses up. Be ready for the "you need a summer job" talk.

Work study. Federal work study is a government-funded program for students who qualify to work on campus in order to earn money for college. (How do you qualify? You guessed it: FAFSA.) If this isn't on your award letter, it doesn't mean you can't find a job on or around campus to fund your expenses from the previous section. It just means you won't be guaranteed an on-campus job when you get there. If this is on your award letter, it's important to know two things: (1) you need to make sure you figure out how to get connected to a job on campus as soon as you get there, and (2) ninety-nine percent of the time, this money is deposited into your bank account (instead of being deducted from your college bill), meaning you can spend it on whatever you like... Be smart and save though, because that money can help pay for next semester.

If there's something on your award letter that doesn't seem to fall into any category described here, call your financial aid office for clarification.

OKAY, YOU'VE FILLED OUT YOUR AWARD LETTER ANALYZER

How does it look? Are your schools roughly equally affordable? Or are some way cheaper than others? Does this influence your decision about where you might go in the fall? Talk this over with your family to make sure everyone's on the same page.

A Word on Student Debt

The national average for total student debt incurred to earn a bachelor degree hovers around $28,000.

Two-thirds of your starting salary is generally accepted as a reasonable amount of college debt. A teacher making $30,000 could have up to $20,000 in debt. A petroleum engineer making $60,000 immediately upon graduation could be $40,000 in debt. If you're not sure what you'll end up majoring in, aim to stay under the $25,000 mark.

Obviously the less debt, the better, but don't feel that you haven't "won" or you're "in trouble" if you end up taking a standard federal student loan.

Bottom line: Some debt is reasonable if needed to achieve your educational and career goals. Too much will cripple your ability to thrive financially later in life—buy a house, buy a car, get married, start a family, travel, retire, etc.

If you've completed these steps, you now understand your award letters and how much you'll be paying for each school. But what if the school you've decided you want to go to most isn't financially feasible?

You have two options. You can rejoice that you put great financial safeties on your list and happily submit your housing deposit to one of those schools! Or you can write a financial aid award appeal letter to that first choice college asking for more aid. How? Like this...

How to Write a Great Financial Aid Award Letter

So you've been accepted to a great college (yay!) only to find out the school isn't giving you enough money (womp womp). What do you do? Accept your fate? Resign yourself to attending your back-up school? Start a GoFundMe campaign? Maybe. But first...

You gotta' wonder: Is this ALL the money the school can offer me? Could it be that, if you ask nicely, the school just might give you a little more? Did they miss something important in your aid application, for example, or did you fail to explain a change in circumstance adequately? Maybe.

You should also go ahead and do it because you can write an appeal letter in an hour, it may be the fastest $2,000 (or $8,000) you ever make, and if you don't ask, you'll never know.

When should you write an appeal letter? As soon as you receive your financial award letter. Because when the money's gone, it's gone. So, like, now.

Just remember the two most important qualities that a financial appeal letter has:

- **Information.** Give the school the information it needs to make a new decision. Bullet point this so that you don't find yourself worrying about "how" to say it.

- **Actually being written and submitted.** I've seen many students that could have appealed but didn't out of fear and ultimately they didn't submit a letter. Just write it. If you have reason to appeal, do so. I tell my students: you don't want to look back years from now and think, "I wonder what would've happened if…" Dispel those future doubts.

And here's an example of how to make that happen:

To the Financial Aid Office at UCLA,

My name is Sara Martinez and I am a 12th grader currently enrolled at Los Angeles Academy. First, I would like to say that I am much honored to have been admitted into this fine school, as University of California Los Angeles (UCLA) is my number one choice.

There is a problem, however, and it is a financial one.

I'd love to attend UCLA—it's near home, which would allow me to be closer to my family, and the Bio department is phenomenal. But, as a low-income Hispanic student, I simply don't feel I can afford it. I'm writing to respectfully request an adjustment of my financial aid award.

Here are some more details of my financial situation. Currently, my father works as an assistant supervisor for American Apparel Co. and he is the only source of income for my family of five, while my mother is a housewife. The income my father receives weekly barely meets paying the bills.

My family's overall income:

Father's average weekly gross pay: $493.30

Father's adjusted gross income: $27,022

Our household expenses:

Rent: $850

Margin notes:

Notice how she reiterates who she is and where she's from, how grateful she is to have been accepted, and that UCLA is her number one choice.

First, she offers two specific reasons that UCLA is right for her. Next, she makes her request really clear. And she does so in a straightforward and respectful way.

She uses her transition sentence to set up what this letter is going to be about. It's really straightforward and explicit. Your letter doesn't have to be fancy; it has to be clear.

It helps to give details of your specific family situation even if you gave these details in your original application.

Again, specifics.
Give them
these numbers
so that, when
they do the
math, they can
see what you
see: there just
isn't enough
money.

Legal Services: $200

Car payment: $230.32

My parents cannot afford to have medical insurance, so they do not have a bill that shows proof of medical insurance. My father's average monthly income is an estimate of $1,973.20 (see attached pay stub). When household expenses such as rent, car payment, legal services, gas bill, and electricity bill are added together the cost is $1,402.70. Other payments such as the phone bill, internet bill, and groceries also add to the list. But in order to make ends meet my father usually works overtime and tailors clothes for people in our neighborhood.

She has already included her dad's pay stub, which saves time. Also, she briefly explains the other costs and how her family is already doing everything it can.

My family is on an extremely tight budget and unfortunately cannot afford to pay for my schooling. I have worked my way up and was recently awarded valedictorian for my class. My goals and my aspiration of becoming a nutritionist have helped me push forward. I appreciate your time in reconsidering my financial aid award. I'm looking forward to becoming a Bruin.

Bonus info: She is VALEDIC-TORIAN! This is also a mini-update, as she wouldn't have known this at the time she applied (November) but did know by the time she wrote the appeal.

Regards,

Sara Martinez

No fancy ending, just your basic sign-off.

Is it okay for a parent to write a financial aid appeal letter?

Yes. While college admission officers generally like to hear directly from students on a variety of things (see page 79 on building an authentic relationship with a college admission officer), sometimes a parent has information a student simply doesn't have. In those cases, it's okay for a parent to write the letter—in fact, sometimes it's better.

Here's an example of an appeal letter written by a parent:

Dear Financial Aid Office,

We appreciate you offering our son Paul a scholarship, but even with your help we cannot afford the tuition. We have asked his grandparents and uncles to help, but they too unfortunately are not able to help pay the tuition. I would use our retirement money for him to attend your school, if we had any retirement fund. We honestly don't know how to make this happen without your help. Next month I will be having a necessary hysterectomy and I will be out of commission for a couple of months and cannot work. I am a first-grade teacher at a small church school with a very small income and we can barely make ends meet.

Your school is the only school Paul wants to attend. He said to us he will not go to college if he cannot go to The New School. None of the other schools offer what The New School can offer him. He has always wanted to be an actor, writer, and director ever since he was five years old. Not only will Paul benefit from attending your school but you will also benefit. If you can offer us more financial help, Paul will be able to attend and graduate as one of your success stories.

Thank you in advance for taking the time to reconsider the amount you have offered Paul.

Sincerely,

Gina and Tom Atamian

Want more? My podcast interview with Jodi Okun covers everything from "The Pause" before the appeal (super important) to how financial aid offices make decisions. Find the link in the Treasure Trove.

In the Treasure Trove, you'll find:
→ A downloadable copy of Amanda Miller's Simple Award Letter Analyzer
→ The link to a site that "decodes" your award letter into three categories: grants/scholarships, work study, and loans
→ The link to find out more about your state's financial aid programs

Chapter 37

How to Decide Where to Attend

Congratulations, you're in! Even better, you're in at multiple schools! Now, how do you pick?

First Figure Out the Financial Situation

If you haven't already, fill out Amanda Miller's Award Letter Analyzer on page 379 (or in the Treasure Trove) to calculate the bottom line for your first year at each school you're considering. Then multiply by four (because you'll be graduating in four years, right?).

Is there a considerable difference? If yes, you'll have to weigh for yourself the benefits of choosing a more expensive school against the reality of likely living with less for longer after you graduate. Ask a counselor, parent, college financial aid officer, or other trusted adult to help make real how much of a difference $10,000 in debt (for example) will make to your life after college. And if you're planning to attend graduate school, then you will want to look even more closely at how much you want to spend on your undergraduate education.

Assuming money isn't a big factor, or the money is similar among different schools, here are...

Three Ways to Decide What Your Heart Wants (in One Day, One Hour, or One Minute)

All three of these exercises are designed to help you tap into feelings you maybe didn't know you had.

1. **One day.** Imagine for the next twenty-four hours you're going to attend School A. If you have a sweatshirt or hat for that school, wear it. Or just say to yourself, "I'm going to [name of school]" a few times throughout the day. See how it feels. Repeat with School B, then C, etc., or try this with multiple schools throughout the same day.

2. **One hour.** Create a good old-fashioned pros and cons list. Ask: What's my *true* intention in going to college (i.e., what do I value most)?

   a. Gainful employment? Research the colleges' post-graduation placement rates and take a look at their office of career services website.

   b. Fulfilling student life experience? Use the student life office to find out what activities thrive on each campus and what portion of students study abroad, play sports, or create art/music/theater. Basically, find out how much you'll get to do the stuff you love.

   c. Building a professional network? Find out through the career services office what industries recent alumni are involved in and how accessible they are to students.

   d. Enriching academic experiences? Look up faculty for departments you're interested in on RateMyProfessor.com. Compare course offerings in the major(s)/department(s) you're interested in.

   If you wanna get fancy, rate each priority from one to ten based on how important it is to you, then add the points for each college. That'll give each college a numerical score. Once you do this, ask yourself, "How do I feel now?" You may be surprised that the highest "score" school isn't actually the one you wanted—in which case you may have your decision.

3. **One minute.** Flip a coin. Heads you go to one school, tails you go to another. Catch the coin and hide the result. Ask yourself, "Which was I hoping would/wouldn't come up?" Then look at the coin and

pay attention to how you feel. Repeat as needed. This is my favorite, fastest way. I did this with my grad school decision and it totally helped me decide.

Once you've done the work to evaluate your financial priorities and (this is important) you've talked to your parents and heard theirs, trust your gut. Then go all in—celebrate and get ready for this exciting next step.

Chapter 38

What to Do If You're Not Accepted Anywhere

Every once in a while I hear about a student who is either rejected by all the schools they applied to or accepted only to schools they can't afford. This is almost always because they didn't have a balanced college list that included at least two to three schools where they were likely to be accepted and that they could afford.

Important: if that thought scares you and you're reading this while you still have a chance to apply to a range of schools, then, phew! Aren't you glad you read this in time? Now please reread the chapter How to Create a Balanced College List. Pay special attention to the part on page 64 about having a balanced list, then research to find two to three schools where you have a very good chance of getting in.

But let's say you didn't do that and are not accepted anywhere. It happens. What to do?

The first thing I would recommend doing is letting yourself be sad for a while. This is the part we sometimes skip. But gosh, allowing ourselves to feel our feelings is really important in life. So give yourself a few days to feel all the things. Or a week. Talk to people who care about you and tell them how you feel. Once you've done that, remember that life is about more than getting into college. That these colleges' decisions aren't a judgment on your character or your worth as a human being. That life will go on. It will.

Then consider these options:

- **Apply to schools that are still accepting applications.** While many colleges send out their decisions by April, a number of schools still accept applications in April, May, and beyond. You'll find a list of schools that often take late applications in the Treasure Trove.

- **Take a gap year.** Rather than taking a year off, think of it as a year on. Create your own "educational" experience, whatever that may look like for you. For resources and ideas, check out www.gapyearassociation.org. Their search feature allows you to search many programs and their planning guides for families. Once you've begun your gap year, you might find either (a) you still want to go to college or (b) you actually don't (see the last option)!

- **Take community college classes.** Earn some college credits and save some money. Future employers don't care as much about where you started as where you finished. And some don't even care too much about the latter.

    Heads up: Be careful about reapplying the following year if you'll need financial aid. Why? Universities will consider you a transfer even if you don't want the credits, and aid is often much less available. Find out more from either your high school counselor or the transfer counselor at your local community college.

    But if none of these is feeling right…

- **Ask yourself:** *Is college right for me?* Perhaps there are options you've not even considered yet. For ideas (and lots of perspective), check out Blake Boles's book *Better Than College: How to Build a Successful Life without a Four-Year Degree.*

Values Check—the Dig Deep, Search-Your-Soul Edition

If you've been rejected everywhere, ask yourself these questions:

1. Why do I want to go to college after all?
2. Was college someone else's idea, or was it truly mine?
3. What values am I hoping to explore there?
4. Could I explore those values in some other way? If so, how?

A Final Request

I told you at the start of this book my goal was to make this process easier, more fun, and more meaningful. I hope I've done that.

I also hope this book has helped you discover more about who you are and what you care about.

If so, here's my request:

Pay it forward.

How? Here are some ideas:

Students:

- Share this book with someone you know.
- Donate it to your high school or local library for others to use.
- Sit down with a ninth or tenth grader and share what you've learned.
- Serve as a mentor to high school students once you're settled into college life.

Counselors:

- Join your affiliate chapter of NACAC and offer to mentor a new counselor.

- Share the free resources in the Treasure Trove.
- Invite a neighboring school or CBO to your college night or fair.
- Volunteer to help one low-income student through the Matchlighters Program: www.collegeessayguy.com/matchlighters

Parents:
- Support your high school teachers and staff as they perform their duties in the process, and pass on any praise about their roles to the administration.
- Encourage other parents to talk about the college process within the framework of values, not of rankings.
- Consider volunteering with—or learning about so you can direct students to—a local college access program (AVID, GearUp, Trio, etc). Often, folks are needed to serve as mentors who cheer on and guide students through this process without needing to be experts.
- Support national and state legislation to increase the number of counselors in public schools.

With gratitude,
Ethan

Appendix and Additional Resources

College Planning Timeline
(a.k.a. What Should I Be Doing Right Now?)

This section is pretty straightforward. It tells you what tasks to prioritize each year of high school in order to prepare for college. For a printable PDF version of this timeline containing links to more resources, check out the Treasure Trove.

Ninth grade

- Do the Values Exercise to determine what's important to you.
- Take a personality assessment to learn more about your strengths, challenges, and communication and learning styles.
- Explore and engage with extracurricular activities (e.g., clubs, sports, community service, fine and performing arts, work, and other in-school or out-of-school activities) that align with your values and strengths.
- Create an activity log to track all your extracurricular activities, summer experiences, academic honors, and other achievements.
- Develop your time management and study skills.
- PSAT: Some high schools allow you to take the October PSAT as a freshman.
- Take an interest assessment to explore possible college majors and careers.
- Plan your high school classes using insight from the previous bullet.
- Meet with your school counselor to explore clubs and classes and discuss

course selection. Start building a relationship with them by doing this regularly.

- Parents: Start exploring how to pay for college.
- Athletes: Familiarize yourself with the NCAA and NAIA athletic recruiting requirements.
- Plan a summer experience that helps you explore a passion or interest.
- Summer reading: Expand your vocabulary and your world.

Tenth grade

- Do the Values Exercise to see if your ever-evolving self has new priorities. If they've changed, assess whether you want to change your current activities so they align with your values.
- Continue participating in nonacademic extracurricular activities. See if you can deepen your involvement or take on a leadership role in the activities you've already been doing. Or step outside your comfort zone and try something new.
- Update your activity log.
- Stay focused on keeping your grades up—this year's grades are important to college admission officers.
- If your school offers higher-level (honors or AP) classes, challenge yourself academically by taking a higher-level class or two in areas that you're interested in.
- Attend a local college fair.
- Meet with your school counselor at least once a year to discuss course selection. Continue building this relationship by asking lots of questions about new courses and suggestions for ways to develop your interests.
- Parents: Continue researching how to pay for college and set up a college budget.
- Visit a college or two locally or while you're on vacation.
- Read more about possible college majors and careers to better plan out your high school classes.
- If you think you may play Division I or II sports in college:
  - Register for the National Collegiate Athletic Association (NCAA) Clearinghouse.

- ➤ Register for the National Association of Intercollegiate Athletes (NAIA) Eligibility Center.
- ➤ Familiarize yourself with National Collegiate Athletic Association (NCAA) requirements. Then double-check that all of your courses are NCAA-approved. Not all high school classes count toward their requirements.
- ➤ Let your high school counselor know you're considering college athletics.
- Testing
  - ➤ If you're taking an AP class this year, consider sitting for the AP exam (May) and the correlating SAT Subject Test (May or June).
  - ➤ If you're taking a precalculus or calculus class in sophomore year, consider taking the Math 2 SAT Subject Test in May or June.
  - ➤ On the fence about which tests to take and when? Check in with your teacher in that subject for some wise counsel.
  - ➤ Take the PSAT if your high school allows you to take the October PSAT as a sophomore.
  - ➤ At the end of the school year, take a practice ACT and SAT to determine which test may be better for you, then set up a testing timeline.
- Summer reading: Continue expanding your vocabulary and your world.
- Continue exploring your interests during the summer. This could be through a job, internship, volunteer experience, or self-designed project.

Eleventh grade

FALL

- Check in with the Values Exercise. Has anything changed?
- Stay consistent with your nonacademic extracurricular activities if your values and priorities haven't changed. If they have, try something new. Continue to look for ways to explore and deepen your interests in these activities. Try a leadership role if you haven't already.
- Continue to update your activity log.
- Start your college search by attending a local college fair and a few college admission rep presentations at your high school (if they are offered).
- Explore your college interests by sorting the college criteria on www. Corsava.com. Then use those preferences to search for a few college matches.

- Start a preliminary list of colleges to visit using the results of your college match searches. Have a family meeting to block out dates for college visits throughout junior year.
- Keep your grades up. Junior year grades are the last ones some schools will see before making an admissions decision.
- Take an aptitude or career assessment such as YouScience or Do What You Are to learn more about your interests and strengths, which will change as you grow and learn.
- Continue challenging yourself academically with higher-level AP or honors classes.
- Schedule a meeting with your school counselor to discuss the colleges you are interested in. Tell them about your college preferences and ask for their suggestions of colleges that might be a good fit for you. Continue to develop your relationship with your counselor.
- Testing
  - Take the PSAT/NSMQT in October. This test qualifies students for the National Merit Scholarship.
  - Stay on track with your ACT/SAT testing timeline and study schedule.
- Athletic Recruitment
  - Double-check that your classes meet the NCAA Clearinghouse requirements
  - Complete online athletic recruitment forms for each college you're considering. You'll find these on the college's website under "athletics."
  - Once you've completed the online recruitment forms, make your sports résumé and recruitment videos.
  - Spread out your correspondence with coaches by sending the résumés and videos a few weeks after you complete the online forms.
- Fine & Performing Arts Students
  - Sign up for Performing & Visual Arts college fairs.
  - Create an admission requirements spreadsheet for fine and performing arts programs.
  - You most likely need to create a portfolio and audition materials, so spend junior year working on pieces.

WINTER & SPRING
- Investigate summer experiences.

- Register for senior year classes. Remember colleges will want to see a strong senior year course load including five academic core classes.
- Continue visiting colleges. Use local colleges to sample certain types of schools (single-sex, small liberal arts, larger university, etc.).
- Start building your college list based on your values and your research.
- Start researching scholarship opportunities.
- Complete the Letter of Rec questionnaire and request letters of recommendation from two academic teachers from junior year.
- Testing
  - Select testing dates. Most likely your first ACT or SAT will take place between December and May.
  - Take the AP/IB exams in May.
  - For highly selective colleges, you may have to take two to three SAT Subject Tests. May or June is likely the best time to schedule these one-hour tests.
- Athletes
  - Send your sports résumé and video to college coaches and fill out the athletic recruitment surveys on the college websites.
- Fine & Performing Arts Students
  - Explore how the audition and portfolio process works for college admission.
  - Build your portfolios and audition videos.
- Set up a meeting with your school counselor to ask questions about college choices, your senior year schedule, testing, and anything else you're curious about.

SUMMER
- Participate in summer experiences (research, reading, internships, fun stuff).
- Refine and finalize your college list. Be sure it reflects a balance of admission probabilities (likely, possible, and reach schools).
- Research the type of applications required for each school on your list, as these vary.
- Write your Common Application personal statement.
- Complete the Common Application.
- Visit more colleges.
- Research the admission requirements and deadlines for schools on your

list and create a spreadsheet to organize information. Research to see if an interview is offered or required at each school.

- Create a scholarship spreadsheet to list deadlines and requirements.

Twelfth grade

AUGUST & SEPTEMBER
- Confirm your final college list, application deadlines, and requirements.
- Write your college-specific supplemental essays.
- Ask an expert outside reader to review your Common Application and personal statement.
- Continue to research scholarships, adding requirements and deadlines to your list.
- Set up on-campus or local rep interviews with colleges.
- Check in with your recommendation writers. Update your Letter of Rec Questionnaire and ask for a letter of recommendation from your school counselor.
- Apply to scholarships throughout the school year.
- Parents: Start preparing financial aid paperwork and develop a deadlines list.

SEPTEMBER–NOVEMBER
- Complete and send out all EA and ED applications no later than late October. (These deadlines are typically around November 1.)
- Many portfolio-based arts programs have December 1 deadlines. And some universities require submission by December 1 to be considered for scholarship opportunities. Schedule a meeting with your school counselor to review your college list to get their feedback and review your application deadlines, and ask any questions you may have.
- Attend high school presentations and programs.
- Apply for financial aid using the FAFSA and CSS/PROFILE (if required).
- Complete final college visits.
- Send test scores to your colleges after checking whether they allow self-reported scores.
- Ask your school counseling office to deliver letters and transcripts to colleges.

DECEMBER

- Regular Decision (RD) deadlines are typically around January 1. Complete and send out all RD applications no later than mid-December. Give yourself a relaxing holiday break by completing your applications before November 15.

JANUARY–MARCH

- January: If deferred, send an email to your region/state/country admission representative. Reaffirm your interest in the school and offer any updates (activities, achievements, awards, etc.).
- Wait for application decisions.

MARCH–APRIL

- Colleges have until April 1 to release decisions.
- Plan visits to accepted colleges, if needed, in order to make your final college choice.
- Attend local admitted student events when possible.
- Evaluate financial aid packages and scholarship offerings to figure out how to pay for college.
- Students need to enroll and submit a deposit by May 1.

MAY

- Take AP/IB exams.
- Notify your school counselor of your college decisions and scholarship opportunities.
- If you've been waitlisted, this is a good time to send (a) your "I'd like to stay on the wait list" form and (b) the email to your designated admission rep that states your interest in the school and offers updates (activities, achievements, awards, etc.).
- Sign up for campus housing if you plan to live on campus.

JUNE–AUGUST

- Continue saving for college.
- Check your email for wait-list notifications.
- Attend orientation sessions.
- Sign up for meal plans and register for classes.
- Find out what you need for your dorm and classes, and go shopping.

- Contact your future roommate(s).
- Make travel and move-in arrangements.
- Set up a bank account on or near campus.
- Continue applying for scholarships.
- Set up a meeting with an academic advisor at your college to plan your classes.

PRE-PROFESSIONAL CAREER HIGH SCHOOL COURSE PLANNING

High school students are encouraged to complete high school courses that are in line with their college major and career goals. For those students who have already identified a pre-professional path, this chart might be helpful. While not exhaustive, it does suggest guidelines for curriculum choices. Don't forget the level of rigor—Honors/AP/IB is always a consideration.

Accounting/Finance/Banking	Engineering	Forensic Science
Accounting Economics IB Mathematics SL/HL Calculus Statistics Computer (Excel/PowerPoint)	AP Calculus AB/BC Multivariable Calculus IB Mathematics SL/HL IB Physics SL/HL AP Physics AP Chemistry Pre-Calculus Robotics AP Computer Science Computer (Coding) Drafting/Design	Anatomy/Physiology AP Psychology IB Biology HL AP Biology Statistics AP Chemistry IB Chemistry HL
Medicine/Dentistry/Veterinary	Law	Pharmacy
Anatomy/Physiology AP Psychology IB Biology HL AP Biology IB Physics SL/HL AP Chemistry IB Chemistry SL/HL Economics	AP Government AP Psychology Speech Drama Statistics IB English HL IB History HL Physics AP U.S. History Journalism AP English	Anatomy AP Psychology AP Chemistry IB Chemistry HL IB Biology HL AP Biology Statistics

Business	Communications	Graphic/Video Game Design
Accounting	Art I, II	Art I, II, III, IV
AP Psychology	Digital Photography	Digital Photography
Business	IB English HL	Graphic Design I, II
Economics	IB Visual Arts SL/HL	IB Visual Arts SL/HL
Computer	Journalism	Computer
IB Business Management SL	Yearbook/Newspaper	Web Design
IB English HL	Music Technology	Computer Modeling
Statistics	Web Design	Animation
Web Design		

Additional Resources for Students, Counselors, and Teachers

At www.collegeessayguy.com, you'll find…

Resources for Students

Blog Posts & Guides

The Free Guide to Writing a Personal Statement

The Great College Essay Test

35+ Best College Essay Tips from College Application Experts

The Free 1-Hour Guide to the UC Personal Insight Questions

How to Write Your UC Activities List

Podcasts

How to Find and Research Great Colleges: The Fiske Guide

Should You Apply Early Decision or Regular Decision?

How to Improve Your Personal Statement in 20 Minutes

What I've Learned from Reading over 10,000 College Essays

Which Schools Are the Most Generous with Financial Aid? (U.S. Version)

Which Schools Are the Most Generous with Financial Aid? (International Version)

17 Things to Do Before Going to College

YouTube

12 College Essay Brainstorming Exercises and How to Use Them (Videos)
9 College Essay Mistakes (And How to Avoid Them!)
Feelings and Needs Exercise
Values Exercise
Essence Objects Exercise

Resources for Teachers and Counselors

Blog Posts & Guides

25+ Amazing 1-Minute Ideas to Take Your College Counseling to the Next Level
Fly-Ins for Counselors
15 Ways to Advocate for Undocumented Youth
How to Write a Letter of Recommendation: Counselor's Guide + Samples
Writing a Recommendation Letter for a Student: Teacher's Guide + Samples
20 Ways Parents Can Support Children Applying to College

Podcasts

Colleges That Change Lives: Great Schools You May Not (Yet!) Know About
Free College Application Tools That Students (and Counselors!) Should Know About
30 Ways to Center Equity and Justice Today
How to Advocate for Undocumented Students

Facebook Groups for Parents

Grown and Flown

Facebook Groups for Counselors

The College Essay Forum for Counselors
College Admissions Counselors Group
ACCEPT (Admissions Community Cultivating Equity and Peace Today)

About the Author

CREDIT: BRAD BUCKMAN PHOTOGRAPHY

Ethan Sawyer is a nationally recognized college essay expert and a sought-after speaker. Each year he helps thousands of students and counselors through his webinars, workshops, articles, products, and books, and works privately with a small number of students.

Raised in Spain, Ecuador, and Colombia, Ethan has studied at seventeen different schools and has worked as a teacher, curriculum writer, voice actor, motivational speaker, community organizer, and truck driver. He is a certified Myers-Briggs specialist, and his type (ENFJ) will tell you that he will show up on time, that he'll be excited to meet you, and that, more than anything, he is committed to helping you realize your potential.

A graduate of Northwestern University, Ethan holds an MFA from UC Irvine and two counseling certificates. He lives in Los Angeles with his beautiful wife, Veronica, and their amazing daughter, Zola.

For more, go to www.collegeessayguy.com.